Allan's Illustrated Edition of Tyneside Songs and Readings: With Lives, Portraits, and Autographs of the Writers, and Notes On the Songs

Thomas & George Allan

ECCENTRICS AND WELL-KNOWN CHARACTERS IN NEWCASTLE-UPON-TYNE.

1 Aud Judy	7 Donald	13 Captain Starkey
2 Jenny Ballo	8 Bugle-Nosed Jack	14 Doodem Daddum
3 Whin Bob	9 Hangy	Dog—"Timour"
4 Jacky Coxon	10 Bold Archy	
5 Pussy Willy	11 Blind Willie	
6 Cull Billy	12 Shoe-tie Anty	

ALLAN'S

ILLUSTRATED EDITION

OF

TYNESIDE SONGS

AND READINGS.

WITH

Lives, Portraits, and Autographs

OF THE Writers,

AND NOTES ON THE SONGS.

REVISED EDITION.

NEWCASTLE-UPON-TYNE:

THOMAS & GEORGE ALLAN,

18 BLACKETT STREET, AND 34 COLLINGWOOD STREET.

SOLD BY

W. ALLAN, 30 GRAINGER STREET; R. ALLAN, NORTH SHIELDS.

LONDON: WALTER SCOTT.

1891

TO

RICHARD OLIVER HESLOP, Esq.

AN ACKNOWLEDGMENT

OF HIS LABOURS

ON

"NORTHUMBERLAND WORDS."

INTRODUCTORY NOTE.

IT is close upon thirty years since we brought out the first edition of this book. In 1872 it was enlarged, and the following from the Introductory Note will show upon what lines.

" Several features, new in local collections, have been introduced. In many of the songs, particularly those of an earlier date, there are allusions to events and persons, without a knowledge of which, the interest of the song is weakened or lost. These allusions, well known at the time the songs were written, have now grown strange to a great many. To remedy this, notes explanatory are given where necessary.

" In previous collections, little has been told about the writers of the songs—the local bards

> ' ——who swept the rustic lyre,
> Their native hills adorning.'

That it should have been so is unfortunate, as, now, the task of supplying the omission is one of difficulty. Like their songs, the singers were, with few exceptions, of humble life, and but little known beyond their own immediate circle. It is from these, now few in numbers, and difficult to trace, that the information in the brief notices now given is obtained. That the information gathered, in several instances, has been so scanty is to be regretted ; but, at least, a little has been obtained which will be interesting to those who take an interest in Tyneside song.

" The older writers wrote for their own amusement, and sung their songs at social meetings amongst their friends ; now Tyneside songs are generally launched into popularity from the stage of the concert hall, music, and dressing in character, being used to add to their effect. Corvan, and, after him, Ridley, followed this course, and made the writing and singing of Tyneside songs their means of livelihood. Joe Wilson and Rowland Harrison are now pursuing a similar course, excepting that Joe never dresses in character, but invariably sings his songs in ordinary dress."

To this we may add :—In the new edition the Notes on the songs and the Lives of the writers have been largely extended, while Portraits and Autographs, some of them rare, have been freely added. For these additional attractions we have been indebted to many kind friends ; their valuable help we here beg to acknowledge with many thanks.

In the present edition a fresh feature is introduced—the writers follow in order of time ; and each song is traced back to its original publication, or as near as can be, and the text revised from the best authority. The emblematic device on the back, the head of the River God, Father Tyne, showing its products and industries, is from Brand's *Newcastle* (1789), where it is given as designed by Sir Wm. Chambers.

CONTENTS.

*a**

CONTENTS.

TYNESIDE SONGS.

WEEL MAY THE KEEL ROW!

The "Tyneside National Anthem," as it has been called, has been claimed—both melody and words—as Scottish. Mr. John Stokoe, in the *Monthly Chronicle*, shows this claim to be unfounded, and proves, by an interesting reference to William Shield, the famous Swalwell musician, that "The Keel Row" was a popular Tyneside melody before 1760. Few melodies, he adds, are so identified with a district as our simple and beautiful melody of the "Keel Row" is associated with Northumbria and Tyneside.

As I went up Sandgate, up Sandgate, up Sandgate,
As I went up Sandgate I heard a lassie sing—
Weel may the keel row, the keel row, the keel row,
Weel may the keel row that my laddie's in!

He wears a blue bonnet, blue bonnet, blue bonnet,
He wears a blue bonnet, a dimple in his chin:
And weel may the keel row, the keel row, the keel row,
And weel may the keel row that my laddie's in!

Ritson's " Northumberland Garland," 1793.

To the above, which may be called the correct version, the following, as heard in the streets of Newcastle, may be added—

As aw was gawn thro' San'get, thro' San'get, thro' San'get,
As aw was gawn thro' San'get aw he'rd th' lasses sing—
Weel may th' keel row, th' keel row, th' keel row,
Weel may th' keel row that maw lad's in!

He wears a blue bonnet, a bunch of ribbons on it;
He wears a blue bonnet, a dimple in his chin:
An' weel may th' keel row, th' keel row, th' keel row,
An' weel may th' keel row that maw lad's in!

THE WAGGONER.

Before William Hedley, with his "Puffing Billy" at Wylam, drove the horse from the waggon-way. The waggoners as thus described would be well known.

Saw ye owt o' ma lad
    Gang doon the waggon-way,
His pocket full o' money,
    And his poke full o' hay?

Chorus—
    Aye, but he's a bonny lad
    As ever ye did see,
    Tho' he's sair pock brocken,
    An' he's blind of an e'e.

There's ne'er a lad like ma lad
    Drives to a staith on Tyne;
Tho' coal black on work days,
    On holidays he's fine.

Ma lad's a bonny lad,
    The bonniest I see,
Wiv his fine posey waistcoat,
    And buckles at his knee.

              Bell's "*Northern Bards,*" 1812.

BOBBY SHAFTOE.

According to Mr. W. Brockie the hero of this song was one of the Shaftoe's of Benwell. A little over a hundred years ago, Robert Shaftoe, the last of the family in the male line, died at the early age of twenty-one; and Miss Shaftoe, afterwards Mrs. Adair, became heiress to the Benwell estate, which she divided and sold, the notorious Andrew Robinson Bowes being one of the purchasers.

Bobby Shaftoe's gone to sea,
With silver buckles at his knee;
He'll come home and marry me,
    Bonny Bobby Shaftoe.

Bobby Shaftoe's bright and fair,
Combing down his yellow hair;
He's ma ain for ever mair,
    Bonny Bobby Shaftoe.

    Bobby Shaftoe's gone to sea, etc., etc.

There are various additional stanzas to this song. An apocryphal verse says—

    " Bobby Shaftoe's getten a bairn
    For to dangle on his arm—
    On his arm, and on his knee ;
    Bobby Shaftoe loves me."

"This song was used for electioneering purposes in 1761, when Robert Shaftoe, Esq., of Whitworth, popularly known as 'Bonny Bobby Shaftoe,' was the favourite candidate at the election here referred to."

    " Bobby Shaftoe's looking out,
    All his ribbons flew about,
    All the ladies gave a shout—
    Hey, for Bobby Shaftoe."

"His portrait at Whitworth represents him as very young and very handsome, and with *yellow* hair. Miss Bellasyse, the heiress of Brancepeth, is said to have died for love of him."

            Sharpe's " Bishoprick Garland," 1834.

THE BONNY PIT LADDIE.

[Ritson's " Northumberland Garland" gives only the first verse.]

THE bonny pit laddie, the canny pit laddie,
    The bonny pit laddie for me, O!
He sits in his hole as black as a coal,
    And brings the white siller to me, O!

The bonny pit laddie, the canny pit laddie,
    The bonny pit laddie for me, O!
He sits on his cracket and hews in his jacket,
    And brings the white siller to me, O!

            Bell's " Northern Bards," 1812.

BONNY KEEL LADDIE.

The *keel* on Tyne and Wear was formerly used for the conveyance of coal from the *dykes*, or staiths, in the upper and shallower reaches of the river to the collier ships at their various berths in the harbour. The foreground of Buck's view of Newcastle, published in 1743, illustrates the old coal *keel*. "These boats are strong, clumsy, and oval, and carry twenty tons apiece; they are navigated with a square sail, but generally by two very large oars— one on the side plied by a man and a boy, the other at the stern, by a single man, serving both as oar and rudder." The word *keel* is in Anglo-Saxon *ceól*, a ship. It is pronounced on the Tyneside to this day *kee-ul*.

Northumberland Words (*Weekly Chronicle*), by R. Oliver Heslop.

My bonny keel laddie, my canny keel laddie,
　My bonny keel laddie for me, O!
He sits in his keel as black as the deil,
　And he brings the white money to me, O!

Ha' ye seen owt' o' my canny man,
　An' are ye sure he's weel, O?
He's geane ower land, wiv a stick in his hand,
　T' help to moor the keel, O!

The canny keel laddie, the bonny keel laddie,
　The canny keel laddie for me, O!
He sits in his huddock and claws his bare buttock,
　And brings the white money to me, O!

UNKNOWN.   *Bell's "Northern Bards,"* 1812.

RIDE THROUGH SANDGATE.

This is a genuine fragment of a ballad relating to Newcastle besieged by Lesley and the Scots army. The blue caps (or Scotchmen) did, however, at last succeed in pulling them down, after a most gallant defence, 19th October, 1644.

RIDE through Sandgate, both up and down,
There you'll see the gallants fighting for the crown :
All the cull cuckolds in Sunderland town,
With all the bonny blue-caps, cannot pull them down.

Sharpe's " Bishoprick Garland," 1834.

THE COLLIER'S WEDDING.

ONLY brief extracts from this old picture of pit life can be given here, as the collection is one of songs; but to the spirit of the work Elswick and Benwell, with their colliers of 150 years ago, are so kindred, that at least room must be found for a few specimens.

The author, Edward Chicken, was born in Newcastle in the year 1698. What little is known of his life has principally been gathered by W. Cail, Esq., who, in 1829, published a new and amended edition of the poem. It thus opens—

" I sing not of great Cæsar's might,
How brave he led his men to fight.

. . . . .

" I choose to sing, in strains much lower,
Of collier lads, unsung before ;
What sport and feasting doth ensue
When such life mortals buckle to."

A description of collier life at that time follows, and of that life the following verse gives a summary—

" And thus the colliers and their wives
Liv'd drunken, honest, working lives ;
Yet still were fond of one another,
And always married thro' each other.

. . . . .

" A collier's daughter, brisk and clean,
Once at a country wake was seen ;

The maid was born in Benwell town,
Was not too fair, nor yet too brown ;
Of beauty she had got her part,
Enough to wound a collier's heart ;
And then her name was up for this—
She loved to spin, but blushed to kiss ;
Her pliant limbs, when music played,
Could humour everything it said ;
For when she tripped it on the plain
To '*Jockey's lost his fellow swain,*'
Her easy steps and airy wheels
Showed she had music in her heels.
She danced so well so very long,
She won the smock and pleased the throng.
"A collier lad was standing by,
And viewed her with a lover's eye."

This viewing "with a lover's eye" leads to the collier lad
going home with her to ask her mother's consent to his suit.

"'Come, Bessy, speak ; what do ye think ?'
The old wife cocked her chin and spoke:
'Why surely, Tom, you do but joke :
If ye're sincere as ye are warm,
And mean to do my bairn nae harm,
Ye knaw our Jenny's on'y young,
And easily may be o'ercome ;
So court her first—hear what she'll say ;
We'll have a drink and fix the day.'
Her daughter Jane, with modest grace,
And fingers spread before her face,
Cried 'Mother, Tommy's won my heart—
If ye'll consent we'll never part ;
I love him as I do my life,
And would like weel to be his wife !'"

.　　　.　　　.　　　.　　　.

The match is settled, the customs common on such occasions are described, and at last the church is reached.

"The gates fly open, all rush in—
The church is full with folks and din ;
And all the crew, both great and small,
Behave as in a common hall :
"For some, perhaps, that were three-score,
Were never twice in church before.
They scamper, climb, and break the pews,
To see the couple make their vows.
With solemn face the priest draws near,
Poor Tom and Jenny quake for fear :
Are singled out from all the band
That round about them gaping stand.

" When they're in decent order got,
  The priest proceeds to tie the knot.
  Then hands are joined, and loosed again,
  And Tommy says, 'I take thee, Jane';—
  Then Jenny looks a little shy,
  And kneels, and says, 'I take Tom-my';
  But here's the blessing, or the curse,
  'Tis done for better or for worse;
  For now they're fairly in for life:
  The priest declares them man and wife.

" Our couple now kneel down to pray,
  Much unacquainted with the way:
  Whole troops of colliers swarm around,
  And seize poor Jenny on the ground."

Rough scenes follow, possibly true of the times described; but of them it may be truly said they are now happily out of date.

WHITE CROSS.

Mr. Cail, in his edition, gives some interesting information about the author, who, it appears, was parish clerk at St. John's. He also followed the profession of a teacher at his residence at the White Cross, Newgate Street. Mr. Cail (1828) came upon an interesting fragment of manuscript left by the poet. It was the title of a song, neatly written, beginning with, "This song is humbly inscribed to Mr. Anthony Meggeson by E. Chicken." This reference to it is all that is left of the song. The author died on the 2nd January 1746, and was buried in St. John's Churchyard, where a tombstone points out his last resting-place. To those wishing to know more about the author and his work, Mr. Cail's most interesting edition, which forms one of the Typographical Reprints, is recommended.

MY EPPIE.

"Acomb, Fallowfield, and Wall lie within about two miles of each other, between Hexham and Chollerford."—BROCKIE.

THERE was five wives at Acomb,
    And five wives at Wa',
And five wives at Fallowfield,
    That's fifteen o' them a'.

They've druken ale and brandy
    Till they are all fu',
And I cannot get home to
    My Eppie I trow,
    My Eppie I trow,
And I cannot get home to
    My Eppie I trow.

The Tyne water's se deep, that
    I cannot wade through ;
And I've no horse to ride to
    My Eppie I trow,
        My Eppie I trow,
        My Eppie I trow,
    And I've no horse to ride to
        My Eppie I trow.

In the Tyne I hev not a boat,
    Nor yet cou'd I row
Across the deep water to
    My Eppie I trow,
        My Eppie I trow,
        My Eppie I trow,
    And I've no horse to ride to
        My Eppie I trow.

                    Bell's " Northern Bards," 1812.

THE NORTHUMBRIAN'S SIGH FOR HIS NATIVE COUNTRY.

AT home wad I be,
And my supper made I see,
And marry with a lass
Of my own country.

If I were at hame,
I wad ne'er return again,
But marry with a lass
In my own country.

There's the oak and the ash,
And the bonny ivy tree;
How canst thou gan away, love,
And leave me?

O stay, my love, stay,
And do not gang away;
O stay, my love, stay
Along with me.

Bell's " Northern Bards," 1812.

———

SAIR FAIL'D, HINNEY.

I was young and lusty,
　I was fair and clear,
I was young and lusty,
　Mony a lang year.

　　Sair fail'd, hinney,
　　　Sair fail'd now,
　　Sair fail'd, hinney,
　　　Sin' I kenn'd thou.

When I was young and lusty,
I could loup a dyke ;
But now, at five-an'-sixty,
Canna do the like.

Then said the awd man
To the oak tree,
" Sair fail'd is I
Sin' I kenn'd thee ! "

Sir C. Sharpe's " Bishoprick Garland."

Sir Cuthbert Sharpe writes :—"This song is ' far north ;' it is admitted
in Bell's *Northern Bards,* and may very possibly belong to the bishoprick,
where it is well known." Ritson, in *Gammer Gurton's Garland,* gives it
differently, and more quaintly :—

" Says t' auld man ti't oak tree,
Young and lusty was I, when I ken'd thee—
I was young and lusty, I was fair and clear—
Young and lusty was I, mony a lang year ;
But sair fail'd is I, sair fail'd now—
Sair fail'd is I, sin' I ken'd thou."

THOMAS WHITTLE.

MR. BROCKIE writes : " In Mackenzie's *Northumberland* we
are told that Cambo was the favourite residence of the
ingenious and eccentric Thomas Whittle, whose comic
productions often beguile the long winter evenings of our
rustic Northumbrians. His parents and the place of his
birth are unknown. His brother, it is said, was parish clerk
of Earsdon, in 1750. Shilbottle, Ovingham, and Long
Edlingham are severally claimed as his birthplace.

"About the beginning of the last century he appeared at
Cambo, mounted on an old goat, and was engaged by a
miller, with whom he continued some years. About the
close of his servitude he became a disciple of Bacchus, and
continued attached to the service of the drouthy god while
he lived. Possessing a fertile imagination, brilliant wit, and
a happy command of language, the temptations to assume
the character of a boon companion were irresistible. His
talents were versatile. Some relics of his workmanship in

painting may be seen at Belsay Castle, Hartburn, Ponteland, and other churches in Northumberland. He died at East Shaftoe, and was buried at Hartburn on the 19th April 1736. An edition of his poetical works was published in 1815." On a contemporary of his, William Carstairs, he wrote a song, three verses of which are given—

WILLIAM CARSTAIRS, SCHOOLMASTER.

Ye muses nine, if ye think fit,
  Instruct my pen to write ;
Apollo, thou great god of wit,
  Come help me to indite.
Let poets, pipers, fiddlers, come,
  In priols or in pairs,
And echo forth as with a drum
  The praise of Will Carstairs.

  .   .   .   .   .

But first I must his pardon crave,
  For making bold and free,
For William was his Christian name,
  And shall be so for me.
But manners must to rhyme give place,
  Or else we spoil our wares,
And Will and William's all one case,
  And equal to Carstairs.

His face is like the midnight moon,
  And stars that shine so bright ;
His nose is like a flaming fire,
  That casts both heat and light ;
It sparkles like the Syrian seas
  When he gets in his airs,
A clown has not the heart to buy
  A beak like Will Carstairs.

  .   .   .   .   .   .

Carstairs, though a poor poet, was vain of his abilities as such. About the year 1731, Thomas Whittle and he being in a large company at the Burnt House* in Newcastle, the conversation turned on their respective merits as disciples of the muses. A wager was soon bet on the subject, and it was agreed that an hour should be allowed for each of them to write satirical verses on the other. The two poets were accordingly placed in separate apartments, and at the expiration of the time specified it was determined, by the throwing of a halfpenny, which of the two should first read his lay.

* The Burnt House finished its long career some twenty years ago, when Messrs. Robinson & Co., Side, bought it, rebuilt, and added it to their large stationery warehouse.

It fell to Whittle's lot, but before he had got to the end, his competitor was so chagrined that he put the concoction of his less fertile brain into the fire. The wager, of course, was won by Whittle's party.

SAWNEY OGILVY'S DUEL WITH HIS WIFE.

GOOD people give ear to the fatalest duel
    That Morpeth e'er saw since it was a town;
Where fire is kindled, and has so much fuel,
    I wou'd not be he that wou'd quench for a crown.
Poor Sawney, as canny a North British hallion
    As e'er crossed the border this million of weeks,
Miscarried and married a Scottish tarpaulin,
    That pays his pack-shoulders, and will have the
        breeks.

It fell on a day, he may well it remember,
    Tho' others rejoiced, yet so did not he,
When tidings was brought that Lisle did surrender,
    It grieves me to think on't, his wife took the gee.
These bitches still itches, and stretches commission,
    And if they be crossed they're still taking peeks,
And Sawney, poor man, was out of condition,
    And hardly well fit for defending the breeks.

She mutter'd and moung'd, and looked damn'd misty,
    And Sawney said something, as who cou'd forbear;
Then straight she began, and went to hand-fisty,
    She whither'd about and dang down all the gear.
The dishes and dublers went flying like fury,
    She broke more that day than would mend in two
        weeks;
And had it been put to a judge or a jury,
    They cou'd not tell whether deserved the breeks.

But Sawney grew weary, and fain would be civil,
   Being auld and unfeary, and failed of his strength ;
Then she couped him o'er the kale pot with a kevil,
   And there he lay labouring all his long length.
His body was soddy, and sore he was bruised,
   The bark of his shins was all standing in peaks,
No stivat e'er lived was so much misused,
   As sare as auld Sawney for claiming the breeks.

The noise was so great all the neighbours did hear them,
   She made his scalp ring like the clap of a bell ;
But never a soul had the mense to come near them,
   Tho' he shouted murder with many a yell.
She laid on whisky-whasky, and held like a steavy,
   Wight Wallace could hardly have with her kept
      streaks,
And never give over until she was weary,
   And Sawney was willing to yield her the breeks.

WHITTLE.   *Bell's " Northern Bards,"* 1812.

LITTLE MOODY, RAZOR-SETTER.

GOOD Master Moody,
My beard being cloudy,
My cheeks, chin, and lips
Like moon i' the 'clipse,
   For want of a wipe.
I've sent you a razor,
If you be at leisure
To grind her, and set her,
And make her cut better,
   You'll e'en light my pipe.

To plant every rural delight,
  Here Nature has lavish'd her skill ;
Here fragrant breezes unite,
  And wanton round Jessamond Mill.

When silence each evening here dwells,
  The birds in their coverts all still,
No music in sweetness excels
  The clacking of Jessamond Mill.

Reclin'd by the verge of the stream,
  Or stretch'd on the side of the hill,
I'm never in want of a theme,
  Whilst leering at Jessamond Mill.

Sure Venus some plot has design'd,
  Or why is my heart never still,
Whenever it pops in my mind,
  To wander near Jessamond Mill ?

My object, ye swains, you will guess,
  If ever in love you had skill ;
And, faith, I will frankly confess,
  'Tis Jenny at Jessamond Mill.

PANDON DENE.

This appears in Bell's *Northern Bards* as " a song published in September
1776, under the name of 'Rosalinda.'" *Richardson's Table Book* has it—
" From *Newcastle Weekly Magazine*, 1777." Neither attempt to tell who
"Rosalinda" was. If a guess might be hazarded, perhaps Miss Harvey,
of Newcastle, might be named. Her life Mr. Welford has lately given in
his "Men of Mark" series. But whoever the writer, the beauties of Pandon
Dene, of which she sings, are now no more. Elderly inhabitants recollect it
something like what it appeared to "Rosalinda," when it extended from
Barras Bridge to about Trafalgar Goods Station. But for some fifty years
the filling-up process has been going on, until now the beautiful ravine or
valley, with its " purling rill," lies buried some seventy feet below. In
Mackenzie's Newcastle a fine view and description of Pandon Dene, as it
appeared in 1821, is given.

WHEN cooling zephyrs wanton play,
Then oft in Pandon Dene I stray;
When sore depress'd with grief and woe,
There from a busy world I go:
My mind is calm, my soul serene,
Beneath the Bank in Pandon Dene.

The feather'd race around me sing,
They make the hills and valley ring;
My sorrow flies, my grief is gone,
I warble with the tuneful throng;
All, all things wear a pleasing mien;
Beneath the Bank in Pandon Dene.

At distance stands an ancient tower,
Which ruin threatens every hour;
I'm struck with rev'rence at the sight,
I pause and gaze with fond delight;
The antique walls do join the scene.
And make more lovely Pandon Dene.

Above me stand the tow'ring trees,
And here I feel the gentle breeze;
And water flows by chance around,
And green enamels all the ground;
Which gives new splendour to the scene,
And adds a grace to Pandon Dene.

And when I mount the rising hill,
And there survey the purling rill;
My eye's delighted—but I mourn
To think of winter's quick return,
With with'ring winds, and frost so keen;
I sighing leave the Pandon Dene.

2

O spare for once a female pen,
And lash licentious wicked men ;
Your conscious cheek need never glow,
If you your talents thus bestow :
Scarce fifteen summers have I seen,
Yet dare to sing of Pandon Dene.

JOHN CUNNINGHAM.

JOHN CUNNINGHAM, "whose name and fame will for ever be identified with Newcastle," was born in Dublin in 1729. His parents, who were of Scottish extraction, seem to have had their share of "fortune's buffets and rewards"—his father rising through winning a prize in a lottery, and falling again as a bankrupt. The son was recalled from the Grammar School at Drogheda—drifted to the theatres, at seventeen wrote a play, "Love in a Mist," which was performed at Dublin, and afterwards at Newcastle—took to the stage, and finally settled at Newcastle as a member of the dramatic company which then travelled the North.

At Newcastle he seems to have won the friendship of Mr. and Mrs. Slack, and for the *Newcastle Chronicle*, of which Mr. Slack was owner, he wrote short notices, and trifles in verse, which added to his income. In 1766 he published his poems by subscription. He was advised by his best friends to dedicate the volume to the celebrated Mrs. Montague, of Denton Hall (just outside of Newcastle), but preferred to dedicate it to David Garrick, and walked the distance from

Newcastle to London with a copy, elegantly bound, only to find himself treated with indifference and neglect. The following extracts from his volume show its character :—

EXTRACT FROM AN ELEGY ON A PILE OF RUINS.

" No—tho' the palace bar her golden gate,
    Or monarchs plant ten thousand guards around,
Unerring and unseen the shaft of fate
    Strikes the devoted victim to the ground.

" What, then, avails Ambition's wide-stretched wing,
    The Schoolman's page, or pride of Beauty's bloom?
The crape-clad hermit and the rich-robed king,
    Levelled, lie mixed promiscuous in the tomb.

. . . .

" Search where Ambition raged with rigour steeled ;
    Where Slaughter like the rapid lightning ran :
And say, while mem'ry weeps the blood-stained field,
    Where lies the chief? and where the common man?

" Vain, then, are pyramids and motto'd stones,
    And monumental trophies raised on high :
For TIME confounds them with the crumbling bones
    That, mix'd in hasty graves, unnotic'd lie.

" Rests not beneath the turf the peasant's head
    Soft as the lord's beneath the labour'd tomb?
Or sleeps one colder in his close, clay bed
    Than t'other in the wide vault's dreary womb ? "

. . . .

On June 20th, 1773, he took his last benefit at Darlington, and returned to Newcastle unwell, where, at his lodgings in Union Street, on September 18th, 1773, he died, in his 44th year, and was buried in St. John's Churchyard, a monument being placed over his grave by Mr. Slack, of the *Newcastle Chronicle.* At this monument, about the year 1820, the poet Gilchrist composed the following :—

" Lament him, ye valleys, ye hills, and ye mountains,
    And mournfully echo his name through the groves;
Lament in your murmurs, ye soft winding fountains,
    Sweet themes of his songs and dear scenes of his loves.
Now jocundly Mirth may out-carol his numbers,
    And fancy with flowerets his bust may entwine—
But these ne'er shall wake from chill Death's icy slumbers
    The Poet who sung on the banks of the Tyne.

" Here sleeps, sons of genius, a spirit undaunted !
　What availed all his merits, so blushing and fair,
Consigned to the earth, with his honours untainted,
　The subject of praise which he never must hear ;
Though his name and his fame will be sung in each ballad
　In ages remote still immortal to shine,
And the green turfy pillow will ever be hallowed
　Of the Poet who sung on the banks of the Tyne."

A POET'S TOMBSTONE.

Ninety-two years after, the monument falling into decay, Jos. Cowen the younger, then as now (1891) proprietor of the *Chronicle*, placed in his memory a memorial window in St. John's Church. In 1887 a subscription, originated by Mr. John Robinson, raised sufficient to restore the decaying tombstone, and thus he lies commemorated both in the church and in the churchyard.

HOLIDAY GOWN.

IN holiday gown, and my new-fangled hat,
　Last Monday I tript to the fair :
I held up my head, and I'll tell you for what—
　Brisk Roger I guessed wou'd be there.
He woos me to marry whenever we meet,
　There's honey, sure, dwells on his tongue ;
He hugs me so close, and kisses so sweet,
　I'd wed—if I were not too young !

Fond Sue, I'll assure you, laid hold on the boy
   (The vixen would fain be his bride),
Some token she claimed, either ribbon or toy,
   And swore that she'd not be deny'd.
A top-knot he bought her, and garters of green,
   Pert Susan was cruelly stung ;
I hate her so much, that, to kill her with spleen,
   I'd wed—if I were not too young !

He whispered such soft, pretty things in mine ear,
   He flatter'd, he promis'd, and swore ;
Such trinkets he gave me, such laces and gear,
   That, trust me, my pockets ran o'er.
Some ballads he bought me, the best he cou'd find,
   And sweetly their burthen he sung ;
Good faith ! he's so handsome, so witty, and kind,
   I'd wed—if I were not too young !

The sun was just setting, 'twas time to retire
   (Our cottage was distant a mile) ;
I rose to be gone—Roger bowed like a squire,
   And handed me over the stile.
His arms he threw round me—love laugh'd in his eye ;
   He led me the meadows among;
There pressed me so close, I agreed, with a sigh,
   To wed—for I was not too young !

JOHN CUNNINGHAM.   *Second Edition.*

A NORTH SHIELDS SONG.

WE'LL all away to the Lowlights,
   And there we'll see the sailors come in ;
We'll all away to the Lowlights,
   And there we'll see the sailors come in.

There clap your hands and give a shout,
And you'll see the sailors go out ;
Clap your hands and dance and sing,
And you'll see your laddie come in.

————

A NEW SONG MADE ON

ALICE MARLEY,

AN ALEWIFE AT PICTREE, NEAR CHESTER-LE-STREET.

The maiden name of Alice, famous as Elsey or Ailcie Marley, was
Harrison. Her husband, Ralph Marley, kept the "Swan" public-house at
Pictree. Alice was a handsome, buxom, bustling landlady, and brought
good custom to the house by her civility and attention. Her end was a sad
one. She suffered from a long illness, and was found drowned in a pond
near Biggs, into which it was supposed she had fallen, and could not
extricate herself.

To its own tune.

ELSIE MARLEY is grown so fine,
She won't get up to serve her swine,
But lies in bed till eight or nine,
And surely she does take her time.

Chorus—
An' div ye ken Elsie Marley, honey ?
The wife that sells the barley, honey ;
She won't get up to serve her swine,
And do you ken Elsie Marlie, honey ?

Elsie Marley is so neat,
It is hard for one to walk the street,
But every lad and lass they meet,
Cries " Div ye ken Elsie Marley, honey ? "

Elsie keeps rum, gin, and ale,
In her house below the dale,
Where every tradesman, up and down,
Does call and spend his half-a-crown.

*Elsie Marley wore a straw hat,
But now she's gotten a velvet cap ;
The Lambton lads mun pay for that,
Do you ken Elsie Marley, honey ?

The farmers, as they come that way,
They drink with Elsie every day,
And call the fiddler for to play
The tune of " Elsie Marley," honey.

The pitmen and the keelmen trim,
They drink bumbo made of gin,
And for the dance they do begin
To the tune of " Elsie Marley," honey.

The sailors they will call for flip,
As soon as they come from the ship,
And then begin to dance and skip,
To the tune of " Elsie Marley," honey.

An' div ye ken, etc.

UNKNOWN. *Ritson's "Bishopric Garland,"* 1784.

* This verse, not in Ritson, is given by Sharpe as current in the neighbourhood. By the Lambton lads were meant the five brothers of the house
of Lambton, all bachelors to a certain period, and all admirers of Elsie
Marley.

DONOCHT HEAD.

Donocht (or Dunnet) Head, the most northerly point of Great Britain.

"' DONOCHT HEAD' is not mine ; I would give ten pounds if
it were." So wrote Burns in 1794 to his friend Thompson,
and further added : " It appeared first in the *Edinburgh
Herald*, and came to the editor with the Newcastle post-
mark on it." The writer of the piece thus praised by Burns
was Mr. George Pickering, at that time a clerk with the
brothers Davidson, attorneys, Newcastle. Dr. Currie, in
his *Life of Burns*, says, " This affecting poem is apparently
incomplete. The author need not be ashamed to own himself.
The piece is worthy of Burns, or of Macniel."

Mr. R. Robinson, bookseller, in his recently published *Thomas Bewick: his Life and Times,* tells a most interesting story relating to Bewick's daughter and this piece. Mr. Robinson was visiting Miss Isabella Bewick; she was then in her ninety-fourth year, and, unlike her usual, seemed indisposed to converse. "Yet, to my surprise," he writes, "she recited, with much feeling, Pickering's beautiful fragment, 'Donocht Head.'" Perhaps the line—

"Full ninety winters hae I seen"

attracted her. Mr. Robinson, on leaving, promised to see her again, but that he was unable to do. Within a month, after a brief illness, the last of the Bewicks had been laid to rest at Ovingham Churchyard.

George Pickering, the author, was born in 1758, and was a native of Simonburn. Mr. Brockie writes, "He was of an unsteady, erratic temperament, and had a very melancholy ending, dying insane at Kibblesworth, on the 28th July 1826, at the house of his sister. He was buried in Lamesley Churchyard, where his sister erected a tombstone to his memory." His poems were published in 1815.

TUNE—"Ye Banks and Braes."

KEEN blaws the wind o'er Donocht Head,
    The snaw drives snelly through the dale,
The Gaber-lunzie tirls my sneck,
    And shivering tells his waefu' tale—
"Cauld is the night, O let me in,
    And dinna let your minstrel fa'!
And dinna let his winding-sheet
    Be naething but a wreath o' snaw.

"Full ninety winters hae I seen,
    And piped where gor-cocks whirring flew;
And mony a day ye've danced, I ween,
    To lilts which from my drone I blew."
My Eppie waked, and soon she cried,
    "Get up, gudeman, and let him in;
For weel ye ken the winter night
    Was short when he began his din."

My Eppie's voice, oh wow! it's sweet,
    E'en though she bans and scaulds a wee;
But when it's tuned to sorrow's tale,
    Oh, haith, it's doubly dear to me.
" Come in, auld carl; I'se steer my fire:
    I'll mak' it bleeze a bonnie flame;
Your bluid is thin, ye've tint the gate;
    Ye shouldna stray sae far frae hame."

" Nae hame hae I," the minstrel said:
    "Sad party strife o'erturned my ha';
And, weeping, at the eve of life,
    I wander thro' a wreath o' snaw."

    .   .   .   .   .

PICKERING.   *Edition* 1815.

THE COLLIER'S RANT.

Sir Cuthbert Sharpe writes:—" This is a true pit song, which few singers can do justice to. Those who have had the advantage of hearing it sung by the late Mr. W. S——, sen., of Pictree, will not readily forget the marvellous effect he produced on his hearers by his powerful voice and genuine humour."

As me and my marrow was ganning to wark
We met with the Devil; it was in the dark;
I up with my pick, it being in the neit,
And knock'd off his horns, likewise his club feet.

Chorus—

    Follow the horses, Johnny, my lad, oh!
    Follow them through, my canny lad, oh!
    Follow the horses, Johnny, my lad, oh!
    Oh, lad, lye away, canny lad, oh!

As me and my marrow was putting the tram,
The lowe it went oot, and my marrow went wrang;
You would have laugh'd had you seen the gam,—
The de'il gat my marrow, but I gat the tram.

> Follow the horses, etc.

Oh, marrow! oh, marrow! what dost thou think?
I've broken my bottle and spilt a' my drink!
I lost a' my shin splints amang the greet stanes;
Draw me t' the shaft, it's time to gan hame.

> Follow the horses, etc.

Oh, marrow! oh, marrow! where hast thou been?
Driving the drift from the low seam,
Driving the drift from the low seam:
Haud up the lowe, lad! de'il stop oot thy een!

> Follow the horses, etc.

Oh, marrow! oh, marrow! this is wor pay week,
We'll get penny loaves, and drink to wor beek;
And we'll fill up our bumper, and round it shall go;
Follow the horses, Johnny, lad, oh!

> Follow the horses, etc.

There is my horse, and there is my tram;
Twee horns full of grease will myek her to gang;
There is my hoggers, likewise my half-shoon,
And smash my heart! marrow, my puttin's a' done!

> Follow the horses, etc.

UNKNOWN.   *Ritson's "Bishopric Garland,"* 1784.

THE LITTLE P. D.

One of the few dialect songs before the time of Thompson, Shield, and Selkirk.

'TWAS between Hebbron an' Jarrow,
    There cam' on a varry strang gale ;
The skipper luik'd oot o' the huddock,
    Crying, "Smash, man ! lower the sail !
Smash, man ! lower the sail !
    Or else to the bottom we'll go !"
The keel an' a' hands wad been lost,
    Had it not been for Jemmy Munro.
                    Fal lal, etc.

The gale blew stranger an' stranger ;
    When they cam' beside the Muck Hoose,
The skipper cry'd oot, "Jemmy, swing 'er !"
    But still wes as fear'd as a moose.
P. D. ran te clear the anchor,
    "It's raffled," right loudly he roar'd ;
They a' said the gale wad sink her
    If it wasn't seun thrawn owerbord.
                    Fal lal, etc.

The laddy ran sweaten, ran sweaten,
    The laddy ran sweaten aboot,
Till the keel went bump 'gainst Jarrow,
    An' three o' th' bullies lap oot.
Three o' th' bullies lap oot,
    An' left nyen in but little P. D.,
Who ran aboot stampin' and cryin',
    "How, smash ! Skipper, what mun a' dee ?"
                    Fal lal, etc.

They all shooted oot frae the Kee—
  "Steer her close in by th' shore,
An' then thraw th' painter t' me,
  Thou cat-faced son of a whore!"
The lad threw the painter ashore,
  They fastened her up to th' Kee;
But whe knaws how far she might gane
  Had it not been for little P. D.

Fal lal, etc.

Then into th' huddock they gat,
  And th' flesh they began to fry;
They talked o' th' gale as they sat,
  An' how a' hands were lost (very nigh).
Th' Skipper roored out for a drink;
  P. D. ran to bring him th' can,
But, odsmash! mun, what d'ye think!
  He coup'd a' th' flesh out o' th' pan.

Fal lal, etc.

UNKNOWN.   *Angus's " Newcastle Garland," about* 1805.

DOL LI A.

A song famous in Newcastle about the years 1792-3-4.

FRESH I'm cum fra Sandgate Street,
                    Do li, do li,
My best friends here to meet,
                    Do li a,
                    Dol li th' dil len dol,
                    Do li, do li,
                    Dol li th' dil len dol,
                    Dol li a.

The Black Cuffs is gawn away,
> Do li, do li,
An' that will be a crying day,
> Do li a, etc.

Dolly Coxon's pawned her sark,
> Do li, do li,
To ride upon the baggage cart,
> Do li a, etc.

The Green Cuffs is cummin in,
> Do li, do li,
An' that 'ill make the lasses sing,
> Do li a, etc.

> *Bell's " Northern Bards,"* 1812.

The "Black Cuffs," the North York Militia. The "Green Cuffs," the 23rd, or Ulster Dragoons.

A YOU A, HINNY BURD.

It's O but I ken well,
> A you, hinny burd,
The bonny lass of Benwell;
> A you a.

She's lang-legg'd and mother-like,
> A you, hinny burd;
See she's raking up the dyke,
> A you a.

The Quayside for sailors,
> A you, hinny burd;
The Castle Garth for tailors,
> A you a.

The Gateshead Hills for millers,
      A you, hinny burd;
The North Shore for keelers,
      A you a.

There's Sandgate for aud rags,
      A you, hinny burd.
And Gallowgate for trolly-bags,
      A you a.

There's Denton and Kenton,
      A you, hinny burd;
And canny Lang Benton,
      A you a.

There's Tynemouth and Cullercoats,
      A you, hinny burd;
And Shields for the sculler-boats,
      A you a.

There's Horton and Holywell,
      A you, hinny burd;
And bonny Seaton Delaval,
      A you a.

Hartley Pans for sailors,
      A you, hinny burd;
And Bedlington for nailers,
      A you a.

UNKNOWN.   *Bell's " Northern Bards,"* 1812.

THE WATER OF TYNE.

As a note to this song, Sir C. Sharpe writes:—"The Tyne divides the counties of Durham and Northumberland, and as one of the parties was evidently on the Durham side of the river, this song may be justly admitted into the 'Garland.' A blue stone marks the boundaries of the counties on Newcastle Bridge, and one-third of it is supported by and belongs to the Bishoprick."

I CANNOT get to my love, if I should dee,
    The water of Tyne runs between him and me;
And here I must stand, with the tear in my e'e,
    Both sighing and sickly, my sweetheart to see.

O where is the boatman? my bonny honey!
    O where is the boatman? bring him to me—
To ferry me over the Tyne to my honey,
    And I will remember the boatman and thee.

O bring me a boatman—I'll give any money
    (And you for your trouble rewarded shall be),
To ferry me over the Tyne to my honey,
    Or scull him across that rough river to me.

UNKNOWN.   *Bell's " Northern Bards,"* 1812.

A SOUTH SHIELDS SONG.

THE sailors are all at the bar,
    They cannot get up to Newcastle;
The sailors are all at the bar,
    They cannot get up to Newcastle.

Up wi' smoky Shields,
    And hey for bonny Newcastle;
Up wi' smoky Shields,
    And hey for bonny Newcastle.

Bell's " Northern Bards," 1812.

Sir C. Sharpe adds—"Of a similar description are the following fragments, which apply to Sunderland :—

> Blow the wind southerly, southerly, southerly,
> Blow the wind southerly, So' and So' West ;
> My lad's at the bar, at the bar, at the bar,
> My lad's at the bar, that I love best.

> We'll all away to Sunniside,
> To Sunniside, to Sunniside,
> We'll all away to Sunniside,
> To see the Fitter's maidens.

> Till the tide comes in, till the tide comes in,
> And we'll sit upon the pier till the tide comes in."

THE TYNE.

"The Tyne" first appeared in Marshall's *Northern Minstrel*, 1806-7. In the same volume, which is made up of four parts, many other songs by the same writer also appeared, and all with the signature J. G., of Newcastle. Bell, in his *Northern Bards*, 1812, reprinted "The Tyne," and gave the author's full name, John Gibson. None of his songs are in the dialect, and excepting "The Tyne," which from its pleasing nature and local subject generally finds a place in Tyneside collections, are forgotten. Mr. Brockie, in his "Local Songs and Song Writers" (*Weekly Chronicle*), says John Gibson was a nephew of the celebrated Thomas Spence, and a very ingenious and promising young man. He died at Liverpool on the 20th of January 1810, aged twenty-two years.

ROLL on thy way, thrice happy Tyne !
Commerce and riches still are thine ;
Thy sons in every art shall shine,
        And make thee more majestic flow.

The busy crowd that throngs thy sides,
And on thy dusky bosom glides,
With riches swell thy flowing tides,
        And bless the soil where thou dost flow.

Thy valiant sons, in days of old,
Led by their Chieftains, brave and bold,
Fought not for wealth, or shining gold,
 But to defend thy happy shores.

So e'en as they of old have bled,
And oft embrac'd a gory bed,
Thy modern sons, by Ridleys led,
 Shall rise to shield thy peace-crown'd shores.

Nor art thou blest for this alone,
That long thy sons in arms have shone;
For every art to them is known,
 And science, form'd to grace the mind.

Art, curb'd by War in former days,
Has now burst forth in one bright blaze;
And long shall his refulgent rays
 Shine bright, and darkness leave behind.

The Muses too, with Freedom crown'd,
Shall on thy happy shores be found,
And fill the air with joyous sound,
 Of—War and darkness' overthrow.

Then roll thy way, thrice happy Tyne !
Commerce and riches still are thine !
Thy sons in arts and arms shall shine,
 And make thee still majestic flow.

GIBSON.   *Marshall's " Northern Minstrel,"* 1807.

BRANDLING.

Like as the brand doth flame and burn,
So we from death to life should turn.

An old rhyme or motto of the Brandling family, whose crest is an oak
tree in flames—perhaps a border beacon.
          Sharpe's "Bishopric Garland."

BRANDLING AND RIDLEY.

Members for Newcastle in seven successive Parliaments.

BRANDLING for ever, and Ridley for aye,
  Brandling and Ridley carries the day !
Brandling for ever, and Ridley for aye,
  There's plenty of coals on our waggon way.
There's wood for to cut, and coals for to hew,
  And the bright star of Heaton will carry us through ;
Ridley for ever, and Brandling for aye,
  There's plenty of coals on our waggon way.

Bell's " Northern Bards," 1812.

THOMAS THOMPSON.

" There's native bards in yon toon,
  For wit an' humour seldom be't,
They sang se sweet in yon toon,
  Gud faith, aw think aw hear them yet."

THE "native bards" thus commemorated who "sang se
sweet in yon toon" the poet might have added were not
the only bards who have sung in praise of "Canny Newcassel." Other bards not native have joined in the strain,
and some of the best songs in its praise are by writers
to whom the old town, however kind, stands but as a
foster-mother. Foremost amongst these must be classed
Thomas Thompson, who, in addition to being one of the
earliest and best of Tyneside writers, may be further
honoured as one of the founders of Tyneside song. Thompson, thus not a native of Newcastle, was born in 1773 in the
neighbourhood of Bishop Auckland, where also his boyhood
was passed, his father, who was an officer, dying of a fever
when his son was young. To Durham as a youth he was
sent to finish his education and enter business. From
Durham to bustling, stirring Newcastle was but a step; that
step while quite a young man he took, and thus from early
manhood until his untimely death, Newcastle, whose praises
with such pride he sung, claimed him as her own.

  Once settled in Newcastle (about 1790), his energy and ability
soon brought him to the front. The times were stirring.

  "Should haughty Gaul invasion threat"

struck the keynote of the period, and Burns but reflected

the feeling which had been aroused by French threats when he joined the Dumfries Volunteers. All over the country volunteer regiments were forming. In one of these, "The Newcastle Light Horse," Thompson, young as he was (about twenty-three), showed the position he had won in the town by being appointed Acting-Quartermaster, and a little later on Captain.

Curiously it is in connection with Burns that we come upon the first trace of Thompson as a writer. He must

THOMAS THOMPSON.

have written much before, but as yet it is untraced. Burns died July 21st, 1796. In the *Newcastle Chronicle*, about six weeks later, an elegy on his death appeared ; it was signed J. H. In the library of the Antiquarian Society, in Bell's "Notes and Cuttings," from which this is condensed, it is said the elegy was a vile heap of plagiarisms. Thompson, young and impulsive, in an anonymous sheet, pointed out these plagiarisms. For that he got no thanks from J. H.

(John Howard), a teacher of mathematics, who had succeeded to the school of the famous Hutton. Howard was one of the "Flying Congress," a company so named from their shifting their meeting-place from one public-house to another according as they found the drink suitable. Thompson, young, and in that drinking age, thus refers to that failing—

> "Think'st thou instead of the Parnassian stream
>   Strong beer can warm thee with a poet's fire ;
> Faith, if thou think'st it, it will prove a dream,
>   Thou'll find a gewgaw where thou'd wish a lyre.
> Beer has no powers poetic of creation."

This exposure produced a reply. Howard confesses to "borrowing a line," compliments his critic "as far surpassing 'Blind Willie,'" writes of his "bombastic thoughts," "ap'd Pindaric strains," brings in "reptile," "assassin," and wants his critic "dragged from his lurking-place." With this reply possibly the inky battle might have ended, but a Dr. Young, a physician of the town, appears to have joined in the fray, and, as Thompson wrote—

> "Throwing thy froth of scandal upon me,"

had gone from house to house.

To the pair Thompson replied in what Bell calls eight pages of rhodomontade, but which more aptly might be called eight pages of fancy, wit, and feeling. He begins his reply by lamenting that he should again have to mount his tired "Pegasus," as

> "'Twas but last night we traversed every clime,
>   Dashing o'er hills and dales, thro' thick and thin,
> In search of thoughts and similies sublime
>   To paint the dimple on my sweetheart's chin."

Yet mount he must—honour calls.

> "But ere we honour's daring call obey,
>   Let us, like pious Christians, down and pray :—
> O Burns ! a youth bred up in Nature's school
>   With bended knee would fain implore thy aid ;
> O give me powers to lash the silly fool
>   Who durst thy honoured mem'ry so degrade.
> 'Twas love of thee that brought me in this scrape,
>   Nor have I half a doit to see a Proctor ;
> Without thy aid I'm sure I can't escape
>   A host like these, led by so great a Doctor.
> O clear pillgarlick from this dreadful strait,
>   Tongue-tye the blockheads, and their malice check ;
> God willing, I would take a broken pate,
>   But verily I fear they'll break my neck."

He then finely puts it is the offence, not the offender, he fights.

> " But tho' with critic eyes his lays I'd scan,
> I'd damn the rhymer, but would save the man ;
> Detest the lays that fann'd the breath of strife,
> Or hurt him in the theatre of life ;
> For could they to his name one stain convey,
> God knows with tears I'd wash that stain away."

After some mock heroic, he proceeds—

> " Permit me now to leave my idle pranks,
> And very gravely offer thee my thanks
>   For telling me I Wyllie* far surpass.
> O Wyllie, thou art Nature's honest child,
> And had but education on thee smil'd,
>   To-day he'd been to thee an empty ass :
> Blind Wyllie, ancient laureate of the Tyne,
> Son of Apollo—thee I'll call divine !
>   Because thy strains, tho' low, are all thy own.
> High then thy head above this reptile rear,
>   For if his lays with thine were shown,
> I'll tell thee honestly how they'd appear :
>   As to the sun would seem a farthing candle,
>   Or thy jig notes to sweetest strains of Handel."

He concludes by announcing he will " lie on his oars awaiting a reply." He might lie ; no reply came ; the inky battle was over.† Bell, in whose interesting volumes of "Notes and Cuttings" this appears, says the best piece of poetry these knights of the quill produced was the following sonnet, written by J. Ingo, the son of a farmer near Benwell :—

SONNET.

TO THOMAS THÓMPSON, ON HIS LATE ADDRESS TO J. HOWARD.

> Struck with strong rapture at the dawning ray
>   Of splendid genius rising in thy mind,
> My dull heart pants to hail ye brightning day,
>   And give th' applause that wit should alway find.
> Shrewdly hast thou exposed the knavish scene,
>   Severely gall'd the vain pretender's pride.
> But for thy muse the theme is far too mean,
>   Thy muse that with such native ease can glide ;
>
> Sing, for I know thou canst, the pleasing pains
>   Of thrilling, melting, nature-cheering love ;
> Or from the deep lyre pour consoling strains,
>   To soothe wan thought in his sequester'd grove.
>
> So shall thy verse on distant ages beam,
> When Howard's sunk in Lethe's morbid stream.

It is sixteen years after this encounter with Howard before

---

* So spelt in the original.
† The two, Thompson and Howard, now lie within a few feet of each other in St. John's churchyard.

we trace Thompson's pen again. Possibly business had grown more pressing; he was young, and had his way to make. At this time, 1796, he was connected with Mr. David Bell, woollen draper, at the lower part of Middle Street, Groat Market side. Five years later (by the *Directory* of 1801), he is on the Quayside as a general merchant, trading as Armstrong, Thompson, & Co. His volunteer duties also would make inroads on his time. His only surviving son, Captain Robert Thompson, has memorials which tell how he devoted himself to his volunteer work. These memorials are two massive silver cups, a large silver vase, and a valuable sword and belt, with the following inscription :—

PRESENTED BY THE
NON-COMMISSIONED OFFICERS AND PRIVATES OF THE
CENTRE TROOP OF THE TYNE LEGION CAVALRY
TO
CAPTAIN THOMAS THOMPSON,
FOR HIS GREAT AND CONTINUOUS EXERTIONS IN
FORWARDING THEIR DISCIPLINE.

At what time he wrote his famous Tyneside songs cannot now be ascertained; his son, who was under four years of age when his father died, has no information. He, as soon as his education was finished (which was at Dr. Bruce's academy), took to the sea; and later on, when papers and relics came to him by the death of members of his family, the chest in which they were being sent to him at Australia was lost by the wreck of the vessel.

It is in 1812, in Bell's *Rhymes of Northern Bards,* that we next trace him. No more "dashing over hill and dale" for "thoughts and similies sublime," "to paint the dimple on his sweetheart's chin." His foot is on firmer if less fanciful ground. On the opening page of Bell's volume we get the first of his dialect songs on which his fame rests. The "New Keel Row" appears there with the initials "T. T.," and with the same initials, towards the end of the volume, his "Canny Newcastle" appears. Of "Jemmy Joneson's Whurry" we find no trace until some years after his death. Another song by him we trace—also in 1812; it appeared in the *Newcastle Advertiser,* and was sung at the Turk's Head Inn, Bigg Market, on Saturday, October 10th. The *Advertiser* introduces the song thus :—

" ELECTION—NEW SONG. We have been favoured by a gentleman with a copy of the excellent song written by Mr. Thompson, and sung by him at the election dinner of this town on Saturday

se-night. We trust the author will not be offended by our thus
giving it publicity."—October 22nd 1812.

This song, not in the dialect, may appropriately be given
here :—

" When joy wakes the muse, though her accents are glowing,
      Yet wildly and hurried they swell thro' the lay :
While ardour less warm might in lines softly flowing,
      Give voice to our feelings, and hail the proud day.
Hail, Ellison,* Senator ! what title greater
      Could call forth thy energies, all thy mind's force ?
Be thou as a star, which responsive to Nature,
      Both cheers and illumines our path in its course.
When won by thy eloquence, warm'd to emotion,
      The Citizens cheer'd thee with plaudits of zeal ;
Each greeting voice swore thee an oath of devotion,
      Thy talents, thy life, to the national weal.

While Wellington, leading the soldiers of Britain,
      Eclipses the glories of Greece and of Rome,
Old England might smile midst the dangers that threaten,
      Did nought vex or bias our Council at home.
A tool to no party, a slave to no passion,
      No wishes but those which from loyalty spring ;
Unmoved by the breeze of political fashion,
      His meed the applause of his country and King.
Thus Statesmen should be, and our country would flourish,
      Still prouder would stand on the records of Fame—
Nor shadows one doubt the warm wishes we cherish,
      Such merits will blazon our Ellison's name.

Hail, Ridley the muse, which, in rude local verses,
      Oft sung of thy sire, bids her greeting be thine ;
With Ellison's worth she thy worth too rehearses,
      And both your proud names in one wreath would entwine.
Alike high in honour, both ardently glowing
      With Patriot Zeal, in Britannia's cause ;
Both proud of the source whence your honours are flowing,
      Our Town's smiling Commerce, its Rights and its Laws.
May health give you powers to keep pace with your spirit ;
      And while in the Senate you worthily shine,
As Burgesses ; Patrons, alike may you merit
      The blessings of every cottage on Tyne."

Before 1812, when we thus get his songs, there is little
doubt Thomas Thompson had prospered and was then
a rising merchant in Newcastle. As Armstrong, Thompson, & Co., he had his offices in the Broad Chare, and
near the Skinner's Burn, at the foot of Forth Banks, his
large timber or raff yard. Cotfield House, on the Wind-

* Cuthbert Ellison, elected M.P. in 1812, succeeding C. J. Brandling
resigned.

mill Hills, Gateshead, overlooking the beautiful valley of the Tyne, was built by him; and about ninety years ago, before either Gateshead or Newcastle had extended westward, Cotfield, in which he lived, would be a most delightful residence. From it he commanded a view of the river, with his yard and mass of floating timber, and when needed, instead of going round by the bridge, a small boat could in a few minutes take him across the Tyne to his yard. How this pleasant prospect was prematurely overcast, and the fortune he had toiled to earn he was not fated to enjoy, cannot be better told than in the following, written some seventy-five years ago, and now for the first time reprinted. Only prefacing it with the introduction that the great flood mentioned, which was so fatal, was one of almost unexampled fury, great damage being done all along the river banks from Hexham to the sea, several lives being lost both at Newcastle and Shields. The flood was caused by a rapid thaw accompanied by a great storm of wind and rain.

From the *Newcastle Weekly Chronicle*, January 14th, 1816.

"From a Correspondent.

"Died on Tuesday morning last, the 9th inst., at his house near the Windmill Hills, Gateshead, Mr. Thomas Thompson, merchant, in the forty-third year of his age. It is with equal regret and sorrow we record the death of one who united in his character every property that constitutes a good, a useful, and a virtuous member of society. He was an excellent husband, a tender father, most affectionate to his relations, and charitable to the distressed. He endeared all (and they were many) who knew him, by a temper good natured in the extreme; for, whether in acts of hospitality or otherwise, he was ever most eager to render himself useful to those who had any claim to his friendship. But, alas! mute is that tongue which so often charmed the social circle, and set the table in a roar. It were unnecessary to say how much his presence was courted wherever humour and vivacity were considered an ingredient contributing to social recreation. There are few in this neighbourhood who have not been interested with his local songs, written by himself in the pure Newcastle dialect, and sung by him with a playfulness and humour that transported every genuine Northumbrian. In 1796, when Britannia's sons eagerly flew to arms in defence of their country and constitution, the deceased became the acting Quartermaster of the Newcastle Light Horse, commanded by that zealous officer, Captain (now Colonel) Burdon; and subsequently, when Colonel Burdon assumed the command of the South Tyne Legion, he was promoted to the rank of Captain in the Cavalry, and on all occasions showed himself an active and able officer. In his commercial transactions he was equally remarkable for that straightforward and liberal conduct which so distinguishes the British merchant. With regret then, no doubt, will the readers learn that the death of the deceased was occasioned by an over-exertion to save his property during the violent storm in the night between the 29th and 30th ult. Too careless of a life in itself so valuable he was seen repeatedly plunging into the river anxious to save his floating timber ere it was swept away by the overwhelming torrent. He, in consequence, caught a severe cold, which ended in an inflammation of the lungs, and all the art of the *materia medica* was unable to arrest the hand of death. Though the writer of this article was warmly attached to him, there is no reader who knew the deceased but will be aware of the strictest adherence to truth, and will long remember the subject of it with affection and esteem."

This loving tribute to the memory of Thomas Thompson could only have been written by one who knew him. Who was the correspondent who sent it? John Shield, author of "My Lord 'Size," doubtless a personal friend, might have done so. Thomas Wilson, a fellow-merchant on the Quay, whose "Pitman's Pay," ten years later, showed such kindred tastes, is another; but perhaps a more likely one still is Robert Gilchrist, then about nineteen years of age, and an ardent admirer of Thompson, as his following lament shows :—

TOMMY THOMPSON.

(Composed extempore.)

All ye whom minstrel's strains inspire,
  Soft as the sighs of morning—
All ye who sweep the rustic lyre,
  Your native hills adorning—
Where genius bids her rays descend
  O'er bosoms bleak and lonesome—
Let every hand and heart respond
  The name of Tommy Thompson.

Chorus—
  His spirit now is soaring bright,
    And leaves us dark and dolesome ;
  O luckless was the fatal night
    That lost us Tommy Thompson.

The lyric harp was all his own,
  Each mystic art combining—
Which Envy, with unbending frown,
  Might hear with unrepining.
The sweetest flower in summer blown
  Was not more blithe and joysome,
Than was the matchless, merry tone
  Which died with Tommy Thomson.

When Thompson died, Gilchrist had published nothing. It was six years after this before his first volume appeared, but it may be, and doubtless was the case, that the young poet had shown to the one he considered his master his early efforts, and had been kindly received. It is all a matter of supposition, but if the supposition be correct, Thomas Thompson would have in his young admirer, Robert Gilchrist, a pupil worthy of himself. Although dying at Cotfield, Gateshead, the body of Thomas Thompson was brought to Newcastle, and laid beside that of his mother in St. John's Churchyard, close to the grave of the poet Cunningham.

A few lines may be devoted to the poet's family. His widow, Jean, died six years after her husband, at the early age of thirty-five years, and was laid beside him in St. John's Churchyard. His youngest son, Bryan, died in 1832 in his sixteenth year, while his eldest son, John, in 1840, returning from Newcastle Races, was killed by jumping from his conveyance, his horse taking fright. Both sons are buried at St. Nicholas'. His daughters, Mrs. Dahl and Mrs. Curry, lived for years in New Bridge Street, and afterwards at Corbridge; there Mrs. Dahl died in 1868, and was buried at Morpeth. Mrs. Curry died at Jersey in 1877, and her brother, Captain Thompson, then returned from New Zealand, knowing how devoted the sisters had been to each other, had the body removed to Morpeth, where they now lie side by side.

Captain Robert Thompson, the sole survivor of the poet's family, only recollects of his father the sad deathbed scene, which, young as he was, stamped itself on his memory. But fortunately amongst the relics, spared by time and wreck, that have come to him, is a beautiful miniature portrait, painted on ivory, nearly one hundred years ago. Most kindly he has sent this from Sussex, where he is spending the evening of his days after a stirring adventurous life abroad. This portrait, which he has heard is a good likeness of his father, is here for the first time copied, and the copying being by the Meisenbach process, every feature and detail in the original is faithfully reproduced.

Of the songs which Thompson left behind him, few though they are in number, yet in all collections they are held amongst the best. W. H. Dawson, in his "Local Poets of Newcastle," contributed to the *North of England Advertiser*, about twenty years ago, after writing of some of the songs popular about the beginning of the century, says :—

"What a relief when Tommy Thompson gave his effusions publicity! What a burst of jovial humour there is in 'Jemmy Johnson's Wherry'; and who that is 'native and to the manner born' knows not the tune of 'Canny Newcassel.'"

And then :—

"Foremost among our local songs is the jovial one of 'Canny Newcassel.' Independent of the interest excited by the connecting links between the locality and the song, it could scarcely have failed in being popular from the hearty geniality of its humour; indeed, it may be said to be one burst of enthusiasm throughout. And at the present day it may be taken as the finest piece of descriptive verse in the dialect. It stands almost unrivalled now, and the only piece to be in any way compared to it is 'My Lord 'Size.'"

Alderman Wilson, author of the famous "Pitman's Pay," before referred to, writes of Thompson's songs :—"It is much to be regretted that neither the author nor his friends ever published his pieces in a collected form. His songs were excellent specimens of the Newcastle dialect happily expressed and pregnant with wit and humour." Readers of this sketch will understand how it was, what the late Alderman so much desired, was not done. The author's sudden death, his widow dying so soon after him, and only young children left, there really was no one to see after collecting his literary work. Yet none the less, the regret expressed by so competent a judge as the author of "The Pitman's Pay" will be shared in by all admirers of Tyneside song.

The late James Clephan, in his exquisite paper, "Over the Churchyard Wall," telling of the quiet sleepers—"Men of Mark" in their day—who lie in Old St. John's, makes no mention of Thomas Thompson, although, in writing of Cunningham, Oviston, and others, he must literally have passed over his grave. In 1889, when Mr. Hay, from information, wrote that Thompson was buried at St. John's, his letter was contradicted, and it was said that the poet lay at the Ballast Hills Burial Ground, so little knowledge had Time, with its deaths and removals, left, of where the author of "Canny Newcassel" lay! None, in fact, seemed to have been aware, when restoring the grave of Cunningham, that one so kindred lay so near, or in the concluding lines of a letter to the *Journal* on the subject that

"Lying for over seventy years so near the grave of Cunningham, that with outstretched arms they might touch each other, poets and lovers of Tyneside poetry have met at Cunningham's grave—restored it, and yet no whisper that so near it was the grave of one whose songs will be sung as long as Cunningham is read."

Photographed by Auty & Ruddock, Tynemouth.

Wishing to give the poet's autograph, and no scrap of his writing unfortunately being to be had from private sources, a visit was made to the Probate Court at Durham, that a tracing might be taken of the signature to his Will There, instead of his signature, as expected, only the initials of his name appeared —T. T. These initials in their brevity recall afresh the sad story of Thomas Thompson's untimely death. Struck down in the prime of life, his fatal illness would find all unprepared, and doubtless at the last moment, when, instead of getting better, as was fondly hoped, he rapidly grew worse, the Will, with its imperfect signature, would be a dying effort.

TRACED AT DURHAM, APRIL 22nd, 1891. PHOTOGRAPHED BY P. M. LAWS.

THE NEW KEEL ROW.

The oldest, and by far the most popular, of all the additions to, or imitations of, the famous fragment, "The Keel Row."

To the Old Tune.

WHE's like my Johnny,
Sae leish, sae blithe, sae bonny?
He's foremost 'mang the mony
   Keel lads o' Coaly Tyne.
He'll set or row so tightly,
Or in the dance so sprightly,
He'll cut and shuffle sightly:
   Tis true—were he not mine.

Chorus.

   Weel may the keel row,
   The keel row, the keel row,
   Weel may the keel row,
     That my laddie's in.
   He wears a blue bonnet,
   A bonnet, a bonnet,
   He wears a blue bonnet,
     A dimple in his chin.

He's ne mair learning
Than tells his weekly earning,
Yet reet frae wrang discerning,
   Tho' brave, ne bruiser he.
Tho' he no worth a plack is,
His awn coat on his back is,
An' nane can say that black is
   The white o' Johnny's e'e.

Each pay-day nearly
He takes his quairt right dearly,
Then talks O latin O cheerly,
   Or mavies jaws away:

How, caring not a feather,
Nelson and he together
The springy French did lether,
    And gar'd them shab away.

Were a' kings comparely,
In each I'd spy a fairly,
An' ay wad Johnny barly,
    He gets sic bonny bairns:
Go bon, the Queen, or misses,
But wad, for Johnny's kisses,
Luik upon as blisses
    Scrimp meals, caff beds, and dairns.

Wour lads, like their deddy,
To fight the French are ready,
But gies a peace that's steady,
    And breed cheap as langsyne;
May a' the press-gangs perish,
Each lass her laddy cherish;
Lang may the coal trade flourish
    Upon the dingy Tyne.

Breet star o' Heaton,
Your ay wour darling sweet 'en,
May Heaven's blessings leet on
    Your leady, bairns, and ye.
God bless the King and Nation,
Each bravely fill his station;
Our canny *Corporation*
    Lang may they sing wi' me—

Weel may the keel row, etc.

THOMPSON.   Bell's " Northern Bards," 1812.

CANNY NEWCASTLE.

Dr. R. S. Watson, in his lecture *A Gossip about Songs*, says :—" I must not speak as fully as I could wish to do of the fine old song 'Canny Newcassel,' and yet I cannot pass it by without remarking that the bard was a cunning philosopher, and had discovered that the fabric of society is built up on clothes, that much majesty may lie in a wig, long before 'Sartor Resartus' puzzled the subscribers to *Frazer's Magazine.*" As illustrating this, the Doctor quotes the climax of the song. Our Newcastle hero is before the king's palace. The wonders of London had failed to move him—

> *He could marrow them all in Canny Newcassel.*

He had seen the King,

> "And aw own he's a guid luikin mannie ;
> But if wor Sir Matthew ye buss iv his wig,
> By gocks he wad just leuk as canny."

" Wor Sir Matthew," whom Northern pride thus placed beside the king, was Sir Matthew White Ridley, of Heaton, then member for Newcastle. The song was written about the time his long career was closing. For eight successive Parliaments he had represented Newcastle ; he died in 1813, in his sixty-seventh year. A fine monument (the face a good likeness), by the great artist Flaxman, is erected to his memory in St. Nicholas'.

'Bout Lunnun aw'd heard sec wonderful spokes,
    That the streets were a' cover'd wi' guineas;
The houses se fine, sec grandees the folks,
    Te them hus i' th' North were but ninnies,
But aw fand ma-sel blonk'd when to Lunnun I gat,
    The folks they a' luck'd wishy-washy;
For gould ye may howk till ye're blind as a bat,
    For their streets are like wors—brave and blashy.

> 'Bout Lunnun then div'nt ye mak' sic a rout,
>   There's nouse there ma winkers to dazzle :
> For a' the fine things ye are gobbin about,
>   We can marra iv canny Newcassel.

A Cockney chep show'd me the Thames' druvy feace,
   Whilk he said was the pride o' the nation,
And thought at their shippin' aw'd maek a haze gaze,
   But aw whop'd ma foot on his noration;
Wi' huz, mun, three hundred ships sail iv a tide,
   We think nouse on't, aw'll maek accydavy,
Ye're a gouck if ye din't knaw that the lads o' Tyneside
   Are the jacks that maek famish wor Navy.

                         'Bout Lunnun, etc.

We went big St. Paul's and Westminster to see,
   And aw warn't ye aw thought they luck'd pretty,
And then we'd a keek at the Monument te,
   Whilk ma friend ca'd the pearl o' the city:
Wey hinny, says aw, we've a Shot Tower se hee,
   That biv it ye might scraffle to heaven,
And if on St. Nicholas ye once cus' an e'e,
   Ye'd crack on't as lang as ye're livin.

                         'Bout Lunnun, etc.,

We trudg'd to St. James's, for there the king lives,
   Aw warn'd ye a gud stare we teuck on't;
By my faicks! it's been built up by Adam's aun neaves,
   For it's aud as the hills by the leuk on't;
Shem bin ye! says I, ye shou'd keep the King douse,
   I speak it without ony malice;
Aw own that wor Mayor rather wants a new house,
   But then wor Infirm'ry's a palace.

                         'Bout Lunnun, etc.

Ah hinnies, out cum the King, while we were there,
    His leuks seem'd to say, "Bairns, be happy!"
So down o' my hunkers aw set up a blare,
    For God to preserve him frae Nappy:
For Geordy aw'd dee—for my loyalty's trig,
    And aw own he's a geud leukin mannie;
But if wor Sir Matthew ye buss iv his wig,
    By gocks! he wad just leuk as canny.

                    'Bout Lunnun, etc.

Ah hinnies! about us the lasses did loup,
    Thick as curns in a spice singin hinnie;
Some aud an' some hardly flig'd ower the doup,
    But aw ken'd what they were by their whinnie.
A'! mannie, says aw, ye hev mony a tite girl,
    But aw'm tell'd they're oft het i' their trappin',
Aw'd cuddle much rather a lass i' the Sworl,
    Than the dolls i' the Strand or i' Wappin'.

                    'Bout Lunnun, etc.

Wiv a' the stravaging aw wanted a munch,
    An' ma thropple was ready to gizen;
So we went tiv a yell-house and there teuk a lunch,
    But the reck'ning, my saul, was a bizon.
Wiv huz i' th' North, when aw'm wairsh i' my way
    (But te knaw wor warm hearts ye yur-sell come),
Aw lift the first latch, and baith man and dame say,
    Cruck yor hough, canny man, for ye're welcome.

                    'Bout Lunnun, etc.

A shillin' aw thought at the play hoose aw'd ware,
    But aw jump'd there wiv heuk-finger'd people,
My pockets gat ripp'd an' aw heard ne mair,
    Nor aw could frae Saint Nicholas' steeple,
Dang Lunnun, wor play-hoose aw like just as weel,
    And wor play-folks aw's sure are as funny:
A shillin's worth serves me to laugh till aw squeel,
    Ne hallion there trimmels ma money.
                      'Bout Lunnun, etc.

The loss o' the cotterels aw dinna regaird,
    For aw've getten some white-heft o' Lunnun;
Aw've learn'd to prefer my awn canny calf-yard,
    If ye catch me mair fra't ye'll be cunnun'.
Aw knaw that the Cockneys crake rum-gum-shus chimes
    To maek gam of wor bur and wor 'parel;
But honest blind Willie shall string this iv rhymes,
    And aw'll sing'd for a Christmas Carol.
                      'Bout Lunnun, etc.

THOMPSON.   *Bell's " Northern Bards,"* 1812.

JEMMY JONESON'S WHURRY.

This song, apparently the last the author wrote, seems not to have been printed during his lifetime. The earliest copy we can trace is in an old chap-book, fourth edition (1823), published by Marshall. As it is the fourth, reckoning back, the first edition would likely be published shortly after Thompson's death, in 1816. Whether through an error in the copy, or by a printer's slip, Marshall, by a simple mistake of two letters, so marred the first line that its meaning has been a puzzle for seventy years. This error finally was corrected, on the authority of the author's son, as told in the following letter :—

    "From the *Weekly Chronicle*, May 25th, 1889.

    "Mr. R. O. Heslop, in his *Northumberland Words*, quoting the opening line of 'Jemmy Joneson's Whurry,'

        'Whei *cavers* biv the chimlay reek,'

raised the question what was the meaning of *cavers*. Partly by the discussion so raised I got, by the kindness of a friend, the address of the author's son, and his letter upon the point is most interesting. Writing with pencil (as owing to an old wound in his knee received at the battle of Navarino in 1827—which occasionally troubles him—he was for the time obliged to keep in a recumbent position, and so unable to use pen and ink), he says that the beginning line, as at present in all collections, is wrong; it should be—

'Whei *cowers* biv the chimlay reek.'

Compare the two versions, how apparent the improvement made by the use of the two right letters. The old uncertain beginning gives place to the natural bold opening—

'Whie (who) cowers biv the chimlay reek,
Begox! it's all a horny,'

as if the hero of the famous voyage was casting back some slur on his daring or courage."

Marshall's unfortunate misprint, now corrected, has been copied into more than our local collections. Macmillan, of London, published in 1866 an edition of songs with music, edited by John Hullah, and "Jemmy Joneson's Whurry," with Marshall's mistake, was in it.

The song relates to a time when steamboats were unknown. Then the conveyance on the Tyne was by wherries, and Jemmy Joneson, whose wherry is here celebrated, was well known to all passengers on the river, but the fame of Jemmy and his wherry was soon to be eclipsed. The *Tyne Steam Packet*, the first steamer on the Tyne, commenced plying on Ascension Day, May 19, 1814.

WHEI cowers biv the chimlay reek,
    Begox! it's all a horney;
For thro' the world aw wisht to keek,
    Yen day when aw was corney;
Sae, wiv some varry canny chiels,
    All on the hop, an' murry,
Aw thowt aw'd myek a voyage to Shiels,
    Iv Jemmy Joneson's Whurry.

Ye niver see'd the church sae scrudg'd,
    As we wur there thegither,
An' gentle, semple, throughways nudg'd,
    Like burdies of a feather;
Blind Willie a' wor joys to croon,
    Struck up a hey-down-derry,
An' crouse we left wor canny toon,
    Iv Jemmy Joneson's Whurry.

As we push'd off, loak ! a' the Key
  To me seem'd shuggy-shooin',
An' tho' aw'd niver been at sea,
  Aw stuid her like a new-on.
And when the Malls began their reels,
  Aw kick'd maw heels reet murry ;
For faix ! aw liked the voyge to Shiels,
  Iv Jemmy Joneson's Whurry.

Quick went wor heels, quick went the oars,
  An' where me eyes wur cassin,
It seem'd as if the bizzy shores
  Cheer'd canny Tyne i' passin.
What ! hes Newcassel now nae end ?
  Thinks aw, it's wondrous, vurry :
Aw thowt aw'd like me life to spend
  Iv Jemmy Joneson's Whurry.

Tyne-side seem'd clad wiv bonny ha's,
  An' furnaces sae dunny ;
Wey, this mun be what Bible ca's
  " The land ov milk and honey ! "
If a' thor things belang'd tiv I,
  Aw'd myek the poor reet murry,
An' cheer the folks i' gannin by
  Iv Jemmy Joneson's Whurry.

Then on we went, as nice as owse,
  Till 'nenst au'd Lizzy Moody's,
A whirlwind cam', an' myed a' souse,
  Like heaps o' babby boodies.

The heykin myed me vurry wauf,
　Me heed turn'd duzzy, vurry;
Me leuks, aw'm sure wad spyen'd a cauf,
　Iv Jemmy Joneson's Whurry.

For hyem an' bairns, an' maw wife Nan,
　Aw yool'd oot like a lubbart;
An' when aw thowt we a' shud gan
　To Davy Jones's cubbart,
The wind bee-baw'd, aw whish'd me squeels,
　An' yence mair a' was murry,
For seun we gat a seet o' Shiels,
　Frev Jemmy Joneson's Whurry.

Wor Geordies now we thrimmel'd oot,
　An' tread a' Shiels, sae dinny;
Maw faix! it seems a canny sprout,
　As big maist as its minny:
Aw smack'd thir yell, aw clim'd thir bree,
　The seet was wondrous, vurry;
Aw lowp'd sec gallant ships to see
　Biv Jemmy Joneson's Whurry.

To Tynmouth then aw thowt aw'd trudge,
　To see the folks a' duckin;
Loak! men an' wives together pludg'd,
　While hundreds stud by, luikin.
Amang the rest, aw cowp'd me creels,
　Eh, gox! 'twas funny, vurry;
An' so aw end me voyge te Shiels,
　Iv Jemmy Joneson's Whurry.

THOMPSON.　　　　　　　　　*From Marshall's Chap-book,* 1828.

WILLIAM PURVIS (BLIND WILLIE).

"Blind Wyllie, ancient laureate of the Tyne."

So in jest Thomas Thompson happily hits off the "minstrel," poor blind Willie, who, hatless in all weathers, for

BLIND WILLIE.

upwards of half a century wandered the streets of Newcastle. John Stokoe, in "The North-Country Garland of Song," has an interesting account of him; from it principally we take the following :—

"William Purvis, son of John Purvis, a waterman, was born in Newcastle, and baptised at All Saints' Church, February 16th, 1752. Blind from his birth, his drifting to music gave him his living, such as it was. Although depending on the charity of the public, street performances were rare with him, his more general custom being to attend some favourite public-house, where he never failed to attract a company to listen to his fiddling and singing the old Newcastle ditties,

> 'Which helped away wi' mony a gill
> 'Mang fuddling men and queerish women.'"

"Buy Broom Busoms" was his favourite song. The melody is said to have been Willie's own composition, but of that Mr. Stokoe says there is no evidence except his partiality for it. The following is the song as it appears in Bell's *Northern Bards:*—

BROOM BUSOMS.

If you want a busom
  For to sweep your house,
Come to me, my lasses,
  Ye ma ha' your choose.

     Buy broom busoms,
      Buy them when they're new,
     Buy broom busoms,
      Better never grew.

If I had a horse,
  I would have a cart ;
If I had a wife,
  She wad take my part.
     Buy broom busoms, etc.

Had I but a wife,
  I care not who she be ;
If she be a woman,
  That's enough for me.
     Buy broom busoms, etc.

If she lik'd a drop,
  Her and I'd agree ;
If she did not like it,
  There's the more for me.
     Buy broom busoms, etc.

To the foregoing Blind Willie (the native minstrel of Newcastle) has added the following simple rhymes :—

> Up the Butcher Bank,
>   And down Byker Chare ;
> There you'll see the lasses
>   Selling brown ware.
>   Buy broom busoms, etc.
>
> Alang the Quayside,
>   Stop at Russell's Entry ;
> There you'll see the beer drawer,
>   She is standing sentry.
>   Buy broom busoms, etc.
>
> If you want an oyster,
>   For to taste your mouth,
> Call at Handy Walker's—
>   He's a bonny youth.
>   Buy broom busoms, etc.
>
> Call at Mr. Loggie's,
>   He does sell good wine ;
> There you'll see the beer drawer,
>   She is very fine.
>   Buy broom busoms, etc.
>
> If you want an orange
>   Ripe and full of juice,
> Gan to Hannah Black's ;
>   There you'll get your choose.
>   Buy broom busoms, etc.
>
> Call at Mr. Turner's,
>   At the Queen's Head ;
> He'll not set you away
>   Without a piece of bread.
>   Buy broom busoms, etc.
>
> Down the river side
>   As far as Dent's Hole ;
> There you'll see the cuckolds
>   Working at the coal.
>   Buy broom busoms, etc.

Bell's " Northern Ballads."

Willie had his regular houses of call, where he was always welcome, and duly served. Thus he used to drop in on his rounds at Messrs. Clapham & Gilpin's chemist's shop, first in Silver Street, and afterwards in Pilgrim Street, for the purpose of getting a dole of Spanish juice, which was never denied him. His invariable address was, "Hinny, doctor, gie us a bit o' Spanish!" uttered in the confident tones of a simple, guileless boy; and "God blish the king—God blish the King; never sheed him—never sheed him; poor shoul—poor shoul!" was his regular form of thanksgiving. Willie's mother, Margaret Purvis, who died in All Saints' poor-house, had reached her hundredth year; and Willie, who breathed his last in the same place on the 20th July 1832, was in his eighty-first year.

An interesting description of Blind Willie is given in the *Monthly Chronicle*, vol. ii. The writer was in a public house when Blind Willie came in. "With the instinct peculiar to blind people Willie made his way instantly to us. We rose at once, and handed him a chair. Willie's dress was generally grey, and he wore buckles, like our keelmen of old. He always went without a hat, and groped his way about wonderfully.

"As soon as Willie got seated, he said, 'Bonny beer, bonny beer.' We took the hint, and at once ordered a pint of beer to be brought to him. Willie went on, 'God blish the king—God blish the king; never sheed him—never sheed him; poor shoul—poor shoul!'

"'Willie,' we said, after he had taken a good draught of the beer—'Willie, we once heard you sing a little song. Will you kindly repeat it?'

"'Shartinly, shartinly, ma chewel.'

"Billy puts down the fiddle, and accompanies a sort of chorus by clapping his knees with both his hands:—

> "For to make the haggish nishe
> They put in some brown spishe.
>   Tarum tickle, tan dum,
>   To the tune o' tan dum,
> Tarum tickle, tan dum.

> "And to make the haggish fine
> They put in a bottle of wine.
>   Tarum tickle, tan dum,
>   To the tune o' tan dum,
> Tarum tickle, tarum tickle tan dum.

"'Ha, ha, ha, ha, ha,' chuckles Billy when he had finished, 'poor shoul, poor shoul!'"

Perhaps there is none of Newcastle's eccentrics more referred to in local song than "Blind Willie." Allusions to him abound. Gilchrist wrote an epitaph on his death, a verse from which may fittingly conclude this.

O wondrous indeed is this bever'ge ethereal!
　The mortal who quaffs it, altho' a mere clod,
Is straightway transformed to a being aerial,
　And moves on earth's surface in fancy a God.
　　　In a bumper is given
　　　A foretaste of Heaven,
All earthly vexations straight cease to annoy;
　　　Whilst laughing and crying
　　　And efforts at flying
Bespeak the soul tost in a tempest of joy.
　　　　For what can so fire us? etc.

Haste, haste to partake on't, ye men of grave faces,
　Ye Quakers, and Methodist parsons likewise;
What tho' ye seem lost to the flexible graces,
　And dormant the risible faculty lies,
　　　One quaff of the vapour
　　　Will cause you to caper,
And swiftly relax your stiff solemnis'd jaws;
　　　You'll acknowledge the change too,
　　　As pleasing as strange too,
And make the air ring with loud ha! ha! ha! ha's!
　　　　For what can so fire us? etc.

Let gin, rum, and brandy grow dearer and dearer,
　Distillers stop working—no toper will mourn;
Of Gas we can make a delectable cheerer,
　Which nor reddens our noses, nor livers will burn;
　　　Unbeholden to whisky
　　　We'll drink and get frisky,
Nor fear that to-morrow our temples may ache;
　　　Neither stomach commotions,
　　　Nor camomile potions,
Shall evermore cause us with terror to quake.
　　　　For what can so fire us? etc.

Let the miser's deep coffers be fill'd to his mind now,
　Let the man of ambition with honours abound;
Give the lover his mistress, complying and kind too,
　And with laurel let Poets and Heroes be crown'd.
　　　Let all be blest round me,
　　　No envy shall wound me,
Contented and cheerful thro' life will I pass,
　　　If fortune befriends me,
　　　And constantly send me
A quantum sufficit of Oxygen Gas.
　　　　For what can so fire us? etc.

This song, clever as it is, appears to have roused the ire
of C. P. (one Charles Purvis), who burlesqued it in the *Tyne
Mercury.* The following extracts give the best points:—

THE BARDS OF THE TYNE.

BY C. P.

Ye sons of Parnassus, whose brains are inspir'd
With envy, or madness, dame dulness, or wine,
Who wish to be flatter'd, or prais'd, or admir'd,
Leave thinking, and fly to the banks of the Tyne.
No wit is requir'd
To make you admir'd ;
Let doggerel run limping thro' each crippled line ;
No humour degrades
Nor genius pervades
The verses sublime of our bards of the Tyne.

· · · · · ·

How sweetly the strains
Must thrill thro' the veins
When Sandgate and Bedlam together combine,
Or "Oxygen Gas"
From the pipe of an ass
Rarifies the dense brains of our bards of the Tyne.

· · · · · ·

Even hydras and bears
Might prick up their ears,
And howl out in concert with Bards of the Tyne.

This is smart, and possibly was intended as a reply to "The Newcastle Bellman," a song supposed to have been written by Shield, in which the *Tyne Mercury* was held up to ridicule. However this may be, Shield appears to have treated it with contempt ; but if he did not notice it, another of the "Bards of the Tyne" (in Bell's *Rhymes*) did. James Stawpert, a clerk with Rayne & Burdon, brewers, on the Quayside, took up the cudgels, and dealt Purvis (whoever he was*) a few smart whacks. Stawpert begins—

" Who's he that with great *Mercury* strides
In imitation's line,
And without reason thus derides
The poets of the Tyne ?

---

* Since writing the above, the following notice of Charles Purvis has been found in Bell's "Notes and Cuttings" :—"Charles Purvis came to Newcastle from near Otterburn, and after being schoolmaster, and afterwards clerk to a merchant upon the Quayside, set up business as a general merchant, in which business he in a short space of time failed, leaving a few empty barrels to pay his creditors with."

> Who, not content with critic's skill,
>   That lets no error pass,
> In passion's cup he dips his quill,
>   And calls his brother—ass."

.   .   .   .   .

He then warns C. P. to forbear, as asses have a trick of kicking, and "OXygen Gas" that he has ridiculed with four letters left off would

> "make thee a monst'rous size,
>   E'en larger than an ass!
>
> I think the appellation suits,
>   Yet this believe from me,
> Had thou not been so fond of brutes
>   I'd not made one of thee."

There is also in the *Northern Songster*, though not in the dialect, some of Shield's brightest songs. Wars and rumours of wars then filled the air, volunteers were arming and drilling all over, Napoleon's legions were gathering at Bologne, and at Newcastle all preparations had been made (if the French came) to remove the people inland to Newburn. Shield, despite the gravity of the times, in them found humorous aspects for his songs. Blackett's Field, just outside the town's wall, where the Central Station partly stands, owing to the crowds attending the drilling of the associated corps, had to be closed against the public. Shield, in his song, "Blackett's Field," made fun of the whole affair. The following verse is one of the best:—

> "Imagine not they warriors brave,
>   To glory who aspire,
> Whilst thus *confin'd* in Blackett's field,
>   Their station much admire!
> Ah! no; in *Heaton cellars* they
>   Would rather chuse to be
> Most jovial, *carrying on the war*,
>   All under lock and key!"

In another song, "O no, my love, no," which appeared in the *Newcastle Chronicle*, he thus jests at the volunteers' trials—

> "Whilst the dread voice of war through the welkin rebellows,
>   And aspects undaunted our volunteers show,
> Do you think, O my Delia! to join the brave fellows
>   My heart beats impatient? O no, my love, no.

At the dawn of the day, their warm beds still forsaking,
  To scamper thro' *bogs*, or where prickly *whins* grow,
When I view them of pastimes so martial partaking,
  Do I sicken with envy ?   O no, my love, no.

.   .   .   .   .   .

Soon war from thy home may a fugitive send thee,
  Soon give thee of keels and their huddocks to know ;
In the voyage to Newburn who'll succour and tend thee ?
  Shall the task be another's ?   O no, my love, no."

.   .   .   .   .   .

This song brought its companion, "Delia's Answer," which Bell, in his "Notes and Cuttings," writes, "I should also suspect to be Shield's." The reply is as bright as the question.   Delia thus answers—

" Whilst the dread voice of war thro' our island rebellows,
  And aspects terrific proud Frenchmen still show,
Do you think, O my Colin ! to join our brave fellows
  I e'er would forbid you ?   O no, my love, no.

.   .   .   .   .   .

Soon war from my home may a fugitive send me,
  And which way, or how, I'm not anxious to know,
For I'll follow the lads that are arm'd to defend me ;
  Shall the task be another's ?   O no, my love, no."

The concluding song in the series, "To Delia," shows him vanquished—

" What though in tented fields of war
  I ne'er aspir'd to shine,
Nor, when *a glorious maim or scar*
  I've seen, e'er wish'd 'twas mine,—
Yet now, since Delia wills it so,
To share heroic toils I go,
  And war's dire chances prove.
Determin'd glory to pursue,
To tranquil joys I bid adieu !—
  Heigho !—'tis all for love !

.   .   .   .

Perhaps the Fates may will it so,
In battle when I meet the foe,
  Thy fortune, *Lutz,* * I'll prove ;
Then, as the trophy proud I lay
At Delia's feet, I'll softly say—
  Heigho !—'tis all for love."

* Lutz, the soldier who captured the invincible standard at the battle of Alexandria.

Perhaps by writing such songs as these John Shield best replied to Charles Purvis, and in the most effective way showed the folly of his attack. While thus engaged the brothers seem to have been prospering in business. The premises in Middle Street were their own. Not a vestige of them now remains, and it is only by referring to old plans of the town, or listening to some of the fast lessening number of old inhabitants who recollect them, that an idea can be got of where, in all probability, "My Lord 'Size" was written. Briefly, their shop was in that lower part of Middle Street which, extending through the block, would face that part of the Cloth Market opposite where the "White Hart" stands.

CLOTH MARKET, IN SHIELD'S TIME.

About the Shields' removal from Middle Street the *Monthly Chronicle*, vol. i., on the authority, I think, of the late venerable Dr. Clark, tells a characteristic story :—

"The poet, who was remarkably quiet and inoffensive, and full of 'the milk of human kindness,' was in temperament the opposite of his brother Hugh, who, while of a generous disposition, was fiery in his temper. Over sixty years ago, when the Middle Street was about being pulled down for improvements, the brothers Shields' shop being amongst those condemned, a fussy attorney one day entered the shop, and, unfortunately for himself, was received by Mr. Hugh. 'Ah!' said he rather haughtily; 'your shop,

Mr. Shield, is wanted for a public improvement, so you must think of moving. We have agreed to give you'—naming the sum. For a moment Mr. Shield glared at him, and then his fiery temper burst out: 'Ye've agreed ti giv. Whe are ye, ye beggar? ye shannit hed—get oot!' 'Oot' for the time being the attorney might go, but the cry for improvements was not to be denied. The shop in Middle Street had to come down, and they removed to Market Lane, when, Hugh Shield having retired from the business, it was carried on as John Shield & Sons. When Hugh, who was unmarried, retired from the business, he bought a small estate at his native place, Broomhaugh, where he spent the remainder of his days. After his death, his brother the poet, who had been living just below St. Andrew's Church, Newgate Street, then gave up business in favour of his sons, and succeeded Hugh at Broomhaugh, where on the 6th of August 1848 he died in his eightieth year."

The late venerable Dr. Clark, who died a few months ago in his eighty-sixth year, had to the last a wonderfully retentive memory. He recollected the author of " My Lord 'Size," and described him as tall and stout, a man about six feet high, and proportionately built. With this description a portrait would have been interesting. It is understood there is one in existence. We wished to give a copy of it, but have not succeeded. Some future publishers, it is to be hoped, may be more fortunate.

Formality or pride seems to have troubled John Shield little. His free and easy nature is shown in his defence of the name of Jack. A copy of this, in manuscript, is in Bell's " Notes and Cuttings"; it also appeared in No. 1 of the *Newcastle Magazine* (Sykes), there with the addition of the lady's name to whom it was addressed.

A DEFENCE OF THE NAME OF JACK.

First inserted in the *Monthly Magazine* for May 1814.

Addressed to Miss Carr, of Dunston.

I heard you say, and griev'd to hear,
The silly name of Jack your ear
   Offended much—good lack !
I grant your *Jack's* a common name,
But that 'tis not unknown to Fame,
   I'll prove t'ye in a crack.

5

How many Bards the praises chant
Of that great warrior *Jack of Gaunt,*
   Renown'd in English story !
And sure, than *Jack of Marlbro's* name,
Ne'er swell'd the martial trump of Fame
   With one of greater glory.

O Albion ! well thy *Jacks* maintain
The envied empire of the main
   (A truth confess'd afar this) :
Among the heroes of the wave,
What name is more renown'd or brave,
   Than that of bold *Jack Jarvis !*

Far, far above the tuneful throng,
Jack Milton soars, unmatch'd in song,
   Bold, too, *Jack Dryden* sings ;
Jack Hopkins took King David's lyre,
And struck it with such strength and fire,
   Fame says he snapp'd the strings.

Survey we now the British stage,
Around the Roscius of the age
   The passions all assemble.
Ah ! who with such resistless art,
Their various impulse can impart,
   As justly fam'd *Jack Kemble !*

Amongst the long robes, do I see
A form, Newcastle ! dear to thee,
   The Chancellor 'tis, I wot.
O say, where shall we find a name
Of higher worth or brighter fame
   Than thy proud boast—*Jack Scott !*

Which of the Philosophic corps,
Shall dare to step *Jack Locke* before,
   And learning : honours claim !
Know you that fearless mother's son
Who scourg'd the Dame of Babylon !
   Jack Calvin was his name.

Behold ambition's sword unblest,
Deep buried in *Jack Hampden's* breast.
   Freedom ! he fell for thee !
But tho' he sunk beneath the wound,
His name shall live, rever'd, renown'd,
   And dear to Liberty !

The patiots fall, no more I mourn,
To Runnimede's fam'd field I turn,
   Where fancy roves at will,
There see—himself to fate resigning—
Poor old King Jack, unwilling, signing
   The Magna Charta Bill.

Thus Heroes, Bards, Reformers, Sages,
Patriots, and Kings, in various ages,
   This famous name hath grac'd ;
Then quickly your opinion change,
That you should not admire 'tis strange,
   And shows a want of taste.

So Ned, Tim, Tom, Will, Kit, Mat, Mick,
Jim, Joe, Nat, Pat, Ben, Bob, Sam, Dick, .
   Are names few think divine ;
But Jack's a name so sweet to hear,
Must charm, methinks, the nicest ear,
   Besides 'tis also mine ! ! !

JACK SHIELD.   *Bell's* " *Cuttings.* "

According to the *Monthly Chronicle*, " Mr. Shield's song-writing proclivities did not commend themselves to the ladies of his household, who did all they could to discourage his poetic flight. It thus happened that he generally wrote his songs when he was away from home on his frequent business journeys in the country. He thus accumulated a great number of manuscript pieces, which were never printed. This was well known to one or two friends. When the furniture and library at Broomhaugh were sold by auction, a near relative instructed the auctioneer to buy the precious manuscript, naming a price which he thought would effectually debar competition. Another gentleman, however, gave a commission to buy the book at any price, and of course got it. The purchaser, we believe, is still alive. If this notice should meet his eye, it may be hoped that he will allow at least a selection from his store to be given to the public." (Nothing has yet appeared.)

In this collection of dialect songs the sentimental have no place, yet in a sketch of the author a little may be allowed, as showing what, as a writer, he was capable of when away from the humorous.

POOR TOM, THE BLIND BOY.

In darkness I wander, led on by poor Tray ;
Ah ! darkness, whose horrors shall ne'er pass away !
The morning, diffusive of rapture and glee,
Returns,—but its radiance ne'er breaks upon me ;
To me it restores no transition of joy,
Nor ends the long night of poor Tom, the blind boy !

My companions rejoice in the sun's cheering light,
Or rapt'rously hail the mild glories of night,
But vainly to me shines the bright orb of day,
And the moon and the stars their effulgence display,
For a sight of their splendours I ne'er shall enjoy ;
All is dark, empty space to poor Tom, the blind boy !

'Tis summer, they tell me—all nature looks gay ;
Vales, woodlands, and mountains, alas ! what are they ?
Hoarse murmurs discover where rushes the flood,
And melody points out the grove and the wood ;
But a sight of their beauties I ne'er shall enjoy ;
All is dark, empty space to poor Tom, the blind boy !

They talk of bright flow'rs which bespangle the ground,
Of birds of gay plume that flit, sportive, around ;
Ah ! the woodbine's sweet fragrance, the lark's cheerful song,
Oft my sadness beguile as I wander along ;
But a sight of their beauties I ne'er shall enjoy ;
All is dark, empty space to poor Tom, the blind boy !

O pity my dreary, my comfortless state !
O pity the want which embitters my fate !
Alas ! the privations, Heav'n gives me to prove,
Your kindness may soften, tho' never remove ;
Relieve then (and bright be the hours ye enjoy !)
The child of misfortune,—poor Tom, the blind boy !

THE VANISHED ROSE RESTORED.

SUNG BY MR. FRITH AT THE NEWCASTLE CONCERTS.

When the forkéd lightnings fly and thunders roll,
  And loud and fierce the madd'ning tempest raves,
Fears for her William wake in Mary's soul,
  Who, far at sea, the rude commotion braves.
     But when the storm is past,
     When hush'd the angry blast,
And o'er the tranquil main the breeze soft whisp'ring blows,
Blest hope her soothing balm bestows,
And back to Mary's cheek restores the vanish'd Rose.

Or when the wintry wind's terrific roar,
  Dread yawns the deep, the mountain-billows rise,
And foaming surges dash along the shore.
    Then tears of anguish stream from Mary's eyes.
      But when the storm, etc.

Or when a tale of shipwreck dire she hears,
  Thro' all her frame a chilly horror creeps,
The sad recital wakes a thousand fears,
  And for her absent love, forlorn, she weeps.

But see ! a ship appears !
And, smiling thro' her tears,
Far o'er the tranquil main a wishful look she throws,
Her William's signal now she knows ;
And whilst her gentle breast with love and rapture glows,
Straight back to Mary's cheek returns the vanish'd Rose.

Marshall's "Northern Minstrel," 1807.

With these graver efforts of Shield's fancy this sketch may close ; only adding that over fifty years ago the Shields left Market Lane for the top of Dean Street. At the end of 1890 they sold the Dean Street premises, and thus closed—after existing for nearly a hundred years—the old business connection of the author of "My Lord 'Size" and his descendants with Newcastle.

To give a copy of the poet's autograph, inquiry was made at the Probate Court, Durham, for his will ; no will of his was there,—in all probability it had been proved at Doctors' Commons, London.

THE BONNY GEATSIDERS, 1805.

"'The Bonny Geatsiders,' a song in praise of the Gateshead Volunteers, a corps raised this war under the command of Cuthbert Ellison, Esq., of Hebburn."—BELL.

AIR—"Bob Crankey."

COME, marrows, we've happened to meet now,
Sae our thropples together we'll weet noo ;
Aw've myed a new sang,
And to sing ye't aw lang,
For it's about the Bonny Geatsiders.

Of a' the fine Volunteer corpses,
Whether footmen or ridin o' horses,
'Tween the Tweed an' the Tees,
· De'il ha'e them that sees,
Sic a corps as the Bonny Geatsiders.

Whilk amang them can mairch, turn, an' wheel sae ?
Whilk their guns can wise off half sae weel sae ?
Nay, for myekin a *crack*
Through England, aw'll back
The corps of the Bonny Geatsiders.

When the time for parading nigh hand grows,
A' wesh theirsels clean i' the sleck troughs;
   Fling off their black duddies,
   Leave hammers and studdies,
And to drill run the Bonny Geatsiders.

To Newcassel, for three weeks up-stannin,
On Permanent Duty they're gannin';
   And sune i' the papers
   We's read a' the capers
O' the corps o' the Bonny Geatsiders.

The Newcasel cheps fancy they're clever,
And are vauntin' and bragging for ever;
   But they'll find theirsels wrang,
   If they think they can bang
At soug'rin' the Bonny Geatsiders.

The Gen'ral sall see they can loup dykes,
Or mairch thro' whins, lair whooles, and deep sykes;
   Nay, to soom (at a pinch)
   Through Tyne wand'ent flinch,
The corps of the Bonny Geatsiders.

Sum think Billy Pitt's nobbit hummin',
When he tells aboot Bonnepart cummin';
   But cum when he may,
   He'll lang rue the day
He first meets wi' the Bonny Geatsiders.

Like an anchor shank, smash! how they'll clatter 'im,
And turn 'im, and skelp 'im, and batter 'im;
   His banes sall, by pring!
   Like a frying-pan ring,
When he meets wi' the Bonny Geatsiders.

Let them ance get 'im into thor taings weel,
Nae fear but they'll give 'im his whaings weel;
    And te Hazlett's* Pond bring 'im,
    And there in chains hing 'im—
What a seet for the Bonny Geatsiders.

Now, marrows, to show we're a' loyal,
And that wi' the King and Blood Royal,
    We'll a' soom or sink,
    Quairts a-piece let us drink
To the brave and the Bonny Geatsiders !

SHIELD.   *Bell's " Northern Bards, 1812. '*

MY LORD 'SIZE; OR, NEWCASTLE IN AN UPROAR.

In former times it was customary for the Judges to go in the town's barge, attended by the Mayor and others of the Corporation, to Tynemouth. On one of the occasions, some years ago, one of the Judges in stepping into or from the barge, slipped into the water. This gave rise to the very ludicrous song entitled, "My Lord 'Size."

THE jailor for trial had brought up a thief,
    Whose looks seem'd a passport for Botany Bay;
The lawyers, some with and some wanting a brief,
    Around the green table were seated so gay;
Grave jurors and witnesses waiting a call :
    Attornies and clients, more angry than wise,
With strangers and town's-people throng'd the Guildhall,
    All waiting and gaping to see my Lord 'Size.

* A pond on Gateshead Fell, so named on account of the body of Robert Hazlett being hung in chains there, September 1770.

Oft stretch'd were their necks, oft erected their ears,
  Still fancying they heard of the trumpets the sound,
When tidings arrived which dissolv'd them in tears,
  That my Lord at the dead-house was then lying
    drown'd!
Straight left *tête-à-tête* where the jailor and thief,
  The horror-struck crowd to the dead-house quick hies,
E'en the lawyers, forgetful of fee and of brief,
  Set off, helter skelter, to view my Lord 'Size.

And now the Sandhill with the sad tidings rings,
  And the tubs of the taties are left to take care;
Fish-women desert their crabs, lobsters, and lings,
  And each to the dead-house now runs like a hare.
The glassmen, some naked, some clad, heard the news,
  And off they ran smoking, like hot mutton pies;
Whilst Castle Garth tailors, like wild kangaroos,
  Came tail-on-end jumping, to see my Lord 'Size.

The dead-house they reach'd, where his Lordship they
    found,
  Pale, stretched on a plank, like themselves out of
    breath;
The Crowner and Jury were seated around,
  Most gravely enquiring the cause of his death.
No haste did they seem in, their task to complete,
  Aware that from hurry mistakes often rise;
Or wishful, perhaps, of prolonging the treat
  Of thus sitting in judgment upon my Lord 'Size.

Now the Mansion-house butler thus gravely depos'd—
  " My Lord on the terrace seem'd studying his charge,
And when (as I thought) he had got it compos'd,
  He went down the stairs and examined the barge.

First the stem he survey'd, then inspected the stern,
    Then handled the tiller and looked mighty wise ;
But he made a false step when about to return,
    And souse in the river straight tumbled Lord 'Size."

Now his narrative ended,—the butler retir'd,
    Whilst Betty Watt mutt'ring (half drunk) thro' her
        teeth,
Declared " in her breest greet consarn it inspir'd,
    That my Lord should se cullishly come by his deeth."
Next a keelman was called on, Bold Archy his name,
    Who the book as he kiss'd shew'd the whites of his
        eyes,
Then he cut an odd caper, attention to claim,
    And this evidence gave them respecting Lord 'Size.

" Aw was setten the keel, wi' Dick Stavers an' Matt,
    An' the Mansion-hoose stairs we were just alangside,
When we a' three see'd something, but didn't ken what,
    That was splashing and labbering aboot i' the tide.
' It's a fluiker,' ki Dick ; ' No,' ki Matt, ' it's owre big,'
    It luik'd mair like a skyat when aw first see'd it rise,
Kiv aw—for aw'd gettin a gliff o' the wig—
    God's marcy ! wye, marrows, becrike, it's Lord 'Size.

"Sae I huik'd him an' hawl'd him suin into the keel,
    An' o' top 'o the huddock aw rowl'd him aboot ;
An' his belly aw rubb'd, an' aw skelp'd his back weel,
    But the wayter he'd drucken it wadn't run oot.
Sae aw browt him ashore here, an' doctors, in vain,
    Forst this way, then that, to recover him tries ;
For ye see there he's lyin' as deed as a stane,
    An' that's a' aw can tell ye aboot my Lord 'Size."

Now the Jury for close consultation retir'd :
  Some *"Death Accidental"* were willing to find,
Some *"God's Visitation"* most eager required,
  And some were for *"Fell in the River"* inclined.
But ere on their verdict they all were agreed,
  My Lord gave a groan and wide open'd his eyes ;
Then the coach and the trumpeters came with great
    speed,
  And back to the Mansion-house carried Lord 'Size.

SHIELD.   *Marshall's "Northern Minstrel,"* 1806.

BOB CRANKEY'S ADIEU.

When going with the Volunteer Association from Gateshead to Newcastle on Permanent Duty.

"Set to music by Thomas Train, of Gateshead, and sung by him at many
public dinners in Newcastle and Gateshead. He humoured this song much,
and it became a great favourite."—BELL.

TUNE—"The Soldier's Adieu."

FAREWEEL, fareweel, ma comely pet !
  Aw's fourc'd three weeks to leave thee ;
Aw's doon for *parm'ent duty* set,
  Oh dinna let it grieve thee.
Ma hinny ! wipe them e'en, sae breet,
  That mine wi' love did dazzle ;
When thy heart's sad, can mine be leet ?
    Come, ho'way, get a jill o' beer
    Thy heart to cheer ;
An' when thou sees me mairch away,
    Whiles in, whiles oot
    O' step, nae doot ;
"Bob Crankey's gane," thou'lt sobbing say,
  "A-sougering to Newcassel ! "

Come, dinna, dinna whinge an' whipe,
  Like yammering Isbel Macky;
Cheer up, ma hinny! leet thy pipe,
  And take a blast o' baccy.
It's but for yen an' twenty days,
  The folks's een aw'll dazzle—
Prood, swagg'rin i' my fine reed claes.
    Ods heft! my pit claes—dist thou hear?
    Are waurse o' wear;
Mind cloot them weel when aw's away,
    An' a posie goon
    Aw'll buy thee soon,
An' thou's drink thy tea—aye twice a-day,
    When aw come frae Newcassel.

Becrike! aw's up tiv every rig,
  Sae dinna doot, my hinny!
But at the Blue stane o' the Brig
  Aw'll hae my mairching Ginny.
A Ginny! wuks! sae strange a seet,
  Ma een wi' joy will dazzle;
But aw'll hed spent that verra neet—
    For money, hinny! owre neet to keep,
    Wad brick my sleep:
Sae smash! aw think'st a wiser way,
    Wi' flesh and beer
    Mysel to cheer,
The lang three weeks that aw've to stay
    A-sougering at Newcassel.

But whisht! the sairgent's tongue aw hear,
  " Fa' in, fa' in," he's yelpin;
The fifes are whuslin' lood an' clear,
  An' sair the drums they're skelpin.

Fareweel, ma comely! aw mun gang
   The gen'rals e'en to dazzle!
But, hinny, if the time seems lang,
      An' thou freets about me neet an' day,
      Then come away,
Seek out the yell-house where aw stay,
      An' we'll kiss an' cuddle;
      An' mony a fuddle
Sall drive the langsome hours away
      When sougering at Newcassel.

SHIELD.   *Marshall's " Northern Minstrel,"* 1807.

THE BARBER'S NEWS;

OR, SHIELDS IN AN UPROAR.

Stephen Kemble, the hero of this song, was the only actor who could play the character of Falstaff without increasing his natural rotundity by means of *stuffing.* The enormous bulk of this gentleman afforded a weighty subject for the joke of the poet, and the temptation could not be resisted. He died on June 6th, 1822, in his 64th year, at the Grove, near Durham. He was formerly manager of the Theatres Royal, Newcastle, Glasgow, and Edinburgh. He also possessed considerable literary talent, having wrote various addresses, songs, etc., which appeared in different journals. Mr. Kemble's remains were interred in the Chapel of the Nine Altars, at the east end of Durham Cathedral, on the north side of the shrine of St. Cuthbert.

TUNE—"O the Golden Days of good Queen Bess."

GREAT was the consternation, amazement, and dismay,
   Sir,
Which, both in North and South Shields, prevail'd the
      other day, Sir;
Quite panic-struck the natives were, when told by the
      barber,
That a terrible Sea-Monster had got into the harbour.
   "Have you heard the news, Sir?" "What news, pray,
      Master Barber?"
   "Oh, a terrible Sea-Monster has got into the harbour."

Now, each honest man in Shields—I mean both North
and South, Sir—
Delighting in occasions to expand their eyes and mouth,
Sir,
And, fond of seeing marv'lous sights, ne'er staid to get
his beard off,
But ran to view the monster, its arrival when he heard of.
Oh, who could think of shaving, when inform'd by the
barber,
That a terrible Sea-Monster had got into the harbour?

Each wife pursu'd her husband, and every child its
mother,
Lads and lasses, helter-skelter, scamper'd after one
another ;
Shopkeepers and mechanics, too, forsook their daily
labours,
And ran to gape and stare among their gaping, staring
neighbours.
All crowded to the river-side, when told by the barber,
That a terrible Sea-Monster had got into the harbour.

It happens very frequently that barbers' news is fiction,
Sir,
But the wond'rous news this morning was truth, no con-
tradiction, Sir :
A something sure enough was there, among the billows
flouncing,
Now sinking in the deep profound, now on the surface
bouncing.
True as Gazette or Gospel were the tidings of the
barber,
That a terrible Sea-Monster had got into the harbour.

Some thought it was a Shark, Sir; a Porpus some con-
ceived it;
Some said it was a Grampus; and some a Whale
believed it;
Some swore it was a Sea-Horse, then owned themselves
mistaken,
For, now they'd got a nearer view, 'twas certainly a
Kraken.
Each sported his opinion, from the parson to the
barber,
Of the terrible Sea-Monster they had got in the
harbour.

"Belay, belay," a sailor cried, "what's that, this thing a
kraken!
Tis no more like one—split my jib!—than it is a flitch
of bacon!
I've often seen a hundred such, all sporting in the Nile,
Sir,
And you may trust a sailor's word, it is a Crocodile, Sir."
Each straight to Jack knocks under, from the parson
to the barber,
And all agreed a Crocodile had got into the harbour.

Yet greatly Jack's discovery his auditors did shock, Sir,
For they dreaded that the Salmon would be eat up by
the Croc., Sir:
When presently the Crocodile, their consternation
crowning,
Raised its head above the waves, and cried, "Help!
O Lord, I'm drowning!"
Heavens! how their hair, Sir, stood on end, from the
parson to the barber,
To find a Speaking Crocodile had got into the harbour.

This dreadful exclamation appall'd both young and old,
    Sir,
In the very stoutest hearts, indeed, it made the blood
    run cold, Sir;
Ev'n Jack, the hero of the Nile, it caused to quake and
    tremble,
Until an old wife, sighing, cried, "Alas! 'tis Stephen
    Kemble!"
    Heav'ns! how were all astonished, from the parson to
      the barber,
    To find that Stephen Kemble was the monster in the
      harbour.

Strait crocodilish fears gave place to manly, gen'rous
    strife, Sir,
Most willingly each lent a hand to save poor Stephen's
    life, Sir;
They dragg'd him, gasping, to the shore, impatient for
    his history,
For how he came in that sad plight to them was quite a
    mystery.
    Tears glisten'd, Sir, in every eye, from the parson to
      the barber,
    When, swol'n to thrice his natural size, they dragg'd
      him from the harbour.

Now, having roll'd and rubb'd him well an hour upon
    the beach, Sir,
He got upon his legs again, and made a serious speech,
    Sir:
Quoth he, "An ancient proverb says, and true it will be
    found, Sirs,
Those born to prove an airy doom will surely ne'er be
    drown'd, Sirs:

For Fate, Sirs, has us all in tow, from the monarch to
the barber,
Or surely I had breathed my last this morning in the
harbour.

" Resolved to cross the River, Sirs, a sculler did I get
into—
(May Jonah's ill-luck be mine, another when I step into !)
Just when we'd reach'd the deepest part, O horror ! there
it founders,
And down went poor Pilgarlick amongst the crabs and
flounders !
But Fate, that keeps us all in tow, from the monarch
to the barber,
Ordain'd I should not breathe my last this morning in
the harbour.

" I've broke down many a stage coach, and many a
chaise and gig, Sirs ;
Once, in passing through a trap-hole I found myself too
big, Sirs ;   .
I've been circumstanc'd most oddly, while contesting hard
a race, Sirs,
But ne'er was half so frightened as among the Crabs and
Plaice, Sirs.
O Fate, Sirs, keeps us all in tow, from the monarch to
the barber,
Or certainly I'd breath'd my last this morning in the
harbour.

" My friends, for your exertions, my heart o'erflows with
gratitude ;
O may it prove the last time you find me in that
latitude !

God knows with what mischances dire the future may
    abound, Sirs,
But I hope and trust I'm one of those not fated to be
    drowned, Sirs."
    Thus ended his oration, Sir, I had it from the barber,
    And, dripping like some River God, he slowly left the
        harbour.

Ye men of North and South Shields too, God send you
    all prosperity!
May your commerce ever flourish, your stately ships still
    crowd the sea !
Unrivall'd in the Coal Trade, till doomsday may you
    stand, Sirs !
And, every hour, fresh wonders your eyes and mouths
    expand, Sirs !
    And long may Stephen Kemble live ! and never may
        the barber
    Mistake him for a monster more, deep floundering in
        the harbour !

SHIELD.   *Bell's " Northern Bards,"* 1812.

CULL, ALIAS SILLY BILLY.

WILLIAM SCOTT, commonly called Cull Billy, was a native
of Newcastle, where he resided along with his mother, a poor
old woman who made her living by hawking wooden ware.
She, like her son, was an object of distress, being not above
four feet high. Billy oft excited compassion while reciting
(which he did with a great degree of exactness and in such a
distinct and clear manner as to surprise many) the Lord's
Prayer, several other prayers, passages of Scripture, etc., to
a numerous audience of boys, who generally repaid his
endeavours for their welfare with a shower of dirt or stones.
Despite his weakness several have felt the power of Billy's

6

wit, which on some occasions has been very severe. Once when a person of the name of —— (not one of the wisest beings in the world) came swaggering out of a tavern while Billy was haranguing the mob at the door,—"Stand out of the way," cries this would-be great man. "Stand out of the way, I never give place to fools." "But I do," cries Billy, bowing, and instantly stepped on the pavement. Another illustration of Billy's ready wit is found in Robert Emery's songs. He calls it

CULL BILLY'S PRIZE.

As Billy Scott was on the trot
　　Along the Pudding Chare,
A shilling on the pavement lay,
　　Which Billy soon, with care,
Into his breeches pocket put,
　　And trotted on with glee ;
A wag, who'd seen him stoop, cried out,
　　" Hold ! that belongs to me ! "

Poor Billy gravely turned about,
　　And thus did him accost—
" Can you, upon your honour, say,
　　You have a sixpence lost ? "
" I have indeed," the wag replied ;
　　Said Bill, " I must away !
See, 'tis a shilling I have found !"
　　So, thank you, sir—good-day."

Billy died at St. John's Poor-house on the 31st July 1831, aged 68 years.

————

REFERENCES TO OLD PLAN ON OPPOSITE PAGE.

The *white spots* on the Plan opposite mark places of interest connected with the writers in this volume :—

WILLIAM ARMSTRONG born. Spot lower right-hand corner.

ROBERT NUNN died. Spot a little above lower left-hand corner.

BEWICK'S workshop; afterwards ⎫
　　　　　　　　　　　　　　　⎬ Spot St. Nicholas' Churchyard.
WILLIAM H. DAWSON'S workshop. ⎭

THOMAS THOMPSON'S shop. Spot Groat Market, Middle Street side.

JAMES MORRISON born. Highest spot Groat Market.

JOHN SHIELD'S shop. Lowest spot Cloth Market, Middle Street side.

GEORGE CAMERON'S shop. Spot Cloth Market—near pant.

WILLIAM OLIVER'S shop. Spot corner of Cloth Market and High Bridge.

JOHN CUNNINGHAM died. Spot Union Street, opposite Oliver, higher up.

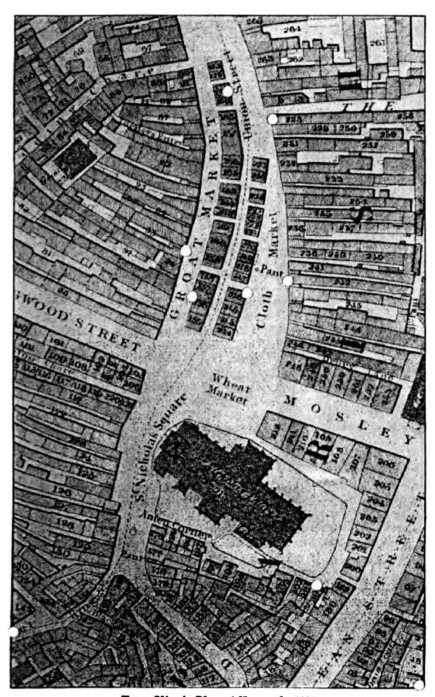

From Oliver's Plan of Newcastle, 1830.

JOHN SELKIRK.

BY his misfortunes, by the wretchedness and want of his later years, and his tragic death, John Selkirk may be called the Otway of the local muse. He was the youngest of the famous three—Thompson, Shield, and Selkirk — who, apparently without concert, simultaneously are found singing of the scenes around them in the dialect as they heard it, and so giving, to what, up to that time, had been considered as less than "airy nothings"—"a local habitation and a name." Nearer to Newcastle than either Thompson or Shield, Selkirk appears to have been born just over "the blue stane o' the brig." Although born in Gateshead, to Newcastle he really belonged, his father, George Selkirk, being a hairdresser in the Close. The Close then, with the old Mansion House, the residence of the Mayor of the year, was something widely different from what it is now, and Selkirk's father would really be in one of the best business parts of the town, and, from what elsewhere appears, a man in a good position.

THE BLUE STONE.*
Photographed by Laws.

Of Selkirk's early life we have little trace. According to a manuscript memorandum in Bell's "Notes and Cuttings," he was a clerk with Messrs. Straker & Boyd, Quayside. In all probability he began his writing early. "Bob Cranky"—bragging Bob—about whom he gives us several songs, is in the form of a broad-sheet in

* This famous stone, formerly on the old Tyne Bridge, was the dividing mark which separated Northumberland from Durham; it is a block of granite six feet long, fourteen and a-half inches wide, and nine inches thick. It was presented by Alderman Cail to the Antiquarian Society, 1887.

Bell's "Cuttings." It is undated, but amongst others with the date 1803. Selkirk then would be just over twenty. The song is there called "The Original Bob Cranky," and though full of minor variations, is essentially the "Bob Cranky's 'Size Sunday" as we now have it. It opens—

> "Ye may luke amang a' your fine vewers,
> Amang banksmen and putters and hewers,
>   Ye'll not find a fellow
>   Drest in blue and yellow
> That lukes owt se fine as Bob Cranky.
>
> On flesh and breed day at Newcassel,
> Wi' fine coat and buttons that dazzel,
>   The little bairns cry—
>   Bonny, bonny, ni, ni,
> When they se the smart, clever Bob Cranky."

It is in the *Northern Minstrel, or Gateshead Songster,* 1806-7, that we first trace his songs with a definite date. This *Minstrel* appears to have been published in four parts. Part I. is dated September 1806, and contains nothing but the run of comic and sentimental songs of the day. Part II. is dated October 1806; and in it we have Shield's famous "Lord 'Size." In his preface the editor says he has been favoured with several *provincial songs*, "some of which it must be allowed have considerable merit," and promises the senders of such one or more copies of the book in which their songs may appear, and finishes by hoping "some mute, inglorious Milton" may through his pages obtain "a local habitation and a name." At the end of his preface, returning to the local, in italics he adds, "Several curious provincial songs have been received, which will appear in the third part." In Part III. the curious provincial songs promised evidently appear, as in it "Blackett's Field," and several of Shield's serio-comic songs appear. The fourth part is undated, but would be in 1807. In that the first song is "Bob Cranky's 'Size Sunday," by J. S., Gateshead. This song is immediately followed by "Swalwell Hoppin'," but to that song there is neither name nor initials. This omission, however, is supplied by Bell's *Rhymes of Northern Bards*, 1812, where "Swalwell Hoppin'" is given with the initials, J. S., Gateshead, and "Bob Cranky's 'Size Sunday" has the author's full name, John Selkirk. His next song, "Bob Cranky's 'Leum'nation Neet," we find in the *Tyne Mercury*, June 7th, 1814; it is in celebration of the general peace of that year, and has the initial " S." After this we trace no more songs ; he appears to have gone to London, and there carried on business as a merchant. About 1830 he is back again to Newcastle, his London career evidently a failure, as he is in poor circumstances. Little more is known about him, until his melancholy death for a while arrested public attention. The account of his death, perhaps, had better be given in the report of the inquest as it appeared in the *Newcastle Chronicle*, November 18th, 1843 :—

" Before William Stoker, coroner for the Borough.

" Another inquest was held on Monday, and by adjournment on Tuesday (at the dead-house), on the body of John Selkirk, aged 60, who fell into the river near Sandgate on Saturday evening, and was drowned. The deceased was a person of singular habits and disposition, and had formerly been a respectable merchant in London ; but latterly was so reduced in circumstances as to subsist upon the charity of the benevolent. For some time past he had slept at nights on the shavings of a joiner's shop in Sandgate, and refused to accept parochial relief. On Saturday evening he was observed to carry a tin bottle to the river to obtain water, when he unfortunately fell in. Verdict—accidental death."

This account is brief, but the other Newcastle papers, the *Courant* and the *Journal*, give still less, and add nothing to the facts above.

In *Songs and Ballads for the People*, 1853, there is a brief sketch of Selkirk, and some interesting additional particulars of the inquest are given by John Bell, land surveyor, Gateshead :—

" James Selkirk, merchant's clerk, Bell's Court, Pilgrim Street, brother of the poet, gave evidence, but did not know what his brother had been doing since (about thirteen years ago) he had returned from London. Andrew Heslop, St. Ann's Street, was the joiner in whose shop amongst the shavings poor Selkirk had slept since May :—" He asked me to let him sleep in my workshop amongst the shavings." He left him in the shop about five o'clock, and did not see him again until after he was drowned —about eight o'clock. To his honour, Mr. David Hamilton Wilson, a guardian of the poor, hearing of Selkirk's distress, visited him and offered him relief, which he respectfully but firmly declined. About a month afterwards Selkirk sent to Mr. Wilson for the loan of £1 (saying he would repay it out of some property in Cannon Street, Gateshead, which he had expectations of obtaining), which was immediately forwarded to him. It is singular that ' Swalwell Hoppin'' and ' Bob Cranky' were the only two songs he ever gave to the world; and whenever he was questioned as to this circumstance, he declined giving any information. Unless Mr. Bell counts the three Bob Cranky songs as really but one, his reckoning is in error. Selkirk has written four. At the conclusion of the inquest, on the same day, November 14th, the body was buried in the Ballast Hills burial-ground."

But for Mr. Bell's most interesting memorandums there is little doubt nothing would have been known relating to Selkirk excepting the names of his songs. A visit lately to the Ballast Hills to try and trace his grave resulted in finding that all books, deeds, etc., had been removed to the Corporation offices. A call there brought out the fact that no "grave plan" existed—nothing by which the locality of Selkirk's, or any particular interment may be traced. The register of burials is there; turning that over, John Bell's information as to the Ballast Hills is verified. The entry runs—

"No. 655.—John Selkirk, Agent. November 14, 1843. From the Dead House. 61 years."

Such is the melancholy record of the unfortunate Selkirk, buried from the dead-house!—a sad ending for one whose life had opened so fair, and whose songs are all of festivity and merriment. Perhaps it is better that over the causes leading to this pitiful ending Time has dropt a veil, and we are left without information as to how the miserable condition of his later years was brought about.

Selkirk has been doubly unfortunate. In worldly circumstances a wreck, even the credit of his songs has partly been given to others. For this his own strange neglect of them may in some way account, coupled with the curious fact that when he wrote there were three all writing Tyneside songs, and all properly using the same signature, "J. S." —John Shield, John Selkirk, James Stawpert. An illustration of this confusion is found in "Bob Cranky's 'Leum'nation Neet." This Bob is one of the bragging Bobs in which Selkirk seemed to delight, and may safely be put down as his. Marshall (1827) prints it without an author's name, but in Davidson's Alnwick edition, Fordyce's Newcastle edition, and all following collections, it is put down as John Shield's. Bell, in his "Notes and Cuttings," in a list of Shield's writings, does not include "Bob Cranky's 'Luem'nation Neet." This, coupled with the internal evidence, should in this case at least give to the unfortunate Selkirk his own.

BOB CRANKY'S 'SIZE SUNDAY.

Dawson, in his *Local Poets*, writes :—"There is little pomp and parade now at an Assize Sunday. In the olden time, when the Judges went to St. Nicholas' Church, the cavalcade was an imposing sight, with Sheriff boys and trumpeters dressed in their gorgeous liveries."

"The first and two last verses were added by J. Bell, bookseller, Quayside."—*Bell's "Notes and Cuttings."*

Ho'WAY and aw'll sing thee a tune, mun,
'Bout huz see'n my Lord at the toon, mun :
    Aw's seer aw was smart, now,
    Aw'll lay thee a quart, now,
Nyen them aw cut a dash like Bob Cranky.

When aw pat on my blue coat that shines se,
My jacket wi' posies se fine se,
    My sark sic sma threed, man,
    My pig-tail se greet, man !
Od smash ! what a buck was Bob Cranky.

Blue stockings, white clocks, and reed garters,
Yellow breeks, and my shoon wi' lang quarters,
    Aw myed wour bairns cry,
    Eh ! sarties ! ni ! ni !
Sic verra fine things had Bob Cranky.

Aw went to awd Tom's and fand Nancy ;
Kiv aw, lass, thou's myed to my fancy !
    Aw like thou as weel
    As a stannin-pye heel,
Ho'way to the toon wi' Bob Cranky.

As up Jenny's backside we were bangin',
Ki Geordy, " How, where are ye gannin' ? "
    "Wey t' see me Lord 'Sizes,
    But ye shanna gan aside us,
For ye're not half se fine as Bob Cranky."

Ki Geordy, "We leeve i' yen raw, weyet,
I' yen corf we byeth gan belaw, weyet,
    At aw things aw've played,
    And to hew aw'm not flayed,
  Wi' sic in a chep as Bob Cranky."

"Bob hez thee at lowpin' and flingin',
At the bool, football, clubby, and swingin':
    Can ye jump up and shuffle,
    And cross ower the buckle,
  When ye dance, like the cliver Bob Cranky?

"Thow naws, i' my hoggars and drawers,
Aw'm nyen o' yor scarters and clawers:
    Fra the trap door bit laddy
    T' the spletter his daddy,
  Nyen handles the pick like Bob Cranky.

"So, Geordy, od smash my pit sarik,
Thou'd best haud thee whist about warik,
    Or aw'll sobble thee body,
    And myek thee nose bloody,
  If thou sets up thy gob to Bob Cranky."

Nan laugh'd—t' church we gat without 'im;
The greet crowd, becrike, how aw hew'd 'em!
    Smasht a keel bully roar'd,
    "Clear the road! whilk's my Lord?"
  Owse se high as the noble Bob Cranky.

Aw lup up, an' catch'd just a short gliff
O' Lord Trial, the Trumpets, and Sheriff,
    Wi' the little bit mannies
    Se fine and se canny,
  Ods heft! what a seet for Bob Cranky!

Then away we off te the yell-hoose,
Wiv a few hearty lasses an' fellows :
    Aw tell'd ower the wig,
    Se curled and se big,
For nyen saw'd se weel as Bob Cranky.

Aw gat drunk, fit, and kick'd up a racket,
Rove my breeks and spoil'd aw my fine jacket ;
    Nan cry'd and she cuddled.
    My hinny, thou's fuddled !
Ho'way hyem now, my bonny Bob Cranky !

Se we stagger'd alang fra the toon, mun,
Whiles gannin', whiles byeth fairly doon, mun ;
    Smasht a banksman or hewer,
    No, not a fine viewer,
Durst jaw to the noble Bob Cranky.

What care aw for maw new suit, a' tatters,
Twe black een ?—od smash a' sic matters !
    When me Lord comes agyen, mun,
    Aw'll strive ev'ry byen, mun,
To bang a' wor consarn, ki Bob Cranky.

O' the flesh and breed day, when wour bund, mun,
Aw'll buy claes far bonnier than thou, mun ;
    For, od smash my neavel !
    As lang as wour yebble,
Let's keep up the day ! ki Bob Cranky.

SELKIRK.   *Northern Minstrel*, 1807.

———

BOB CRANKY'S COMPLAINT.

ODD, smash ! 'tis hard aw can't rub dust off,
To see ma Lord wi' wig se fine toss'd off,
    But they mak a sang, man,
    Aw can't tell how lang, man,
All myeking a gam o' Bob Cranky.

Ma blue coat and pigtail's my awn, wyet,
And when to Newcassel I gang, wyet,
    Aw like to show town folks,
    Whe se oft ca' us gowks,
They ar'n't se fine as Bob Cranky.

If aw fin' the owther, as sure as a'm Bob,
A'll mak him sing the wrang side o' his gob,
    A'll gi' 'im sick sobbling,
    A'll set him hyem hobbling,
For myeking a gam o' Bob Cranky.

A'll myek his noodle as reed as ma garters ;
A've a lang stick, as weel as lang quarters ;
    Whilk a'll lay ower his back,
    'Till he swears ne'er to mak
Ony mair sangs o' Bob Cranky.

Aw wonder the maist how he did spy,
What was dyun when nobody was by—
    Some conj'rer he maun be,
    Sic as wi' Punch aw did see,
Whilk myed the hair stand o' Bob Cranky.

Our viewer sez aw can't de better
Than send him a story cull letter.
    But writing a'll let rest :
    The pik fits ma hand best ;
A pen's owr sma for Bob Cranky.

Nan, whe a'll marry or it's very lang,
Sez, "Hinny, din't mind the cull fellow's sang,
    Gif he dis se agyen,
    Our schyulmaister's pen
Shall tak pairt wi' ma bonny Bob Cranky.

"Ize warrn't, gif aw weer my pillease,
An ma hat myed of very sma strees,
    He'll be chock full o' spite,
    An about us will write,
An say Ize ower fine for Bob Cranky."

"Sure, Bobby," says she, "his head's got a crack."
"Ne maiter," sed I, an' gov her a smack.
    " Pilleases are tippy,
    Like shugar's thy lippy,
And thou shalt be wife to Bob Cranky."

The Crankies, farrer back nor I naw,
Hae gyen to 'Sizes to see trumpets blaw,
    Wi' white sticks an' Sheriff ;
    But warn't myed a sang of,
Nor laugh'd at like clever Bob Cranky.

Lord 'Sizes cums but yence a year, wyet!
To see his big wig a've ne fear, wyet!
So be-crike! while aw leeve,
Tho' wi' lang sangs a'm deave'd,
Me Lord at the church shall see Cranky!

SELKIRK. *Bell's " Northern Bards,"* 1812.

SWALWELL HOPPING.

The scenes here described are now unknown. A few scattered ginger-bread and fruit stalls are all that remain of the glories, such as they were, of Swalwell Hopping. The large ironworks of Ambrose Crowley, which, fifty years ago, gave employment to great numbers of workmen, have gradually decayed, until the winter of 1862 all that remained of the famous ironworks were sold, and Crowley's works now exist but in memory.—*Note to* 1872 *edition.*

TUNE—" Paddy's Wedding."

LADS! myek a ring,
An' hear huz sing
The sport we had at Swalwell, O;
Wour merry play
O' th' Hoppen' day,
Ho'way, marrows, an' aw'll tell you, O.
The sun shines warm on Whickham Bank,
Let's aw lye doon at Dolly's, O,
An' hear 'boot monny a funny prank
Play'd by the lads at Crowley's, O.

There was Sam, O zoons!
Wiv's pantaloons,
An' gravat up ower his gobby, O;
An' Willie, thou,
Wi' th' jacket blue,
Thou was the varra Bobby, O.

There was knack-kneed Mat, wiv's purple suit,
    An' hopper hipp'd Dick, aw yellow, O;
Greet Tom was there, wi' Hepple's aud coat,
    An' bucksheen'd Bob fra Stella, O.

      When we wour drest,
      It was confest
We shem'd the cheps frae Newcassel, O:
      So away we set
      To wour town gyet,
To jeer them aw as they pass'd us, O;
We shouted some, and some dung doon,
    Lobstrop'lus fellows we kick'd them, O;
Some culls went hyem, some crush'd to toon,
    Some gat aboot by Whickham, O.

      The spree com on—
      The hat was won
By carrot-pow'd Jenny's Jackey, O;
      What a fyece, begok!
      Had buckle-mouth'd Jock,
When he twined his jaws for the baccy, O:
The kilted lasses fell tid pell mell,
    Wi' Tally-i-o the Grinder, O:
The smock was gi'en to slavering Nell—
    Ye'd dropp'd had ye been behind her, O.

      Wour dance began
      Awd buck-tyuth'd Nan,
An' Geordy, thou'd Jen Collin, O;
      While the merry black,
      Wi' monny a crack,
Set the tamboreen a-rolling, O.

Like wour forge hammer, we bet se true,
   An' shuk Raw's hoose se soundly, O;
Tuff canna cum up wi' Crowley's crew,
   Nor thump the tune se roundly, O.

    Then Gyetside Jack,
    Wiv's bloody back,
Wad dance wi' goggle-ey'd Mally, O;
    But up cam Nick,
    And gav him a kick,
And a canny bit kind of a fally, O.
That day a' Hawks's blacks may rue—
   They gat monny a varra sair clanker, O,
Can they de ouse wi' Crowley's crew,
   Frev a needle tiv a anchor, O?

    What's that to say
    To the bonny fray,
We had wi' skipper Robin, O?
    The keel-bullies aw,
    Byeth greet an' sma',
Myed a beggarly tide o' the hoppen, O.
Gleed Will cried "Ma-a!" up lup awd Frank,
   An' Robin that marry'd his dowter, O,
We hammer'd their ribs like an anchor shank,
   They fand it six weeks after, O.

    Bald-pyet Jone Carr
    Wad hev a bit spar,
To help his marrows away wid, O;
    But poor aud fellow,
    He'd getten ower mellow,
So we down'd byeth him an' Davy, O.

Then Petticoat Robin jumpt up agyen,
    Wiv's gully to marcykree huz aw,
But Willanton Dan laid him flat wiv a styen :
    Hurro ! for Crowley's crew, boys aw.

        Their hash was sattled,
        So off we rattled,
An' we jigged it up se hearty, O !
        Wi' monny a shiver,
        An' lowp se clivvor ;
Can Newcassel turn oot sec a party, O ?
When, wheit dyun ower, the fiddlers went,
    We stagger'd ahint, see merry, O,
An' thro' wour town, till fairly spent,
    Roar'd, "Crowley's crew an' glory, O."

SELKIRK.   *Marshall's " Northern Minstrel," 1807.*

BOB CRANKY'S LEUM'NATION NEET.

In celebration of the General Peace of 1814. The song shows how
elaborate had been the illuminations.

LORD 'Sizes leuks weel in coach shinin',
Whese wig wad let Nan's heed an' mine in ;
        But a bonnier seet
        Was the Leum'nation neet,—
It dazzled the e'en o' Bob Cranky.

Aboot seven aw gov owr warkin',
Gat beard off, an' put a white sark on ;
        For Newcasslers, thowt aw,
        Gif they dinn't see me braw,
Will say, " What a gowk is Bob Cranky ! "

Aw ran to the toon without stoppin',
An' fand ilka street like a hoppin';
    An' the foak stud se thick,
    Aw sair wish'd for ma pick,
To hew oot a way for Bob Cranky.

The guns then went off fra the Cassel,
Seun windors war a' in a dazzle;
    Ilka place was like day,
    Aw then shooted, "Hurray!
There's 'Plenty an' Peace' for Bob Cranky!"

Sum windors had pictors se bonny,
Wi' sma' lamps aw can't tell how mony;
    Te count them, awm shure,
    Wad bother the Viewer—
A greater Goggriffer than Cranky.

Aw seed croons myad o' lamps blue an' reed,
Whilk aw wad na like put on mi heed!
    "G. P. R." aw seed nex,
    For oor Geordy Prince Rex;—
Nyan spelt it se weel as Bob Cranky.

Sum had anchors of leet high hung up,
To shew foak greet Bonny was deun up;
    But, far as aw see, man,
    As reet it wad be, man,
Te leet up the pick o' Bob Cranky.

A leg of meat sed, "Doon aws cummin',"
But sum chep aw seun fand was hummin';
    For aw stopp'd bit belaw,
    Haddin oot a lang paw,
But mutton cam ne nearer Cranky.

A cask on the Vicar's pump top, man,
Markt " Plenty an' Peace," gard me stop, man ;
    Thinks aw te me-sell,
    I'se here get sum yell,
But only cau'd waiter gat Cranky.

Bonny, shav'd be a bear, was then shot, man,
An' be auld Nick weel thump'd in a pot, man ;
    But aw thowt a' the toon
    Shuddint lick him when down,
Tho' he'd a greet spite te Bob Cranky.

Yen Price had the cream o' the bowl, man,
Wi' goold lamps clagg'd close cheek by jowl, man ;
    It was sic a fine seet,
    Aw cou'd glower'd a' neet,
Had fu' been the wame o' Bob Cranky.

Ne mair seed aw till signal gun fir'd,
Out went the leets, an' hame aw gat, tir'd ;
    Nan ax'd 'boot Leum'nations,
    Aw bad her hae patience,
An' first fetch sum flesh te Bob Cranky.

Aw tel'd her what news aw had hard, man,
That shuggar was sixpence a pund, man,
    An' good beef at a groat :—
    Then oor Nan clear'd her throat,
An' shooted oot, " Plenty for Cranky ! "

'Twas a' lees—for when Nan gang'd te toon,
An' for yen pund a sixpence pat down ;
    Fra shop she was winnin',
    When Grosser, deuce bin him,
Teuk a' the cheap shuggar fra Cranky.

But gif Peace brings another gran' neet,
Aw think foak shou'd hae Plenty te eat:
    Singin' hinnys, awm shoor,
    An' strang yell at the doowr,
Wad better nor candles please Cranky.

Then agyan, what a sheym an' a sin!
Te the Pit dinner nyan ax'd me in:
    Yet aw work like a Turk,
    Baith wi' pick, knife, and fork,—
An' whese mair a Pittite nor Cranky?

Or what cou'd ye a' de without me,
When cau'd ice an' snaw cum aboot ye?
    Then sair ye wad shiver,
    For a' ye're se cliver,
An' lang for the pick o' Bob Cranky.

S * * * *   *Tyne Mercury*, June 1st, 1814.

JAMES STAWPERT.

"NEWCASTLE FAIR," by J. S. With this signature the song appears in Bell's *Rhymes*, and is another illustration of the confusion caused by the strange coincidence of three writers, all at one period, using the same initials—J. S. John Bell, in one of his volumes of broad-sheets, now in the possession of R. Welford, Esq., settles which of the three— John Shield, John Selkirk, or James Stawpert—this J. S. belongs to, by adding in ink to the initials *James Stawpert*. Stawpert is the least known of the three. It will be remembered he was the one who took up the cudgels in defence of "The Bards of the Tyne" against Charles Purvis. Two additional songs by him, "John Diggons" and "Trafalgar's Battle," appear both in Bell's *Rhymes* and Angus' *Garlands*. Neither are in the dialect, although both show their northern origin. "John Diggons," a country lad singing of Nelson's death, thus refers to our Lord Collingwood—

> " But now I'm determined, since this is the case,
> To write to Lord Collingwood straight for a place,
> For they say he's right fond of a North-country face ;
> So I may chance to revenge Nelson's wrongs,
> So I may chance to revenge Nelson's wrongs.
>
> Adieu, then, my friends, your best wishes I'll take.
> Oh ! send them all good for your *Collingwood's sake !*
> For your country and you his life's olt been at stake ;
> Then bless him, and thank his brave tars !
> Then bless him, and thank his brave tars ! "

In "Trafalgar's Battle" he further refers to Newcastle's great naval hero—

> " 'Tis Collingwood he, our townsman and friend,
> May heaven send angels his life to attend,
> To guard him through dangers on ocean's great space.
> Returning in peace may we all see his face,
> To bless him, caress him,
> In kind words address him,
> Ye Britons and *Sons of the Tyne.*"

James Stawpert, according to Bell's "Notes," was a clerk with Messrs. Burdon & Rayne, brewers, Quayside ; and this scrap of information about him is really all that is known. His songs show they were written about 1805. Then he would be on the Quayside, daily meeting with Thomas Thompson and Thomas Wilson, and would have as a fellow-clerk the unfortunate John Selkirk. Of his further career we have no trace.

NEWCASTLE FAIR; OCTOBER 1811.

THE PITMAN A-DRINKING OF JACKY.*

TUNE—"Drops of Brandy."

HA' ye been at Newcastle Fair ?
And did you see ouse o' great Sandy?
Lord bliss us ! what wark there was there,
And the folks were drinking of brandy.
Brandy, a shilling a glass !

* English Gin. This liquor has various names in different parts of the country. At a village in the western part of Northumberland the editor (Bell's *Rhymes*) heard it called Blue Dick.

Aw star'd, an' thought it was shameful,
Never mind, says aw, canny lass,
  Give us yell, and aw'll drink ma wame full.
            Rum te idily, etc.

Says she, Canny man, the yell's cawd;
  It cums frev a man they ca' Mackey,
And my faith! it's byeth sour and awd;
  Ye'd best hev a drop o' wour Jacky.
Yor Jacky! says I, now what's that?
  Aw ne'er heerd the nyem o' sic liquor.
English gin, canny man, that's flat!
  And then she set up a great nicker.
            Rum te idily, etc.

Says I, divent laugh at poor folks,
  But gang and bring some o' yur Jacky;
Aw want nyen o' yur jibes or jokes:
  I' th' meantime aw'll tyek a bit backy.
Aw just tyuk a chew o' pig tail,
  She brought in this Jacky se funny;
Says she, Sir, that's better than ale,
  And held out her hand for the money.
            Rum te idily, etc.

There's threepence to pay, if you please:
  Aw star'd an' aw gyep'd like a ninny:
Odsmash thee! aw'll sit at ma ease,
  An' not stir till aw've spent a half-guinea.
Aw sat an' aw drank till quite blind,
  Then aw gat up te gang te the door,
But deel smash a door cou'd aw find!
  An' fell flat o' ma fyess on the floor.
            Rum te idily, etc.

There aw lay for ever se lang,
    And dreamt about rivers and ditches;
When waken'd, was singing this sang—
    "Smash, Jacky, thou's wet a' ma breeches!"
An' faith! but the sang it was true,
    For Jacky had been se prevailing,
He'd whistled himsel' quickly through,
    An' the chairs an' tables were sailing.
                        Rum te idily, etc.

Then rising, aw went ma ways hyem,
    Aw knock'd at the door, and cry'd, Jenny!
Says she, Canny man, is te lyem,
    Or been wadin' in Tyne, ma hinny?
I' troth, she was like for te dee,
    An' just by the way to relieve her,—
The water's been wadin' through me,
    An' this Jacky's a gay deceiver.
                        Rum te idily, etc.

STAWPERT.   *Bell's "Northern Bards,"* 1812.

THE PITMAN'S REVENGE AGAINST BONAPARTE.

"THIS Tyneside song, written nearly seventy years ago, and published in all collections since, is now printed with the author's name for the first time. The author, George Cameron, was for many years a hairdresser in the Cloth Market. When the song was written, about 1804, Napoleon's legions lay at Boulogne waiting a favourable opportunity to cross the Channel. How volunteer associations to resist this threatened invasion were formed has already been told. In one of the volunteer regiments then formed George Cameron was sergeant. Whilst occupying that position, he wrote the song, and sung it amongst his fellow volunteers at a meeting held at the Three Indian Kings on the Quayside. The song was greatly admired, being most appropriate to

the times. It was afterwards borrowed by a comrade, who, unknown to the author, got it printed. These facts are well remembered by his daughter, Mrs. G. Halliday, of this town."

The above note appeared in the 1872 edition of this collection. Mrs. Halliday's son George (since dead), who then was carrying on in Collingwood Street the old-established business of a saddler left him by his father, happening to come into the publisher's, which was next door to

A NEWCASTLE. VOLUNTEER.

his own shop, he saw the proofs of the song-book lying about, and remarked, " I wonder if my grandfather's song is there." Further conversation brought out the facts related above, and another equally interesting. Mr. Halliday repeated the first verse of the song as he had learned it from his mother, and then it was found he gave one line more in the first verse than was in the book. This difference brought out the fact that Bell, who had printed the song, by some error had missed a line in the first verse, all the verses having nine lines except the first, which only had eight. The eighth line in the first verse is the one Mr. Halliday restored, after its omission in all collections for nearly seventy years. It might also be mentioned that Bell (1812), in printing the

song, gave no author's name.   Marshall (1827) also printed
it without a name; but Davidson, in his Alnwick edition (about
1840), and Fordyce, in his collection (1842), both printed the
song, and ascribed it to John Shield.   This error is now
corrected.   By the kindness of J. C. Halliday (a grandson),
we also give an autograph of the author, taken from his old
family Bible, now in the possession of Mrs. Richardson, a
grand-daughter of the poet.

George Cameron

This appears to have been the only song Cameron wrote.
He died June 20th, 1823, aged 55 years, and was buried in
St. Nicholas' Churchyard.

HA'E ye heerd o' these wondrous Dons
        That myeks this mighty fuss, man,
Aboot invadin' Britain's land?
        I vow they're wondrous spruce, man:
But little de the Frenchmen ken
About wor loyal Englishmen;
Wor collier lads are for cockades,
They'll fling away their picks an' spades
        For guns te shoot the French, man.
                        Tol lol de rol, de rol de rol.

Then te parade the Pitmen went,
        Wi' hearts byeth stoot an' strang, man;
Gad smash the French! we are se strang,
        We'll shoot them ivry one, man!
Gad smash me sark! if aw wad stick
Te tummel them a' doon the pit;
As fast as aw cud thraw a coal
Aw'd tummel them a' doon the hole,
        An' close her in aboon, man.
                        Tol lol, etc.

"Heeds up!" says one, "ye silly sow!
  Ye dinna mind the word, man!"
"Eyes reet!" says Tom, "an' wi' a dam,
  And march off at tbe word, man!"
Did ever mortals see sic brutes,
Te order me to lift maw kutes?
Ad smash the fyul! te stand an' talk
How can he learn me te walk,
  That's walked this forty year, man!
                                    Tol lol, etc.

But shud the Frenchmen show thor fyece
  Upon wor waggon-ways, man,
Then there upon the road, ye knaw,
  We'd myek them end thor days, man.
Ay, Bonaparte's sel aw'd tyek,
An' thraw him i' the burnin' heap,
An' wi' greet speed aw'd roast him deed;
His marrows, then, aw waddent heed—
  We'd pick oot a' thor een, man.
                                    Tol lol, etc.

Says Willy Dunn to loyal Tom,
  "Yor words are a' a joke, man:
For Geordy winna hae yor help,
  Ye're sic kamstarie folk, man."
"Then Willy, lad, we'll rest in peace,
I' hopes that a' the wars may cease;
But aw's gie ye, Wull, te understand,
As lang as aw can wield my hand,
  Thor's nyen but George shall reign, man!"
                                    Tol lol, etc.

" Eneuf of this hes shure been said,"
   Cried cowardly Willy Dunn, man :
" For shud the Frenchmen cum this way,
   We'd be ready for te run, man."
" Gad smash ye, for a fyul ! " says Tom,
" For if aw cudden't use my gun,
  Aw'd tyek me pick and hew them doon,
  An' run an' cry thro' a' the toon,
     ' God save greet George, wor king, man ! ' "
                          Tol lol, etc.

CAMERON.

HENRY ROBSON.

As far back as 1812, in Bell's *Rhymes of Northern Bards*, the following notice of Henry Robson appears :—

" The author of ' The Collier's Pay Week ' was born at Benwell, near Newcastle, and is now residing at the latter place, where, besides the above, he has written several pieces of poetry possessing a considerable degree of merit."

The piece of poetry, to which this was a note, is about forgotten. It was a song, " The Tyne." Perhaps its best lines were the chorus—

" Flow on, lovely Tyne, undisturbed be thy motion ;
  Thy sons hold the threats of proud France in disdain :
As long as thy waters shall mix with the ocean,
  The fleets of Old England will govern the main."

Generally, and it may be added unfortunately, Bell's references to the writers in the *Bards* are of the scantiest. How he came to notice Robson so specially might possibly be that as a printer Robson worked with Angus, who printed Bell's volume, and so they came together.

The introductory set of verses in the volume on "Northumberland Minstrelsy," signed H. R., in all probability are also Robson's. They begin—

" With taste so true and genius fine
  The blythsome minstrels of lang syne
  Sung sweetly 'tween the Tweed and Tyne."

With Angus at that time, as an apprentice, would be Robert Emery, then a youth in his eighteenth year. He in all probability would assist in setting up Bell's volume, and from it may have got that "bent" to local song which in after years produced "Hydrophobia," "Jean Jamieson's Ghost," etc. "The Collier's Pay Week" is Robson's best piece. As a slight sketch it may fairly stand beside the fuller and more finished "Collier's Wedding" and "Pitman's Pay." As a dialect writer Robson has done little; his taste evidently "did not that way tend." Even when, as in the "Collier's Pay Week," his subject is local, his treatment has little of the dialect in it.

As a printer he was for many years with Mackenzie & Dent, publishers of local works, and is said to have had a small press at home, where he printed his pieces for distribution amongst his friends. In his later years he appears to have written little. At his death, which occurred at Grenville Terrace on December 21st, 1850, he had reached the ripe age of 75 years, and by a brief obituary notice which then appeared, "he had worked 60 years as a printer, was the oldest member of the profession in the town, and was much respected by a numerous circle of friends."

———

THE COLLIER'S PAY WEEK.

(A Picture of Benwell Pit Life about the year 1800.)

As far back as 1644 mention is found of the colliers of Benwell. The Milbank MS. states, in that year, during the siege of Newcastle, it was the Benwell and Elswick colliers who undermined and blew up the walls of the town.

THE baff week is o'er—no repining—
    Pay-Saturday's swift on the wing;
At length the blythe morning comes shining,
    When kelter makes colliers sing.
'Tis Spring, and the weather is cheary,
    The birds whistle sweet on the spray;
Now coal working lads, trim and airy,
    To Newcastle town hie away.

Those married jog on with their *hinnies*,
　　Their canny bairns go by their side;
The daughters keep teasing their minnies,
　　For new clothes to keep up their pride;
They plead—Easter Sunday does fear them,
　　For if they have nothing that's new,
The *Crow*—spiteful bird!—will besmear them,
　　Oh, then, what a sight for to view!

The young men, full blithesome and jolly,
　　March forward, all decently clad;
Some lilting up, "*Cut-and-dry Dolly*,"
　　Some singing "*The Bonny Pit Lad.*"
The pranks that were play'd at last binding
　　Engage some in humorous chat;
Some halt by the wayside on finding
　　Primroses to place in their hat.

Bob Cranky, Jack Hogg, and Dick Marley,
　　Bill Hewitt, Luke Carr, and Tom Brown,
In one jolly squad set off early
　　From Benwell to Newcastle town:
Such hewers as they (none need doubt it)
　　Ne'er handled a shovel or pick;
In high or low seam they could suit it,
　　In regions next door to Old Nick.

Some went to buy hats and new jackets,
　　And others to see a bit fun;
And some wanted leather and tackets
　　To cobble their canny pit shoon.

Save the ribbon Dick's dear had requested
   (Aware he had plenty of chink),
There was no other care him infested,
   Unless 'twere his care for good drink.

In the morning the dry man advances
   To purl shop to toss off a gill,
Ne'er dreading the ills and mischances,
   Attending on those who *sit still.*
The drink Reason's monitor quelling,
   Inflames both the brain and the eyes;
The enchantment commenc'd, there's no telling
   When care-drowning tipplers will rise.

O MALT! we acknowledge thy powers,
   What *good* and what *ill* dost thou brew!
Our good *friend* in moderate hours—
   Our *enemy* when we get fu';
Could thy vot'ries avoid the fell furies
   So often awaken'd by thee,
We would seldom need judges or juries
   To send folk to Tyburn tree!

At length in Newcastle they centre—
   In Hardy's,* a house much renown'd,
The jovial company enter,
   Where stores of good liquor abound:
As quick as the servants could fill it
   (Till emptied were quarts half-a-score),
With heart-burning thirst down they swill it,
   And thump on the table for more.

* Sign of the Black Boy, Groat Market.

While thus in fine cue they are seated,
  Young Cock-fighting Ned from the Fell*
Peep'd in—his *"How d'ye?"* repeated,
  And hop'd they were all very well;
He swore he was pleased to see them—
  One rose up to make him sit down,
And join in good fellowship wi' them,
  For him they would spend their last crown.

The liquor beginning to warm them,
  In friendship the closer they knit,
And tell and hear jokes—and, to charm them,
  Comes Robin, from Denton Bourn Pit:
An odd, witty, comical fellow,
  At either a jest or a tale,
Especially when he was mellow,
  With drinking stout Newcastle ale.

With bousing, and laughing, and smoking,
  The time slippeth swiftly away!
And while they are ranting and joking,
  The church clock proclaims it mid-day.
And now for black puddings, long measure,
  They go to Tib Trollibag's stand,
And away bear the glossy rich treasure
  With joy, like curl'd bugles in hand.

And now a choice house they agreed on,
  Not far from the head of the Quay;
Where they their black puddings might feed on,
  And spend the remains of the day.

            * Gateshead Fell.

Where pipers and fiddlers resorted,
  To pick up the straggling pence,
And where the pit lads often sported
  Their money at Fiddle and Dance.

Blind Willie the fiddler sat scraping.
  In a corner just as they went in ;
Some Willington callants were shaking
  Their feet to his musical din.
Jack vow'd he would have some fine cap'ring,
  As soon as their dinner was o'er,
With the lassie that wore the white apron,
  Now reeling about on the floor.

Their hungry stomachs being eased,
  And gullets well cleared with a glass,
Jack rose from the table, and seized
  The hand of the frolicsome lass.
"Ma hinny !" says he, "pray excuse me—
  To ask thee to dance aw make free :"
She replied, "I'd be loth to refuse thee !
  Now, fiddler, play 'Jigging for me.'"

The damsel displays all her graces,
  The collier exerts all his power ;
They caper in circling paces,
  And *set* at each end of the floor ;
He jumps, and his heels knack and rattle,
  At turns of the music so sweet,
He makes such a thundering brattle,
  The floor seems afraid of his feet.

This couple being seated, rose Bob up,
  He wished to make one in a jig;
But a Willington lad set his gob up,—
  O'er him there should none "*run the rig;*"
For now 'twas his turn for a caper,
  And he would dance first as he'd rose;
Bob's passion beginning to vapour,
  He twisted his opponent's nose.

The Willington lads for their Franky,
  Jump'd up to revenge the foul deed;
And those in behalf of Bob Cranky
  Sprung forward—for now there was need.
Bob canted the form, with a kevel,
  As he was exerting his strength,
But he got on the lug such a *nevel*,
  That down he came all his long length.

Tom Brown, from behind the long table,
  Impatient to join in the fight,
Made a spring, some rude foe to disable,
  For he was a man of some might:
Misfortune, alas! was attending,
  An accident fill'd him with fear:
An old rusty nail his flesh rending,
  Oblig'd him to slink in the rear.

When sober, a mild man was Marley,
  More apt to join friends than make foes;
But, rais'd by the juice of the barley,
  He put in some sobbling blows.

And Cock-fighting Ned was their Hector,
  A courageous fellow and stout :
He stood their bold friend and protector,
  And thump'd the opponents about.

All hand-over-head topsy-turvy,
  They struck with fists, elbows, and feet ;
A Willington callant, called Gurvy,   .
  Was top-tails toss'd over the seat.
Luke Carr had one eye closed entire,
  And what is a serio-farce,
Poor Robin was cast on the fire,
  They cudn't hae serv'd him much warse.

Oh, Robin ! what argued thy speeches ?
  Disaster now makes thee quite mum :
Thy wit could not save the good breeches
  That mensefully cover'd thy bum.
To some slop-shop now thou may go trudging,
  And lug out some squandering coins ;
For now 'tis too late to be grudging—
  Thou cannot go home with bare groins.

How the wayfaring companies parted
  The Muse chooseth not to proclaim ;
But 'tis thought that, being rather down-hearted,
  They quietly went "toddling hame."
Now, ye Collier callants, so clever,
  Residing 'tween Tyne and the Wear,
Beware, when you fuddle together,
  Of making too free with strong beer.

H. ROBSON.   *Bell's " Northern Bards,"* 1812.

8

THE SANDGATE LASSIE'S LAMENT.

TUNE—"The Bonny Pit Laddie."

THEY'VE prest my dear Johnny,
Se sprightly and bonny——
Alack! I shall ne'er mair d' weel, O!
The kidnapping squad
Laid hold of my lad
As he was unmooring the keel, O!

Chorus.

O, my sweet laddie,
My canny keel laddie,
Se hansum, se canty, and free, O!
Had he staid on the Tyne,
Ere now he'd been mine,
But, oh! he's far ower the sea, O!

Should he fall by commotion,
Or sink in the ocean,
(May sic tidings ne'er come to the Key, O!
I could ne'er mair be glad,
For the loss of my lad
Wad break my poor heart, and I'd dee, O!

O, my sweet laddie, etc.

But should my dear tar
Come safe from the war,
What heart-bounding joy wad I feel, O!
To the church we wad flee,
And married be,
And again he shall row in his keel, O!

O, my sweet laddie, etc.

H. ROBSON.   *Bell's "Northern Bards,"* 1812.

O, my sweet laddie,
My cannie keel laddie,
Se handsum, se canty, and free, O!
Tho' far from the Tyne,
I still hope he'll be mine,
And live happy as any can be, O!

O, my sweet laddie, etc.

H. ROBSON.   *Bell's " Northern Bards,"* 1812.

TILL THE TIDE CUMS IN.

WHILE strolling down sweet Sandgate Street,
A man-o'-war's blade I chanc'd to meet;
To the sign of " The Ship " I haul'd him in,
To drink a good glass, till the tide came in.

Till the tide came in, etc.

I took in tow young Squinting Meg,
Who well in the dance could shake her leg;
My friend haul'd Oyster Mally in,
And we jigg'd them about till the tide came in.

Till the tide came in, etc.

We boos'd away till the break of day,
Then ask'd, What shot we had to pay?
" You've drank," said the host, " nine pints of gin!"
So we paid him his due—now the tide was in.

Now the tide was in, etc.

H. ROBSON.   *Marshall's Collection* (1827).

MA' CANNY HINNY.

WHERE hast'te been, ma' canny hinny?
    An' where hast'te been, ma' bonny bairn?
Aw was up an' down seekin' ma' hinny,
    Aw was thro' the toon seekin' for my bairn;
Aw went up the Butcher Bank and down Grundin Chare,
Call'd at the Dun Cow, but aw cuddent find thee there.

    Where hast'te been, ma' canny hinny?
    An' where hast'te been, ma' bonny bairn? etc.

Then aw went t' th' Cassel Garth, and caw'd on Johnny
        Fife;
The beer-drawer tell'd me she ne'er saw thee in her life.

            Where hast'te been? etc.

Then aw went into the Three Bulls' Heads, and down the
        lang stairs,
And a' the way alang the Close, as far as Mr. Mayor's.

            Where hast'te been? etc.

Fra there aw went alang the brig, an' up t' Jackson's
        Chare,
Then back again t' the Cross Keys, but cuddent find thee
    · there.
            Where hast'te been? etc.

Then comin' out o' Pipergate, aw met wi' Willy Rigg,
Whe tell'd me that he saw thee lukin' ower the brig.

            Where hast'te been? etc.

Cummin' alang the brig again, aw met wi' Cristy Gee,
He tell'd me 'et he saw thee gannin down Humeses'
    Entery.
            Where hast'te been? etc.

Where hev aw been ? aw sune can tell ye that ;
Cummin up the Kee, aw met wi' Peter Pratt,
Meetin' Peter Pratt we met wi' Tommy Wear,
An' went t' Humeses t' get a gill o' beer.

There's where a've been, ma' canny hinny,
There's where a've been, ma' bonny lam'.
Wast'tu up an' down seekin' for yur hinny ?
Wast'tu up and down seekin' for yur lam' ?

Then aw met yur Ben, an' we were like to fight ;
An' when we cam to Sandgate it was pick night.
Crossin' th' road, aw met wi' Bobby Swinny :
Hing on th' girdle, let's hev a singin' hinny.

Aw my sorrow's ower now, a've fund my hinny,
Aw my sorrow's ower now, a've fund my bairn ;
Lang may aw shout, ma' canny hinny,
Lang may aw shout, ma' bonny bairn.

UNKNOWN.   *Bell's " Northern Bards,"* 1812.

CHILDREN'S RHYMES.

Repeated by children when rain is falling—especially a summer's shower.

RAIN, rain, gan away,
Cum another summer's day.

Repeated by children when snow is falling.

KEEL-BULLY, keel-bully, ploat yor geese,
Cawd days an' winter neets.

A SUNDERLAND SONG.

OH! the weary Cutter, and oh! the weary Sea,
Oh! the weary Cutter, that stole my laddie from me;
When I look'd to the Nor'ard, I look'd with a wat'ry eye,
But when I look'd to the South'ard, I saw my laddie
    go by.

Sharpe's " Bishoprick Garland."

ANDREW CARR.

As I went to Newcastle,
    My journey was not far,
I met with a sailor lad,
    Whose name was Andrew Carr.

        And hey for Andrew, Andrew,
          Ho for Andrew Carr;
        And hey for Andrew, Andrew,
          Ho for Andrew Carr.

Good fortune attend my jewel,
    Now he's sail'd o'er the bar,
And send him back to me,
    For I love my Andrew Carr.

        And hey for Andrew, Andrew, etc.
Bell's " Northern Bards," 1812.

NORTHERN NURSERY SONG.

My bairn's a bonny bairn, a canny bairn, a bonny bairn,
My bairn's a canny bairn, and never looks dowley;
My bairn's a canny bairn, a canny bairn, a bonny bairn,
My bairn's a bonny bairn, and not a yellow-yowley.

Sharpe's " Bishoprick Garland."

WILLIAM STEPHENSON.

WILLIAM STEPHENSON, one of the earliest of Tyneside writers, was a native of Gateshead, where he was born on June 28th, 1763. At Gateshead, with James Atkinson, of

Church Street, he served his apprenticeship to the clock and watchmaking, and continued in that line until a severe accident disabled him, and rendered a lengthened stay in the country necessary for the recovery of his health. When he returned, he resolved to leave the watchmaking for a more congenial line. He was a scholar, and possessing literary tastes, the life of a schoolmaster appeared more attractive to him. He opened his school on the Church

Stairs, Gateshead, and his venture succeeding, he continued there during the greater part of his life.

In 1812 we find his "Quayside Shaver" in Bell's volume, and there also his "Skipper's Wedding," but the "Wedding" then under the title of "The Invitation." These two are by far his best songs. In 1832 he collected his songs and poems into a volume, which he inscribed to the Rev. John Collinson, then Rector of Gateshead. The principal piece is entitled "The Retrospect," and begins—

> "Gateshead is nought like what it was,
>   When first a boy I knew it;
> I had such sport and merry days,
>   When I went scampering through it."

A description of Gateshead as it was follows, introducing the eccentrics and well-known characters of the time, including the "Man who built a house and stole the stones," "Lowp, Peter, lowp," and possibly in these four lines the original of his "Quayside Shaver"—

> "Tom Tough and wife, both he and she
>   Bought up old pewter cuttings;
> She went and shav'd upon the Quay,
>   And he made soldiers' buttons"—

the whole poem being a curious and interesting picture of Gateshead 100 years ago.

His works are not numerous. "The Retrospect" occupies one-third of the 112 pages of the volume. Amongst his songs, of which there are only six, he places "The Age of Eighty." It is a good specimen of his graver pieces, and begins—

AGE OF EIGHTY.

> Now past the gay season and sunshine of youth,
>   Whose scenes are no longer endearing,
> I clearly perceive, in the mirror of truth,
>   The close of life's day now appearing.
> Tho' pleasing to some their past follies may seem,
>   Not thinking on matters more weighty,
> Like me will discover 'tis all but a dream,
>   If they live to the hoary age Eighty.
>
> Replete with old age yet contentment I know,
>   In my cot on the side of a mountain,
> Where streams of fruition abundantly flow
>   From rectitude's chrystalline fountain.

Prosperity's smiles, or adversity's frowns,
    Shall never divert or affright me ;
And sweet rosy health all my happiness crown,
    Tho' now at the hoary age Eighty.

His singing of "The Age of Eighty" seems a poetical licence, in which he a little anticipated the flight of time, as at his death, which occurred at Gateshead on August 12th, 1836, he would be in his seventy-third year. The portrait and autograph are from the volume published by his son (a copy of which was kindly lent by Matthew Mackey, Jun.).

THE QUAYSIDE SHAVER.

As far back as 1812 Bell writes as if the "Quayside Shaver" then was a thing of the past. His note runs—"Formerly on the Sandhill, and afterwards on the Quay, near the Bridge, were people (chiefly women) who, in the open street, on Market Days, performed the office of barber." Bell does not mention it, but it is said the "Quayside Shavers" prospered through only charging half what was charged at the shops.

ON each market day, Sir, the folks to the Quay, Sir,
    Go flocking with beards they have seven days worn,
And round the small grate, Sir, in crowds they all wait, Sir,
    To get themselves shav'd in a rotative turn.
Old soldiers on sticks, Sir, about politics, Sir,
    Debate—till at length they quite heated have grown;
May nothing escape, Sir, until *Madam Scrape*, Sir,
    Cries "Gentlemen, who is the next to sit down?"

A medley the place is, of those that sell laces,
    With fine shirt-neck buttons, and good cabbage nets,
Where match-men, at meeting, give a kind greeting,
    And ask one another how trade with them sets;
Join'd in with *Tom Hoggers* and little *Bob Nackers*,
    Who wander the streets in their fuddling gills;
And those folks with bags, Sir, who buy up old rags, Sir,
    That deal in fly-cages and paper wind-mills.

There pitmen, with baskets, and gay posey waistcoats,
  Discourse about nought but whee puts and hews best;
There keelmen just landed, swear, may they be stranded,
  If they're not shaved first, while their keel's at the *Fest!*
With face of coal dust, would frighten one almost,
  Thro' off hat and wig, while they usurp the chair;
While others stand looking, and think it provoking,
  But, for the insult, to oppose them none dare.

When under the chin, Sir, she tucks the cloth in, Sir,
  Their old quid they'll pop in the pea-jacket cuff;
And while they are sitting, do nought but keep spitting,
  And looking around with an air fierce and bluff.
Such tales as go round, Sir, would surely confound, Sir,
  And puzzle the prolific brain of the wise;
But when she prepares, Sir, to take off the hair, Sir,
  With lather she whitens them up to the eyes.

No sooner the razor is laid on the face, Sir,
  Than painful distortions take place on the brow;
But if they complain, Sir, they'll find it in vain, Sir,
  She tells them, "there's nought but what *Patience* can
      do:"
And as she scrapes round 'em, if she by chance wound 'em,
  They'll cry out as tho' she'd bereav'd them of life,
"'Od smash your brains, woman! aw find the blood's
      comin',
  Aw'd rather be shav'd with an aud gully knife!"

For all they can say, Sir, she still rasps away, Sir,
  And sweeps round their jaw, the chop torturing tool;
Till they in a pet, Sir, request her to whet, Sir;
  But she gives them for answer, "Sit still, you poor fool!"

For all their repining, their twisting and twining,
 She forward proceeds, till she's mown off the hair;
When finish'd cries, "There, Sir!" then straight from the
  chair, Sir,
 They'll jump, crying, "Daresay you've scrap'd the bone
  bare!"

W. STEPHENSON, Sen.   { *"Bell's Bards"* and
              { *Author's Volume*, 1832.

———

THE SKIPPER'S WEDDING.

GOOD neighbours, I'm come for to tell ye,
 Our Skipper and Mall's to be wed;
And if it be true what they're saving,
 Egad we'll be all rarely fed!
They've brought home a shoulder of mutton,
 Besides two fine thumping fat geese,
And when at the fire they're roasting,
 We're all to have sops in the greese.
     Blind Willy's to play on the fiddle.

And there will be pies and spice dumplings,
 And there will be bacon and peas;
Besides a great lump of beef boiled,
 And they may get crowdies who please;
To eat of such good things as these are,
 I'm sure you've but seldom the luck;
Besides, for to make us some pottage,
 There'll be a sheep's head and a pluck.
     Blind Willy's to play on the fiddle.

Of sausages there will be plenty,
    Black puddings, sheep fat, and neats' tripes;
Besides, for to warn all our noses,
    Great store of tobacco and pipes;
A room, they say, there is provided
    For us at "The Old Jacob's well;"
The bridegroom he went there this morning,
    And spoke for a barrel o' yell.
                    Blind Willy's to play on the fiddle.

There's sure to be those things I've mention'd,
    And many things else; and I learn,
There's white bread and butter and sugar,
    To please every bonny young bairn.
Of each dish and glass you'll be welcome
    To eat and to drink till you stare;
I've told you what meat's to be at it,
    I'll tell you next who's to be there.
                    Blind Willy's to play on the fiddle.

Why there will be Peter the hangman,
    Who flogs the folks at the cart-tail,
Au'd Bob, with his new sark and ruffle,
    Made out of an au'd keel sail!
And Tib on the Quay who sells oysters,
    Whose mother oft strove to persuade
Her to keep from the lads, but she wouldn't,
    Until she got by them betray'd.
                    Blind Willy's to play on the fiddle.

And there will be Sandy the cobbler,
    Whose belly's as round as a keg,
And Doll, with her short petticoats,
    To display her white stockings and leg;

And Sall, who, when snug in a corner,
  A sixpence, they say, won't refuse;
She curs'd when her father was drowned,
  Because he had on his new shoes.

> Blind Willy's to play on the fiddle.

And there will be Sam the quack doctor,
  Of skill and profession he'll crack;
And Dick who would fain be a soldier,
  But for a great hump on his back;
And Tom in the streets, for his living,
  Who grinds razors, scissors, and knives;
And two or three merry old women,
  That call "Mugs and doubles, wives!"

> Blind Willy's to play on the fiddle.

But I had forgot neighbours nearly,
  For to tell ye—exactly at one,
The dinner will be on the table,
  And music will play till it's done.
When you'll be all heartily welcome,
  Of this merry feast for to share;
But if you won't come at this bidding,
  Why then you may stay where you are.

> Blind Willy's to play on the fiddle.

W. STEPHENSON, Sen.   *Author's Volume*, 1832.

NEWCASTLE ON SATURDAY NIGHT.

A Picture of Saturday Night One Hundred Years Ago.

YE Muses, oh! mount on Aonian wing,
    And leave the fam'd fount, and Pierian shades,
All haste to Newcastle, and aid me to sing,
    The time when her sons have release from their trades;
But hard words and Greek'um, let learned folks seek 'em,
    Who epic, and tragic, bombastic would write,
While loudly we'll sing O, in plain English lingo,
    The stir at Newcastle on Saturday Night.

Here barbers their gimcracks in readiness getting,
    Hot water and looking-glass, shaving-cloth clean,
Their towels and lather-box,—razors are whetting,
    To mow the ripe harvest that grows on the chin;
When into the shop, Sir, with long beards you pop, Sir,
    There get yourselves painted all over with white,
And one may suppose, Sir, fast hold of your nose, Sir,
    They'll smooth off your phiz on a Saturday Night.

Then see that you pop in, nor dare to delay, Sir,
    Nor turn Sabbath breaker, the clergy's strict rule,
But be wise and beware of a Sunday morn razor,
    And always avoid the chap-torturing tool,
Else with smart on your chin, Sir, you'll grumble and
        grin, Sir,
    Sure as the dull edge on your front should alight;
But ask him to whet, Sir, he'll cry in a pet, Sir,
    "Then come and be shav'd on a Saturday Night!"

Of Hawks' smithies, no more heard the din is,
  Round the door of the warehouse the workmen arrange,
While old Tommy Youll with his bank notes and guineas,
  Is puffing and running about to get change;
When reckon'd they ne'er stop, but jog to the beer shop,
  Where fumes of tobacco and stingo invite,
And the oven inhabits great store of Welch rabbits,
  To feast jov'al fellows on a Saturday Night.

While cheerful liquor around they are pushing,
  The many-mouth'd chorus melodious flies,
Tho' oft interrupted by merchants who rush in,
  With do you want crabs, or with hot penny pies;
Perhaps you may chuse, Sir, to pore o'er the news, Sir,
  To see whether matters go wrong or go right,
All ranks and conditions commence politicians,
  While set in the alehouse on Saturday Night.

While over the tankard such joys they are raising,
  Full often will fate their enjoyments annoy.
A good scolding wife puts her unwelcome face in,
  An intruding guest, she breaks thus on their joy:
" What, here again Harry, ne langer ye's tarry,
  Od swell ye come hyem, or I'll close up your sight."
" Nay, now he says jewel, ye'll not be se cruel,
  To begrudge one a drop on a Saturday Night."

Here wives with their baskets are to and fro walking,
  In shambles to bargain with butchers for meat,
While some ballad singer by slowly is stalking,
  And warbles so sweetly his lays in the street;

Here's Calender's crying, and people come buying,
   Around the hoarse fellow in crowds such a sight,
And as suits your palates, confessions and ballads
   Are all at your service on Saturday Night.

As through the dark alleys if slily one passes,
   What fun we may have if an ear we will lend;
Such sighs and soft wishes, from lads and from lasses,
   Who tell their fond tales at an entry end;
When he to his true love cries, "Sally, adieu, love!"
   And kisses and squeezes his deary so tight,
She, blushing, says "Fie, Sir!" and softly will cry, "Sir,
   Do stay a bit longer; 'tis Saturday Night."

Now, if for variety, Sir, you be craving,
   Here's fruit and here's butter, here's flesh and here's
      fish,
Here's buying and selling, and courting and shaving,
   And drinking and smoking—what else can you wish?
With courting and joking, and drinking and smoking,
   We'll put wrinkled sorrow and care to the flight,
And over the stingo we'll laugh loud and sing O,
   And merrily welcome each Saturday Night.

JOHN LEONARD.

JOHN LEONARD is the author of but one song which finds
its way into dialect collections, "Winlaton Hopping." He
has written much beside, but it is of a political and general
character. In the Reference Library, Newcastle, there is a
manuscript volume of his poetry extending to some three or
four hundred pages, foolscap size. In a note in the volume
he tells that it was partly written during a three months'
imprisonment. What sort of imprisonment this was, where,

or how brought about, is not said. The Irish question then, as now, seems to have been to the front, as Leonard, in the volume, has two pieces—one on Charles James Fox, who is highly praised, and a companion piece on William Pitt, who is thus denounced—

> Who raised the torch and flaming brand
>   Which scorch'd so long Hibernia's land,
> Where thousands perish'd on the strand ?—
>
> > 'Twas Pitt.
>
> Who swore he'd make the Irish free,
>   If to the Union they'd agree,
> Who from his sacred oath did flee ?—
>
> > 'Twas Pitt.

Besides this manuscript volume, which appears to have been written about 1813, Marshall, of Gateshead, published a small collection of his poems (some 36 pages) in 1808.

Fac-simile of John Leonard's writing and autograph (reduced scale) from the manuscript in the Reference Library, kindly lent by the Committee.

Photographed by Mr. P. M. Laws, Blackett Street.

About Leonard himself little appears to be known. In all probability he would be born in Gateshead, where his father, George Leonard, was a gardener, and a man of some means, as he owned property in High Street, near Jackson's Chare—possibly Leonard's Court. When it is added that the poet was brought up to the trade of a joiner, the little that is known about him is told. When and where he died we have no record. Apparently it was not in Gateshead, as St. Mary's register has been searched from 1813 to 1852 without finding any entry of his burial.

WINLATON HOPPING.

Winlaton Hopping, always held on the Monday and Tuesday following the 14th of May, is an old institution. It still survives, but shorn of much of its former popularity.

YOU sons of glee, come list to me,
    You who love mirth and toping, O,
You'll ne'er refuse to hear the muse
    Sing of Winlaton Hopping, O.
To Tenche's Hotel let's retire,
    To spend the night so neatly, O;
The fiddle and song you'll sure admire,
    Together they sound so sweetly, O.
                              Tal lal la, etc.

With box and dice you'd Sammy spy,
    Of late Sword-dancers' Bessy, O—
All patch'd and torn with tail and horn,
    Just like a Dei'el in dressy, O;
But late discharg'd from that employ,
    This scheme came in his noddle, O;
Which fill'd his little heart with joy,
    And pleas'd blithe Sammy Doddle, O.

Close by the stocks, his dice and box
    He rattled away so rarely, O;
He did engage, youth and old age,
    Together they play'd so cheerly, O:

While just close by the sticks did fly,
    At spice on knobs of woody, O:
" How ! mind my legs !" the youngsters cry,
    "Smash ! see, thou's drawn the bloody !" O.

Rang'd in a row, a glorious show
    Of spice, and nuts for cracking, O ;
And handsome toys for girls and boys,
    Did grace Winlaton Hopping, O.
Each to the stalls led his sweet lass,
    And treat her there so sweetly, O ;
And then retir'd to drink a glass,
    Or shuffle and cut so neatly, O.

You men so wise who knowledge prize,
    Let not this scene confound ye, O ;
At Gardner's door you might explore
    The world a' running round ye, O :
Blithe girls and boys on horse or chair,
    Did fly round without stopping, O ;
Sure Blaydon rare can't compare
    With Winlaton's fam'd Hopping, O.

The night came on, with dance and song
    Each public-house did jingle, O ;
All ranks did swear to banish care,
    The married and the single, O :
They tript away till morning light,
    Then slept sound without rocking, O ;
Next day got drunk in merry plight,
    And jaw'd about the Hopping, O.

At last dull care his crest did rear,
    Our heads he sore did riddle, O ;
Till Peacock drew his pipes and blew,
    And Tenche he tun'd his fiddle, O ;

Then Jack the Glazier led the van,
  The drum did join in chorus, O—
The old and young they danced and sang,
  Dull Care fled far before us, O.

No courtier fine, nor grave divine,
  That's got the whole he wishes, O,
Will ever be so blithe as we,
  With all their loaves and fishes, O:
Then grant, O Jove! our ardent pray'r,
  And happy still you'll find us, O;—
Let pining Want and haggard Care,
  A day's march keep behind us, O.

LEONARD.   *Author's Manuscript*, 1813.

WILLIAM MITFORD.

FOLLOWING closely on the three founders of Tyneside Song comes William Mitford; and here again Newcastle is unable to claim our writer as her own. Like many more, he is hers only by adoption, his birthplace being Preston, near North Shields. Mitford, who was born on April 10th, 1788, had the misfortune to lose his parents when quite a child, and was brought to Newcastle by his uncle when between three and four years of age. Of his early life there is little or no record. His schooling past, he was apprenticed to a shoemaker in Dean Street (Dean Street then had been but lately opened, and was a fashionable part). The father of Willie Armstrong (afterwards noted in Tyneside Song) was a master shoemaker there, and possibly it was with him that Mitford learned his trade.

The next record we have of him is in connection with his famous songs. In 1816, Marshall, in the Cloth Market, published *The Budget; or, Newcastle Songster.* This is the earliest trace we have of Mitford as a writer. The *Budget* is written entirely by him; it contains eleven songs. On the second page is the following—half title, half dedication :—

THE
FEAST OF MOMUS; OR,
ODDFELLOWS' CABINET
FOR 1816,
CONTAINING A
COLLECTION OF SONGS,
CHIEFLY IN THE NEWCASTLE DIALECT, NEVER
BEFORE PUBLISHED,
IS DEDICATED, BY PERMISSION,
TO THE
LOYAL UNION LODGE OF ODDFELLOWS,
BY THE AUTHOR,
BROTHER MITFORD.

In this " Feast of Momus ; or, Oddfellows' Cabinet " we
have Mitford's best songs. His " Cappy," " The Courtship," and " X. Y." are there. In the course of years he

wrote many more, but while they all show his genius as a
song-writer, his early work is his best. Seven years after

this we have his next public appearance, but not this time in verse. In July 29th, 1823, the Cordwainers of Newcastle celebrated the festival of St. Chrispin, their patron saint, by holding a coronation (the first for thirty-four years) in the court of the Freemen's Hospital, Westgate (now the Police Station), and afterwards walking in procession through the principal streets of the town. Mitford, as a shoemaker, was one of them, and being well known through his local songs, he was selected to act the part of the bishop in the ceremonies. And on that occasion he assumed the lawn sleeves, mounted his spectacles, and acted the part to perfection.

His company being now much sought after through the celebrity of his songs, he left his shoemaking and opened a public-house on the edge of the Leazes, near to the Spital Tongues, which he called the " North Pole." Here, through his lively disposition, and possessing the qualification of singing his own songs, he succeeded in doing a good business. While residing there he wrote a song which he called " The North Pole," descriptive of the place and its attractions, and often sung it amongst his visitors. The last verse runs—

> " A social squad, I like it much,
> When Gill comes down to air his crutch,
> And Jack gets up to show you a touch—
>   You never now get at the Pole, sir.
> Here Winter never spoils our cheer,
> Though he comes more than once a year ;
> Then come, my lads, whose hearts are prime,
> Dispose yourselves at regular time,
> And see an Old Boy, who can chant a rhyme,
>   With his frosty face at the Pole, sir.
>   Hokey, pokey, etc."

After a time, leaving the " North Pole" for a more central situation, he removed to the " Tailors' Arms" at the " head of the Side," where he is thus referred to in 1834 by William Watson, a brother poet, in his song of the " Newcastle Landlords "—

> " M stands for Mitford—he kept the North Pole,
> Just over the Leazes—a dull looking hole ;
> Now our favourite poet lives at head of the Side—
> Here's success to his muse—long may she preside !"

By industry and attention Mitford was in time enabled

to leave his public-house, and to pass the evening of his life independent of the cares of business. In a house of his own in Oyster Shell Lane, at the head of Bath Lane, he died on the 3rd of March 1851, in his sixty-third year, and was buried at Westgate Cemetery, Arthur's Hill. We give a view of the house in which he died, and showing the bay window put in by himself, from which in his day, however it may be now, there was a fine open view of gardens, trees, and fields.

Perhaps there is no Tyneside song more known out of the district than Mitford's "Pitman's Courtship." The hero's dreams of happiness, homely simplicity, and happy mingling of the hetrogeneous stock of articles sold in a "huickstery way" in the pit villages, can be appreciated by many to whom the majority of Tyneside songs are riddles.

The portrait of Mitford on a previous page is copied from an oil painting in the possession of the poet's grandson. By the courtesy of the family this portrait is for the first time allowed to be copied. Mr. Laws has photographed it, and by the Meisenbach process, which reproduces every detail of the original, the portrait has been reproduced.

Photo.   Auty & Ruddock, Tynemouth.

Robert Emery, Mitford's friend and fellow-poet, wrote the following acrostic on his death.

W eep ! Northumbria's Bard is dead !
I n evil hour Death's arrow sped :
L ife felt the shock—the mortal fell :
L ight soared the soul, and sighed farewell !
I n freedom's wilds it travels far,
A nd beams beyond the evening star !
M ourn on, ye mighty Sons of Tyne !

M ourn for your Bard, whose lyre divine,
I n mirthful hour, inspired each heart,
T hus fallen beneath the tyrant's dart.
F ame hovers o'er his honoured bier—
O 'er all Northumbria once held dear.
R ide on, grim Death ! though dust's thy claim,
D eathless is our Minstrel's name !

William Mitford

This autograph is traced from the poet's signature to his
will at the Probate Court, Durham. Although only forty
years have passed since Mitford died, yet his munuscripts
have been so dispersed that an autograph was not otherwise
to be had.

TYNE FAIR.

In commemoration of the great frost in the winter 1813-14, when the
Tyne was frozen over for three weeks.

SINCE in cold there are some who don't wish to come
      out,
While others, confin'd, cannot ramble about ;
To those in such cases I'll offer a line,
While the ice is so thick upon Newcastle Tyne.

> Lol de lol, etc.

Jackey Frost, when he came, made the keelmen con-
      trive,
While the river was frozen, how they should best thrive ;
When one of them open'd a prospect so nice,
"'Od smash ye ! let's heave out wor planks on the ice."

I was going 'mongst the rest, the amusement to share,
When " Pay for the plank, sir!" says one with an air;
Slipt my hand in my pocket without e'er a frown,
And this knight of the huddock led me carefully down.

Huts, soldiers, and fiddlers arrested my view;
But something fell out, when away they all flew:
Fell out, did I say? why, I think 'twas fell in,
For they spy'd a gay barber sous'd up to the chin.

There were some rowley-powley, tetotum, dice-box,
While others, for liquor, were fighting game cocks;
While Neddy the Bellman—his bell tinkled on—
Said, a Cuddy Race started exactly at one.

O'er this fine icy walk, too, each belle had her beau,
Don skaiters cut figures their skill for to show;
All striving who'd get the most praise at the skait,
From the Member of Parliament down to the sweep.

A marine next went half down, whose paws on the ice
Went as fast as a cat's when she's kidnapping mice:
I began now to think 'twas a dangerous place,
When a Keel-Bulley roar'd, " Clear the road for a race."

The winning post seem'd a grand sight for a glutton,
For there hung suspended a plump leg of mutton;
Its rump orange laurels display'd to the view,
Which Cud Snapes after winning bedizen'd his brow.

This race was scarce done when another began,
'Tween knack-kneed Mall Trollop and bow-legged Nan:
This filly race made the folks round them to flock,
But knack-kneed Mall Trollop came in for the smock.

Hats, stockings, and hankerchiefs, still hung as prizes,
Was run for by skaiters and lads of all sizes;
Razor-grinders quite tipsy, with Bambro' Jack,
And God save the King, sung by Willy the Black.

Before I came home I'd a peep through the bridge,
Where a horse ran about with a man in a sledge;
I was bidding farewell to this cool winter's treat,
When in Will Vardy's tent I made choice of a seat.

"A game at quoits," says the landlord, "will finish the
    day.
With the tent pins for hobs ye may lather away;"
But the cords were soon cut, made him sulky and glum,
For down came the tent and three bottles of rum.

So now to conclude—here's wishing fresh weather,
That the poor and the rich may rejoice altogether;
Let's fill up our glasses and loyally sing,
Long live the Prince Regent, and God save the King.

Lol de lol, etc.

MITFORD.   *"The Budget"* (1816).

X Y Z AT NEWCASTLE RACES, 1814.

X Y Z, a famous racehorse, and the winner for four consecutive years—
viz., 1811-1812-1813-1814 of the Gold Cup, then the great prize at the Newcastle meeting. The Northumberland Plate, now the great race, had then
no existence.

SMASH! Jemmy, let us buss, we'll off
    An' see Newcassel races:
Set Dick the Trapper for some syep,
    We'll seun wesh a' wor faces.

There'll ne'er a lad in Percy Main,
Be bet this day for five or ten ;
Wor pockets lin'd wiv notes an' cash,
Amang the cheps we'll cut a dash—
    For X Y Z, that bonny steed,
      He bangs them a' for pith and speed,
        He's sure to win the Cup, man.

We reach'd the Moor, wi' sairish tews,
    When they were gaun to start, man :
We gav a fellow tuppence each,
    To stand upon a cart, man ;
The bets flew round frae side to side,
'' The field agyen X Y !" they cried ;
We'd hardly time to lay them a',
When in he cam—Hurraw ! hurraw !
    "Gad smash !" says I, " X Y's the steed,
      He bangs them a' for pith an' speed,
        We never see'd the like, man."

Next, to the tents we hied, te get
    Some stuffin for wor bags, man :
Wi' flesh we gaily pang'd wor hides—
    Smok'd nowse but patent shag, man.
While rum an' brandy soak'd each chop,
We'd Jackey an' fine ginger pop ;
We gat what made us winkin' blin'—
When drunkey aw began te sing—
    "Od smash ! X Y, that bonny steed,
      Thou bangs them a' for pith an' speed,
        We never see'd the like, man !"

Next up amang the shows we gat,
  Where folks a' stood i' flocks, man,
To see a chep play Bob and Joan,
  Upon a wooden box, man :
While bairns an' music fill'd the stage,
An' some, by gox ! were grim wi' age ;
When next au'd grin a poyney brought,
Could tell at yence what people thowt !
    " Od smash ! " says I, if he's the breed
    Of X Y Z, that bonny steed,
      Thou never see'd his like, man ! "

But, haud ! when we cam' to the toon,
  What thinks tou we saw there, man ?
We see'd a Blackey puffin, swetten,
  Suckin in fresh air, man ;
They said that he could fell an ox—
His name was fighting Mollinox ;
But ere he fit another round,
His marrow fell'd him te the groond.
    " Od smash ! " says aw, " if thou's sec breed
    As X Y Z, that bonny steed,
      Thou niver see'd his like, man ! "

Next board the steamer-boat we gat,
  A laddie rang a bell, man :
We haddent sitten verra lang,
  Till baith asleep we fell, man,
But the noise seun myed poor Jemmy start—
He thowt 'twas time to gang to wark,
For pick an' hoggers roar'd oot he—
An' myed sec noise it waken'd me,
    " Od smash ! " says I, " X Y's the steed,
    He bangs them a' for pith an' speed,
      Aw niver see'd his like, man."

When landed, straight off hame aw gans,
  An' thunners at the door, man ;
The bairns lap ower the bed wi' fright,
  Fell smack upon the floor, man ;
But to gar the wifey haud her tongue,
Show'd her the kelter aw had won ;
She with a cinder brunt her toes,
An' little Jacob broke his nose—
    The brass aw've getten at the race
    Will buy a patch for Jacob's face—
    So now my sang is deun, man.

MITFORD.   *" The Budget"* (1816).

CAPPY;

OR, THE PITMAN'S DOG.

The "highwayman fellow," whose bludgeon laid Cap on his back, W. H. Dawson writes, "was at that time custodian of our Norman keep, and kept watch and ward over malefactors, until the large 'stone jug' in Carliol Square was finished in 1828, and made ready for their reception. He was a gross, vulgar fellow, with a 'patch on his cheek,' and the name of Cappy stuck to him ever after the song appeared. Whether it was his by right before the song appeared we cannot say, but we find him so designated in a song written in February 1826, when he was keeper of the Castle. The circumstances that gave rise to the disaster of poor Cappy was a raid on the dogs similar to that perpetrated by the police in Newcastle in 1860."

TUNE—"Chapter of Donkeys."

IN a town near Newcassel a Pitman did dwell,
Wiv his wife nyemed Peg, a Tom Cat, and himsel;
A Dog, called Cappy, he doated upon,
Because he was left him by great Uncle Tom.

    Weel bred Cappy, famous au'd Cappy,
    Cappy's the Dog, Tallio, Tallio.

His tail pitcher-handled, his colour jet black,
Just a foot and a half was the length of his back,
His legs seven inches frev shoulders to paws,
And his lugs like twe dockins hung ower his jaws.
    Weel bred Cappy, etc.

For huntin of vermin reet clever was he,
And the house frev a' robbers his bark wad keep free;
Cou'd byeth fetch and carry,—cou'd sit on a stuil,
Or, when frisky, wad hunt water rats in a puil.
        Weel bred Cappy, etc.

As Ralphy to market one morn did repair,
In his hat-band a pipe, and weel kyem'd was his hair,
Ower his arm hung a basket—thus onward he speels,
And enter'd Newcassel wi' Cap at his heels.
        Weel bred Cappy, etc.

He haddent got farther than foot o' the Side,
Before he fell in with the dog-killing tribe;
When a highwayman fellow slipt round in a crack,
And a thump o' the skull laid him flat on his back.
        Down went Cappy, etc.

Now Ralphy *extonished*, Cap's fate did repine,
While its eyes like twee little pyerl buttons did shine;
He then spat on his hands, in a fury he grew,
Cries, "Gad smash! but I'se hev satisfaction o' thou
        For knocking down Cappy," etc.

Then this grim luiking fellow his bludgeon he rais'd,
When Ralphy ey'd Cappy, and then stuid amaz'd,
But fearin' beside him he might be laid down,
Threw him into the basket and bang'd out o' town.
        Away went Cappy, etc.

He breethless gat hyem, and when lifting the sneck,
His wife exclaim'd, Ralphy, thou's suin gettin back!
Gettin' back, replies Ralphy, I wish I'd ne'er gyen,
In Newcassel they're fellin dogs, lasses, and men.
        They've knock'd doon Cappy, etc.

If aw gan te Newcassel when comes wor pay week,
Aw'll ken him agyen by the patch on his cheek ;
Or if iver he enters wor toon wiv his stick,
We'll thump him about till he's black as au'd Nick,

   For killing au'd Cappy, etc.

Wiv tears in her eye Peggy heard his sad tale,
And Ralph wiv confusion and terror grew pale,
While Cappy's transactions with grief they talk'd o'er,
He crap oot o' the basket quite brisk o' the floor.

   Weel deun Cappy, etc.

MITFORD.   "*The Budget*," 1816.

THE PITMAN'S COURTSHIP.

"For a picture painted by the pen, drawn in the fond imagination of the lover, gilding the honeyed future, 'The Pitman's Courtship' is a gem that will ever be redolent of domestic bliss."—W. H. DAWSON.

      TUNE—"The Night before Larry was Stretched."

QUITE soft blew the wind from the west,
  The sun faintly shone in the sky,
When Lukey and Bessy sat courting,
  As walking I chanc'd to espy;
Unheeded I stole close beside them,
  To hear their discourse was my plan ;
I listen'd each word they were saying,
  When Lukey his courtship began.

Last hoppen thou won up my fancy,
  Wi' thy fine silken jacket o' blue ;
An' smash if thor Newcassel lyedys
  Cou'd marrow the curls o' thy brow;

That day aw whiles danc'd wi' lang Nancy,
  She coudn't like thou lift her heel:
My grandy lik'd spice singing hinnies,
  Ma comely, aw like thou as weel.

Thou knaws, ever since we were littel,
  Together we've ranged through the woods,
At neets hand in hand toddled hyem,
  Varry oft wi' howl kites and torn duds:
But now we can tauk about mairiage,
  An' lang sair for wor weddin' day;
When mairied thou's keep a bit shop,
  An' sell things in a huikstery way.

An' to get us a canny bit leevin,
  A' kinds o' fine sweetmeats we'll sell,
Reed harrin, broon syep, and mint candy,
  Black pepper, dye-sand, an' sma' yell;
Spice hunters, pick shafts, farden candles,
  Wax dollies wi' reed leather shoes,
Chawk pussy-cats, fine curley greens,
  Paper skyets, penny pies, and huil doos.

I'se help thou to tie up thy shuggar,
  At neets when frae wark I get lowse!
An' wor Dick that leeves owr by High Whickham,
  He'll myek us broom buzzums for nowse,
Like an image thou's stand owr the coonter,
  Wi' thy fine muslin, cambricker goon:
An' te let the fokes see thou's a lyedy,
  On a cuddy thou's ride to the toon.

There's be matches, pipe-clay, an' broon dishes,
  Canary seed, raisins, and fegs;
And, to please the pit laddies at Easter,
  A dish full o' giltey paste eggs;

Wor neibors, that's snuffers an' smokers,
  For wor snuff and backey they'll seek,
An' to show them we deal wi' Newcassel,
  Twee Blackeys sal mense the door cheek.

So now for Tim Bodkin I'se send,
  To darn my silk breeks at the knee,
Thou thy ruffles and frills mun get ready,
  Next Whitsunday mairied we'll be.
Now aw think it's high time to be steppin,
  We've sittin tiv aw's about lyem,
So then, wiv a kiss and a cuddle,
  These lovers they bent their ways hyem.

MITFORD.   "*The Budget,*" 1816.

THE MAYOR OF BORDEAUX; OR, MALLY'S MISTAKE.

On the night of June 27th, 1815, the bells of the town began to ring at half-past ten, and continued at intervals until after midnight. The cause of the uncommon occurrence was the arrival in Newcastle of Count Lynch, Mayor of Bordeaux; he was on his way to visit his relative, John Clavering, Esq., of Callaly. Count Lynch was in favour of the Old French Monarchy, and against Napoleon. He was the first in France to hoist the white flag, and surrendered Bordeaux to the British arms. The rejoicings were renewed when, next morning, June 28th, the mail arrived confirming the great victory at Waterloo.

As Jacob sat loosin his buttons,
  And rowlin his great backey chow,
The bells in the toon 'gan to tinkle;
  Cries Mally, What's happen'd us now?
Ho! jump and fling off thy aud neet-cap,
  And slip on thy lang-quarter'd shoes,
Ere thou gets hauf way up the Key,
  Ye'll meet sum that can tell ye the news,
                          Fol de rol, etc.

As Mally was puffin and runnin,
  A gentleman's flonkey she met;
"Canny man, ye mun tell us the news,
  Or ye'll set wor aud man i' the pet."

10

"The Mayor of Bordeaux, a French noble
    Has com'd to Newcastle with speed :
To-night he sleeps sound at wor Mayor's,
    And to morn he'll be at the Queen's Head."
                      Fol de rol, etc.

Now Mally thank'd him wiv a curtsey,
    And back tiv her Jacob did prance :
"*Mary Mordox, a fine fitter's Leady's
    Com'd ower in a coble frae France.*"
"Mary Mordox, a fine fitter's Leady !
    Ise war'nt she's some frolicksome jade,
And com'd to Newcassel for fashions,
    Or else to suspect the Coal Trade.
                      Fol de rol, etc.

"So to Peter's thou's gan i' the mornin,
    Gan suin and thou'll get a good pleyce ;
If thou canna get haud of her paw,
    Thou mun get a guid luick at her feyce :
And if ye can but get a word at her,
    And mind now ye divent think shem,
Say, 'Please ma'm, they ca' my wife Mary,
    Wor next little bairn's be the syem.'"
                      Fol de rol, etc.

So betimes the next mornin' he travels,
    And up to the Queen's Head he goes,
Where a skinny chep luik'd frev a winder,
    Wi' white powther'd wig an' lang nose :
A fine butterflee coat with gowld buttons,
    A man ! how the folks did hurrow ;
Aw thowt he'd fled frae sum toy-shop i' Lunnin,
    Or else frae sum grand wax-work show.
                      Fol de rol, etc.

Smash! Mally, ye've tell'd a big lee,
　For a man's not a woman aw'll swear;
But he hardly had spoken these words,
　Till oot tumbled a cask o' strang beer;
Like a cat Jackey flang his leg ower,
　Ay, like Bacchus he sat at his ease,
Tiv aw's fuddled, odsmash! ye may tauk
　Yor French gabberish as lang as ye please.
　　　　　　　　　　　　　　Fol de rol, etc.

They crusht sair, but Jack never minded,
　Till wi' liquor he'd lowsened his bags;
At last a great thrust dang him ower,
　He lay a' his lang length o' the flags;
Iv an instant Mall seiz'd his pea jacket,
　Says she, Is thou drunk, or thou's lyem?
The Mayor's o' wor box! smash, aw'm fuddled!
　O Mally, wilt thou lead me hyem?
　　　　　　　　　　　　　　Fol de rol, etc.

MITFORD.　　　　　　　　　　　　　*"The Budget,"* 1816.

THE PITMAN'S SKELLYSCOPE.

Sir David Brewster's "KALEDEOSCOPE." Sir David's invention, when first brought out about 1820, was a wonderful success. 200,000 were said to have been sold in London in a week or two. It is now comparatively forgotten.

OH! Tommy, lad, howay! aw's myek thou full o' play;
　Aw'm sartin that thou'll byeth skip an' lowpey-O:
Aw've sic a bonny thing, an' it's myed o' glass an' tin,
　An' they say its nyem's a bonny Gleediscowpey-O.
　　　　　　　　　　Skellyscowpey-O, etc.

A gawn alang the close, a bit laddy cock'd his nose,
   An' was keekin throu'd aside the Jabel Growpey-O :
Aw fand that he wad sell'd ; se, odsmash ! aw'm proud
     te tell'd !
   For twee shillin' bowt his bonny Gleediscowpey-O.

Wey, then aw ran off hyem—Nan thowt me myekin gyem,
   Said, My Deavy* for a new-aw'd had a cowpey-O :
But she gurn'd, ay, like a sweeper, when aw held it tiv
     her peeper,
   See'd church-windors through my bonny Gleedis-
     cowpey-O.

Then the bairns they ran like sheep, a' strove to hev a
     peep,
   Frae the awdest lass, ay, doon to the dowpey-O :
There Dick dang ower Cud, myed his nose gush out o'
     blood,
   As he ran to see the bonny Gleediscowpey-O.

There was dwiney little Peg, not se nimmel i' the leg,
   Ower the three-footed stuil gat sic a cowpey-O ;
And Sandy wiv his beak, myed a lump i' mother's cheek,
   Climbin' up to see the bonny Gleediscowpey-O.

But she held it tiv her e'e, ay, till she could hardly see,
   Oh ! then aboot the marketin she thowty-O ;
Wey, Lukey, man ! says she, 'stead o' shuggar, flesh, an'
     tea,
   Thou's fetch'd us hyem thy bonny Gleediscowpey-O.

     * "Davy," a term for the Safety Lamp.

She struck me wi' surprise while she skelly'd wiv her
    eyes,
And aw spak as if aw'd gettin a bit rowpey-O!
So, neighbours, tyek a hint, if ye peep ower lang ye'll
    squint,
For aw think they're reetly nyem'd, a Gleediscowpey-O.

MITFORD. *Marshall's Collection*, 1827.

THE WONDERFUL GUTTER.

In 1824, when the question was "Rail" or "Canal" between Newcastle
and the west, this song was written. At a public meeting Willy Armstrong,
father of Lord Armstrong (see last verse), advocated the canal. The rail
won, but the canal still (1891) has advocates who dream of its great future.

SINCE Boney was sent to that place owre the sea,
We've had little to talk of, but far less to dee;
But now they're a' saying, we seun will get better,
When yence they begin with the wonderful Gutter,

      The greet lang Gutter, the wonderful Gutter:
      Success to the Gutter! and prosper the Plough!

The way now aw ken—when aw was at the toon,
Aw met Dicky Wise near the Rose and the Croon;
And as Dicky reads papers, and talks about Kings,
Wey he's like to ken weel aboot Gutters and things;

      So he talk'd owre the Gutter, etc.

He then a lang story began for to tell,
And said that it often was ca'd a Cannell;
But he thowt, by a Gutter, aw wad understand,
That it's cutten reet through a' the Gentlemen's land.

      Now that's caw'd a Gutter, etc.

Now, whether the sea's owre big at the West,
Or scanty at Sheels—wey, ye mebby ken best;
For he says they can team, ay, without any bother,
A sup out o' yen, a' the way to the tother,

　　　　　By the great lang Gutter, etc.

Besides, there'll be bridges, and locks, and lairge keys,
And shippies, to trade wiv eggs, butter, and cheese;
And if they'll not sail weel, for want o' mair force,
They'll myek ne mair fuss, but yoke in a strang horse,

　　　　　To pull through the Gutter, etc.

Ye ken there's a deal that's lang wanted a myel,
When they start wi' the Gutter 'twill thicken their kyell;
Let wages be high, or be just what they may,
It will certainly help to drive hunger away,

　　　　　While they work at the Gutter, etc.

There's wor Tyne Sammun tee 'ill not ken what's the
　　matter,
When they get a gobful o' briny saut watter;
But if they should gan off it's cum'd into my nob,
For to myek some amends we mun catch a' the cod,

　　　　　That sweems down the Gutter, etc.

So come money and friends; support Willy Airmstrang,
In vent'rin a thoosan ye canna get wrang;
While we get wor breed by the sweet o' wor broo,
Success to the Gutter! and prosper the Plough!

　　　　　The great lang Gutter, etc.

MITFORD.　　　　　　　　　　*Marshall's Collection,* 1827.

THE BEWILDERED SKIPPER.

TUNE—"The Bewildered Maid."

SLAW broke the leet 'boot fower yen morn,
When the Deevil aw seed, as sure as thou's born;
His lang beerd hung doon frae his greet lantern jaw,
His eyes wes like sawsers, his mooth filled wi' straw.

Oh, where de ye cum frae, sweet Deevil! oh, where?
But aw gat for an answer a greet ugly blare;
Wor merry lads lay snorin' on the huddock's hard bed;
Here's Aud Nick at the hatch—give him battle, aw said.

The tide rummel'd by, as they luckt up forlorn—
Whist! whist! Oney luik, there's his club feet an' horn!
Says they, Te gie battle, a' hands i' wor keel,
Te Hawthorn's aud goat, 'twad sure bang the Deil!

Cum in, gentle Willy, says they, frae the storm;
In wor huddock lie doon, keep yor aud carkish warm;
If cawd deed ye'd freetened wor skipper se brave,
We'd myed ye follow his byens to the grave.

MITFORD.   *"Bards of the Tyne,"* 1849.

THE SANDGATE GIRL'S LAMENTATION.

I WAS a young maiden truly,
    And lived in Sandgate Street;
I thought to marry a good man,
    To keep me warm at neit.
        He's an ugly body, a bubbly body,
            An ill-far'd, ugly loon;
        And I have married a keelman,
            And my good days are done.

Sum good-like body, sum bonny body,
   To be with me at noon ;
But last I married a keelman,
   And my good days are done.
              He's an ugly body, etc.

I thought to marry a parson,
   To hear me say my prayers ;
But I have married a keelman,
   And he kicks me down the stairs.
              He's an ugly body, etc.

I thought to marry a dyer,
   To dye my apron blue ;
But I have married a keelman,
   And he makes me sorely rue.
              He's an ugly body, etc.

I thought to marry a joiner,
   To make me chair and stool ;
But I have married a keelman,
   And he's a perfect fool.
              He's an ugly body, etc.

I thought to marry a sailor,
   To bring me sugar and tea ;
But I have married a keelman,
   And that he lets me see.
              He's an ugly body, etc.

UNKNOWN.   *Bell's "Northern Bards,"* 1812.

THE HALF-DROWNED SKIPPER.

TUNE—"Chapter of Donkeys."

T'OTHER day up the water aw went in a boat,
Aw brush'd up my trousers, put on my new coat ;
We steer'd up wor boat 'langside ov a keel,
And the luiks of the skipper wad frighten'd the deil.
Fol de rol, etc.

So thinks aw, wi' the keel we'll gan a' the way,
And hear a few words that the skipper may say,
For aw wes sure if owt in the keel wes deun rang,
The skipper wad curse, ay, an' call every man.
Fol de rol, etc.

Noo we'd just getten up te the fam'd Skinners' Burn,
When the skipper bawl'd oot that the keel wes te turn,
Whey, he shooted and roar'd like a man hung i' chains,
And swore by the keel he wad knock oot thor brains.
Fol de rol, etc.

The little Pee-dee jump'd aboot on the deck,
An' the skipper roar'd oot he wad sure smash his neck ;
What for, says the Pee-dee, can one not speak a word ?
So he gav him a kick—knock'd him plump owerboard.
Fol de rol, etc.

There was nyen o' the bullies e'er lost a bit time,
But flung thor greet keel huiks splash into the Tyne,
They browt up the Pee-dee just like a duck'd craw,
An' the skipper wi' laughin fell smack ower an' a'.
Fol de rol, etc.

Noo the keelmen bein tired of thor skipper se brave,
Not one e'er attempted his life for te save,
They hoisted thor sail,—and we saw no more,
But the half-drown'd skipper wes swimmin ashore.
Fol de rol, etc.

UNKNOWN.   *Marshall's Collection,* 1827.

WRECKENTON HIRING.

The author of "Wreckenton Hiring" is unknown. The King Pit at
Wreckenton, which is mentioned in the song, has been laid in for many
years. From one who hewed in it about the year 1820 we learn that the
song was a favourite one then, and regularly sung at pay-nights by the
pitmen. In all probability it was written about that time.

Note to 1872 *Edition.*

O, LADS and lasses, hither come,
To Wreckenton, to see the fun,
And mind ye bring your dancing shoon,
    There'll be rare wark wi' dancin', O ;
And lasses, now, without a brag,
Bring pockets like a fiddle bag,
Ye'll get them crammed wi' mony a whag
    Of pepper kyek an' scranchim, O.

And, Bess, put on that bonny goon
Thy mother bought thee at the toon,
That straw hat, wi' the ribbons broon,
    They'll a' be bussed that's coming, O.
Put that reed ribbon round thy waist,
It myeks thou luik sae full o' grace,
Then up the lonnen come in haste,
    They'll think thou's com'd fra Lunnon, O.

Ned pat on his Sunday's coat,
His hat and breeches cost a note,
With a new stiff'ner round his throat,
    He luiked the very dandy, O :
He thought that he was gaun to choke,
For he'd to gyep before he spoke :
He met Bess at the Royal Oak,
    They had byeth yell and brandy, O.

Each lad was there wi' his sweetheart,
And a' was ready for a start,
When in com Jack wi' Fanny Smart,
    And brought a merry scraper, O :
Then Ned jumped up upon his feet,
An' on the table myed a seet,
Then bounced the fiddler up a heet,
    Saying, " Play, an' we will caper, O."

Now, Ned and Bess led off the ball,
" Play ' Smash the windows,' " he did call ;
" Keep in yor feet," says Hitchy Mall,
    " Learn'd dancers hae sic prancin', O."
Now, Ned was nowther laith nor lyem,
An' faith he had byeth bouk and byen,
Ye wad thought his feet was myed o' styen,
    He gav sic thuds wi' dancing, O.

Now, Jackey Fanny's hand did seize,
Cried, " Fiddler, tune your strings to please,
Play ' Kiss her weel amang the trees,'
    She is my darlin', bliss her, O !"
Then off they set, wi' sic a smack,
They myed the joints a' bend and crack ;
When duen, he took her round the neck,
    An' faith, he diddent miss her, O.

The fiddler's elbow wagged a' neet,
He thought he wad dropt off his seet,
For deil a bit they'd let him eat,
    They were sae keen o' dancing, O :
Some had to strip their coats for heat,
And sharts and shifts were wet wi' sweet ;
They crammed their guts, for want o' meat,
    Wi' gingerbreed and scranchim, O.

Now cocks had crawn an hour or more,
And ower the yell pots some did snore ;
But how they luikt to hear the roar
    Of Matt, the King Pit caller, O !
"Smash him !" says Ned, "he mun be rang,
He's callin' through his sleep, aw's war'n ;"
Then shootin' to the door he ran—
    "Thou's asleep, thou rusty bawler, O !"

Now, they danced agyen till it was day,
Then hyemwards singin' tyuk their way.
Suen Wreckenton will bear the sway—
    Wor taxes will be 'bolished, O ;
Backey and tea will be sae cheap ;
Wives will sit up when they should sleep ;
An' we'll float in yell at wor pay week—
    Then Wreckenton for ever, O !

UNKNOWN.   *Marshall's Collection,* 1827.

CANNY SHEELS.

In Davidson of Alnwick's collection of Tyneside Songs, 1840, we first
meet John Morrison's "Canny Sheels." In Fordyce's "Song Book," 1842,
there is a second song by him, "Permanent Yeast," but it is much inferior
to the first. Of the author we have no trace.—Evidently a Sheels man,
he contrives to cap Thompson, who, in making "Canny Newcassel" marrow
the "Seets o' Lunnin," had not done amiss.

'BOUT Newcassel they've written sae mony fine sangs,
    And compar'd their bit place unti Lunnun ;
What a shem that 'tiv Sheels not a poet belangs,
    For to tell them they lee wi' their funnin.
They may boast o' their shippin without ony doubt,
    For there's nyen can deny that they've plenty ;
But for every yen they are gobbin about,
    Aw'm sure we can show them, ey twenty !

Let them haud their fule gobs then and brag us ne mair,
  Wi' their clarty bit au'd Corporation ;
For it's varry weel knawn Sheels pays her full share,
  For te keep Mister Mayor iv his station.

They hev a bit place where they myek a few shot,
  Lunnun's Column tiv it's like a nine-pin ;
And St. Nicholas' compar'd wi' St. Paul's an' what not,
  Wey it's a yuven compar'd tiv a limekiln.
If their Shot Tower sae hee was plac'd on wor Sand
    End,
  'Side wor Light House to scraffle to glory ;
Their journey to heaven wad suen hev an end,
  For by gox they'd ne'er reach the first story.
                                    Let them haud, etc.

They call their Infirm'ry a place for a king,
  To be stow'd 'mang the sick, lyem, and lazy ;
If a Sheels man had ventur'd to say sic a thing,
  The blind gowks wad a' said he was crazy.
'Bout their Custom House, tee, they myek a great rout,
  That the e'en o' the folk it diz dazzel ;
But if a' gans reet, Sheels, without ony doubt,
  Will suen 'clipse that at Canny Newcassel.
                                    Let them haud, etc.

Then they brag they leuk bonny, fresh-coloured and gay,
  And the Lunnun folk a' wishey washey ;
But L——d put it off tiv a far distant day,
  That there's one on huz here leuks sae trashy.
Then they boast o' Sir Matthew—but never inquire
  If the foundation's good that he stood on ;
But if he comes up to wor canny au'd Squire,
  Then becrikes he is nowse but a good 'un.
                                    Let them haud, etc.

But the Squire, canny man, he's gyen frae the toon,
　And aw'm sure on't the poor sairly miss him ;
For oft as aw waulk Pearson's Raw up and doon,
　Aw hear the folk cry, Heaven bliss him !
Yet aw hope, an' aw trust, he'll seun find his way hyem,
　And aw's sure aw'll be glad to hear tell on't ;
For aw've varry oft thowt—did ye ne'er think the syem,
　Since he's gyen Sheels hezzent luik't like the sel on't.

Let them haud, etc.

Then lang life to the King and wor awn noble Duik,
　May Sheels lang partake of his bounty ;
For Newcassel, ye ken, if ye e'er read a buik,
　Is at yence byeth a toon and a county.
Northumberland's Duik may still shew his sel there,
　But his int'rest frae Sheels ne'er can sever ;
So aw'll gie ye just now, shou'd aw ne'er see ye mair,
　Wor Duik and wor Duchess for ever !

Let them haud, etc.

JOHN MORRISON.　　　　　　　　　　*Davidson's Collection*, 1840.

COALY TYNE.

Written during the trial of Queen Caroline in 1820.　(See last verse.)

TUNE—"Auld Lang Syne."

TYNE RIVER, running rough or smooth,
　Makes bread for me and mine ;
Of all the rivers, north or south,
　There's none like coaly Tyne.

　　　So here's to coaly Tyne, my lads,
　　　　Success to coaly Tyne ;
　　　Of all the rivers, north or south,
　　　　There's none like coaly Tyne.

Long has Tyne's swelling bosom borne
  Great riches from the mine,
All by her hardy sons uptorn—
  The wealth of coaly Tyne.

Our keelmen brave, with laden keels,
  Go sailing down in line,
And with them load the fleet at Shields,
  That sails from coaly Tyne.

When Bonaparte the world did sway,
  Dutch, Spanish, did combine;
By sea and land proud bent their way,
  The sons of coaly Tyne.

The sons of Tyne, in seas of blood,
  Trafalgar's fight did join,
When led by dauntless Collingwood,
  The hero of the Tyne.

With courage bold, and hearts so true,
  Form'd in the British line;
With Wellington, at Waterloo,
  Hard fought the sons of Tyne.

When peace, who would be Volunteers?
  Or Hero Dandies fine?
Or sham Hussars, or Tirailleurs?—
  Disgrace to coaly Tyne.

Or who would be a Tyrant's Guard,
  Or shield a libertine?
Let Tyrants meet their due reward,
  Ye sons of coaly Tyne.

Let us unite with all our might,
   Protect Queen Caroline ;
For her we'll fight, both day and night,
   The sons of coaly Tyne.

UNKNOWN.   *Marshall's Collection,* 1827.

———

WALKER PITS.

TUNE—"Off she goes."

IF I had another penny,
   I would have another gill ;
I would make the fiddler play
   "The Bonny Lads of Byker Hill."

   Byker Hill and Walker Shore,
      Collier lads for evermore !
   Byker Hill and Walker Shore,
      Collier lads for evermore !

When aw cam to Walker wark,
   Aw had ne coat, nor ne pit sark ;
But noo aw've getten twe or three—
   Walker Pit's dyun weel for me.

   Byker Hill and Walker Shore, etc.
   Bell's " Northern Bards," 1812.

———

THE FISHER'S GARLAND.

ROXBY and Doubleday, inseparably associated through
their famous fishing songs, were yet unlike in age, Roxby
being so much the elder of the two that Doubleday might
have been his son.   Their lives have been so often told that
the briefest summary must suffice.   Robert Roxby, born at
Needless Hall, by the failure of his trustee, had to turn to
business, and his long life was spent as a clerk, at first with

Sir W. Loraine and afterwards with Sir M. W. Ridley, at their banks at Newcastle. He died July 30th, 1846, in his seventy-ninth year, and lies in St. Paul's disused burial-ground at the top of Westgate Hill. Thomas Doubleday, poet, politician, and merchant, was least successful as the last, to which he was trained. As a poet, lyrical and dramatic, he took high rank. In the stormy Reform Bill, and early Chartist agitation days he was a prominent figure. Business, unfortunately, was not to his taste, and there he was unsuccessful. The latter part of his life was spent in comparative retirement. His beautiful song, "The Auld Fisher's Lament," written in 1841, possibly is not all fancy, but may, in some measure, be a reflection of his own altered circumstances. Although in the original *Garland* signed R. R., Mr. Crawhall writes, the manuscript is Roxby's, but the lyric is from Doubleday's pen.

THE AULD FISHER'S LAST WISH.

TUNE—"My Love is Newly Listed."

THE morn is grey, and green the brae, the wind is frae the wast ;
Before the gale the snow-white clouds are drivin', light and fast ;
The airly sun is glintin' forth, owre hill, an' dell, an' plain,
And Coquet's streams are glitt'rin' as they rin frae muir to main.

. . . .

My Sun is set ; my eyne are wet ; cauld poortith now is mine,
Nae mair I'll range by Coquetside, and thraw the gleesome line ;
Nae mair I'll see her bonnie streams in spring-bright raiment drest,
Save in the dream that stirs the heart, when the weary e'e's at rest.

Oh ! were my limbs as ance they were, to jink across the green ;
And were my heart as light again as sometime it has been ;
And could my Fortunes blink again, as erst when youth was sweet,
Then Coquet—hap what might beside—we'd no be lang to meet.

Or had I but the Cushat's wing, where'er I list to flee,
And wi' a wish might wend my way owre hill, an' dale, an' lea ;
'Tis there I'd fauld that weary wing ; there gaze my latest gaze ;
Content to see thee once again—then sleep beside thy Braes !

DOUBLEDAY. "*Fisher's Garland,*" 1841.

At Gosforth, on the outskirts of Newcastle, where his latter years were passed, the strife and passion of party politics forgotten, he died, universally respected, on December 18th, 1870, in his eighty-first year.

Strictly the "Garlands" do not come into this collection, but in everything, except the dialect, they are so local and akin that specimens may be given.

Dr. Watson, in his *Gossip about Songs*, thus writes of them :—"There are no fairer streams than those which flow amongst the hills of mountainous Northumberland ; and time was when they were as famous for their angling qualities as for their intrinsic beauty. What fisher but knows how through the long hours of the summer day some verse of song haunts his brain? And surely the best of all sporting songs are those of dear old Robert Roxby, and his far greater and as lovable companion, Thomas Doubleday. Their Coquet-dale angling songs are as truly a pride to Newcastle as the steeple of St. Nicholas', or Thomas Bewick's birds. Where else will you find such words wedded to such tunes? Not a detail of the sport is lost, and yet they are full of nature's poetry, instinct with melody as 'the stream that I love best.'"

COQUET SIDE.

This Garland, the joint production of Robert Roxby and Thomas Doubleday, appeared as a broadside. One hundred and ninety-six copies were printed for Emerson Charnley, December 20th, 1828. First three verses by Roxby, last three by Doubleday.

TUNE—"They may rail at this life."

THE lambs they are feeding on lonely *Shill-moor*,
　　And the breezes blow softly o'er dark *Simonside ;*
The birds they are lilting in ev'ry green bower,
　　And the streams of the *Coquet* now merrily glide.
The primrose is blooming at *Halystane Well*,
　　And the bud's on the Saugh and the bonny birk tree ;
The moorcocks are calling round *Harbottle Fell*,
　　And the snaw wreaths are gane frae the *Cheviots* so hie.

The mist's on the mountain, the dew's on the spray,
　　And the Lassie has kilted her coats to the knee ;
The Shepherd he's whistling o'er *Barraburn* brae,
　　And the sunbeams are glintin' far over the sea.
Then we'll off to the *Coquet*, with hook, hair, and *heckle*,
　　With our neat taper Gads, and our well-belted Creels,
And far from the bustle and din o' Newcastle,
　　Begin the campaign at the streams o' *Linn-shiels*.

The " Nimrod " may brag of his horns and his hounds,
　And of louping o'er hedges and ditches may rave ;
But what's all their clamour, their rides and their rounds,
　Compar'd with the murmur of Coquet's clear wave?
And " Ramrod " may crack of his pointer so staunch,
　And may tramp till he's weary o'er stubble and lea ;
But what's all the fun of the dog and the gun,
　Compar'd with the "Lang-rod" and "*thrawing the flee*"?

More big of our Conquests than great Alexander,
　We'll rise to our sport with the morning's first beam ;
Our creels shall grow heavier as onward we wander,
　And levy large tribute from pool and from stream.
We'll plunder the deeps, and the shallows we'll tax well,
　Till *Sharperton, Hepple,* and *Thropton* are past ;
We'll halt near the " Thrum " for a dinner with *Maxwell,*
　But land at our old Home of Weldon at last.

Now Crag-end is past, and now *Brinkburn* is nearest,
　Now the green braes of *Tod-stead,* the pride of the vale ;
Then hey ! for fam'd *Weldon,* to anglers the dearest,
　Old Weldon, whose cellars and streams never fail ;
There we'll talk of our triumphs, and boast of our
　　slaughter,
　　How "we hook'd him, and play'd him, and kill'd him
　　so fine ; "
And the battles, so gloriously finish'd in water,
　Again and again we'll fight over in wine.

Here's good luck to the Gad, and success to each friend
　　on't ;
　If e'er prayer of mine can have interest above,
May they run their line smoothly, nor soon see an end on't,
　And their course be as clear as the streams that they
　　love !

May the current of life still spread glitt'ring before them
  And their joys ever rise as the season draws nigh;
And if e'er—as 'twill happen—Misfortune comes o'er
    them,
  Oh! still may her dart fall as light as their fly!

ROBERT ROXBY.   *"Fisher's Garland,"* 1823.
THOMAS DOUBLEDAY.

————

THE AULD FISHER'S FAREWEEL TO COQUET.

Mr. Crawhall writes:—"Two hundred and ninety copies were printed for
Emerson Charnley, March 26th, 1825, and one hundred copies presented to the
author (Robert Roxby), though the Garland is the joint production of
Roxby and Doubleday." Roxby writing the first, and Doubleday the last
three verses. It was often Doubleday's fortune thus to finish. Roxby
would begin, get stranded, and as he told Doubleday when writing the first
Garland, "If it was to be finished, he (Doubleday) must do it."

TUNE—"Gramachree."

COME bring to me my limber gad
  I've fish'd wi' mony a year,
An' let me hae my weel-worn creel,
  An' a' my fishing gear;
The sunbeams glint on *Linden-Ha*,
  The breeze comes frae the west,
An' lovely looks the gowden morn
  On the streams that I love best.

I've thrawn the *flee* thae sixty year,
  Ay, sixty year an' mair,
An' monie a speckled troutie kill'd
  Wi' *heckle*, heuk, an' hair.
An' now I'm auld an' feeble grown,
  My locks are like the snaw,
But I'll gang again to Coquet-side,
  An' take a fareweel thraw.

O, Coquet! in my youthfu' days
    Thy river sweetly ran,
. An' sweetly down thy woody braes
    The bonnie birdies sang;
But streams may rin an' birds may sing,
    Sma' joys they bring to me,
The blithesome strains I dimly hear,
    The streams I dimly see.

But ance again, the weel-kenn'd sounds
    My minutes shall beguile,
An' glistering in the airly sun
    I'll see thy waters smile;
An' Sorrow shall forget his sigh,
    An' Age forget his pain,
An' ance mair, by sweet Coquet-side,
    My heart be young again.

Ance mair I'll touch wi' gleesome foot
    Thy waters clear and cold,
Ance mair I'll cheat the gleg-e'ed trout,
    An' wile him frae his hold;
Ance mair, at *Weldon's* frien'ly door,
    I'll wind my tackle up,
An' drink " Success to Coquet-side,"
    Though a tear fa' in the cup. ·

An' then farewell, dear Coquet-side!
    Aye gaily may thou rin,
An' lead thy waters sparkling on,
    An' dash frae linn to linn;

Blithe be the music o' thy streams
An' banks through after-days,
An' blithe be every fisher's heart
Shall ever tread thy Braes.

ROBERT ROXBY.
THOMAS DOUBLEDAY.   *"Fisher's Garland,"* 1825.

THE COQUET FOR EVER.

1st and 5th verses.

Mr. Crawhall writes :—"Four hundred copies of this Garland, the joint production of Roxby and Doubleday, were printed for Emerson Charnley, April 15th, 1826." Again Roxby did the first and Doubleday the last three verses.

TUNE—"Oh, whistle and I'll come to you, my lad."

I HAVE sung thee, clear Coquet—I'll sing thee again
From *Harden's* bleak fell to the deep-rolling main,
And the *Alwine* and *Wreigh* in the garland shall shine,
For they mix, lovely river, their waters wi' thine.
In my youth I have danced on your bonny green braes;
In my old age I think on these dear happy days;
In your streams I have angled and caught the scaled fry,
And your streams they shall live, tho' their beds should
        run dry.

Chorus—And your streams, etc.

Oh, how should a fisherman ever be old?
There's wrinkles in Glory, there's wrinkles in Gold;
And Love has his sorrows as well as his joys,
And power is made up but of glitter and noise.
Such gewgaws as these let the fisherman scorn—
He's glorious at night, and light-hearted at morn;
With a cheek full of health, be it hot, be it cold,
Oh, how should a fisherman ever be old?

Chorus—Oh, how, etc.

ROBERT ROXBY.   *"Fisher's Garland,"* 1826.
THOMAS DOUBLEDAY.

THE IMPATIENT LASSIE.

Like the "Garlands," "Cumberland Songs" scarcely belong to this collection, but as dialect songs they are so much akin that a specimen may be given. The author of the "Cumberland Ballads," etc., begins a memoir of his life in the following words:—"At six o'clock, on the snowy morning of February 1st, 1770, I beheld the light of this world, and first drew breath at the Dam Side, parish of St. Mary, in the suburbs of this ancient city (Carlisle); a poor little, tender being, scarce worth the trouble of rearing." He was the youngest of nine children, born of parents getting up in years, whom poverty had with all their kindred kept in bondage, knowing only hard labour and crosses. At an early age he was placed in a charity school. His schooling over, he was put to learn the business of a calico printer. In 1794, in London, he wrote his first song, "Lucy Gray,' which was sung at Vauxhall Gardens. It would be some ten years after that before his first volume of Cumberland songs was printed. His life was a chequered one. His gift of song may have led him into temptation,—towards the end of his life he gave way to drink, and fell into poor circumstances. He died at Carlisle on September 26th, 1833. In Carlisle Cathedral a marble monument is erected to his memory.

TUNE—"Low down in the Broom."

DEUCE tek the clock; click-clackin' sae
    Still in a body's ear;
It tells and tells the time is past,
    When Jwohnnie sud been here:

Deuce tek the wheel! 't will nit rin roun—
    Nae mair to-neet I'll spin;
But count each minute wi' a seegh,
    Till Jwohnnie he steels in.

How neyce the spunky fire it burns,
    For twee to sit beseyde!
And theer's the seat where Jwohnnie sits,
    And I forget to cheyde!

My fadder, tui, how sweet he snwores!
    My mudder's fast asleep—
He promis'd oft, but, oh! I fear
    His word he wunnet keep!

What can it be keeps him frae me?
   The ways are nit sae lang!
An' sleet an' snaw are nought at aw,
   If yen wer fain to gang!

Some ither lass, wi' bonnier faice,
   Has catch'd his wicked e'e,
An I'll be pointed at, at kurk—
   Nay! suiner let me dee!

O durst we lasses nobbet gang,
   An' sweetheart them we leyke!
I'll run to thee, my Jwohnnie, lad,
   Nor stop at bog or deyke:

But custom's sec a silly thing—
   For men mun hae their way,
An' monnie a bonnie lassie sit,
   An' wish frae day to day.

But whist!—I hear my Jwohnnie's fit—
   Aye! that's his varra clog!
He steeks the faul yeat softly tui—
   Oh! hang that cwoley dog!

Now hey for seeghs, an' sugar words,
   Wi' kisses nit a few—
O but this warl's a paradise,
   When lovers they pruive true!

ANDERSON.   *Wigton Edition,* 1808.
   July 31st, 1802.

ROBERT GILCHRIST.

ROBERT GILCHRIST, one of the brightest of Tyneside writers, was born at Gateshead, in the parish of St. Mary's, on September 8th, 1797. Although Gateshead born, it is with Newcastle that his name is most intimately connected, as there his father carried on business as a sailmaker; and there also he was apprenticed to William Spence to learn the same business.

From an early age he appears to have had a passion for poetry, as in 1818, when he would be twenty-one, we find a

few of his youthful companions presenting him with a silver medal and inscription, as a mark of their appreciation of his poetical abilities. In the same year he took up his freelage, and so stood charged with a musket for the defence of the town. The year before this, he had been drawn by ballot for the militia, and had either to serve or find a substitute. A substitute he found, not in a "Gallowgate," but a

"High Bridge" lad, one Matthew Winship, a shoemaker, who was sworn in in his stead.

Reduced copy of Medal, with Gilchrist's Autograph.

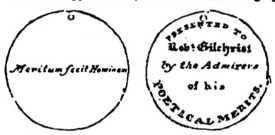

In 1822, his first book (a small one of 24 pages), *Gothalbert and Hisanna*, appeared. It was published by Mitchell, of the *Tyne Mercury*. In a brief introduction he writes—

"This whimsical poem is the offspring of a few leisure hours. . . . Though it takes the appearance of burlesque, the characters are nothing less than real life."

The real life he thus refers to is soon seen to be his own. The hero, "Gothalbert," is Gateshead born, and was at nineteen

"A viewly lad, of grave yet sprightly mien."

Gilchrist's passion for the country appears in—

"Alone—on foot—how often forth he hied,
Alike o'er nations and a country-side."

And there can be no doubt his father and mother are thus described—

> "He knew no luxuries, ever bluntly spoke,
> And seldom rov'd beyond his chimney smoke.
>
> .   .   .   .   .   .
>
> Alike revered in country, town, or city—
> Too poor for envy, and too rich for pity.
> Nor less exalted was Gothalbert's mother—
> The world has seldom boasted such another."

The poem then goes on to tell in a strained and half-burlesque tone of the loves of "Gothalbert and Hisanna." At best it is but a fragment; he has called it a whimsical poem. It is all that; it is essentially a youthful production, and laid him open to the ridicule which T. Ferguson, of Bishopwearmouth, cast upon him. Why T. Ferguson should so criticise it, and have printed a special condemnation of it does not appear, but none the less, in *Gothalbert of the Tyne*, in a mock Miltonic strain, he lays on with right good will—as

> "Of *Bob's* first "lucubrations," and the *fruit*
> Of his pedantic *muse*, whose *mortal taste*
> Brought *trash* into the world—likewise his *woe*
> For loss of *Anna*, I attempt to sing."

Ferguson further describes his piece as "a humorous satire on all 'Would-be Wits' and conceited Rhymesters, whose heterogeneous compositions being so tinctured with vanity, egotism, folly, and impertinence, are justly considered, by men of taste and impartiality, as inimical to the dignity of the muses." A few lines from the satire itself will show the author's skill—

> "Ye tuneful 'verse inspiring' maids,
> Who rove amidst Parnassian shades,
>
> .   .   .   .   .   .
>
> Assist my lays whilst I expose
> The gross impertinence of those
> Who, like the tinker tribe on asses,
> Infest the precincts of Parnassus,
> And most presumptuously aspire
> To strike with hands profane the lyre,
> Without once saying, 'By your leave.'"

By whatever urged, the satire is clever. Like Gilchrist's own rhyme, it is only a fragment, and appears never to have been finished.

Two years after this, in 1824, also printed by Mitchell, there appeared his *Collection of Original Songs, Local and Sentimental*. With one or two exceptions, in this work of thirty-six pages, the songs on which his fame rests appear.

In his address he writes—"I offer to the public *part* of the poetical effusions composed during a life spent in incessant toil from the early age of twelve years." The remaining part, to which he refers, appeared two years later, in 1826, and makes a volume of ninety pages. The publisher this time—not Mitchell, but W. Boag. No local songs are amongst them; the pieces generally are sentimental, with part of a religious character. In this tendency to sing of sacred themes, Gilchrist's rather peculiar religious opinions may be traced, he being one of the Glassites, a body originating in Newcastle, and called after their founder. The opening piece in his volume begins—

> "A voice was heard on Zion's hill,
>   Round which in dust her temples lay;
> There songs of praise were wont to thrill,
>   But Salem's fame had passed away.
>
> .   .   .   .
>
> From Jesse's Root a Branch shall spring,
>   A Star whose brightness ne'er shall dim;
> Of monarchs He shall be the King—
>   Yea, all the earth shall kneel to Him."
>
> .   .   .   .

A little further on is a kindred piece, a verse from which runs—

> "'Twas thus the Prince of Minstrels sung,
>   Ere Bethlehem's Star, with purest beam,
> Had o'er the earth its radiance flung—
>   And yet this star was David's theme.
> He saw—(through future ages dim)—
>   He saw in that predicted hour,
> The Star which ne'er should rise to him,
>   Though then he knew its healing power."
>
> .   .   .   .   .

In the same volume his beautiful lines on St. Nicholas' Church appear—

ON ST. NICHOLAS' CHURCH.

> "Lo! here shall stand the boast of lyric page,
> The growing wonder of each coming age,
> This goodly fabric, which, sublimely high,
> Doth raise its spires as if to reach the sky;
> Its lanthorn and eliptic arches bold
> Seem light as air, yet mighty strength unfold.
> Bright structure! where no beauteous form is lacked!
> So great, so chaste, so vast, yet so compact!
> Such comely symmetry, such matchless grace,
> Was ne'er before beheld by mortal face!

Oh, enter here, and feel without controul
Devotion pour her softness on the soul ;
And hear the organ, which, like Sion's lyre,
With strains celestial fills the spacious choir ;
Or see the grave, where sad and sacred gloom
Shows peerless beauty wasting in the tomb,
And manly vigour mouldering in decay,
Like withered flowers vilely cast away.
Be warned, be wise, improve thy mortal span :
All serves to prove—the vanity of man."

These extracts give a fair idea of Gilchrist away from his dialect songs. His 1826 volume seems to have been his last. What he wrote after appeared only in slips, newspapers, etc. His marriage with Miss Morrison and his father's death would take place about this time, and the battle of life would have to be begun in earnest. His father died in 1829, and he succeeded to the business, which he carried on at the old premises, near the Custom House, on the Quayside. Although brought up to the business, and consequently master of it, yet it never seems to have done much for him. Perhaps he was too much of the old school; perhaps too much given to his books and writing. But whatever the cause, in business he was not very successful.

OLD HOUSE, SHIELDFIELD.
Photo. Auty & Ruddock, Tynemouth.

His love of the country and long walking tours have already been alluded to. One may be more particularly recorded. In 1821 he wagered a shilling with a Mr. R. White, possibly

the historian of "Otterburn," that he would walk from Newcastle to Edinburgh by a circuitous route of 125 miles
without his expenses amounting to 12s.   He won this
wager by showing a balance-sheet with distances and
route all marked down, and 3s. 7d. to spare, his expenses
only amounting to 8s. 5d.   One of his shorter country
rambles after his marriage, of which he has left an account,
reads curiously now.   It was a three-mile walk into the
country to Dr. Headlam's house (now Captain Noble's) at
Jesmond Dene.   He describes leaving home, the old house
facing Shieldfield Green, and from beginning to end of
his ramble there was nothing but green country walks all
the way to Jesmond Dene.   His married life appears to
have been spent in this old Shieldfield house, and to it he
seems to have been much attached.   Time, which has
made such marvellous changes since then, and transformed
his country walk into a tramway ride, was beginning its
changes, and his old house (in 1838) was threatened with
destruction.   To a Mr. Foggin, who either owned or had
some say in it, he makes the old house send a humble
petition to be allowed to stand.   Part of the verses run—

.   .   .   .   .   .

" Let innovations e'en go on,
    I'll be despite all dogging,
A good old house when all are gone,
    My canny Mr. Foggin.

My tenant tunes the rustic reed,
    And tells a good old story ;
One of the true old English breed—
    An antiquated Tory.
In future years should he be fam'd—
    Then times most ample log in ;
Your kind forbearance shall be nam'd,
    My canny Mr. Foggin."

Besides the old house's petition, we have the poet directly
addressing John Clayton, who appears also to have had to
do with it.   The last verse is given—

" Then say the word, my lease renew,
    And win a wreath of glory ;
A bard of Tyne will sing of you,
    All in my upper storey.
Who lays disporting hands on me,
    All ills may pour his pate on ;
So be advised, and let me be,
    My canny Mr. Clayton."

The petitions were successful, the old house was spared, and in it he was to spend his days. He seems to have been proud of the old place. In the second number of the *Conversazione*, a small fortnightly publication issued in 1829 by W. Boag, there is an account, partly descriptive, partly legendary, of it by him. In the same number he has "Fragmento." Two of these fragments, of which there are nine, here follow; they show him in a moralising mood:—

> "Content is great, perchance a sole domain—
> Let him that's poor be happy 'tis no worse;
> He has but little reason to complain,
> Whose greatest burden is an empty purse.
> 'Tis better far, less daintily to feast,
> Than have the bailiff running in one's track:—
> Old shoes serve well (in summer time, at least);
> An old coat, too, sits easy on the back.
>
> .   .   .   .   .   .
>
> Death is an honest radical reformer,
> That all states to an equal level brings—
> Allotting each of cold, cold earth a corner,
> Where humble peasants slumber with their kings.
> Here is to folly, vice, deceit, and pride,
> To fame and frippery, an endless end—
> The deadliest foes sleep calmly side by side,
> And in one common clay their ashes blend."

Another of his "Fragments" begins—

> "Many have eulogised the pipe and pot—
> Such are not powers the minstrel should invoke."

Akin to this wholesome teaching is the following interesting note on his song, "The Quack Doctors" (not in this collection):—

> "I have often reflected with satisfaction that my compositions conveyed a proof that it was very possible to be humorous and harmless at the same time. The foregoing composition is a slight departure from this salutary principle, and which I sincerely regret. I would wish it expunged from my works, and certainly in case of another edition, it should not be republished. Some may consider me too squeamish in this respect, but (if there were no other reason) the popularity of the other (and many subsequently composed) local songs is the best testimony that native humour needs not the aid of either invective personality or the least indecency. It may be very possible to excite laughter at the expense of worthy persons, but this no one can reflect upon without experiencing a feeling of disapprobation. "*July* 29, 1829.   "R. G."
> From the original manuscript (never before published).

That his teaching is true we only need to turn to his own

gems of Tyneside songs, which, without the least objectionable touch, charm alike by their rich humour and easy versification. As a Freeman in the ": good old days" when the "barges" was an event, he was foremost in the Freemen's steamboat, which formed part of the pageant, and a new local song by him at the dinner was the event of the day. His unquenchable humour and buoyancy of spirit were shown in his last illness. His complaint, an internal cancer, was one from which he, as well as his friends, knew he could not recover. The late Dr. Clark used to tell how, visiting him in company with a friend, Gilchrist, suffering as he was, had them both ill with laughter before their visit ended, as he told them, in a manner which he did to perfection, a story about a South Shields pilot. According to Dr. Clark, Gilchrist had a slight cast in his eye, and when telling a humorous story this eye did half the business ; others who recollect Gilchrist cannot recall this cast, which at all events must have been slight.

About the last piece he would write is the following "Sonnet on the Shortest Day." It is so appropriate and characteristic that we give it here—

> " I always lov'd the shortest day,
>   Though dull the aspect of the year,
>   Each hearth beams forth a kindlier ray,
>   Reminding us of Christmas cheer !
>   And friends assemble far and near,
>   With lightened hearts and humours gay ;
>   And dearest ties seem still more dear,
>   Rang'd round the board of Christmas Day.
>   Long may such scenes on England smile,
>   As times and seasons pass away,
>   And still more free from guilt and guile,
>   Lur'd by the Star of Bethlehem's ray,
>   To where is neither storm nor strife,
>   Nor shortest day, nor longest life."

Dec. 21st, 1843.   Robert Gilchrist.

On the 11th of July 1844 he died in his old house at Shieldfield, aged 47 years, and was buried at the East Ballast Hills burial-ground. John Luke Clennell, likely the son of Bewick's noted pupil, thus wrote of his old friend—

> " If honest, manly, unpretending worth
>   May justly claim from us a tribute dear,
> And those who were respected whilst on earth,
>   Deserve a passing dirge sung o'er their bier,
> Then may I write me Robert Gilchrist here.

No vain and empty words are these to tell
  A tale of sorrow in an idle rhyme ;
I knew the simple-hearted fellow well,
  And felt his kindness also many a time.
Thus it is fitting memory should dwell
  In pensive sadness on a man who gave
  Good cause for us to sorrow o'er his grave,
And that the Muse bear record with a sigh,
  When now it is the poet's lot to die.

July 16*th*, 1844.   JOHN LUKE CLENNELL.

The following notes, signed "R. G.," are from Gilchrist's manuscript—now for the first time printed.

THE COLLIER'S KEEK AT THE NATION.

The following song was written in reprobation of the attempts of many designing individuals to stir up a spirit of Republicanism in the minds of those honest, well-meaning, and industrious members of the community.

NEWCASTLE, *July* 30*th*, 1829.   R. G.

Huz Colliers, for a' they can say,
  Hae byeth heads and hearts that are sound—
And if we're but tuen i' wor way,
  There's few better cheps above ground.
Tom Cavers and me, frae West Moor,
  On a kind ov a jollification,
Yen day myed what some folks call a tour,
  For a keek at the state o' the nation.

We fand, ere we'd lang been on jaunt,
  That the world wasn't gannin see cliver—
It had gettin a Howdon-Pan cant,
  As aw gat once at wor box-dinner.
Monny tyels, tee, we heard, stiff and gleg—
  Some laid a' things stright as a die—
Some crook'd as a dog's hinder leg,
  Or, like wor fitter's nose, all a-wry.

Yen tell'd me, may heart for to flay
  (Thinkin' aw knew nowt about town),
Out o' may three-and-sixpence a-day,
  The King always gat half-a-crown.

Aw said they were feuls not to ken
　　That aw gat a' the brass me awnsel'—
Ga' wor Peg three white shillins, and then
　　Laid the rest out on backey and yell!

They blabb'd oot that aw was mistuen—
　　That maw brains sairly wanted *seduction*—
Without *animal* Parliaments seun,
　　We wad a' gan te wreck and *construction*—
That we'd wrought ower lang for wor lair—
　　That landlords were styen-hearted tykes—
For their houses and land only fair,
　　To divide them and live as yen likes!

To bring a' these fine things about
　　Was as easy as delving aslent is—
Only get some rapscallion sought out,
　　And to Lunnin sent up to present us.
Thinks aw to mysel' that's weel meant—
　　There's wor Cuddy owre laith to de good,
We'll hev him to Parliament sent,
　　Where he'll bray, smash his byens, for his blood.

Then, says aw, Tommy, keep up thy pluck,
　　We may a' live to honour wor nation—
So here's tiv Au'd England, good luck!
　　And may each be content in his station.
Huz Colliers, for a' they can say,
　　Hae byeth heeds and hearts that are sound—
And if we're but teun i' wor way,
　　There's few better cheps above ground.

GILCHRIST.　　　　　　　　　　　*Author's Edition*, 1824.

————

BOLD ARCHY DROWNDED.

Archibald Henderson was a man of great stature and immense muscular power, but very inoffensive in his manners. There were many excellent traits in his character; among the rest his filial attachment to his mother is worthy of being recorded. His mother was a little woman; but it was no uncommon sight to behold her leading Archy out of any wrangling he might happen to be engaged in; for Archibald, though not a quarrelsome man, had his struggles of competition, but the voice of his mother in one moment charmed him into meekness, and he would follow her with the docility of a child. Archibald was never married. He once confessed himself a little enamoured of a pretty servant girl who resided upon the Quayside. The highest compliment that Archy paid her was by observing that she was *almost* as *canny* a woman as his mother !

Archibald Henderson died May 14th, 1828, aged 86 years.

A production, in which I attempted to honour his memory, appeared in the Poets' Corner of the *Tyne Mercury*, May or June 1828.

ON THE DEATH OF BOLD ARCHY,

WHO DIED MAY 14TH, 1828.

BOLD ARCHY'S deed, and lang for him will poor Newcassel fret,
Her sun of glory has gaen doon, her brightest star is set ;
Frae the *blue-staen* tiv *Causey Brig*—frae *Tinmouth* bar reet round by *Stella*,
Not yen remains tiv fill the place left vacant by this honest fellow.

Weel may *Jack Steenson* dool his dreed and drink his sorrow dry—
Weel might *blind Willy* shake his head, and lay his fiddle by ;
For though he vow'd t' play ne mair when he lamented *Captain Starkey*,
He slacken'd all his fiddle strings in memory of poor BOLD ARCHY.

BOLD ARCHY was a lad o' spunk, yet not a saucy tyke,
And, as I've heard *blind Willy* say, I never saw his like ;
As meek as ony sucking pet, with fist of oak and arm o' thunner,
He wadn't see the weak one wrang'd, he'd swallow'd a' Newcassel seunner.

The funeral flag hung drooping law as Archy's corpse went by,
And monie gaz'd, and monie a tear was wip'd frae monie an eye ;
And every one the truth confest—warm was the heart, now still an' caller,
So lay him softly in the sod, fam'd man of might, and prince o' valour.

Fareweel ! fareweel !—my local harp I'll bury with the brave—
And here I'll plant my local wreath to flourish on his grave ;
Byeth English and outlandish *nyems* shall one day pass oblivion's portal,
But Archy's shall survive them a', it weel desarves to be immortal.

NEWCASTLE, *May* 15, 1828.

Numerous might be the anecdotes related of Archibald Henderson's good humour and astonishing athletic powers. I decline further enumeration of them, satisfied that they will not escape observation from the able pen and consummate ability of Mr. John Bell.

QUAYSIDE, *July* 30th, 1829.   R. G.

BOLD ARCHY DROWNDED.

TUNE—"The Bold Dragoon."

AWILE for me yor lugs keep clear, maw spoke aw'll
    briefly bray,
Aw've been see blind wi' blairin that aw scarce ken what
    to say,—
A motley crew aw lately met, my feelins fine had sairly
    wounded,
By axin if aw'd heer'd the news, or if aw'd seen *Bold*
    Archy drownded.

The tyel like wildfire through the toon suin cut a dowly
    track,
An' seem'd to wander up an' doon wi' Sangate on its back ;
Bullrug was there—*Golightly's Will*—ti croon the whole,
    au'd *Nelly Marchy*,
Whee as they roond the Deed-house thrang'd whing'd
    oot in praise ov honest Archy.

Waes ! Archy lang was hale an' rank, the king o' laddies
    braw—
His wrist was like an anchor-shank, his fist was like the
    claw—
His yellow waistcoat flowered se fine, myed tyeliors lang
    for cabbage-cuttings ;
It myed the bairns to glower amain, an' cry "Ni, ni,
    what bonny buttons !"

His breeches an' his jacket clad a body rasher straight—
A bunch o' ribbons at his knees—his shoes an' buckles
    bright ;
His dashing stockins, true sky-blue, his gud shag hat,
    although a biggin,
When cock'd upon his bonny head, luiked like a pea
    upon a middin.

The last was he to myek a row, yit foremost in the fight,
The first was he to right the wrang'd, the last to wrang
    the right;
They said sic deeds, where'er he'd gyen, cud not but
    meet a noble station;
Cull-Billy * fear'd that a' such hopes were built upon a
    bad foundashin.

For *Captain Starkey* word was sent to come without
    delay—
The Captain begged to be excused, and come another
    day,
When spirits strong and nappy beer, with bread and
    cheese might make him able
To bear up such a load of grief, and do the honours of
    the table.

Another group was then sent off, an' browt *Blind Willie*
    doon,
Whee suen began a simfinee wi' fiddle oot o' tune :—
"Here Archy lies, his country's pride, oh ! San'gate,
    thou will sairly miss him,
Stiff drownded i' the ragin tide, powl'd off at last—
    eehoo ! 'od bliss him !"

While thus they mourn'd, byeth wives an' bairns, young
    cheps and au'd men grey,
Whee shud there cum but Archy's sel', to see about the
    fray.—

---

* William Scott was an inmate of St. John's poor-house; a very harmless
creature, and once much pestered by the wantonness of the boys in the
streets of Newcastle. He was very good-natured. When I was a schoolboy
I used to stop and ask him to spell any hard word, and it is a singular truth
that I never once found him in the wrong. Numerous anecdotes are
recorded of William's wit and presence of mind which would have done
credit to many of greater eminence.

July 30, 1829.   R. G.

Aw gav a skrike, for weel ye ken a seet like this wad be
    a shocker,
"'Od smash! here's Archy back agyen,—slipped oot, by
    gox, frae Davy's locker."

Aboot him they a' thrang'd an' ax'd what news frae
    underground?
Each tell'd aboot their blairin, when they ken'd that he
    was drown'd.
"Hoots!" Archy moung'd, "it's nowt but lees,—to the
    Barley Mow let's e'en be joggin,
Aw'll tyek my oath it wasn't me, because aw hear it's
    Archy Loggan.

To see bold Archy thus restor'd, they ga sic round
    hurraws,
As myed the very skies to splet, an' deav'd a flight o'
    craws;
To the Barley Mow for swipes o' yell, they yen an' a'
    went gaily joggin,
Rejoiced to hear the drownded man was nobbit little
    Archy Loggan.

GILCHRIST.   *Author's Edition,* 1824.

A VOYAGE TO LUNNIN.

The following song owes its origin to my first sea voyage, but I have made
very free with facts. A full account of the voyage and consequent land
excursions will be found in my memoirs yet unpublished.

SHIELDFIELD, *July* 29, 1829.   R. G.

LANG years ower meadows, moors, and muck,
    I cheer'ly on did waddle—
Se various is the chance o' luck
    Between the grave and cradle.

When wark at hyem turn'd rather scant,
  Aw thought 'twas fair humbuggin';
An' so aw even teuk a jaunt,
  Faiks, a' the way to Lunnin.

Lord Howick was my chosen ship,
  Weel rigg'd byeth stem and quarter,
The maister was a canny chep—
  They ca'd him Jacky Carter.
Wi' heart as free frae guilt as care,
  I pack'd up all my duddin,
And shipp'd aboard—the wind blew fair—
  Away we sail'd for Lunnin.

Safe ower the bar a-head we tint—
  The day was fine and sunny,
An' seun we left afar behint,
  Wor land o' milk and honey;
But few their dowly thoughts can tyem—
  May-be the tears were comin'—
Sair griev'd, ne doubt, to pairt wi' hyem,
  Though gaun to keek at Lunnin.

Fareweel, Tyne Brig and cannie Kee,
  Where aw've seen monny a shangy,—
Blind Willey, Captain Starkey tee—
  Bold Archy and great *Hangy.*
Fareweel *Shoe Ties, Jack Tate, Whin Bob,*
  Cull Billy, and *Jack Cummin,*
Aud Judy, Jen Baloo—aw'll sob
  Your praises a' at Lunnin.

Some such as me the hyke myed sick,
  An' gar'd them rue their roamin':
Still forward plung'd wor gallant ship,
  An' left the water foamin'.
Waes me! but 'tis a bonny seet,
  O land o' beef an' puddin'!
To see thy tars, in pluck complete,
  Haud fair their course for Lunnin!

Hail, Tyneside lads! in collier fleets,
  The first in might and motion—
In sunshine days or stormy neets
  The lords upon the ocean.
Come England's foes—a countless crew—
  Ye'll gie their gobs a scummin',
And myek them a' the day to rue,
  They glibb'd their jaws at Lunnin.

I thought mysel' a sailor good,
  And flir'd while some lay sprawlin',
Till where the famous Robin Hood
  Sends out his calms or squallin'—
'Twas there aw felt aw scarce ken how—
  For a' things teuk a bummin',
And myed me wish, wi' retch and spew,
  The ship safe moor'd at Lunnin.

As round by Flambrough Head we shot,
  Down cam' a storm upon us—
Thinks aw, we're fairly gyen to pot—
  O dear!—hev mercy on us!
Ower northern plains 'twill dowly sound,
  And set their eyes a runnin',
When they shall tell that aw was drown'd,
  Just gannin' up to Lunnin.

To cheer wor hearts in vain they brought
   The porter, grog, and toddy—
Maw head swam round whene'er aw thought
   Upon a fat pan-soddy.
"O what the plague fetch'd us frae hyem!"
   Some in the glumps were glummin';
I could hae blubber'd, but thought shyem,
   While gaun a voyage to Lunnin.

'Cross Boston Deeps how we did spin,
   Skelp'd on by noisy Boreas,
Up Yarmouth Roads, and seun up Swin,
   The water flew before us.
O glorious seet! The Nore's in view—
   Like fire and flood we're scuddin';
Ne mair we'll bouk wor boily now,
   But seun be safe at Lunnin.

Hail, bonny Thames! weel smon thy waves!
   A world might flourish bi' them—
An', faiks, they weel deserve the praise
   That a' the world gies ti them.
O lang may commerce spread her stores,
   Full on thy bosom dinnin'—
Weel worthy thou to lave the shores
   O' sic a town as Lunnin.

Seun Black Wall Point we left astern,
   Far ken'd in dismal story—
An' Greenwich Towers we now discern,
   Au'd England's pride and glory.
Sure Nature's sel' inspir'd my staves,
   For aw began a crunnin',
An' blair'd, "Britannia rules the waves!"
   As by we sail'd for Lunnin.

Fornenst the Tower, we myed a click,
    Where traitors gat their fairins,
And where they say that hallion Dick
    Yence scumfish'd two wee bairns.
Hitch, step, and loup, aw spang'd ashore,
    My heart reet full o' funnin'—
An' seun forgat the ocean's roar,
    Amang the joys o' Lunnin.

GILCHRIST.   *Author's Edition,* 1824.

THE AMPHITRITE.

The following production records some of the ludicrous mistakes made by the intrepid navigators of the coal keels. They are a healthy race of men, and for strength and activity have long been justly famous. Intelligence is making rapid advances amongst them.
    July 30, 1829.   R. G.

FRAE Team Gut to Whitley, wi' coals black and brown,
For the *Amphitrite* loaded, the keel had come doon;
But the bullies ower neet had their gobs se oft wet,
That the nyem o' the ship yen an' a' did forget.

To find out the nyem, now each worried his chops,
An' claw'd at his hips fit to murder the lops—
When the Skipper, whe' hunger, was always most bright,
Swore the pawhogger luggish was called Empty Kite.

Frae the Point roond the Girt, a' the time sailin' slow,
Each bully kept bawlin', "*The Empty Kite, ho!*"
But their blairin' was vain, for nee Empty Kite there,
Tho' they blair'd till their kites were byeth empty an'
    sair.

A' slaverin' the Skipper ca'd Geordy and Jim,
For to gan to Newcassel and ax the reet nyem ;
The youngest he thowt myest to blame in this bore,
So P D an' his marrow were e'en pawk'd ashore.

Up Shields Road as they trudged i' their meyst worn oot
    soles,
Oft cursin' the Empty Kite, Skipper, an' coals ;
At the sign o' the Coach they byeth ca'd it befell,
To mourn their hard case an' to swattle some yell.

Here a buck at a sirloin hard eatin' was seen,
Which, he said, wi' the air myed his appetite keen ;
"Appetite ! " cried the bullies—like maislins they stared
Wide gyepin wi' wonder, till "Crikes ! " Jemmy blair'd.

" *The Appetite*, Geordy ! smash, dis thou hear that ?
The varry ootlandish cull nyem we forgat ;
Bliss the dandy ! for had he not tell'd uz the nyem,
To Newcassel we'd wander'd byeth weary and lyem ! "

To Shields back they canter'd, and seun frae the keel,
Roar'd, "The Appetite, ho ! " 'neuf to frighten the deil,
Thus they fund oot the ship, cast the coals iv a swet,
Still praisin' the dandy that day they had met.

Then into the huddock, weel tir'd they all gat,
An' of Empty Kite, Appetite, lang they did chat,
When the Skipper discovered (mair wise than a king),
Tho' not the syem word, they were much the syem thing.

GILCHRIST.   *Author's Edition*, 1824.

BLIND WILLIE'S SINGING.

William Purvis was the well-known native minstrel of Newcastle-upon-Tyne. He was a very harmless character, and if not blind from his birth, was so from a very early period of life. It is a singular fact that he always spoke as if he possessed the sense of sight, for nothing was more common than to hear him express an ardent wish to see the king, for poor Billy was very loyal. When Lord Stowell visited Newcastle, William told him (on being presented to his lordship) that he was glad to see him (Lord Stowell) look so well! Billy could never be prevailed upon to wear a hat. Lord Stowell gave him one, and desired him to use it. Willie did so for half a day, and could suffer it no longer, appearing once more with his bare head exposed to all the transitions of the weather. His memory was very tenacious; any simple rhymes communicated to him he never forgot. Any one presenting him with a halfpenny, and telling him their name, might be assured their name, voice, and bounty would be retained in grateful remembrance. William was an inhabitant of the poor-house of All Saints, but wandered much about the town, distinguishing every street, alley, house, or shop with astonishing exactness. Even when a change of tenants took place, he soon discovered it, and would, in passing, pronounce the name of the new occupier. He was universally a favourite, and few passed him without showing their sympathy and respect for *Poor Blind Willie.*

July 30th, 1829.   R. G.

TUNE—" Jimmy Joneson's Whurry."

YE gowks that 'bout daft Handel swarm,
  Your senses but to harrow—
Styen deaf to strains that myest wad charm
  The heart iv a wheelbarrow.
To wor Keeside awhile repair,
  'Mang Malls an' bullies pig in,
To hear encor'd, wi' monny a blair,
  Poor au'd *Blind Willie's* singin.

To hear fine Sinclair tune his pipes
  Is hardly worth a scuddock—
It's blarney fair, and stale as swipes
  Kept ower lang i' the huddock.
Byeth Braham an' Horn behint the wa'
  Might just as weel be swingin,
For a' thor squeelin's nowt at a'
  Beside Blind Willie's singin.

Aboot " *Sir Maffa* " lang he sung,
  Far into high life keekin,
Till by " *Broom buzzoms* " roundly swung,
  He ga' their lugs a sweepin.
A stave yence myed *Dumb Bet* to greet,
  Se fine wi' cat-gut stringin—
Bold Archy said it was a treat
  To hear Blind Willie singin.

Aw've heard it said, *Fan Welch*, one day,
  On pepper'd oysters messin,
Went in to hear him sing an' play,
  An' get a moral lesson ;
She vow'd 'twas hard to haud a heel,
  An' thowt (the glass whilst flingin)
Wi' clarts they should be plaister'd weel,
  That jeer'd Blind Willie's singin.

It's fine to hear wor Bellman talk,
  It's wond'rous fine an' cheerin
To hear *Bet Watt* an' *Euphy Scott*
  Scold, fight, or bawl fresh heerin ;
To see the keels upon the Tyne,
  As thick as hops, a' swimmin,
Is fine indeed, but still mair fine
  To hear Blind Willie singin.

Lang may wor Tyneside lads se true,
  In heart byeth blithe an' mellow,
Bestow the praise that's fairly due
  To this bluff, honest fellow—
And when he's hamper'd i' the dust,
  Still i' wor memory springin,
The times we've run till like te brust,
  To hear Blind Willie singin.

But may he live to cheer the *bobs,*
  That skew the coals te shivers,
Whee like the drink te grip their gobs,
  And burn their varry livers.
So, if you please, aw'll myek an end,
  My sang ne farther dingin,
Lest ye may think that aw pretend
  To match Blind Willie's singin.

GILCHRIST.   *Author's Edition,* 1824.

THE LAMENTATION
ON THE DEATH OF CAPTAIN STARKEY.

Benjamin Starkey was an inhabitant of the Freeman's Hospital in Newcastle-upon-Tyne. He told me he never could account for the term Captain preceding his name. He was diminutive in his figure, but uncommonly polished in his manners, taking off his hat and kissing his hand with an air of excessive good breeding, and which at the same time bore no resemblance of either affectation or buffoonery. He was vain of being accounted company for the great, and would converse familiarly of his *friends,* Sir Matthew Ridley and Charles Brandling, Esq. Starkey wrote a good hand, and was in the habit of giving *promissory* notes for certain pence he had borrowed from certain persons. He was fond of being treated to a glass of ale, and very grateful for trifling favours. Any one showing him kindness or treating him with deference were for ever entitled to a polite bow from Benjamin Starkey, who died July 9th, 1822, an old man (in his 65th year).

July 30th, 1829.   R. G.

"WHAT! is he gyen?" *Bold Airchy* said, and moungin'
    scratch'd his head—

"O can sic waesome news be true?—Is *Captain Starkey*
    dead?

Aw's griev'd at heart—push round the can—seun empty
    frae wor hands we'll chuck it—

For now we'll drink wor last to him, since he hez fairly
    kick'd the bucket.

"My good shag hat ne mair aw'll wave, his canny fyece to see—
Wor bairns' bairns will sing o' him, as Gilchrist sings o' me—
For O! he was a lad o' wax! Aw've seen him blithe
    and offen mellow—

He might hae faults, but wi' them a' we've seldom seen
    a better fellow.

"Yen day they had me drown'd for fun, which myed the
    folks to blair;

Aw myest could wish, for his dear syek, that aw'd been
    drown'd for fair.

On monny a day when cannons roar, yen loyal heart
    will then be missin'—

If there be yell, we'll toast his nyem—if there be nyen,
    he'll get wor blissin'."

Blind Willie then strumm'd up his kit wi' monny a
    weary drone,

Which *Thropler*, drunk, an' *Cuckoo Jack** byeth answer'd
    wiv a groan.

"Nice chap! poor chap!" Blind Willie said; "my
    heart is pierc'd like onny riddle,

To think aw've liv'd to see him dead—aw never mair 'ill
    play the fiddle.

* Cuckoo Jack has been for many years in the service of the Corporation
as one of the barge-rowers. He was remarkable for his skill in the recovery
of anything lost by accident in the river—the bodies of persons drowned,
boats sunk for many years, watches and money, and innumerable other
materials, being by honest Jack's dexterity brought to light and restored to
their owners for a trifling remuneration. Jack was much valued as a
dexterous and good-natured individual.

July 30, 1829.   R. G.

"His gam is up, his pipe is out, an' fairly laid his craw—
His fame 'ill blaw about, just like coal dust at Shiney-
    Raw.
He surely was a joker rare—what times there'd been for
    a' the nation,
Had he but liv'd to be a Mayor, the glory o' wor
    Corporation.

"But he has gi'en us a' the slip, and gyen for evermore—
Au'd Judy and *Jack Coxon* tee, hae gyen awile before.
An' we maun shortly follow them, an' tyek the bag, my
    worthy gentles—
Then what'll poor Newcassel dee, deprived of all her
    ornamentals?

"We'll moralize—for dowly thowts are mair wor friends
    than foes—
For death, like when the tankard's out, brings a' things
    tiv a close.
May we like him, frae grief an' toil, when laid in peace
    beneath the hether—
Upon the last eternal shore, a' happy, happy meet
    together!"

GILCHRIST.   *Author's Edition*, 1824.

———

BLIND WILLIE'S DEETH.

TUNE—"Jimmy Joneson's Whurry."

As aw was gannin up the Side,
    Aw met wi' drucken Bella;
She rung her hands, and sair she cried,
    He's gyen at last, poor fellow!
O hinny, Bella! whe is't that's gyen?
    Ye gar my blood run chilly;
Wey, hinny, deeth hes stopt the breeth
    O' canny aud Blind Willie.

God keep us, Bella, is that true?
   Ye surely are mistaken!
O, no! aw've left him just a-now,
   And he's as deed as bacon.
Aw tied his chaffs, and laid him oot—
   His flesh just like a jelly—
And sair, sair, aw was put aboot
   For canny aud Blind Willie.

Then off aw went as fast as owt,
   Ti see poor Willie lyin;
When aw gat there, maw heart was sair,
   Ti see his friends a' sighin.
Around his bed they hung their heeds,
   Just like the droopin lily:
And aw wi' them did de the syem
   For canny aud Blind Willie.

Ne mair, said aw, we'll hear him sing,
   Ne mair he'll play the fiddle!
Ne mair we'll hear him praise the king—
   No! no! cried Jimmy Liddle.
His days are past—he's gyen at last,
   Beside his frind, Sir Billy,
The parish chiel, that preach'd se weel.
   We'll mourn for him an' Willie.

His bonny corpse crowds cam to see,
   Which myed the room luik dowley;
And whe was there amang them tee,
   But noisy Yellow Yowley;
She throo the crowd did push her way—
   Wi' drink she seem'd quite silly—
And on her knees began to pray
   For canny aud Blind Willie.

13

They tell'd us a' to gang away,
　Which myed us varry sorry ;
But Beagle Bet wad kiss his lips,
　Before they did him bury.
He's buried noo—he's oot o' seet—
　Then on his grave se hilly,
Let them that feel take their fareweel,
　O' canny aud Blind Willie.

NUNN.　　　　　*Fordyce's " Newcastle Song Book," 1842.*

"The Death of Blind Willie" has generally been ascribed to Gilchrist.
There, however, is little doubt but it is Robert Nunn's.

MORE INNOVATIONS.

Grainger's great improvements set speculation astir. Some of the innovations dreamt of in the song are now accomplished facts ; others again, the
reader will see, are yet to come.

TUNE—" The Bold Dragoon."

NEWCASSELL'S sore transmogrified, as every one may see,
But what they've duen is nowt to what they still intend
　　t' de :
There still remains some sonsy spots, pure relics of our
　　ancient features,
Of which our canny town shall brag, while Gyetshead
　　boasts sand beaters !

The scrudg'd up foot of Pilgrim Street they surely will
　　not mend,
'Tis such a curiosity—a street without an end !
Should they extend it to the Quay, and show All Saints'
　　Church so neatly,
It might look fine, but I'm afraid 'twould spoil the
　　Butcher Bank completely !

Of pullin' down the Butcher Bank it grieves one's heart
　　to speak ;
From it down every Quayside Chare there's such a
　　glorious keek !

The shambles, too, a bonny sight, the horse and foot-
ways nice and narrow;
Say what they will, seek through the world, the Butcher
Bank is bad to marrow!

Our fishwives, too, might well complain, forced off the
Hill to move,
Where they so long had squall'd in peace, good fellow-
ship, and love:
The brightest day will have an end, and here the
Sandhill's glory closes,
Now flies and fumes no more will make the gentles stop
their ears and noses.

'Tis said they mean to clear away the houses in the Side,
To set off old St. Nich'las' Church, so long our greatest
pride;
But where's the use of making things so very grand and
so amazing,
To bring daft gowks from far and near to plague us with
their gob and gazing.

The Middle Street's to come down next, and give us
better air,
And room to make to hold at once the market and the
fair;
Well may Newcassel grieve for this, because, in hot or
rainy weather,
It look'd so well to see the folks all sweltered in a hole
together!

The Tyne's to run out East and West; and, 'stead of
Solway boats,
Our Greenland ships at Carlisle call, and not at Johnny
Groat's;

Dull may we be at such a change: eh! certies, lads,
 haul down your colours!
'Twould be no wonder now to see chain bridges ruin all
 the scullers.

  GILCHRIST.   *Fordyce's " Newcastle Song Book,"* 1842.

  To this song Gilchrist has left no manuscript notes. The notes already
given are in an interleaved copy of his songs—evidently intended for a
new edition.
  The portrait of Gilchrist on page 169 is copied, by the kindness of the late
Dr. George N. Clark, from a scarce lithograph of the Herbage Committee,
of which Gilchrist was a member. The portrait was photographed by
P. H. Laws, and reproduced by the Meisenbach process.

THE CORN MARKET.

A LAMENT.

  The following clever song appears in Fordyce's Collection (1842). No
author's name is given, but evidently he was no unpractised hand.
The local improvements of Grainger could not be carried out without
injuriously affecting the interests of some; and this witty production is
interesting as showing the spirit of opposition Grainger encountered in
beautifying his native town.—*Note to* 1872 *edition.*
  To the above, which appeared in the 1872 edition, it may be added that
Grainger intended the Central Exchange (Art Gallery) to be the Corn
Market. At the time, about 1838, a model of the new building was
exhibited showing men carrying sacks of corn on their backs. The song,
besides appearing in Fordyce's volume, seems also to have been printed as a
broadsheet. We have come across a copy, possibly the original publication;
it is printed by W. Boag, is undated, and, like the volume, is without an
author's name. The author, as a guess, possibly Gilchrist.

          TUNE—"The Bold Dragoon."

O HINNEY Grainger, haud thy hand, thou'll turn us upside
 doon,
Or faith aw'll send for Mr. Brand, te claw thy curly
 croon ;
For what thou's myed the Major's dene, wor thenks are
 due, and thou shalt hae them ;
But noo the law toon folk complain, thou wants to tyek
 thor Egypt frae them.

        Whack, row de dow, etc.

Most folk like the better half, but thou wad swalley all,
Poor hoose or jail may tyek the rest, gie thou but
    Elswick Hall.
Wor cooncil's cliver, thor's ne doubt, but they'll find oot,
    tho' rather late on,
How cool the divil walks aboot, in the smooth shape of
    J——y C——n.

Thou's getten a' the butcher meat, the taties, tripe, and
    greens,
And, not content wi' this, thou wants te tyek wor corn,
    it seems ;
For Mosley Street and mercy's sake, sic wicked thowts
    at once abandon,
Or else wor canny aud law toon it winnet hev a leg te
    stand on.

The wheel o' fortune will stand still, the bees forsyek
    the hive,
Thor'll be ne wark for Sinton's Mill, the White Horse
    winnet drive ;
Poor Mrs. French and Temperance Hall ne mair need
    recommend their diet,
The farmers will forget te call, Hell's Kitchen very sel
    turn quiet.

The *Chronicle* may doze in peace—Lord Grainger says,
    "Sleep on l"
The bugs may tyek anuther leese, thor race is not yet
    run ;
Aud Nichol still may fairly say, frae Hepple's up to
    Humble's hoose end,
He feeds a lively host each day, aw'll say, at least a
    hundred thoosand.

The White Swan suen 'ill be agrund, the Black Boy turn
  quite pale ;

The Black Bull wi' the blow be stunn'd ; the Lion hang
  his tail ;

Tom Heron's Cock 'ill craw ne mair ; the aud Blue
  Bell be dumb for iver ;

An', just te myek the Keeside stare, thou'd better send
  doon for the river.

ANONYMOUS.   Broadsheet printed by W. Boag about 1838.

JAMES MORRISON.

JAMES MORRISON, author of " Newcastle Noodles " and
" Burdon's Address," was a native of Newcastle, being born,
about the year 1800, in Morrison's Court, Groat Market.
He served his apprenticeship as a painter, and worked for

GROAT MARKET IN MORRISON'S TIME.

some years as a journey-
man in his native town ;
after which (somewhere
about the year 1830) he
went to Edinburgh. With
his removal from New-
castle, the little that is
known of his life abruptly
ends. Whether he settled
in Edinburgh, or made it
but a halting-place for
further journeys, is not
known. His two songs
were popular in their day ;
but the subjects being of
a temporary interest, they
are now less known.
" Burdon's Address " is
found in Marshall's Chap-
books, 1823, and "New-
castle Noodles" in Marshall's volume, 1827. Beyond the
interest attached to him as a writer of Tyneside songs,
his name is additionally interesting on account of his

relationship to the celebrated Dr. Morrison, he being a nephew of that eminent scholar : who, from a joiner's bench, in the Groat Market, by study and self-denial, raised himself to a foremost rank amongst the scholars of his day. Dr. Morrison, in 1824, when famous as a Chinese missionary and scholar, during a brief visit to England, did not forget his old friends, or the scene of his early struggles, but preached in the Presbyterian Chapel, High Bridge; and thus, in a measure, repaid the kindness of his old minister, the Rev. A. Laidlaw, who had greatly assisted him in his studies whilst a youth. His great works were, the compilation of a Chinese dictionary, and, in conjunction with Mr. Milne, making a translation of the Scriptures into the Chinese language. He died at Canton, on the 1st of July 1834, in his fifty-second year.

BURDON'S ADDRESS TO HIS CAVALRY.

This witty parody refers to the great strike amongst the sailors at Shields, in 1815. Thomas Burdon was lieut.-colonel of the Tyne Hussars, who were sent to assist in keeping order. For his services on that occasion he was knighted by the Prince Regent, in May 1816.

TUNE—"Scots wha hae.'

SOLDIERS whom Newcastle's bred,
View your Cornel at your head,
Who's been called out of his bed
        To fight with sword in hand.
Now's the time, ye sons of Mars,
You've to conquer British tars,
Who've broke out in civil wars
        At Shields and Sunderland.

But, my lads, be not alarm'd,
You've to fight with men unarm'd,
Who in multitudes have swarm'd.
        We will make them flee.

Come, then, my noble sons of Tyne,
And let your valour nobly shine;
There at last has come a time
    To show your bravery.

Then they cried out, every man,
Cornel, we'll dee a' we can;
So away to Shields they ran,
    Their lives in jeopardy.
But they had no call to fight,
The Marines had be't them quite;
Yet the Cornel's made a Knight
    For the victory!

JAMES MORRISON.   *Marshall's Chap-Book*, 1823.

THE NEWCASTLE NOODLES.

In December 1819 the Northumberland and Newcastle Volunteer Corps of Yeomanry was formed, Charles John Brandling, Esq., being chief in command. About that time, political agitation was rife in the district. As the parties who took an active part in raising the new corps were generally opposed to political reform, the new force was considered by the reforming party as a menace against them, and they showed their dislike by calling them, in derision, "Noodles."

TUNE—"Canny Newcassel."

BE easy, good folks, for we're all safe enough,
    Better fortune seems now to attend us;
And two canny fellows, both lusty and tough,
    Have raiséd a new corps to defend us:
Men sound, wind and limb, good sighted and stout,
    That can fight well, without being daunted;
Free from all diseases, such like as the gout,
    And can jump, or be ready when wanted.

Chorus.
Then if any invaders should dare us to fight,
    Let it be on the shore or the river;
Bold Archy* the Noodle and Tommy the Knight,†
    Will guard and protect us for ever.

* Archibald Reed, at that time Mayor.
† Sir Thomas Burdon, colliery owner, also a large brewer.

The Noodles have ne'er been at battle as yet,
    Nor been brought down by scanty provision;
So to try them whenever his worship thinks fit,
    He'll find them in famous condition.
In all their manœuvres there's scarcely a flaw,
    They're quite up to the science o' killing;
For the Noodle drill-sergeant's a limb o' the law,
    And an old practis'd hand at the drilling.
        Then if any invaders, etc.

Misfortunes, however, will sometimes attend,
    For, one morning, by danger surrounded,
A poor fellow splintered his fore-finger end,
    And, of course, in the service was wounded.
'Tis true a sair finger's a very bad thing,
    But it didn't diminish his beauty;
So, the next day, he just popp'd his arm in a sling,
    And, Briton-like, went upon duty.
        Then if any invaders, etc.

They have all been abroad, and as far too as Shields,
    But to walk there was no easy matter:
So, for fear that their boots should go down in the heels,
    They took the steamboat down the watter.
Their warlike appearance was awfully grand;
    When they fired it sounded like thunder,
Which put all the natives o' Shields to a stand,
    And left them for ages to wonder.
        Then if any invaders, etc.

What a pity they cannot get medals to buy,
    It greatly would add to their grandeur:
" There's Waterloo soldiers!" the strangers would cry,
    And think Archy was great Alexander.

These mighty Preservers if death cannot save,
    But send one or two of them bummin';
The rest o' the Noodles would fire o'er his grave,
    And tell the below-folks he's comin'.
             Then if any invaders, etc.

JAMES MORRISON.   *Marshall's Collection*, 1827.

GREEN'S BALLOON.

The local poets have not let ballooning go unsung. Mitford has left us Bob Cranky's account of Sadler's balloon ascent, 1815. Oliver has a song on Green's ascent (apparently the first of the four). But the unknown author of the following has evidently been in a happier vein than either of his popular rivals—his song is by far the best.

Messrs. Green ascended in their grand Coronation Balloon, from the Nuns' field* in Newcastle, four times—on Wednesday, May 11th; Whit-Monday, May 23rd; Monday, May 30th; and on Race Thursday, July 14th, 1825.

                              TUNE—"Barbara Bell."

Now just come and lissen a while till aw tell, man,
    Of a wonderful seet t'other day aw did see:
As aw was gaun trudgen alang by mysel, man,
    Aw met wi' wor skipper, ay just on the Key.
O skipper, says aw, mun, wye where are ye gannen?
    Says he, Come wi' me, for aw's gaun up the toon;
Now just come away, for we munnet stand blabbin,
    Or we'll be ower lang for to see the Balloon.
                      Right fal de, etc.

The balloon, man, says aw, wye aw never heard tell on't,
    What kind o' thing is it? now skipper tell me:
Says he, It's a thing that gans up by the sel' on't,
    And if ye'll gan to the Nuns' Gate, man, ye'll see.

* On the Nuns' field, Nuns' Street, and Grainger's New Markets are now built. It extended from the back of Newgate Street nearly to where Earl Grey's monument stands.

So to the Nuns' Gate then we went in a hurry,
    And when we gat there, man, the folks stood in crowds;
And aw heerd a chep say, he wad be very sorry,
    If it went to the meun, reet clean thro' the clouds.

                    Right fal de, etc.

We stared and luik't round us, but nought could we see,
        man,
    Till a thing it went up as they fir'd a gun:
Cried the skipper, Aw warn'd that's the little Pee-dee,
        man,
    Gyen to tell folks above 'twill be there varry suen.
Then a' iv a sudden it cam ower the house-tops, man,
    It was like a hay-stack, and luikt just as big;
Wiv a boat at the tail on't, all tied tid wi' ropes, man,
    Begox! it was just like wor aud Sandgate gig.

                    Right fal de, etc.

And there was two cheps that sat in the inside, man,
    Wi' twe little things they kept poweyin her roun';
Just like wor skipper when we've a bad tide, man:
    Aw warn'd they were fear'd that the thing wad come
        doun;
And still the twe cheps kept poweyin her reet, man,
    For upwards she went, ay clean ower the toon:
They powey'd till they powey'd her reet out o' seet, man,
    That was a' that we saw o' this grand air balloon.

                    Right fal de, etc.

The skipper cam to me, tuik haud o' my hand, man,
    Says, What do ye think o' this seet that's been given?
Says aw, Aw can't tell, but it's a' very grand, man;
    Aw wish the cheps byeth safely landed in heaven.

'Twad be a good plan to tyek's up when we're deed, man,
　For which way we get there 'twill be a' the syem ;
And then for wor Priests we'd stand little need, man :
　So me an' the skipper we went wor ways hyem.

Right fal de, etc.

UNKNOWN.   *Marshall's Collection*, 1827.

_____

WILLIAM WATSON.

WILLIAM WATSON, author of "Dance to thy Daddy,"
"Thumping Luck to yon Town," and other popular Tyneside
songs, appears to have been by trade a shoemaker, and,
like many of the sons of St. Crispin, an active politician.
At election times he turned his poetical abilities to account,
and helped the man of his choice by writing election songs,
etc. His songs appear to have been written between the
years 1820 and 1840, as his "Newcassel Races" is in
Marshall's Collection of Newcastle Songs, published 1827,
and his later pieces in Fordyce's collection, published in
1842. His "Thumping Luck," one of the best of our
Tyneside songs, is said to have been written in London,
while he was away for a time from Newcastle.

The above sketch appeared in our 1872 edition. Some
fifteen years after the following letter, which explains itself,
appeared in the *Evening Chronicle*.

The *Evening Chronicle* had reprinted "Dance to thy
Daddy," and wrote that the author was a shoemaker.

"SIR,—I beg to draw your attention to the introductory remarks
on the author of 'Dance to thy Daddy' (William Watson), who is
there stated as being a shoemaker. This is not so, as he was a
fellow-shopmate with me in the employment of John Richardson,
painter, 29 St. Nicholas' Churchyard, Newcastle. He was in
London previous to that, and wrote the song of 'Thumping Luck'
when his affections prompted his return to Newcastle. To Newcastle he came back by sea in the London trader, the *Barefoot*,
about 1829 or 1830. He remained in the above shop until after
the time you mention, 1840. He resided in St. Martin's Court,
Newgate Street. It may be interesting to know that he was a very
talented workman, and of a kind and genial nature.

"His brother John was a very talented engraver on glass, mainly
of local views, such as St. Nicholas' Church, etc., and he exhibited

several of his artistic works on glass in the two Polytechnic Exhibitions held in Newcastle, and, being silvered on the back, they were objects much admired by the visitors. His youngest brother, Nathaniel—a hairdresser by trade—was a great musical genius, a fine flute player, and an interesting convivial companion. I write thinking the correction about this local author might be worthy of a place in the *Evening Chronicle.*—Yours, etc.,
"42 Dean Street, Nov. 23rd, 1885.   "JOHN BROWN."

This interesting letter corrects the error of Watson being a shoemaker. How he came to be classed as one arose in the following way:—When bringing out the previous edition, coming to Watson's songs, to the question who or what he was, there was no answer; previous collections told nothing. Mr. Sewell, already referred to, was then seen. He recollected Watson; he had seen him in a house in the Groat Market at some social club, but beyond that he knew little. About his business he could not tell; thought he was a shoemaker; but there was a Mrs. Watson lived about the White Swan Yard, she might be a relative. A visit was made to her; she was found in a clean, plain room, up a flight of stairs in the yard. No information was to be got there: "It

PAINTERS, GLAZIERS, JAPANNERS, &c.

Imitators of Woods and Marbles.

REDUCED COPY OF WATSON'S BUSINESS CARD (1820).

wassent maw man, hinney; he was a mason, and never wrote sangs." Mr. Sewell recollected another Watson, who had a shop in Pilgrim Street. On the chance that he might be of the family, Mr. Sewell called upon him; it was another miss. Nothing more being to be gleaned, the impression that he was a shoemaker was then put into the sketch.

Getting a trace through Mr. Brown's note, a little additional has been gleaned. Before Watson went to London he was in business for himself, and from what has been told appears to have had the ball of fortune at his foot; but his failing was that of too many—company. As a writer and singer his company was courted. Business appears to have fallen off, and then, about 1823, he sailed for London. By the kindness of his nephew, Mr. John Watson, we have seen a letter of his written from London in 1826. In it he tells his brother Nathaniel he sends him a parcel of manuscript (songs) which he wants him to get printed. He adds that many of the songs have been well taken with in London, and copies are wanted there. Whether the songs thus sent were ever printed in a separate form is very doubtful. His nephews—sons of his brothers John and Nathaniel—have never seen them, and know nothing of the manuscript, which, in fact, they never saw. Most likely the songs only appeared in collections. One of his songs, "Newcassel Races," is in Marshall's song-book as early as 1827, the remainder (likely part of the packet) are in Fordyce's collection, 1842. It may be mentioned here that Fordyce, like Marshall, published chap-books; so that while the volume is dated 1842, the songs may have been printed in the chapbooks earlier.

Affectionate Brother J. M. Watson

The autograph given above is from the London letter already referred to. His portrait we should also have liked to have given. Many years ago one (an oil painting) was in the possession of the family, but now, and for many years past, all trace of it has been lost. By St. John's register of burials he died at his residence, St. Martin's Court, Newgate Street, on February 4th, 1840, aged forty-four years, and was buried in St. John's Churchyard. Another "Man of Mark," if but a minor one, whose lying at St. John's has been overlooked.

————

NEWCASSEL RACES.

It's hae ye heard the ill that's duen?
Or hae ye lost? or hae ye won?
Or hae ye seen the mirth and fun
    At fam'd Newcassel Races, O?

The weather fine, and folks se gay,
Put on their best, and bent their way
To the Toon Moor, to spend the day
    At fam'd Newcassel Races, O !

There shows of all sort you may view,
Polito's grand collection too ;
Such noise, an' din, an' lili-bulloo,
    At fam'd Newcassel Races, O !
There sum on horses sat astride,
An' sum in gigs did snugly ride,
Wi' smart yung wenches by their side,
    Luik'd stylish at the Races, O !

A tailor chep aw chanc'd to spy,
Wes sneekin' thro' the crood se sly,
For he'd tyen the darlin' ov his eye
    To swagger at the Races, O !
He says, "My dear, we'll see the show."
"Egad !" says she, "I do not know,
It looks so vulgar and so low,
    We'd better see the Races, O !"

Noo, sum were singin' songs se fine ;
An' sum were lyin' drunk like swine ;
Sum drank porter, uthers wine ;
    Rare drinkin' at the Races, O !
Sum gat hyem midst oots an' ins ;
Sum had black eyes an' broken shins ;
An' sum lay drunk amang the whins,
    A-cummin' frae the Races, O !

Let iv'ry one his station mense,
By acting like a man o' sense :
'Twill save him mony a pund expense
 When he gans to the Races, O !
Kind friends, I would you all advise,
Gud coonsel ye shud ne'er despise ;
The world's opinion always prize,
 When ye gan to the Races, O !

WATSON.   *Marshall's Collection*, 1827.

THUMPING LUCK.

"Canny Newcassel," so often sung of and celebrated by its own bards, has never been more fortunate in its fond admirer than in William Watson. His "Thumping Luck" will always remain a happy expression of the feeling of every true son of "Canny Newcassel" to the famous old town of his birth.—*Note from* 1872 *edition.*

TUNE—"Gang ne mair to yon toon."

HERE's thumping luck to yon town,
 Let's have a hearty drink upon't,—
O the days I've spent in yon town,
 My heart still warms to think upon't ;
For monie a happy day I've seen,
 With monie a lass so kind and true,—
With hearty chiels I've canty been,
 And danc'd away till a' was blue.

Chorus.
Here's thumping luck to yon town,
 Let's have a hearty drink upon't,—
O the days I've spent in yon town,
 My heart still warms to think upon't.

There's famous ale in yon town,
　　Will make your lips to smack again ;
And many a one leaves yon town,
　　Oft wishes they were back again ;
Well shelter'd from the northern blast,
　　Its spires and turrets proudly rise,
And boats and keels all sailing past
　　With coals, that half the world supplies.
　　　　　　Here's thumping luck, etc.

There's native bards in yon town
　　For wit and humour seldom be't ;
And they sang se sweet in yon town,
　　Gud faith, I think I hear them yet :
Such fun in Thompson's voyage to Shields,
　　In Jemmy Joneson's wherrie fine—
. Such shaking heels and dancing reels,
　　When sailing on the coaly Tyne.
　　　　　　Here's thumping luck, etc.

Amang the rest in yon town,
　　One Shield was fam'd for ready wit—
His " Lord 'Size " half drown'd in yon town,
　　Gud faith, I think I hear it yet :
Then Mitford's muse is seldom wrong,
　　When once he gives the jade a ca',
And Gilchrist, too, for comic song,
　　Though last, he's not the least of a'.
　　　　　　Here's thumping luck, etc.

May the sun shine bright on yon town,
　　May its trade and commerce still increase,
And may all that dwells in yon town
　　Be blest with fond, domestic peace ;
I4

For, let me wander east or west,
  North, south, or even o'er the sea,
My native town I'll still love best—
  NEWCASTLE is the place for me.
        Here's thumping luck, etc.

WATSON.   *Fordyce's "Newcastle Song Book,"* 1842.

––––––––––

DANCE TO THY DADDY.

TUNE—" The Little Fishy."

COME here, my little Jackey,
Now I've smoked my backey,
Let's have a bit crackey
Till the boat comes in.

> Dance to thy daddy, sing to thy mammy,
> Dance to thy daddy, to thy mammy sing;
> Thou shalt have a fishy on a little dishy,
> Thou shalt have a fishy when the boat comes in.

Here's thy mother hummin',
Like a canny woman;
Yonder comes thy father,
Drunk—he cannot stand.

> Dance to thy daddy, sing to thy mammy,
> Dance to thy daddy, to thy mammy sing;
> Thou shalt have a fishy on a little dishy,
> Thou shalt have a haddock when the boat
> comes in.

Our Tommy's always fuddlin',
He's so fond of ale,
But he's kind to me,
I hope he'll never fail.

> Dance to thy daddy, sing to thy mammy,
> Dance to thy daddy, to thy mammy sing;
> Thou shalt have a fishy on a little dishy,
> Thou shalt have a codling when the boat
> comes in.

I like a drop mysel',
When I can get it sly,
And thou, my bonny bairn,
Will lik't as well as I.

> Dance to thy daddy, sing to thy mammy,
> Dance to thy daddy, to thy mammy sing;
> Thou shalt have a fishy on a little dishy,
> Thou shalt have a mack'rel when the boat
> comes in.

May we get a drop
Oft as we stand in need;
And weel may the keel row
That brings the bairns their bread.

> Dance to thy daddy, sing to thy mammy,
> Dance to thy daddy, to thy mammy sing;
> Thou shalt have a fishy on a little dishy,
> Thou shalt have a salmon when the boat
> comes in.

WATSON.   *Fordyce's "Newcastle Song Book,"* 1842.

NEWCASTLE LANDLORDS. 1834.

An interesting list of names and characteristic descriptions.

KIND friends and acquaintance, attention I claim,
While a few jolly landlords in this town I name;
In alphabet order my song it is penn'd,
And I hope, for joke's sake, it will never offend.

> *Chorus.*
> Then hey for good drinking,
> It keeps us from thinking,
> We all love a drop in our turn.

A stands for Armfield, a good hearty blade,
Tho' he's left the Nag's Head, still follows his trade;
At the foot of the Market you'll find his new shop,
Where many an old friend still calls in for a drop.

B stands for Burns, of the Theatre square;
She's an orderly woman—good drink is sold there;
If I wanted a wife, I should readily choose
This amiable widow to govern my house.

C stands for Cant, sign of the Blue Bell,
Who keeps a good house, and good porter doth sell;
Quarrelling or fighting is there seldom seen,
She's a canty old widow, but rather too keen.

D for Dixon, who once kept the Unicorn—Ho!
And D stands for Dixon, White Hart, you well know;
Then there's Dixon, Quayside, just a little way down—
Were the three fattest landlords in all the whole town.

E stands for Eggleton, Fighting Cocks Inn,
Tho' old, took a young wife, and thought it no sin;
F for Finlay, his shop's corner of Pudding Chare,
And good wine and spirits you'll always get there.

G for Gibson, the Blue Posts, in Pilgrim Street,
Where a few jolly souls oft for harmony meet;
H for Hackworth in Cowgate, Grey Bull is the sign—
Only taste his good ale—faith, you'll say it's divine.

H stands for Heron, the sign of the Cock;
H for Hall, near Nuns' Gate keeps a snug oyster shop;
H stands for Horn, and he's done very weal,
Since he bother'd the heart of sly Mrs. Neil.

I stands for Inns—we've the best in the North,
There's the King's Head, the Queen's Head, the
    George, and the Turf;
The old Crown and Thistle, and Miller's Half Moon,
Well known to the trav'lers who frequent the town.

K stands for Kitchen, Hell's Kitchen 'twas nam'd,
And long for good ale and good spree has been fam'd;
In each parlour, in vestry, or kitchen you'll find
The beer drawer, Mary, obliging and kind.

L stands for Larkin—he's left the Black Boy,
Once fam'd for Patlanders and true Irish joy;
On the Scotswood New Road a house he has ta'en,
Where I hope the old soul will get forward again.

M stands for Mitford—he kept the North Pole,
Just over the Leazes, a dull-looking hole;
Now our favourite poet lives at Head on the Side,
Here's success to his muse—long may she preside.

N stands for Newton, sign of the Dolphin,
Who the old house pull'd down, built it up like an inn;
They say he found gold—how much I can't tell,
But never mind that, he's done wonderful well.

O stands for Orton—he keeps the Burnt House,
Once fam'd for the knights of the thimble and goose;
And O stands for Ormston at Pandon—O rare!
Temptation enough for young men that go there.

P stands for Pace, sign of the White Swan,
Who, for to oblige, will do all that he can;
A convenient house, when you marketing make,
To pop in and indulge yourself with a beef-steak.

R stands for Ridley and Reed, you all know,
And R stands for Richardson—all in a row;
First, Three Tuns, the Sun, and the old Rose and Crown,
And their ale's good as any at that part of the town.

S for Sayers, Nag's Head—he keeps good mountain
    dew ;
Only taste it, you'll find what I tell you is true.
S for Stokoe, wine merchant, foot of St. John's Lane ;
For good stuff and good measure we'll never complain.

T for Teasdale, the Phœnix—a house fam'd for flip ;
T for Teasdale, who once kept the sign of " The Ship" :
And W for Wylam, a place more fam'd still ;
Sure you all know the Custom-House on the Sandhill.

Robin Hood, Dog and Cannon, and Tiger for me,
The Peacock well known to the clerks on the Quay ;
The Old Beggar's Opera for stowrie, my pet,
Mrs. Richardson's was—and she cannot be bet.

There's the Black Bull, and Grey Bull, well known to
    a few ;
Black, White, and Grey Horse, and Flying Horse too.
The Black House, the White House, The Hole in
    the Wall,
And the Seven Stars, Pandon, if you dare to call.

There's the Turk's Head, Nag's Head, and Old Barley
    Mow,
The Bay Horse, the Pack Horse, and Teasdale's
    Dun Cow :
The Ship and the Reel, the Half-Moon and the Sun ;
But I think, my good friends, it is time to be done.

Then, each landlord and landlady, wish them success,
Town and trade of the Tyne, too—we cannot do less ;
And let this be the toast when we meet to regale—
" May we ne'er want a bumper of Newcastle ale."

WATSON.   *Fordyce's " Newcastle Song Book," 1842.*

WILLIAM ARMSTRONG.

WILLIAM ARMSTRONG, author of "Lizzie Mudie's Ghost," and other popular songs, was born in the Painter Heugh, Newcastle, about the year 1804. His father was a tradesman of the town, carrying on business in Dean Street as a shoemaker. Apparently not caring for his father's business, he was bound to Mr. Wardle, a painter, at the White Cross, Newgate Street; and after serving his apprenticeship, worked for some years as a journeyman in this town. The songs of "Willie Armstrong," as he was familiarly called by his friends, are of the broad Newcastle class. Their subjects generally being some laughable extravagance ascribed, as circumstances suited, to the pitmen or keelmen of the Tyne. He was, in addition to his popularity as a writer, much admired as a singer; and at convivial meetings sung his own songs with great success. As a member of the "Stars of Friendship" (a social club), he was highly esteemed; his double gifts as writer and singer making him a general favourite. Somewhere about the years 1833-34 he left his native place for London. Of his life after he removed from Newcastle we have been unable to gather any information.

The information in the above sketch was gathered from Mr. Sewell, silversmith, Dean Street, then one of the old standards of the town. In 1872, when the previous edition of this book was brought out, he was the only one we could find who knew anything of Armstrong. Mr. Sewell has now (1891) been dead some years, and further inquiries in other quarters have resulted in nothing. Armstrong appears to have left no trace. Mr. Sewell, it may be added, was one of the Stars of Friendship with Armstrong, and as lads they were companions, and often together. Despite this intimacy, about his songs, beyond the fact that he wrote them, Mr. Sewell had no recollections. He recollected more about Armstrong as a boy, and then, as he put it, he was never out of mischief.

We are unable to give either portrait or autograph of this, if rough, at least amusing writer. The earliest of his songs we can trace is the "Jenny Howlet," in one of Marshall's Chap-Books, 1823. The rest appeared in Marshall (1827), the later in Fordyce (1842).

THE JENNY HOWLET;

OR, LIZZIE MUDIE'S GHOST.

The scene of the following laughable incident is laid at Hebburn Quay, nigh to Jarrow, where near the shore stood a public-house at one time kept by the Lizzie Mudie whose ghost was supposed to have jeered the enraged skipper.

SUM time since a skipper was gawn iv his keel,
His heart like a lion, his fyece like the deil ;
He was steering his-sel, as he'd oft duin before,
When at Au'd Lizzie Mudie's his keel ran ashore.

>   Fal de ral la, etc.

The skipper was vext when his keel gat ashore,
So for Geordy and Pee-dee he loudly did roar ;
They lower'd the sail—but it a' waddent de,
So he click'd up a coal, an' maist fell'd the Pee-dee.

>   Fal de ral la, etc.

In the midst of their trouble, not knawn what to do,
A voice from the shore gravely cried out Hoo! Hoo!
How noo, Mister Hoo! Hoo! is thou myekin fun?
Or is this the first keel that thou e'er saw agrun'?

>   Fal de ral la, etc.

Agyen it cried Hoo! Hoo! the skipper he stampt,
An' sung oot for Geordy to heave oot a plank ;
Iv a raving mad passion he cursed and he swore,
Aw'll hoo-hoo ye, ye beggar, when aw cum ashore.

>   Fal de ral la, etc.

Wiv a coal in each hand, ashore then he went,
To kill Mister Hoo-Hoo it was his intent,
But when he gat there, O what his surprise !
When back he cam runnin—Oh ! Geordy, he cries.

>   Fal de ral la, etc.

Wey, whe dis thou think hez been myekin this gam,
Aw'll lay thou maw wallet thou'll not guess his nyem!
"Is't the ghost of au'd Lizzie?"—Oh no, no, thou fool, it
Is ne ghost at all, but—an au'd Jenny Howlet!

Fal de ral la, etc.

ARMSTRONG.   *Marshall's Chap-Book*, 1823.

THE BABOON.

SUM time since sum wild beasts thor cam te the toon,
And in the collection a famous baboon,
In uniform drest;—if maw story yor willin'
To believe, he gat lowse, an' ran te the High Fellin'.

Fal de rol la, etc.

Three pitmen com up—they war smokin' thor pipe—
When strite in afore them Jake lowp'd ower the dyke;
"Ho, Jemmy! smash, marrow! here's a reed-coated Jew,
For his fyece is a' hairy, an' he hez on ne shoe!"

"Wey, man, thou's a fuil! for ye divent tell true,
If thou says 'at that fellow was iver a Jew:
Aw'll lay thou a quairt, as sure as me nyem's Jack,
That queer-luckin' chep's just a Rooshin Cossack!

"He's ne volunteer—aw ken biv his wauk;
And if he's ootlandish we'll ken biv his tauk,
He's a lang sword ahint him—ye'll see'd when he turns;
Ony luik at his fyece!—smash his byens, how he gurns!"

Tom flung doon his pipe an' set up a greet yell—
"He's owther a spy or Bonnypairty's awnsel!"
Iv a crack the High Fellin' wes in full hue an' cry,
To catch Bonnypairt, or the hairy French spy.

The wives scamper'd off for fear he shud bite ;
The men folks an' dogs ran te grip him se tight :
" If we catch him," said they, "he'll hev ne lodgin' here,
Ne, not e'en a drop o' Reed Robin's sma' beer !"

ARMSTRONG.   *Marshall's Collection*, 1827.

THE GLISTER.

SOME time since a Pitman was tyen varry bad,
So ca'd his wife Mall te the side of his bed ;
" Thou mun run for a docter, the forst can be fund,
For maw belly's a' rang, an' aw'm varry fast bund."

" Wey, man, thou's a fuil, aw ken thou's fast boon,
Wi' thy last bindin munny thou bowt this new goon :
Ne docter can lowse thou one morsel or crum,
For thou's bun te Tyne Main for this ten month te
      cum."

" Aw divvent mean that,—maw belly's se sair,
Run fast, or aw'll dee lang afore ye get there !"
So away Mally ran te thor awn docter's shop,
" Gie me somethin for Tom, for his belly's stopt up."

A glister she gat—and ne langer she'd wait,
But strite she ran hyem an' gat oot a clean plate :
" Oh Tommy, maw Tom, ony haud up thy heed,
Here's somethin 'll mend thee, suppose thou wes deed.

" Thou mun eat up that haggish, but sup the thin forst,
Aw's frighten'd that stopple it will be the worst."
" Oh Mally ! thou'll puzzen poor Tom altegither,
If aw drink a' the thin an' then eat up the blethur."

He managed it a' wiv a greet deal to do :
"Oh Mally, oh Mally ! thoo's puzzen'd me noo."
But she tuik ne notice of poor Tommy's pain,
But straight she ran off te the docter's again.

"Oh docter, maw hinny ! Tom's tyened a' thegither,
He supp'd up the thin, then he eat up the blethur ;
The blethur was tuif, it myest stuck iv his thropple ;
If he haddent bad teeth he wad eaten the stopple !"

"Oh woman, you have been in too great a hurry,
'Stead of mendin your husband, you'll have him to bury,
'Stead of makin him better, poor Tommy must go,
For you've put in his mouth what we put up below."

ARMSTRONG.   *Marshall's Collection*, 1827.

———

THE FLOATIN' GRUNSTAN.

TUNE—"*Derry down.*"

NOT lang since sum keelmen wer' gaun doon te Sheels,
When a hoop roond sum froth cam alangside thor keel.
The Skipper saw'd first, an' he gov a greet shoot,
How, begger, man, Dick, here's a grunstan afloat.

Derry down, etc.

Dick leuk'd, an' he thowt that the Skipper was reet,
So they'd hev her ashore, an' then sell her that neet :
Then he jumped on te fetch her—my eyes !—what a
    splatter,
Ne grunstan wes there, for he fand it wes watter.

Derry down, etc.

The Skipper astonished, quite struck wi' surprise,
He roar'd oot te Dickey when he saw him rise—
How, smash, marrow—Dick, ho! what is thou aboot?
Cum here, mun, an' let's hae the grunstan tyen oot.

Derry down, etc.

A grunstan! says Dick—whey, ye slaverin cull,
Wi' watter maw belly an' pockets are full;
By the gowkey, aw'll sweer that yor drunk, daft, or
    doatin'—
It's ne grunstan at a', but sum aud iron floatin'.

Derry down, etc.

ARMSTRONG.   *Marshall's Collection*, 1827.

THE SKIPPER IN THE MIST.

A FOG on the Tyne plays the deuce 'mang the keels,
As wor skipper once fund as he sailed doon te Sheels;
The fog com se thick, wig in hand, he did roar,
"Aw mun lay by my swape—Geordy, lay by your oar!

Derry down, etc.

"Now, hinnies, me marrows! come tell's what to dee,
Aw's frightened wor keel will seun drive out to sea!"
So the men an' their skipper each sat on their buttock,
An' a council they held, wi' their legs down the huddock.

Derry down, etc.

Says Geordy, "We canna be very far down,
Wi' the wash o' my oar, aw hev just touched the grund;
Cheer up, my awd skipper, put on yor awd wig,
We're between the King's Meedows an' Newcassel Brig."

Derry down, etc.

The skipper, enraged, then declared he kenn'd better,
For at the same time he had smelt the salt wetter;
"And there's Marsden Rock, just within a styen thraw,
Aw can see't throo the mist, aw'll swear by my reet paw.

> Derry down, etc.

"The anchor let's drop till the weather it clears,
For fear we be nabb'd by the French privateers!"
The anchor was dropt; when the weather clear'd up,
They fund th' keel moor'd at th' awd Javil Group.

> Derry down, etc.

The skipper was vex'd, and he curs'd and he swore,
That his nose had ne'er led him se far wrang before;
But what most of all did surprise these four people
Was Marsden Rock chang'd into Gateshed Church
steeple.

> Derry down, etc.

ARMSTRONG.   *Fordyce's " Newcastle Song Book," 1842.*

BILLY OLIVER'S RAMBLE BETWEEN BENWELL AND NEWCASTLE.

"Billy Oliver's Ramble" is first met in Marshall's Chap-Books, 1823. No author is given, and although the song has been very popular and often printed, none have given an author's name. H. Robson, who wrote "The Collier's Pay Week," was born in Benwell; he was writing in 1823, and may have written it. The names of others then writing, as Shield, Armstrong, Watson, Oliver, etc., might be given. Possibly the author, owing to his song holding the pitman so much up to ridicule, may have judged it best to " lie low."

The popularity of this song brought out a parody, " My Nyem is Willy Dixon." It appeared in Fordyce's 1842 volume.

ME nyem it's Billy Oliver,
  Iv Benwell town aw dwell;
An' aw's a clever chep, aw's shure,
  Tho' aw de say'd me-sell.
Sec an a clever chep am aw, am aw, am aw,
     Sec an a clever chep am aw.

There's not a lad iv a' wur wark,
   Can put or hew wi' me ;
Nor not a lad iv Benwell toon,
   Can coax the lasses sae.

               Sec an a clever chep, etc.

When aw gans tiv Newcassel toon,
   Aw myeks me-sell sae fine,
Wur neybors stand and stare at me,
   And say, "Eh ! what a shine ! "

               Sec an a clever chep, etc.

An' then aw walks wi' sec an air,
   That, if the folks hev eyes,
They a'wis think it's sum great man,
   That's cumin i' disguise.

               Sec an a clever chep, etc.

An' when aw gans down Westgate Street,
   An' alang biv Denton Chare,
Aw whussels a' the way aw gans,
   To myek the people stare.

               Sec an a clever chep, etc.

An' then aw gans intiv the Cock,
   Ca's for a pint o' beer ;
An' when the lassie cums in wid,
   Aw a'wis says, Maw dear !

               Sec an a clever chep, etc.

An' when aw gets a pint o' beer,
   Aw a'wis sings a sang ;
For aw've a nice yen aw can sing,
   Six an' thorty vairses lang.

               Sec an a clever chep, etc.

An' if the folks that's i' the house
  Cry, " Haud yur tongue, ye cull ! "
Aw's sure to hev a fight wi' them,
  For aw's as strang as ony bull.

> Sec an a clever chep, etc.

An' when aw've had a fight or twee,
  An' fairly useless grown;
Aw back, as drunk as aw can be,
  To canny Benwell toon.

> Sec an a clever chep, etc.

ANONYMOUS.   *Marshall's Chap-Book*, 1823.

THE DEVIL; OR, THE NANNY GOAT.

"The Shields Song Book, being a Collection of comic and sentimental songs never before published, Written by Gentlemen of the neighbourhood. South Shields, printed by C. W. Barnes, Thrift Street, 1826." Such is the title of the book (about 24 pages) from which the three following songs are taken. Who these gentlemen of the neighbourhood were the book does not say. All the songs are anonymous, and inquiries lately to trace the writers of them have resulted in little. The *Shields Gazette* a few months ago kindly inserted an inquiry, but nothing came of it. A Shields gentleman recollects the printer of the book, Mr. Barnes. It appears somewhere between five and ten years after issuing the book he left the printing and started as an auctioneer; that of course was long ago, and for many years he has been dead. Possibly from what is known of Mr. Barnes he may have had to do, at least, with the writing of some of the songs. The comic dialect songs are the best in the book, and resemble very much Armstrong's humorous productions.

A copy of the "Shields Song Book" is in the Public Library, South Shields.

SOME bullies gaun doun i' their keel late at night,
Met sic a still gale that it ga' them a fright;
Now, aw think this might be just about twelve o'clock,
And the keel at that time was abreest Howdon Dock.

> Fal lal la, etc.

The bullies and pee-dee a' huddl'd thegither,
Yen an' a' did agree it was terrible weather;
To bring her up there then they thowt it wad be
The best plan, so they got her in close to the quay.

So they a' got below, an' they started to gob;
Seun a chep's turnip field they agreed for to rob;
So the pee-dee was left i' the keel biv hees-sel,
An' for robbing he thowt they wad sure gan to hell.

As they were returning agyen frae the fields,
A Nanny Goat followed them close by their heels;
She was eating the skins as they threw them away,
For she liked them far better than any new hay.

When the bullies had getten agyen to their keel,
The pee-dee he ax'd them if they'd seen the deil;
The Nanny by this time had getten aboard,
So they thowt he was coming—they call'd on the Lord.

Now Nan couldn't find either skins, beef, or bread,
So she went to the huddock an' popp'd down her head,
And seeing them champ what she thowt was her share,
Stretch'd her neck an' jaws wide, and gov a greet blare.

The bullies didn't know how this devil to lay,
However, they thowt 'twas the best plan to pray;
So the skipper roar'd out iv a terrible swe't,
"Our Fetheers chart in Heven—is the beggar gyen
　　yet?"

The prayer not being answer'd, they started to bubble,
For they thowt they were left by the father in trouble;
So they fell on their faces, and stopping their breath,
Swore they'd rather die there as be dragg'd to their death.

The innocent pee-dee thowt he'd nowt to fear,
So he'd venture on deck and see if all was clear;
When the Nanny saw pee-dee she blar'd out a note,
And their devil prov'd only a poor Nanny Goat.

ANONYMOUS.   *Shields Song Book*, 1826.

———

THE CLIFFS OF VIRGINIA.

TUNE—"Drops of Brandy."

SOME brave lads in their keel left the spout,
    It blew a fresh breeze from the west;
Now happy they were without doubt,
    And to Providence left all the rest.
The breeze seun increased to a gale,
    The tide ran down rapid and rough,
For safety they teuk in the sail,
    For by this time they'd most had eneugh.
                    Rum ti iddity, etc.

To stop her they now were not able,
    Says the skipper, "We'll drive to the ocean,
Thraw ower the chain-anchor and cable,
    For of sic a trip aw ha' ne notion."
The keel by this time was near swamp'd,
    So they threw all the coals overboard;
The skipper he shouted and stamped,
    And for the help of good Providence roar'd.

On the deck they could no longer stand,
    So they pray'd both for succour and shelter,
Bid adieu to their awn native land,
    And to the huddock they ran helter-skelter:

15

There they rattled and tumbled about,
  They pray'd for their bairns and wives,
And if Providence spar'd, without doubt,
  They surely wad mend all their lives.

This night spent in devotion and fasting,
  They long'd for to see the sun rise ;
Skipper swore his repentance was lasting,
  If it wasn't the deil d—n his eyes.
The gale being entirely hush'd,
  And the sun was beginning to shine ;
Up his heed then he carefully push'd,
  And he says, "Lads, we'll ne'er see the Tyne."

The skipper roar'd out for Ben Mackey,
  To see the high cliffs of Virgini,
Where they grow all the green tea and baccy ;
  Ay, as sure as I'm living, my hinny.
The folks aw believe are all wild,
  An' sure they will some of us fry ;
But now we're all meekness and mild,
  We needn't mind how seun we die.

A steamer seun cam within hail—
  They ax'd skipper how he got there :
"We gat here during the last heavy gale ;
  If ye please, sur, what land is that there ?"
"Wey divn't you knaw Tynemouth Cassell ?"
  "Od, smash me, a' tuek'd for Virgini's."
So they row'd hard an' strang for Newcassell,
  And lang'd for a kiss o' their hinnies.

ANONYMOUS.   *Shields Song Book*, 1826.

THE SKIPPER'S MISTAKE.

TUNE—"The Chapter of Accidents."

Two jovial souls, two skippers bold,
  Were sailing down one morning
In their keel black as the deil,
  All fear and danger scorning.
The sky luck'd bright and seem'd to promise
  A fair and glorious day, man;
But soon a mighty mist came on,
  And they cud not see their way, man.

Fal lal la, etc.

They pull'd about fra' reet to left,
  But not knowing what to do, man;
When poor pee-dee began to fret
  Lest they should gaun to sea, man.
Says Geordy, " Should wor voyage be lang,
  We've little stuffing for wor gut, man;
There's nowt but raw tates and caud cabbage,
  Some tripe and a nowt foot, man."

They got down as far as Jarrow slake,
  When Geordy bawl'd aloud, man:
" Smash marrow, you're a bit of a scholar,
  Can't you find our latitude, man?
Run the ways into the huddock, Jack,
  And fetch up the reada-ma-deasy, man,
And let's see where abouts we are,
  To keep wor minds easy, man."

They studied hard, byeth lang and sair,
  Though hardly they cud read, man;
When Jack suddenly starts up,
  " Aw hev it i' my heed, man.

Let's pray to Heaven to keep us free
  Frae all danger and mischance, man;
We're ower the bar, there's nowt left for us,
  But either Holland or France, man."

At length the day began to clear,
  The sun peep'd through the dew, man;
When lo, aud-fashion'd Jarrow kirk
  Appear'd fair to their view, man.
They laugh'd and crack'd about the joke,
  And Geordy said, "Smash marrow, man,
Instead of being at Holland or France,
  We're only off at Jarrow, man."

May wealth and commerce still increase,
  And bless our native isle, man;
And make each thriving family
  In prosperity to smile, man;
And the coal trade flourish more and more,
  Upon our dingy Tyne, man.

ANONYMOUS.   *Shields Song Book*, 1826.

––––––

WILLIAM OLIVER.

WILLIAM OLIVER, whose "Newcassel Props" is justly
esteemed as one of the best of the old Tyneside songs, was
born in the Side, Newcastle-on-Tyne, on the 5th February
1800. His father was a cheesemonger, who during the
latter part of his life carried on business on his own account
in the Side. The business selected for his son was that of
a draper and hatter; and the earlier part of the poet's life
was passed with Mr. Bowes, at the Bridge End, Gateshead,
following that occupation. Eventually leaving Mr. Bowes,
he joined with his brother Timothy, who carried on business
as a grocer at the corner of the High Bridge, in the Cloth
Market, and with his brother he remained until his death.

From a collection of his songs and poems, published in 1829, and inscribed to Robert Bell, Esq., Mayor of Newcastle, we extract the following :—

TO THE MECHANICS' INSTITUTE OF NEWCASTLE-UPON-TYNE.

Hail ! Temple of Science, break forth in thy splendour,
  And scatter around thee a halo of light ;
Strike off the fetters of genius, and lend her
  The pinions of learning to aid in her flight.

Illumine the mind of the genius, who, friendless,
  And struggling with poverty, kneels at thy shrine ;
Enrich from thy treasure, so varied, so endless ;
  Though fortune disowns him, adopt him as thine.

Oh ! say, can the 'vantage of fortune or birth ;
  Can heraldry's pomp, or the pageant's glare ;
Can the proudest of titles, unhallowed by worth,
  With the name of a Watt or a Bewick compare ?

How vain are the efforts of marble and sculpture
  O'er the tombs of the worthless a radiance to shed !
The blazoned escutcheon, the gorgeous sepulchre,
  Are vain, for how soon is their memory dead !

The stirring political agitation of the years preceding the passing of the great Reform Bill of 1832 found in him an ardent sympathiser ; and his lines to the memory of Riego, the Spanish patriot, and "England, Awake," are spirited pieces in praise of liberty. The songs in the volume are few, and form but a small part of the work. They, like the old local songs, relate to events and eccentrics of the town. They are cleverly written, and were highly popular in their day, when the events and characters to which they referred were well known. Time has a little lessened their popularity ; but there is little doubt his songs—especially the "Newcassel Props"—will always retain a high position amongst the best of Tyneside songs. The author died, at the comparatively early age of forty-eight, on the 29th October 1848, and was buried at the Westgate Cemetery, Arthur's Hill.

The preceding sketch of Oliver appeared in our 1872 edition. The information there was got from his brother Timothy. Time has made changes since then. Timothy is now dead, and as both brothers were unmarried, further information is difficult to obtain. From the little fresh we have gleaned, it appears his father before he opened in the Side was a cheesemonger, doing business at the Old Market Cross. Years after, the making of Grey Street by Grainger finished this old market, but a remnant of its site may still be seen in the open square opposite Watson's gates, High Bridge. It also appears, the poet, about 1830, before he joined with his brother Timothy, had a try at business on his own account as a hatter. The venture was made in the Side, near his birthplace. It was short and unsuccessful, and after that came the joining with Timothy.

Social meetings, held at public-houses amongst the tradesmen, after business hours, appears then to have been the rage, and William Oliver, a writer and singer of Tyneside songs, would be a welcome member. "Sons of Apollo," "Stars of Friendship," "Corinthian Society," these are some of the names that have been handed down. "The Corinthian Society" seems to have been Oliver's favourite. In his volume several of the poetical addresses which he delivered before the members are given. In addition to these, we have been favoured by Mr. W. H. Hastings with the loan of an old manuscript volume which belonged to his father. His father was one of the old Corinthians, and the volume contains poetical pieces by various members, some, as Oliver and W. Gill Thompson, well known, others, as R. Hobkirk and P. Galloway, but little, if ever known, and now about forgotten. A few extracts from the old manuscripts may be interesting.

The praise of Corinth and the local Corinthians are thus sung—

. . . .

"   Go find me a diadem pleasing for ever,
        All are sullied by age and impaired by decay ;
     But this I have wreath'd for you perishes never,
        Its charms are for ever unfading and gay.
     'Tis the crown of true friendship, the faithful may share it,
        And boast it the choice and the pride of the Tyne.
     I have wreath'd it, Corinthians accept it and wear it—
        The garland of Corinth enwreathed with the vine."

Delivered June 4th, 1827.   D. H. (LIKELY D. HOBKIRK).

Three months later the Corinthians listen to the following and six more verses—

"   Companions of my social hours,
        The circling year is on the wane ;
     Withering are the mountain flowers,
        The daisy's dying on the plain.

. . . . . .

Oh, here then on each meeting night
Let varied themes still roll along,
Till every eye beams with delight,
Till every heart be linked to song."

Delivered August 29th, 1827. P. G. (LIKELY P. GALLOWAY).

Unsigned, but between two pieces, the one by Thompson and the other by Oliver, is a short piece in which the writer sings of the fall of Corinth, and of its Tyneside successor. The following is an extract :—

•   •   •   •   •

" Corinth no longer in her grandeur smiles,
Mute is the harp where dreary ruin reigns.

•   •   •   •   •

Yet other lands have caught the glowing strain
The pensive melody, the martial song.
Corinth, thy ancient harp resounds again
Where rolls the Tyne its beauteous banks among."

•   •   •   •   •

May 21st, 1830. UNKNOWN.

The first, fifth, and sixth verses from a piece by W. O. (Oliver) may finish these—

" I cannot enwreath in the garland I bring
The rarest of flowers in their odours and hue ;
To the wild strains of fancy their beauties I fling,
The breath of the heart is the odour for you.

•   •   •   •   •   •

The favoured to fortune, the strangers to care,
May boast of their transient, fanciful bliss ;
But oh, in their toil after pleasure, how rare
Do they taste of a heart-leaping moment like this.

Then pledge me once more in a bumper, and swear,
With the heart on the lip and the soul in the eye,
That the couch of the mourner will still be your care,
As the Angel of Mercy ye still will be nigh."

Delivered Dec. 27th, 1830. W. O. (LIKELY WILLIAM OLIVER).

Death breaks into the Corinthian band. Alexander Donkin, a young man of twenty-four, dies on February 12th, 1825. Two of his friends lament him ; a verse from each follows :—

" Thou sleepest now, and what shall make thee
Break thy slumbers so profound ;
A thousand thunders will not wake thee
Till the judgment trump shall sound."

W. O. (WILLIAM OLIVER).

"No! thoughts of him shall never perish
In a true Corinthian breast;
Corinthians will his memory cherish,
Till like himself they glide to rest."

P. G. (P. GALLOWAY).

Another of the Corinthians, Richard Young, dying, Oliver and Hobkirk both have very feeling pieces on his untimely death:—

To the Memory of RICHARD YOUNG, who died November 4th, 1831, aged 29.   Deeply and deservedly regretted.

Corinth, a light hath left thee now,
    A gem which ne'er can be restored;
The dauntless heart, the manly brow,
    Hath left thy friendship-circled board.
Mute is the tongue, which the heart unveil'd,
And the heart is at rest that never quailed.

Farewell, the grateful task be ours to keep
    Thy name and virtues from oblivion's wave;
To mourn thy early call to that long sleep,
    And lay thy failings with thee in the grave;
To wear thee in "our heart of hearts" embalmed,
Until, like thee, we lie in death becalmed.

Nov. 4th, 1831.   WILLIAM OLIVER.

To the Memory of R. YOUNG.

(4th verse.)
I could have wished once more to say farewell,
    And once again to clasp thy hand in mine;
It may not be, not even friendship's spell
    Can win a smile back to those lips of thine.

Nov. 8th, 1831.   D. HOBKIRK.

These selections give a fair idea of the contents of the old book, and show the taste current some sixty years ago.

On the publication of his volume in 1829 Oliver appears to have had a taste of the political partisan criticism too common at the time. It was the eve of the great Reform Bill, and political feeling ran high. Oliver appears to have been a Whig. This was enough for *The Northern John Bull.* Catching at some trifling allusions in his songs as an excuse, it fastened on them, and reminded Oliver that he should be the last to write of personal appearances, as about himself they could a tale unfold, . . . and if he did not beware, they would. . . . These ungenerous threats, there is little doubt, referred to a slight lameness or deformity in one of Oliver's legs, which, while little, yet in walking could be detected. It also would refer to a cast which Oliver had in the eye, which was slight, and ought not even by inference to have been brought against him.

Through the courtesy of Matthew Mackey, Jun., Esq., we are enabled to give the following autograph and *fac-*

Tell me not, that hearts can sever
Once by sacred Friendship join'd
Clouds may come but warm as ever
The sun of kindness smiles behind.
Soon his beams the cloud dispels
And heart to heart, past scenes compels

William Oliver

June 10th 1829.

Photographed by P. M. Laws (slightly reduced).

simile of the poet's handwriting, which is in a copy of his poems, formerly belonging to Joseph Crawshaw, Esq.

Perhaps a few lines from his piece on the death of C. J. Brandling, M.P., may come in here. The open-handed bounty of the Brandlings is yet spoken of, and Oliver but put into verse the feeling their generosity had raised.

ON THE DEATH OF (FEB. 1, 1826) C. J. BRANDLING, M.P.

He is gone—the poor man's ready friend,
The orphan's father, and the widow's stay;
The prop of age, the best of masters, sleeps
Now in the tomb! But words are idle all,
And marble far too cold to speak his praise.
On a nobler monument his virtues
Shall be graven,—on many a swelling heart,
Whose sorrows he hath lightened, and made glad.

A portrait of Oliver would have been an interesting addition; but while several recollect him, none have a likeness. At his favourite Corinthian Society, which was held at the Blue Posts, Pilgrim Street, he delivered a poetical address on the closing of the season on Whit-Tuesday, May 27th, 1828. From this piece, which is the last in his volume, we take the closing verses.

VERSES ADDRESSED TO THE CORINTHIAN SOCIETY ON CLOSING FOR THE SEASON, WHIT-TUESDAY, MAY 27TH, 1828.

When from this circle I depart,
  I quit the early friends I gained;
I leave the generous open heart,
  Aye, and a crown, for I have reigned
O'er those whom love not fear could quell,
To whom I ne'er would say—farewell.

The time will come, it must be so,
  Yet ere I quit this cherished scene,
Assure my heart before I go
  To rest beneath my shroud of green,
Your thoughts will sometimes stray and dwell
On him who bids ye now—farewell.

Beneath his "shroud of green" he lies in Westgate Hill Cemetery. No stone marks his grave, which may be found near the centre of the Cemetery, and just behind the tombstone of one George Elliott. An elder tree marks the spot.

———

THE NEWCASSEL PROPS.

TUNE—"The Bold Dragoon."

OH, waes me, wor canny toon, it canna stand it lang—
The props are tumblin one by one, the beeldin seun mun
    gan;
For deeth o' late hez no been blate, but sent some jovial
    souls a joggin,
Aw niver grieved for Jacky Tate, nor even little Airchy
    Loggan.

But when maw lugs was 'lectrified wi' Judy Downey's
    deeth,
Alang wi' Heuffy Scott aw cried, till byeth was oot o'
    breeth ;
For greet an' sma', fishwives an' a', luik'd up te her wi'
    veneration—
If Judy's in the courts above, then for Aud Nick ther'll be
    ne 'cation.

Next Captain Starkey teuk his stick, and myed his final
    bow,
Aw wonder if he's scribblin yet, or what he's efter now;
Or if he's drinkin gills o' yell, and axin pennies te buy
    baccy—
If not allowed where Starkey's gyen, aw'm sure that he'll
    be quite unhappy.

Jack Coxon iv a trot went off one mornin varry seun—
Cull Billy said he'd better stop, but deeth cried, Jacky,
    come !
Oh, few like him could lift thor heels, or tell what halls
    were in the county ;
Like mony a proud black-coated chiel, Jack lived upon
    the parish bounty.

But cheer up, lads, an' dinna droop, Blind Willie's ti the
    fore,
The blythest iv the motley groop, an' fairly worth the
    score ;
O, weel aw like te hear him sing, 'bout young Sir Mat
    an' Dr. Brummel—
If he but lives to see the king, thor's nyen o' Willie's
    frinds need grummel.

Cull Billy, tee, wor lugs te bliss, wiv news 'bout t'other
    warld,
Aw move that when wor Vicar dees, the place for him be
    arl'd;
For aw really think, wiv half his wit, he'd myek a reet
    gud pulpit knocker,
Aw'll tell ye where the berth wad fit, he hugs se close
    the parish copper.

Another chep and then aw's deun, he bangs the tuthers
    far,
Yor mevies wonderin whe aw mean—ye gowks! it's
    Tommy Carr!
When lodgin's scairce just speak ti him, yor hapless case
    he'll surely pitty,
He'll 'sist upon yor gannin in, te sup wi' Scott, an' see
    the Kitty.

OLIVER.   *Author's Edition,* 1829.

———

THE BONASSUS.

About 1821, Wombwell, with his collection of wild beasts, came to Newcastle, with an extra attraction in the form of a rare animal, which he
called a "Bonassus." It was puffed as a great curiosity, and made a considerable stir at that time. The wonderful "Bonassus" was, in reality, a
buffalo.

TUNE—" Jemmy Johnson's Wherry."

LET Wombwell, James, an' a' the pack
    Iv yelpin' curs, beef-eaters,
Ne mair aboot Bonasses crack,
    Them queer, ootlandish creturs.
Be dumb, ye leeing, yammerin' hoonds!
    Nor wi' yor clavers fash us;
For suen aw'll prove wor canny toon
    Can boast its awn Bonassus.

It chanced when honest Bell was mayor,
  An' gat each poor man's blessin'—
When cheps like Gee an' Tommy Carr
  Gat monny a gratis lessin'—
Then Bell refused te stand agyen,
  Tired iv the sitiwation,
An' ne awd wife wad tyek the chain
  Iv a' wor Corporation.

The folks iv Sheels hez lang begrudg'd
  The Custom Hoose beside us;
This was the time, they reetly judg'd,
  Ti cum se fine 'langside us.
They had a chep (Wright was his nyem),
  Ti poor folk rether scurvy,
They sent him up wor heeds te kyem,
  An' turn us topsy-turvy.

He suen began ti show his horns,
  An' treat the poor like vassals:
He sent the apple wives te mourn
  A month i' wor aud Cassel.
The *timber marchints* will ne mair
  Wiv "ten a penny" deave us:
They sweer if Wright's ti be wor mayor,
  That i' the dark they'll leave us!

The drapers next he gov a gleece,
  'Bout thor unruly samples:
Bund ower the cloots te keep the peace,
  Wiv strings to the door stanchels.
The tatee market iv a tift—
  (Ye heuxters, a' resent it!
My certies! but that was a shift!)
  Ti the Parade Grund sent it.

Ye gowks! frae Sheels ye've oft slipt up,
   When ye had little 'cashun,
Te see wor snobs thor capers cut,
   Or Geordy's Coranashun.
Now altegither come wonce mair,
   Wor blissins shall attend ye,
If ye'll but rid us i' wor mayor,
   I' hacknies back we'll send ye.

OLIVER.   *Author's Edition*, 1829.

TIM TUNBELLY.

The name given by W. A. Mitchell to a series of letters he wrote for his
paper, *The Tyne Mercury.* The letters began in October 1821, and lasted a
little over a year. Tim, with an unsparing hand, exposed the abuses then
existing in the unreformed Corporation. In 1828 the letters were reprinted
in volume form, price five shillings.

Now lay up your lugs, a' ye freemen that's poor,
   An' aw'll rhyme without pension or hire—
Come listen, ye dons, that keep cows on the Moor,
   Though ye couldn't keep them iv a byre—
An' a' ye non-freemen wherever ye be,
   Though dame Fortune has myed sic objections,
That you're neither o' Town nor o' Trinity free,
   To be brib'd an' get drunk at elections.

When aw was but little, aw mind varry weel
   That Joe C——k was the friend o' the freemen—
Aw mysel' heard him say, his professions to seal,
   He wad care very little to dee, man.
Corporation corruptions he sair did expose,
   And show'd plain whee was rook and whee pigeon—
While El——h, the cobbler, in fury arose,
   And pummell'd Sir M——w's religion.

Some sly common councilman happen'd to think
    That the patriots each had a pocket—
So they sent Joe an order for wafers and ink,
    And the Custom-House swallow'd the prophet.
Now if ever these worthies should happen to dee,
    And Au'd Nick scamper off wiv his booty,
Just imagine yoursels what reformin there'll be,
    If belaw there's nee printin nor duty.

But there's honest folk yet now, so dinna be flaid,
    Though El——h and Joe hes desarted—
For a chep they ca' Tunbelly's ta'en up the trade,
    And bizzy he's been sin' he started :
Aboot town-surveyin' he's open'd wor eyes,
    And put Tommy Gee in a pickle—
He's gi'en to Jack Procter a birth i' the skies,
    And immortal he's render'd Bob Nichol.

Now, if ony refuse to the freemen their dues,
    They're far greater fules than aw thowt them—
Let R——y ne mair stand godfather ti cows,
    Nor his cousin swear on—till he's bowt them.
Niver mind what the cheps o' the council may say,
    He'll seun sattle obstropolous Billy—
Ne mair he'll refuse for a way-leave to pay,
    For fear o' the ditch and Tunbelly.

The good that he's duen scarce a volume wad tell,
    But there's one thing that will be a wonder—
If Tunbelly losses conceit iv his sel'
    Till his head the green sod be laid under.

But we a' hae wor likens, what for shouldn't Tim ?
   An' aw'm shure he a mense to wor town is—
So fill up yor glasses once mair to the brim,
   And drink to the Newcassel JUNIUS.

OLIVER.   *Author's Edition,* 1829.

THE NEWCASTLE MILLERS.

Written on the great prize fight, at Barlow Fell, between Jim Wallace and Tom Dunn, fought on the 25th October 1824, for forty sovereigns. Wallace was the victor.

TUNE—"The Bold Dragoon."

Now hail, thou pride iv a' the Tyne, my glorious native
    toun !
As lang as aw can cum ti time, thy nyem shall ne'er gan
    doun ;
Fame hez been lang, wi' glorious moves, the pages i' thy
    hist'ry filling,
But now she sports her boxing-gloves, an' nowt gans
    doon but rings an' milling.

The fancy lads that thou can boast wad tyek an 'oor ti
    tell,
Let Cockneys tawk o' Moulsey Hurst, we'll crack iv
    Barlow Fell.
Jim B——n hez up te Lunnin gyen, ti show them hoo ti
    hit an' parry ;
But still we've bits iv blud at hyem, that for a croon wad
    box Aud Harry.

The greet turn-up we've had between Jim Wallace an'
    Tom Dunn,
Sum wished that day they'd nivver seen, an' that boxers
    a' were hung ;

The butcher lads had a' ti pay, sum pawn'd thor watches, sum thor horses,
An' a' the Tuesday neet, they say, that Morpeth turnpike rung wi' curses.

The 'prentice lads that stole away ti see the champions peel,
They'll mind o' that, for mony a day they walked upon a wheel:
Their half-'oor time they learn'd ti keep, a sitiwation rether tryin',
Just like the chep iv Collingwood Street, that's huggin' tiv his nose a lion.

Let men iv science bounce and swell, gi'e me the glass ti swing,
A nice snug room for Barlow Fell, filled wiv a jovial ring;
Then them that will may tyek thor bangs, the science that aw most delight in
Is drinkin' yell an' hearin' sangs, let Dunn an' Wallace tyek the fightin'.

OLIVER. *Author's Edition*, 1829.

THE LAMENT.

TUNE—"The Bold Dragoon."

A BARD hez said that "dowly thowts are mair wor frinds than foes"—
As frinds are rether scarce, ye ken, aw've browt a mournful dose;
Deeth rammels on throo lane an' square, an' wiv his dart byeth wives an' men pricks,
Od bliss him! wad he oney spare wor canny toon her greet eccentrics.

16

Bet Watt an' *Soulger Mally's* gyen!—Yence mair his
    dart he threw,
An' slew the bonniest an' the last—the maid they called
    Balloo:
Ti hear her sweer how oft aw've staid, an' gazed upon
    her linsey-winsey;
But Jenny's cracks are now aw laid aboot her bruther,
    greet Lord Linsay.

Mysell aw suen began ti hug when *Crummy* was laid law,
Aw thowt the yell wad be a drug, 'twas sartin shure ti
    fa';
Ti see him drink, that was a treat,—his thropple seemed
    a hogshead funnel;
An' now that Crummy's lost his feet, it sarves, aw fancy,
    for a tunnel.

A story yence myed Sandgate ring, the Keyside a' luik
    blue—
'Twas then a hoax, or sum sic thing, but noo it's cum
    ower true;
Oh, had it been a duke or lord, aw wonder whe wad
    cared a scuddick;—
Bold Archy's popped at last owerbord, slipt withoot bait
    intiv his huddick.

His cradle was the keel deck, where Britannia seeks her
    tars—
She quickly spied the hero there, an' called him ti the
    wars;
He thump'd the Spanish Dons, 'twas said, till they roared
    oot for peace like ninnies,
For yence, at least, was Archy paid his good shag hat
    chock full iv ginnies.

Men are se dwiney nooadays, that honest Archy cam
    Ti gi' the world, as Shakesperre says, asshurance iv a
      man ;
Ti see him cummin' up the Kee, se independent, stiff,
    an' starchy—
His like agyen we'll nivver see—peace ti the byens iv
    poor Bold Archy !
    OLIVER.   *Author's Edition*, 1820.

THE NEW MARKETS.

"The completion of the New Markets at Newcastle, by Richard Grainger,
was celebrated by a public dinner on the 22nd of October 1835. The Mayor
presided, and nearly 2000 individuals sat down under one roof (that of the
Green Market), which forms but a mere section of the splendid erections.
These markets are the most magnificent in the world." . . .—*Richardson's
Table-Book.*

Besides Oliver, both Mitford and Gilchrist have songs on the opening of
the New Markets.

    TUNE—" Canny Newcassel."

WEY, hinnies, but this is a wonderful scene,
    Like sum change that yen's seen iv a playhoose ;
Whe iver wad thowt that the aud Major's dene
    Wad hae myed sic a capital wey-hoose?
Where the brass hez a' cum frae nebody can tell,
    Some says yen thing, and some says another ;
But whe iver lent Grainger 't, aw knaw very well
    That they mun hev at least had a fother.

Chorus.
Aboot Lunnen, then, divvent ye myek sic a rout,
    For thor's nowt there maw winkers ti dazzle ;
For a bell or a market thor issent a doot,
    We can bang them at canny Newcassel.

Wor gratitude Grainger or sumbody's arl'd,
    Yet still mun it myeks yen a' shuther,
Te see sic a crood luikin' efter this warld
    Where the Nuns used ti luik for the tuther.

But see yor awn interest—dinna be blind,
  Tyek a shop there whativer yor trade is;
Genteeler cumpany where can ye find
  Then wor butchers, green wives, an' tripe ladies?
                              Aboot Lunnen, etc.

Ti see the wives haggle aboot tripe an' sheep heeds,
  Or weshing thor greens at a foontain,
Where the bonny Nuns used te be tellin' thor beeds,
  An' had nowt but thor sins ti be coontin';
There the talented lords o' the cleaver an' steel
  May be heard on that classical grund, sir,
Loodly chantin' the praise o' thor mutton an' veal,
  Tho' thor loosin' a happney a pund, sir,
                              Aboot Lunnen, etc.

When them queer Cockney folk cum stravagin' this way
  (Tho' aw've lang thowt we'd gettin' aboon them),
They'll certainly now hae the mense just te say,
  That we've clapt an extingisher on them.
It's ne use contendin'—they just may shut up,
  For it's us can astonish the stranger :
They may brag o' thor lords, an' thor auld King ti
    boot,
  What's the use on't ?—they hevint a Grainger.
                              Aboot Lunnen, etc.

OLIVER.   *Fordyce's " Newcastle Song Book,"* 1842.

NEWCASTLE IMPROVEMENTS.

R. Charlton, whose name appears but once in local collections, differs
from his contemporaries in this :—they sing of material improvements, as
new streets, markets, etc; he notices the social changes, and some of them
not kindly.   The song is clever, and appears in Marshall's 1827 volume,
but who the author was, beyond the record of his name, we have no trace.

WHAT a cockneyfied toon wor Newcassel hez grown,
   Wey, aw scarce can believe me awn senses;
Wor canny au'd customs for ever ha'e flown,
   An' there's nowt left ahint for to mense us:
The fashions fra Lunnin are now a' the go,
   As there's nowt i' wor toon to content us—
Aw'll not be harpris'd at wor next 'lection day,
   If twe Cockneys put up to 'present us.

Times ha'e been when a body's been axt out to tea,
   Or to get a wee bit of a shiver,
Wor hearts were sae leet we ne'er thowt o' the caw'd,
   Or the fear o' wet feet plagu'd us niver;
But i' blanket coats now we mun get muffled up,
   For fear that the caw'd should approach us—
And to hinder a spark gettin' on to wor breeks,
   We mun jump into fine hackney coaches.

Aw've seen when we've gyen in a kind freenly way
   To be blithe ower a jug o' good nappy—
The glass or the horn we shov'd round wi' the pot,
   For then we were jovial and happy:
But now we mun all hev a glass t' worsels,
   Which plainly appears, on reflection,
We thinks a' wor neighbours ha'e something not nice,
   And are frighten'd we catch the infection.

The very styen pavement they'll not let alyen,
   For they've tuen'd up and putting down gravel;
So now, gentle folks, here's a word i' yor lugs—
   Mind think on't whenever ye travel:
If in dry dusty weather ye happen to stray,
   Ye'll get yor een a' full o' stour, man—
Or, if it be clarty, you're sure for to get
   Weel plaister'd byeth hint and afore, man.

If a' their improvements aw were for to tell,
  Aw might sit here and sing—aye, for ever ;
There's the rum weak as watter i'stead o' the stuff
  That was us'd for to burn out wor liver ;
Aw's fair seek and tir'd o' the things that aw've sung,
  So aw think now aw'll myek a conclusion,
By wishing the cheps iv a helter may swing,
  That ha'e browt us tiv a' this confusion.

CHARLTON.   *Marshall's Collection*, 1827.

THE NEWGATE STREET PETITION TO MR. MAYOR.

About the destruction of this famous gate in the old town wall, Mackenzie, in his *Newcastle*, writes :—"In June 1823 workmen began to pull down Newgate. At this time a clever *jeu d'esprit* was privately circulated, purporting to be the petition of the inhabitants of Newgate to the Mayor, praying for the preservation of this ancient building ; and which was understood to be from the pen of a gentleman well known for his poetic talents and his many local and humorous productions."

This, there is little doubt, refers to John Shield—although Bell, in his manuscript list of Shield's pieces, does not include this "Newgate Street Petition." The petition embodied the opinions of a great many of the influential inhabitants—but, as in a later case (the destruction of the "Carliol Tower"), they went for nothing.

ALACK ! and well-a-day !
    Mr. Mayor, Mr. Mayor ;
We are all to grief a prey,
    Mr. Mayor :
They are pulling Newgate down,
That structure of renown,
Which so long hath graced our town,
  . Mr. Mayor, Mr. Mayor.

Antiquarians think't a scandal,
    Mr. Mayor, Mr. Mayor ;
It would shock a Goth or Vandal,
    They declare :

What! destroy the finest *Lion*
That ever man set eye on !
'Tis a deed all must cry fie on,
    Mr. Mayor, Mr. Mayor.

St. Andrew's Parishioners,
    Mr. Mayor, Mr. Mayor,
Loud blame the Gaol Commissioners,
    Mr. Mayor ;
To pull down a pile so splendid
Shows their powers are too extended,
And *The Act* must be amended,
    Mr. Mayor, Mr. Mayor.

If *Blackett Street* they'd level,
    Mr. Mayor, Mr. Mayor,
Or with *Bond Street* * play the devil,
    Who would care ?
But on *Newgate's* massive walls,
When destruction's hammer falls,
For our sympathy it calls,
    Mr. Mayor, Mr. Mayor.

'Tis a Pile of ancient standing,
    Mr. Mayor, Mr. Mayor,
Deep reverence commanding,
    Mr. Mayor :
Men of *Note* and *Estimation*,
In their course of *Elevation*,
Have in it held a station,
    Mr. Mayor, Mr. Mayor.

    * *Now called Prudhoe Street.*

'Tis a first-rate kind of College,
    Mr. Mayor, Mr. Mayor,
Where is taught much useful knowledge,
    Mr. Mayor :
When our fortunes "gang aglee,"
If worthy Mr. Gee*
Does but on us turn his key,
    All's soon well, Mr. Mayor.

In beauty nought can match it,
    Mr. Mayor, Mr. Mayor :
Should you think we *throw the Hatchet*,
    Mr. Mayor :
John Adamson,† with ease
(In purest *Portuguese*),
Will convince you, if you please
    To consult him, Mr. Mayor.

He'll prove t'ye in a trice,
    Mr. Mayor, Mr. Mayor,
'Tis a pearl of great price,
    Mr. Mayor :
For of ancient wood or stone,
The value—few or none
Can better tell than John,
    Mr. Mayor, Mr. Mayor.

Of this edifice bereft,
    Mr. Mayor, Mr. Mayor,
To the neighbourhood what's left?
    Mr. Mayor :

* The gaoler of debtors' prison.
† The famous Portuguese scholar and translator of "The Luciad.'

The *Nuns' Gate*, it is true,
Still rises to our view,
But that Modern Babel few
    Much admire, Mr. Mayor.

True, a building 'tis, *unique*,
    Mr. Mayor, Mr. Mayor,
A charming *fancy-freak*,
    Mr. Mayor:
But candour doth impel us
To own that strangers tell us
The *Lodge* of our *Oddfellows*,
    They suppos'd it, Mr. Mayor.

Still if *Newgate's* doomed to go,
    Mr. Mayor, Mr. Mayor,
To the *Carliol Croft**—heigh-ho!
    Mr. Mayor,
As sure as you're alive
(And long, sir, may you thrive),
The shock we'll ne'er survive,
    Mr. Mayor, Mr. Mayor.

Then pity our condition,
    Mr. Mayor, Mr. Mayor,
And stop its demolition,
    Mr. Mayor;
The Commissioners restrain
From causing us such pain,
And we'll pay and ne'er complain,
    The *Gaol Cess*, Mr. Mayor.

ANONYMOUS.   *Marshall's Collection*, 1827.

* Where the new gaol in place of Newgate was to be built.

THOMAS MARSHALL.

THOMAS MARSHALL, most favourably known as a local writer, was a native of Newcastle. He served his apprenticeship as a brush-maker with Mr. Laidler, now of Pilgrim Street, but at that time carrying on business at the Carpenters' Tower, and afterwards worked for many years as a journeyman at the same shop. In 1829 he published a collection of his songs. Like his two best known pieces, "Blind Willie" and "Euphy's Coronation," they are full of allusions to local eccentrics. Newcastle in his day had a famous collection of these worthies, and in his songs he appears to have delighted in recording their grotesque bynames, and faithfully preserving their most marked peculiarities. Towards the latter part of his life he seems to have written little. He died suddenly, about the year 1866, having attained a little over his sixtieth year.

To the above, which appeared in the 1872 edition, may be added some interesting memorandums gathered by Mr. Hay from Marshall's old shop-mates at Byers & Co.'s, successors to Laidler & Nicholson. Marshall appears to have been for years foreman at the brush works, and his autograph, here given, is reproduced from his signature to

the weekly pay-sheet. In appearance he was slight, dark, and a little under the middle height. At his work he would often break out with Watson's "Thumping Luck to yon Town," a favourite song of his. Music appears to have been his fancy, as for years he was one of the Guild of Bell-ringers of "All Saints' Church." His death was sudden. The last entry of his pay in the shop books is on December 29th, 1866; two days later, on New Year's Eve, he died at his residence, Shield Street, Shieldfield, from a paralytic attack, and was buried at All Saints' Cemetery on the 2nd of January 1867. Entering the cemetery, his grave is on the right-hand side of the main walk, about one-third of the way up and about ten yards from the edge of the walk. No stone marks the spot.

Marshall appears to have begun and finished his writing early; he would be only twenty-one when his collection of songs (24 pages) was published. If he wrote anything after this it is untraced, as nothing appears to have found its way into local collections. Silver Street, it may be added, appears to have been Marshall's birthplace, and of his family he had but one son, a young man who died some time before his father.

––––––––

EUPHY'S CORONATION.

TUNE—"Arthur McBride."

TE the Fish Market wor gannin, the queen is proclaim'd,
Aud Euphy's thor choice—for beauty lang fam'd;
They've geen her full power—now she's justly ordain'd;
    So they've gyen te croon honest aud Euphy!
The Market wes crowded the queen for te view:
Euphy sat for promotion, drest up wi' new;
The procession appeared with the flag—a true blue!
    And then they surrounded aud Euphy.

The procession wes headed by Barbara Bell;
She wes followed by chuckle-heed Chancellor Kell;
Mally Ogle appear'd wi' a barrel o' yell,
    Te drink te the health ov aud Euphy.
Honest Blind Willie, tee, gaw them a call;
Thor wes great Bouncin Bet, Billy Hush, and Rag Sall,
The Babe o' the Wood, wi' Putty-mouthed Mall,
    A' went te croon honest aud Euphy.

Thor wes a grand invitation for byeth greet an' sma';—
Her subjects assembl'd did loudly hurra!
She wes nobly supported by bauld Dolly Raw,
    At the croonin of honest aud Euphy.
But Ralphy the Hawk wes in prey for a job,
Wiv his small quarter-staff wished te silence the mob;
He wes mum when he gat the beer cask tiv his gob,
    At the croonin of honest aud Euphy.

Euphy and Madge wes the gaze i' the show ;
They were lang loodly cheer'd by the famous Jin Bo ;
Te preserve peace an' order there wes barrel-bag'd Joe,
    At the croonin of honest aud Euphy.
Te make an oration wes the Chancellor's wish,
While his turbot-heed sweel'd like a smokin het dish ;
Bauld Dolly Raw stopt his gob wiv a cod-fish,
    At the croonin of honest aud Euphy.

By greet Billy Hush, Euphy Queen wes declared ;
Te move frae the Market her subjects prepared :
Te the aud Custom-hoose the procession repair'd,
    Te drink at the cost of aud Euphy.
Fine Barbara Bell grand music did play,
Which elevated the spirits of young Bella Grey :
"Keep your tail up!" she wad sing a' the way,
    At the croonin of honest aud Euphy.

Te lead off the ball for the Queen they did cry :
Te please all her people, she wes there te comply ;
Peggy Grundy wad follow, wi' big Bob an' X Y,
    Te assist in the dance wi' Queen Euphy.
The dancin wes ended—doon te dine they a' sat ;
Roast beef an' pig cheek—a gud swig followed that ;
The fragments were reserved in Chancellor Kell's hat,
    At the croonin of honest aud Euphy.

The Chancellor's gob wes beginnin te swet :
He swill'd it away till he gat ower wet ;
He wes led te the tower by young Beagle Bet,
    Frae the croonin of honest aud Euphy.
Bella Roy wes beginnin te produce all her slack :
She wes teun hyem on a barrow by wise Basket Jack ;
The sport wes weel relish'd by Billy the Black,
    At the croonin ov honest aud Euphy.

A speech wes now myed frae the Queen i' the chair—
Te study thor gud she wad tyek a greet care;
They a' had her blissin—what cud she say mair?
    God bliss the Queen, honest aud Euphy.
Wi' cheers for the Queen the hoose oft did ring;
By their humble request she "The Keel Row" did sing;
They a' happy retired wi' "God save the King!"
    Frae the croonin of honest aud Euphy.

MARSHALL.   *Author's Edition*, 1829.

BLIND WILLIE V. BILLY SCOTT.

TUNE—"Fie, let's away to the Bridal."

BLIND WILLIE, one morning, was singin'
    At the sign o' the "Bunch o' Grapes,"
Te amuse the folks he was beginnin'
    Wi' aud Sir Matthew's mistakes.
Sumbody shoots, "Here's Mister Scott cummin!"
    Willie instantly wished for te see;
"Aw'll tell ye the truth, withoot funnin,
    He once half-a-croon gav te me!"
                        Fal lal, etc.

Willie now thowt they were gamin,
    For Mister Scott's cummin seem'd lang,
Till he heard a voice gravely exclaimin,
    "Poor William!—poor blind man!"
Willie bawls oot—"Ye canna deceive me!—
    Ye needn't think aw'm se silly;
Aw's not such a feul, ye'll believe me,—
    It's not Mister Scott, but Cull Billy!"
                        Fal lal, etc.

"Blind man, come, don't be so mulish,
   If I'm silly, no doubt I'm not right;
You for to say that I'm foolish!
   Thank God! I'm endued with my sight!"
"But, Cull Billy, what browt ye here now?
   Nebody can say that it's reet.
Gan away, or aw'll blind ye wi' beer now,
   For cummin te myek gam o' maw seet!"

                         Fal lal, etc.

"You stand on a groundless foundation,
   What else can such as you think?
You indulge yourself in dissipation,
   You are both blind and stupid with drink!"
Willie sat an' heard Cull Billy pratting,
   Quite heedless tiv a' the abuse:
His hand on his knee he kept clapping—
   "Cull Billy's cum fra the madhoose!"

                         Fal lal, etc.

Billy now turned quite ootrageous,
   At Blind Willie's nose tuik a grip:
His haud he suin disengages,
   For Willie began hard te kick.
Willie still gav him greet provocation,
   His raillery still wadn't cease;
Billy went oot wiv a vile execration,
   Te gan tiv a justice for peace.

                         Fal lal, etc.

Willie fand hissel reythur twisted,
   His nose was beginnin te bleed;
He wad gan te the Mayor, he insisted,
   And let his reet worshipful see'd.

Willie oft loodly did grummel—
"The divil brust Cull Billy's bags :
When the aud wife let the pie tummel,
He sat doon an' dined on the flags ! "

Fal lal, etc.

Willie tuik a consideration,
He thowt the subject shud drop ;
He allowed he'd gi'en provocation,
But further mischief he wad stop.
Te finish the pack, anuther gill he got,
But with an oath he did declare,
The varry first time he *saw* Billy Scott,
He wad take him before Mister Mayor.

Fal lal, etc.

MARSHALL   *Author's Edition*, 1829.

TARS AND SKIPPERS.

This song is a relic of the old resurrection days. The Burke and Hare
excitement caused a great many country churchyards to be regularly
watched, the people forming themselves into gangs or sets of watchers. This
does not appear to have been the case in Newcastle. Here, according to old
inhabitants, watching was common, but it was done by friends of the
deceased, or by parties engaged by them for that purpose.

TUNE—"Derry Down."

FOUR hardy Jack tars, wi' a noble intent,
To protect the remains of a messmate they went,
To the Ballast Hills arm'd, just about the midwatch,
To prevent resurrectionists moving his hatch.

Derry down.

Each tar took his post, no way daunted with fear,
When two drunken skippers near the place did appear ;
While stawping alang, it dropt into their head,
They wad byeth gan an' watch a friend they had dead.

Derry down.

The tars, now alarm'd, they prepared for attack—
Ower a styen byeth the skippers now fell on their
    back ;
O Lord ! exclaim'd Jacky, we cannot lie here,
Or we'll byeth be tyen off by resurrectioners, aw fear !
                       Derry down.

Who's there ? cried the tars, or who may you be?
Ax about ! replied Jacky, what's that to ye?
We're not robbers like ye—what else can wi say?—
Come here for to carry the dead folks away.
                       Derry down.

Here's me and friend Ralph knew a friend down
    the shore,
For pulling, wi' him neyn could touch the oar ;
So me and my neighbour's just come for to see
If his body's·tuen off by sic robbers as ye.
                       Derry down.

A signal for action—the tars gave a cough,
To the skippers' amazement, a pistol went off—
The skippers byeth drunk, now sober did feel,
To get out o' their way, they byeth tuik to heel.
                       Derry down.

Ralphy, he thowt 'twould been a terrible job,
If they'd byeth gettin a plaister clapp'd on their gob;
For the skippers tuik the tars for resurrection men—
The tars tuik the skippers to be just the syem.
                       Derry down.

MARSHALL.   *Author's Edition*, 1829.

WEEL MAY THE KEEL ROW

THAT GETS THE BAIRNS THEIR BREED.

WEEL may the keel row, the keel row, the keel row,
Weel may the keel row,
And better may she speed ;
Weel may the keel row, the keel row, the keel row,
Weel may the keel row,
That gets the bairns their breed.

We tyuk wor keel up to the dyke,
Up to the dyke, up to the dyke,
We tyuk wor keel up to the dyke,
An' there we gat her load ;
Then sail'd away doon to Shields,
Doon to Shields, doon to Shields,
Then sail'd away doon to Shields,
And shipp'd wor coals abroad.

Singin'—Weel may the keel row, etc.

Then we row'd away up to the fest,
Up to the fest, up to the fest,
We row'd away up to the fest,
Cheerly every man ;
Pat by wor geer and moor'd wor keel,
And moor'd wor keel, and moor'd wor keel,
Pat by wor geer and moor'd wor keel,
Then went and drank wor can.

Singin'—Weel may the keel row, etc.

Our canny wives, our clean fireside,
Our bonny bairns—their parents' pride,
Sweet smiles that make life smoothly glide,
We find when we gan hyem ;

17

They'll work for us when we get au'd,
They'll keep us frae the winter's cau'd,
As life declines they'll us uphaud—
When young we uphaud them.

Singin'—Weel may the keel row, etc.

UNKNOWN.   *Marshall's Collection*, 1827.

THOMAS WILSON.

"Honour and shame from no condition rise;
Act well your part, there all the honour lies."

THOMAS WILSON, trapper boy, schoolmaster, merchant, and
poet, is a fine example of what natural ability, joined to high

character, can raise a man to, however lowly may be the lot
in which he is born. Thomas Wilson, who, as a song-

writer, comes into our list, was born at Gateshead Low Fell, on November 14th, 1773. At the age of eight he was sent down the pits as a trapper boy, and there often eighteen out of the twenty-four hours were spent in darkness sitting behind his door.

Possibly it was a little recollection of this olden time Wilson introduced into—about the latest piece he wrote—"The Market Day" (published when he was over eighty). It is "Pay Week," the husband is ready for Newcastle; the wife has all her wants told,

> " When just as he was gawn to leave,
>   A little curly-heeded callant
> Tuik deddy softly by the sleeve,
>   And said, 'Eh! fetch me hyem a ballant.'"

The fancy and the taste which prompted such a request, if not his own, seem to have been strong in the trapper boy; he determined to better his lot, and set about educating himself. This he did with much self-denial, and with such success that he qualified himself for the office of school-master. This was but a step to further progress. After a while he obtained a clerk-ship on the Quay, which, after a few changes, led up to a partnership with Mr. Losh. This two years later (1807), by the addition of Mr. Bell, became the famous Tyneside firm of Losh, Wilson, & Bell.

What Armstrong's and Palmer's are to-day, employing their thousands and enriching the district, that Losh, Wilson, & Bell were in their day on the Tyne. His pro-

FELL HOUSE.
From a Painting by Carmichael.

gress now, to adopt the language of a present-day politician, would be one of "leaps and bounds," and he was enabled to accomplish what had long been a cherished object—a residence on the spot where he was born. Fell House was the realisation of this, and at Fell House, Gateshead, the rest of his long life was passed.

For a life of Wilson the reader may refer to Routledge's edition of his works, which is published at a popular price. Here we can only touch upon a few points. In 1826, in the *Newcastle Magazine*, appeared the first part of his famous "Pitman's Pay." The second part appeared the following year, and two years later came the conclusion. The opening of this picture of pit life, one hundred years ago, begins—

> " I sing not here of warriors bold,
> 　　Of battles lost or victories won,
> Of cities sack'd or nations sold,
> 　　Or cruel deeds by tyrants done.
>
> I sing the pitmen's plagues and cares,
> 　　Their labour's hard and lowly lot,
> Their homely joys and humble fares,
> 　　Their pay-night o'er a foaming pot."

This leads up to a description of the varied scenes that a pay-night shows in a public-house. The picture is one drawn before the rise of the teetotal movement had told upon the drinking habits of the country, and when the drinking was the freer from the fact that

> "The 'Caller' dizn't call te-morn."

The night thus wears on; the men, half drunk, are sought for by their wives. Here is one little gem of a picture.

> " Here Nanny, modest, mild, an' shy,
> 　　Took Neddy gently by the sleeve:
> 'Aw just luik'd in as aw went by—
> 　　Is it not, thinks te, time te leave?'
>
> 'Now, Nan, what myeks thi fash me here—
> 　　Gan hyem and get the bairns te bed;
> Thou knaws thou promis'd me maw beer,
> 　　The varry neet before we wed.'
>
> 'Hout, hinny, had thy blabbin' jaw,
> 　　Thou's full of nought but fun an' lees;
> At sic a kittle time, ye knaw,
> 　　Yen tells ye onything te please.

'Besides, thou's had eneugh o' drink,
　And mair wad only myek thee bad ;
Aw see thy een begin te blink,
　Gan wi' me, like a canny lad.'

' O Nan, thou hez a witchin' way
　O' myekin' me de what thou will,
Thou needs but speak, and aw obey,
　Yet there's ne doubt aw's maister still.' "

More like this is to be found in the poem ; to that the reader is referred. Here we can only add W. H. Dawson's appreciative notice of Wilson, taken from his *Local Poets :*—

"Graceful and easy in the measured flow of his melody, like some weird sage who casts the glamour over his victim, he holds his reader spell-bound. In all his efforts he betrays a master mind. Never flagging in interest for one moment, 'The Pitman's Pay' may vie in descriptive power with McNiel's beautiful poem of 'Will and Jean,' whilst its declamatory portions are no way inferior to Wilson's well-known 'Watty and Meg.' . . . We are not aware of any single work which so thoroughly exhibits every trait of the pitman's character, his feelings and failings, his passions, prejudices, and predilections. It is a perfect gem from beginning to end. In the portrait of the miner, nothing that was essential to the correctness of the picture has been omitted. The poet has not been sparing of their foibles, but he does it with a tenderness that shows he treats of men who are endowed with failings common to humanity."

Wilson was over fifty when he printed his " Pitman's Pay," and of his miscellaneous pieces, none go further back than 1824. Possibly some of them might have been written earlier ; if so, he seems to have left the printing of them until his business had brought him leisure. A few extracts from his short miscellaneous pieces may be given. The following, from " The Petition of the Old Apple Tree threatened with Destruction," is feelingly put—

" Your children all have round me played,
　As happy as the day was long,
And oft, with longing eyes, surveyed
　The tempting prize my leaves among.

　　.　　　.　　　.　　　.　　　.　　　.

Nay, I have borne them on my arms,
　And helped them up to pluck my fruit,
For those below, urged by my charms,
　To scramble after at the root ;
Then, still let them quite happy be,
　In climbing up their favourite tree."

Next, a mouse running across the road before him in winter (January) sets him musing : his musings are after the style of Burns' famous lines on *his* mouse, and thus conclude—

> " Come, then, ye daft and thriftless crew,
> And in this mousely mirror view
> Yourselves displayed in colours true,
> 　　With a' your pride :
> With boasted human reason, too,
> 　　Your steps to guide.
>
> 　·　　·　　·　　·　　·　　·
>
> Then learn, ere hirplin' age appears,
> When friendship aft a cauldness wears,
> Which fills the aged een wi' tears,
> 　　The heart wi' grief,
> To live so that the closing years
> 　　Mayn't need relief."

Old age creeping over him, he thus breaks out in " Long, Long Ago "—

> " Oh, memory ! paint me those days of delight
> 　　Long, long ago—long, long ago !
> When every hour scattered joys in its flight
> 　　Long, long ago—long ago.
> Give me a glimpse of the form I held dear,
> Recall me the smile which at all times could cheer—
> The sound of that voice I delighted to hear
> 　　Long, long ago—long ago ! "

In keeping with this love of the old is the following interesting account of the closing years of his long and active life :—

" His seat at the office window was regularly taken, even when he was eighty years of age, and for some time afterwards. His arm-chair at home he occupied still longer—a chair which his muse has immortalised in lines concluding—

> ' *Thy* joints are creaking now with age,
> *Mine* get more rigid daily too ;
> A few more seasons in this stage
> Must bring us to our last adieu.
> And when the curtain falls at last,
> Should any one our story tell,
> May this the sentence be that's pass'd—
> They both their parts have acted well.'

The prayer is fulfilled. The gentle poet, with full faith in the Christian verities, calmly passed away on the 9th of May 1858, in the eighty-fifth year of his age, drawing his last breath as he had done his first on the day of rest and peace. His remains were interred in his family vault at St. John's, Gateshead Fell."—*Routledge's Edition.*

To the courtesy of Mrs. Cook (daughter of the poet) we are indebted for the portrait of Thomas Wilson, the view

of Fell House, and for the loan of the original manuscript
from which this reduced copy of a page of "The Pitman's

Pay" has been photographed. The autograph is from a

presentation copy of "The Pitman's Pay" made by the
author to the late Dr. George N. Clark.

THE WASHING-DAY.

Copy of original note sent with "The Washing-Day" to the Editor of the *Newcastle Magazine* :—

"November 7th, 1831.

"DEAR SIR,—Below you have a trifle descriptive of a washing-day in a poor man's cottage, to be said or sung to the tune of 'There's nae Luck aboot the House.' If you think they merit a place in the local department of the *Newcastle Magazine* they are much at your service. I was led to this subject by seeing a song under this name in a collection published in this town by Marshall, wherein the matter does not seem to me to be in keeping with the operation described. I have availed myself of the author's ideas so far as they suited my purpose, and how far I have improved the sketch of this important day by the addition of my own I will leave you and your readers to determine.—Yours, etc.,   "W. T."

"W. T.," his initials reversed, was Wilson's usual signature in the *Newcastle Magazine.* The *Magazine* just at the time was discontinued, and the song did not appear.

TUNE—"Nae Luck about the House."

OF a' the plagues a poor man meets
    Alang life's weary way,
There's nyen amang them a' that beats
    A rainy weshin' day;
And let that day come when it may,
    It a'ways is maw care,
Before aw break maw fast to pray
    It may be fine and fair.

Chorus.

For it's thump ! thump ! souse ! souse !
    Scrub ! scrub away !
There's nowt but glumpin' i' the house
    Upon a weshin' day.

For sud the morn when SALL turns oot
    Be rainy, dark, or dull,
She cloots the bits o' bairns aboot,
    And packs them off to skuel.

In iv'ry day throughout the week
  The good man hez his say,
But this, when if he chance to speak,
  It's "Get oot o' maw way!"

      For it's thump, thump, etc.

Her step hez stern defiance in't,
  She luiks a' fire and tow,
A single word, like sparks frae flint,
  Wad set her iv a low;
The varry claes upon her back,
  Se pinn'd and tuck'd up are,
As if they'd say to bairns and JACK,
  "Come near me, if you daur!"

      For it's thump, thump, etc.

The cat's the pictur o' distress,
  The kitlins daur nut play,
Poor PINCHER niver shows his fyece
  Upon this dreary day;
The burd sits mopin' on the balk,
  Like somethin' iv a flay,
The pig's as hungry as a hawk,
  The hens lay all away.

      For it's thump, thump, etc.

The hearth is a' wi' cinders strewn,
  The floor wi' dirty duds,
The hoose is a' torn'd upside doon,
  When SALL is i' the suds;

But when the fray's a' ower an' deun,
　　And a's hung up to dry,
A cup and blast o' baccy suin
　　Blaws a' bad temper by.

　　　　Then the thump ! thump ! souse ! souse !
　　　　　Scrub ! scrub away !
　　　　Myek ne mair glumpin' i' the house
　　　　　Until neist weshin' day.

T. WILSON.　　　　　　　　　　　　　*Author's Edition*, 1848.

CARTER'S WELL.

For nearly 150 years Carter's Well has been famed. The water at first came from the side of the hill; the supply was scanty, the inhabitants often waiting until midnight and taking it up with a saucer. When Sheriff Hill Colliery commenced the owners improved the supply. On the colliery ceasing to work, the inhabitants (Thomas Wilson as chairman of the committee) put the well into a thorough state of repair.

　　　　　　　　　　　　TUNE—" Mrs. Johnson."

WOR faithers o' " the olden time "
The praises sung in sparklin' rhyme
Of rosy wine and nectar prime,
　　For gods and men the dandy ;
But they'd ha'e tell'd a diff'rent tyel
Had they knawn owt o' Cairter's Well,
The Helicon o' Gyetside Fell,
　　Or sec a thing as brandy.
　　　　　　　　　　But they'd ha'e tell'd, etc.

Ne other spring wiv it can vie,
It is a tap that ne'er runs dry—
A cellar where a rich supply
　　Suits iv'ry rank and station.

And if awd age myeks tipple fine,
Wors mun, aw think, be quite divine,
For it's a batch of Adam's wine
 We gat at the Creation.
     And if awd age, etc.

And iver since we've swigg'd away
Frae flowin' cans, day efter day;
We've cheer'd and soaked wor drouthy clay
 Wi' Cairter's iverlastin'.
But mony think a drop or two
Of brandy, rum, or mountain-dew,
Wad help a deal to get us through,
 When care's the mind ow'rcastin'.
     And if awd age, etc.

Let sic te Hetherington's repair,
And sit an' sip their mixtur' there;
And if for toddy they declare,
 "At eight the kettle's boilin'."
But gi'e me Cairter's caller spring,
For mixtur' just the varry thing;
We then care ower the shoother fling,
 And gi'e wor wigs an oilin'.
     And if awd age, etc.

And then for news there's nowt can beat
The well where all the lasses meet,
An' gi'e their tongues a pleasant treat
 On village speculations.
The coortin that's te " callin " led,
The couples that are suin te wed,
When the last bride will get her bed,
 And sec like gleg occasions.
     And if awd age, etc.

OPENING OF THE NEWCASTLE AND CARLISLE RAILWAY.

June 18th, 1838.

A day of great rejoicing. The Corporations of Newcastle, Gateshead, and Carlisle attended. Thirteen engines and a hundred and twenty carriages, taking well on to four thousand passengers, made the opening journey.

Strange as it may sound now, when all are so accustomed to the convenience of the "Central," the first Newcastle station was in the Close. The railway itself ran only to the Redheugh, close by the water's edge, the Gateshead station, where it finished, being about the junction of the Redheugh and the Teams. A steamboat took the passengers across the Tyne from the Close station to Redheugh, where the line began. T. Wilson, as an Alderman of Gateshead, would attend the opening.

Mems. from Richardson's "Table Book":—

1835. Railway opened between Hexham and Blaydon. A stage coach then took the passengers from Bigg Market to Blaydon.

1837. Railway opened from Redheugh to Blaydon.

LASS! lay me out maw Sunday claes,
Te-morn's te be the day o' days—
   The railroad's gaun te oppen;
And we'll be there amang the rest,
Buss'd as aw was iv a' maw best
   At the last Westgate Hoppin'.

. . . . . .

Aw'll tell thou mair when aw come back,
For then we'll hev a sappy crack
   'Boot a' aw've heerd and seen.

. . . . . .

Now, hinny, here aw's back agyen,
Thou'll think aw's flaid maw time aw've tyen,
   Aw've been se lang i' comin.
But when twee sic awd standards meet,
The pain o' pairtin's varry greet,
   Thow knaws, maw bonny woman.

We left the Heugh i' gallant style,
And shot away for awd Carlisle,
   Snug seated i' the *Queen*,
Amang the swarms wor canny toon
And Gyetshed planted up and doon
   Te see se rare a scene.

Wi' murth and fun the country rung,
The lairks and linties roun us sung;
　　And when the day was sunny,
The scenery rich and richer grew,
Until we seem'd just glidin through
　　A land o' milk and honey.

We suin reech'd Gilsland's famish wells,
Which, when a lung or liver fyels,
　　Or other ailin maiters,
Myek sick folk flee frae doctors' pills
Te souk health frae the heather hills,
　　Or draw it frae the waiters.

　　.　　　.　　　.　　　.

Could but the folks of awd lang syne
Luik out upon this bonny line
　　And see what we are deein,
They could, aw think, compare 't wi' nowse
But Clootie's gang a' brocken lowse,
　　And frae his clutches fleein.

It was a pleasant seet te see
Wor canny town and Carlisle tee,
　　Byeth yit se hale and hearty,
In spite of a' the Border frays
In which they fowt i' former days,
　　The bravest o' their party.

And now the travellers wi' their trains
Will thraw young blood into the veins
　　O' Carlisle's murry city.
And Grainger may some efternuin
Slip ower and touch her up when duin
　　Here wi' her canny titty.

What lots o' brass it mun ha'e tyen,
And labour frae lang-heeded men,
   Te join this ancient pair—
Te myek them, as it war, shake hands,
And knit them close iv iron bands
   Te separate ne mair.

T. WILSON.   *Author's Edition,* 1848.

THE MOVEMENT.

WHERE canny Newcassel will gan te at last
   Is far ayont maw understandin';
But if it gans on as its duin for years past,
   It'll suin about Hexhim be landin'.

For toon within toon, and street efter street,
   Grainger pops up—without ever heedin'
How they're to be fill'd, unless some new leet
   Shows him folks will like rabbits be breedin'.

But this railroad-pace of increasin' wor race
   Wad be torn'd topsy-torvy by steamin';
The folks now-a-days hev ne dwellin'-place,
   Of hoose or of hyem niver dreamin'.

This howiver, ne doot, is Grainger's luik-out,
   The greet Court-and-Market-exchanger;
And wors iv'ry inch o' the grund to dispute,
   When the props o' wor toon are in danger.

The Markets are gyen, exceptin' just yen
   Which the Cooncil kept out of his clutches;
And the Courts he'll grab suin, if they let him alyen,
   But the day he'll repent he them touches.

For the *crabby* awd dealers in *ling*, *cod*, and *brats*,
   And the *vurgins* that tempt us wi' nice *maiden skyet*,
Will niver aw hope be the *gudgeons* or *flats*
   Te *floonder* aboot i' this huge movement-*net*.

He'll neist try the Quay—the Custom Hoose tee—
   The Brig—and wor awd coaly River;
But in spite o' the warst that a' Grainger can dee,
   They're wor awn, and we'll keep them for iver.

They're cronies we've lang been accustom'd to see,
   For some o' them battled afore lang and sair;
And though we're grown grey i' the cause o' the Quay,
   We hev pluck eneugh left for a few tussels mair.

They're fixtors, some awd-fashioned bodies may say,
   But where can we now for sec rarities surch?
For a man walkin' off wiv a Play-hoose te-day,
   May te morn slip away wi' St. Nicholas' Chorch.

Let the Trinity folks o' their moorin's tyek care,
   Let them double their watch—or as sure as a gun
They'll wyeken some morn leavin' Trinity Chare,
   And driftin' tiv Elswick afore a' be duin.

The Radical movement is now all the go,
   But little like wors as ye'll easily guess,
When aw tell ye that Grainger can move te and fro
   A chorch or a chapel like figurs at chess.

The Cooncil, then, led by wor brave BRITISH TAR,*
   Mun battle and watch for wor canny awd toon;
And byeth tar and feather the hallion that dar'
   Te hoist his-sel up by haulin' huz *doon*.

T. WILSON.   *Author's Edition*, 1843.
            * George Straker, Esq.

THE PEA JACKET.

The author, in a note to this song, writes :—"At the time those emblems of civic dignity, Aldermen's gowns, went out of fashion, a new species of attire—to wit, 'Pea Jackets'—came up. The lines on 'The Pea Jacket' embody the feelings of an honest keelman, expressed to his wife on witnessing the metamorphosis which the 'male creatures' had undergone."

WEY, Mally, maw hinny! what thinks te aw've seen,
  And aw niver saw nowt half se dashin'?
Aw've seen i' the toon, if aw may trust maw een,
  Maw Pea just the pink o' the fashion!

Frae the cut and the claith and the hornbuttons tee,
  Aw said te mawsel, aw was sarten
The fellow had snaffled maw best Sunday Pea
  Thou a'ways said aw was se smart in.

If he'd breeches on, a' lowse at the knee,
  And a chow iv his cheek o' rag backy,
Thou'd sworn as he swagger'd doon Newcastle Quay
  That he was thy awn canny Jacky.

Wor skipper cam up and aw tell'd him maw tyel,
  The Pea i' maw heed a'ways runnin';
"Wey, man," says he, "surely thou isn't thyself
  Not te knaw what's been gaun on in' Lunnen.

"The awd Corporations, the Doctors a' say,
  That meet at the hoose call'd St. Stephen,
Are at their last gasp, and by next New Year's Day
  There winnet be yen o' them leevin'.

"It lang hez been said they war gannin' te pot,
  But wor awn set it a' doon for leein',
Till the Mayor and the Aldermen a' teuk the rot,
  And are now just like rotten sheep deein'.

" Aw've just been up street—the toon's iv a low,
  And aw's frighten'd some mischief is brewin',
As a deed Corporation's not worth an awd chow,
  An' aw wadn't say much for the new un.

"For the cock'd hat and goon that govern'd the toon,
  I' the days of awd Alderman Blackett,
The Alderman myekin' are gawn te lay doon,
  An' put on a keelman's PEA JACKET!"

T. WILSON.   *Author's Edition*, 1843.

A GLANCE AT POLLY TECHNIC.

"A collection of the most splendid productions of nature and art ever
exhibited in Newcastle," this, the first Polytechnic Exhibition, was opened
April 6th, 1840. It had a threefold object—to raise funds for the North
of England Fine Arts Society, the Newcastle Mechanics' Institute, and
the Gateshead Mechanics' Institute. The Polytechnic closed with upwards of £1,500 as a clear surplus to divide amongst the three institutions.
It was here that John Watson, the brother of the author of "Thumpin'
Luck," exhibited specimens of his beautiful engravings on glass. (See Life
of William Watson, page 205.)

Aw'VE travelled East as weel as West,
  At Carlisle and the sea aw've been,
And i' maw time aw think the myest
  Of a' the marvels here aw've seen.

At Grainger's warks aw've wonder'd sair,
  Aw've stared at a' the feats o' steam,
But at the 'Sociation* mair—
  Till now of a' that's grand the cream.

But this is all a bagay tyel,
  For now the seet just torns maw brain,
Sin' POLLY TECHNIC cam hersel
  Wiv a' her wonders in her train.

* The British Association's visit to Newcastle, 1838. The "wise week"
was crowded with meetings, lectures, exhibitions, etc.

She's gyen an' ransack'd iv'ry pairt,
 For rarities of iv'ry kind,
As weel of Natur as of Airt,
 The pith o' mony a maister-mind.

Aw glower'd aboot the Pictur Place,
 Aw ax'd for Judy o' the Hutch,
But Judy's fyece aw cudn't trace—
 The want o' Judy vex'd me much.

． ． ． ． ． ．

There's Belted Will the Border chief,
 If he wad speak, could thraw some leet
On where se rankly prowled the thief
 That honest men war bad te meet.

And here's maw horny-letter'd frien',
 The corner-styen of a' wor lare,
It is the finest thing aw've seen—
 O dear! aw's glad te see it there.

Some feuls may giggle at the nyem
 O' byeth the Hornbuick and Tom Thumb;
But where is it if not frae them
 That a' yor Polly Technics come?

The "branks," a kind o' brake, is here,
 Wor faithers, when a' else was vain,
Compell'd the noisy jades te weer
 Whene'er their clappers ran amain.

Eh! "nick-sticks! nick-sticks!" what are they?
 O! now aw hae'd:—they're used at hyem,
And when kept decently in play
 The branks was but an empty nyem.

And here's wor hatless Minstrel * tee,
  That roam'd aboot wor canny city,
And charm'd the guzzlers o' the Quay
  Wi' mony a simple hyem-spun ditty.

Aw think aw hear him fiddlin' still,
  And on Sur Maffa sweetly strummin,
Which help'd away wi' mony a gill
  'Mang fuddlin' men and queerish women.

But aw mun end maw simple tyel—
  It's now ower lang, aw sadly fear ;
Te Polly praise there's nyen can fyel—
  Wor bairns will praise her mony a year.

T. WILSON.   *Author's Edition*, 1843.

THE MARKET DAY.

OH ! hinny Jack, aw've wearied sair
  To see thee come back frae the pay,
That aw may get it ettled reet :
  Te-morn, thou knaws, is market day.

Aw gat the bits o' bairns te bed,
  Conn'd ower the things we wanted myest ;
But 'til aw knaw'd what thou had myed,
  Maw ettlin' was but nobbut guessed.

Aw's glad te see it is se much,
  And noo hev hopes to get the goon
Thou promised, in thy wily way,
  The varry furst good fortnith's hewin'.

          * Blind Willie.

This mun stand furst upon the list
  That sadly croods maw muddled brain;
And, just like wanderin' iv a mist,
  Te fix the rest seems all in vain.

Thou munnet Bobby's clogs forget
  That we hev promised him se lang,
Te keep him frae the cawd and wet
  He's barefoot trudged for weeks amang.

And little Sall wants varry sair
  A bit new ribbon for her hat;
She says, "Aw's sure ye this mun spare:
  Ye knaw aw've lang expected that."

Thou wants some odds and ends thysel':
  Thy panties luick but varry bare:
Thy coat's beginnin' sair te fyell,
  At elbows it wants some repair.

    .   .   .   .   .

Thou'll mebby call at Alder Dunn's
  To see if maw bit hat be duin,
For aw've te stand for Nelly's bairn
  In it, neist Sunday efternuin.

Now, just as he was gawn te leave,
  A little curly-heeded callant
Tuik deddy softly by the sleeve,
  And said, "Eh! fetch me hyem a ballant,

"Or else some funny story buick
  That aw may read tiv Uncle Joe,
As he sits laughin' i' the nuick—
  He diz enjoy these worthies so.

" The feats of Hickathrift and Hood
    All pass with *him* for Gospel truth,
And ony doot he nivir could
    Admit, e'en frae the preacher's mooth."

Noo, hinny! mind thou comes suin hyem,
    Aw'll hev a white kyeck for thy tea,
Thou knaws the treat's nut like the syem
    Withoot thy canny company.

T. WILSON.   *"Northern Tribune,"* 1854.

THE COAL TRADE.

TUNE—" The Keel Row."

GOOD people, listen while I sing
The source from whence your comforts spring,
And may each wind that blows still bring
    Success unto the Coal Trade.
Who but unusual pleasure feels
To see our fleets of ships and keels?
Newcastle, Sunderland, and Shields
    May ever bless the Coal Trade.

May vultures on the caitiff fly,
And gnaw his liver till he die,
Who looks with evil, jealous eye
    Down upon the Coal Trade.
If that should fail, what would ensue?
Sure ruin, and disaster, too !
Alas, alas ! what could we do,
    If 'twere not for the Coal Trade?

What is it gives us cakes of meal?
What is it crams our wames sae weel
With lumps of beef and draughts of ale?
    What is't but just the Coal Trade?
Not Davis' Straits, or Greenland oil,
Nor all the wealth springs from the soil,
Could ever make our pots to boil,
    Like unto our Coal Trade.

Ye sailors' wives that love a drop
Of stingo fra the brandy shop,
How could you get one single drop
    If it were not for the Coal Trade?
Ye pitman lads, so blithe and gay,
Who meet to tipple each pay day,
Down on your marrow bones and pray,
    Success unto the Coal Trade.

May Wear and Tyne still draw and pour
Their jet black treasures to the shore,
And we with all our strength will roar,
    Success unto the Coal Trade!
Ye owners, maisters, sailors, a',
Come shout till ye are like to fa';
Your voices raise—huzza! huzza!
    We all live by the Coal Trade.

This nation is in duty bound,
To prize those who work underground,
For 'tis well known this country round
    Is kept up by the Coal Trade.
May Wear, and Tyne, and Thames ne'er freeze,
Our ships and keels will pass with ease,
Then Newcastle, Sunderland, and Shields
    Will still uphold the Coal Trade.

I tell the truth, you may depend,
In Durham or Northumberland,
No trade in them could ever stand,
    If it were not for the Coal Trade.
The owners know full well 'tis true,
Without pitmen, keelmen, sailors too,
To Britain they might bid adieu,
    If it were not for the Coal Trade.

So to conclude, and make an end
Of these few lines which I have penn'd,
We'll drink a health to all these men
    Who carry on the Coal Trade:
To owners, pitmen, keelmen too,
And sailors, who the seas do plough,
Without these men we could not do,
    Nor carry on the Coal Trade.

UNKNOWN.   *Marshall's Collection, 1827.*

THE COLOURS.

Written on the memorable election for the County of Northumberland
in 1826, when there were four candidates. The contest lasted from the
20th of June to the 6th of July, and the numbers polled for each candidate
were:—The Hon. H. T. Liddell, 1562; M. Bell, Esq., 1380; T. W. Beaumont, Esq., of Bywell, 1835; and Lord Viscount Howick (who declined the
contest on the 3rd), 976.
    Robert Surtees, historian of the county of Durham, born in Durham City,
died at his seat at Mainsforth on the 11th February 1834, aged 55 years.

O'ER Northumbria's hill and dale,
    Far and wide the summons flew;
Dallying with the summer gale,
    Four gay banners court the view.

Where bright beauty's glance is beaming,
    Lasses' love, and lads' delight,
See young *Liddell's* colours streaming
    ~~broad fond of~~ *pink* and *white.*

Unstain'd and true see deep *true blue*
  With lighter tints combine,
For honest *Bell* the triumph swell,
  And deck the coaly Tyne.

From *Hexham's* towers, from *Bywell's* bowers,
  From *Allen's* wilder shade,
While *Beaumont's* name loud bands proclaim,
  Glints forth the *White Cockade.*

From mountains rough, old *blue* and *buff,*
  That oft has won the day,
Is loath to yield, untried the field,
  And waves once more for *Grey.*

Two must win, though *four* may woo,
  Mingle, while ye mingle may,
Pink and *white*, and *buff* and *blue*,
  In a medley strange and gay.

Gay fleeting colours shift and blend
  Beneath the sunbeam bright;
Two may last to six years' end,
  And two *must* fade ere night.

'Twas thus Northumbria's genius spoke,
  And cast a pitying glance behind,
As from old *Alnwick's* bowers she broke,
  And mounted on the eddying wind.

She raised on high the bonny *Bell*,
  And *Liddell's* red rose streaked with pale;
The blue and buff, and the White Cockade,
  She scattered on the rising gale.

SURTEES.   *Richardson's Table-Book*, 1842.

DAVID ROSS LIETCH.

ALTHOUGH not in the dialect, "The Cliffs of Old Tyne-mouth," from its interesting local subject, as well as its popularity, may fittingly find a place in this collection. The author, David Ross Lietch, was born at North Shields, and for some years practised there as a medical man. In 1838 appeared his volume, *Poetic Fragments.* "The Cliffs" (apparently a later production) is not in it, but it contains many very fine pieces. The following, "Red Eric and Lord Delaval," from its spirited nature and local character, becoming very popular, Wilson, in one of his famous "Tales of the Borders," publishing it :—

RED ERIC AND LORD DELAVAL.

Red Eric, the Dane, o'er the ocean has come ;
His course was as swift as the wind-driven foam ;
As the storm-risen sea rushes wild o'er the strand,
He has swept the fair shores of Northumbria's land.
There was wailing and weeping in cottage and hall,
O'er the plundered domain of the Lord Delaval.

The gallant young baron went forth with his train,
To bring home a bride to his princely domain—
'Twas the Lady Edith, the flower of the Tyne—
In beauty, how peerless ! in grace, how divine !
Oh, ne'er was there maiden, in cottage or hall,
More fair than the bride of the brave Delaval !

The bridal train trooped a-down Hallowell Dale ;
The last rays of sunlight yet gleamed on their mail,
And brightened their banners and steel-headed spears—
When, hark ! a loud wail fills each warrior's ears ;
And the towering flames leapt aloft o'er the wall,
And whirled round the castle of Lord Delaval.

His vassals came crowding, in tears, round their lord ;
They had fled from the fierce Scandinavian horde ;
Their daughters were stolen, dishonoured their dames,
Their cattle were slaughtered, their roofs were in flames ;
Thus wretched they knelt, and for vengeance did call
On Eric the Bloody, from Lord Delaval.

Dark red grew his brow, and his glances more keen,
He leapt from his steed, and he knelt on the green ;
Then, raising his helm—"May I never," he cried,
" Press the couch of Editha, my beautiful bride,
If aught else I think of, ere vengeance shall fall
On the savage destroyer of fair Delaval.

"On the land, on the ocean, by night or by day,
Alone, or amid his barbaric array
Of savage despoilers, I swear to pursue,
And my steel in the best of his blood to imbrue ;
Or a blood-bolter'd corse 'neath his weapon to fall—
St. Cuthbert, so speed me ! " quoth brave Delaval.

Again to her home Lady Edith has gone,
And away rode her lord on his war-steed alone.
He sought every bay, and each cliff on the coast,
For the ships of the fierce Scandinavian host ;
And often in rage on Red Eric did call—
"Fierce savage ! prepare thee to meet Delaval !"

As the gates of the abbey of Tynemouth he passed,
The warder was fled, and the gates were all fast ;
But a warrior stood near, in full armour arrayed.
Him courteous saluting, brave Delaval said—
"Know'st thou aught of Red Eric, whom fiends shall enthral,
For the woes he has wrought upon fair Delaval ? "

"Leave thy steed and I'll show thee," the warrior cried.
In an instant brave Delaval stood by his side.
"Dost thou see those dark galleys drawn up on the sand,
And their crews round their watch-fires that blaze o'er the
        strand ?
Then these are the Norsemen who fired your fair hall,
And I am Red Eric, thy foe, Delaval ! "

"Ha ! have I then got thee ? " the Baron exclaimed,
And forth in the moonlight his falchion flamed ;
And there, all unseen, was such valour displayed
As the sun should have witnessed, the world have surveyed.
Oh ! ne'er did such strokes upon habergeon fall,
As when Bloody Eric fought Lord Delaval.

They struck, and they parried, they wounded, they bled,
Till the turf which they trampled grew slippery and red ;
Their bucklers were splintered, their helmets were riven,
In their flesh the sharp edge of the fragments were driven,
Till a heart-splitting stab caused Red Eric to fall,
With a howl of despair, before brave Delaval.

He has hacked off the head, ere the blood ceased to flow
He has hied to the horde who were feasting below—
He flung it among them ; his war-cry he raised—
The Norsemen all rushed to their galleys amazed ;
They have left the lost maidens, their plunder, and all,
And have fled, terror-stricken, before young Delaval.

Nor yet they escaped ; for a tempest arose,
And wrecked on her beach fair Northumbria's foes :
Some perished, engulfed iu the depths of the waves,
And some to the serls they had mocked became slaves.
Now, his bride in his arms, and his knights in his hall,
Oh ! who is so happy as brave Delaval ?

The ballad of " Red Eric " is not Dr. Lietch's only contribution to the popular Border Tales ; several stories by him also appear. Towards the end of his life the author retired to the Lake district, where he died on August 16th, 1881. He lies in Crossthwaite churchyard, not far from the grave of Southey.

In connection with this song, some forty years ago, John— familiarly known as Jack—Dent, when in his cups (and he was often so), used to claim the authorship. Dent was one of the old band of Black House amateurs, and wrote a good many pieces; perhaps his best was his lines on seeing Joe Wilson's portrait in Mr. France's window :—

"Hail, youthful Bard of Coaly Tyne,
  Child of the musing dream,
I've scann'd that thoughtful brow of thine,
  And thus it prompts my theme.

. . . . .

Hold fast the Bard's unfading crown,
  Ne'er sell thy pen for lucre ;
The poet's thoughts are not his own,
  They live but for the future.

I would not play the critic's part,
  Nor speak one word to wound thee ;
My worst wish is—thou honest heart,
  May fortune smile around thee."

That his talk of the authorship was only idle (although he had his supporters) is best seen in this : about 1870 he collected his pieces into a small volume, and " The Cliffs " is not there. Poor Dent towards the end grew erratic ; shortly after Ned Corvan's death he was found in St. Andrew's churchyard pulling at the grass and scratching the soil. When asked why he was doing that and what he wanted, his only answer was, he wanted to find Ned Corvan's grave. He died shortly after.

THE CLIFFS OF OLD TYNEMOUTH.

TUNE—" The Meeting of the Waters."

OH ! the Cliffs of old Tynemouth they're wild and they're
    sweet,
And dear are the waters that roll at their feet ;
And the old ruin'd Abbey, it ne'er shall depart :
'Tis the star of my fancy, the home of my heart.

Oh! 'twas there that my childhood fled cheerful and gay,
There I loitered the morning of boyhood away ;
And now as I wander the old beach alone,
The waves seem to whisper the names that are gone.

'Twas there with my Alice I walked hand-in-hand,
While the wild waves in moonlight leapt o'er the bright
    sand ;
And sweet were the echoes of the dark Cliffs above,
But, oh ! sweeter her voice as she murmured her love.

Other lands may be fairer, but nought can be seen
Like the shore where our first love and boyhood have
    been ;
Oh ! give me the Cliffs and the wild roaring sea—
The Cliffs of old Tynemouth for ever for me.

    DR. LIETCH.   *Broadsheet about 1843.*

ROBERT EMERY.

ROBERT EMERY, author of the celebrated Tyneside songs,
"Sandgate Pant," "Hydrophobie," etc., was born on the
26th of September 1794, at Edinburgh ; but his parents
removing to Newcastle when he was very young, all the
associations of his long life are connected with "Canny
Newcassel." He served his apprenticeship as a printer with

Mr. Angus, bookseller and printer, in the Side. Whilst there he made his first appearance as an author, by writing children's nursery rhymes for the penny and halfpenny books sold by his master. During his apprenticeship the great frost of 1813–14 occurred. He had as a fellow-apprentice one Thomas Binney, who was bound in the same establishment, learning the business of a bookbinder. Being com-

Photo.   Bannister.

panions, they agreed between them to write a song about the severe frost, then the great topic of the day. Robert wrote the first and second verses. Unfortunately, the first verse of this interesting joint production is all that is preserved, and it most curiously, through being printed on silk, and kept within the case of a large old-fashioned watch which he wore. It ran as follows :—

GREAT FROST ON THE RIVER TYNE,

January and February 1814.

" Behold the Coaly Tyne, now frozen o'er,
  That lately ships of mighty burden bore ;
  Where watermen, for want to row in boats,
  Make use of tents to get their pence and groats."

The remainder of the song was written by his fellow-apprentice, Thomas Binney, who, from this lowly beginning in life, has gradually risen, until now we find him the Rev. Thomas Binney, the celebrated preacher, who has officiated for so many years at the Weigh House Chapel, London, and who is generally admitted to be one of the most able, if not the ablest man in the Independent body.* After Robert's apprenticeship expired, he worked journeyman for many years at the different printing offices in the town, writing songs upon the various topics of the day, many of them becoming highly popular, "Sandgate Pant" and "Hydrophobie" especially so. Amongst Tyneside songs there are few so popular as his. They are found in all collections ; and it is to be regretted that he did not carry out the intention he had of publishing a collected edition of his songs, as they would have been an interesting contribution to local literature. As it is, they are scattered about in various collections ; many of them were only printed in sheets by himself, and are now very scarce. About the year 1850 he began business as a printer on his own account in Silver Street, in premises belonging to himself. Here he continued for about twenty years. About a year before his death he left Silver Street, and removed to more extensive premises at the foot of Pilgrim Street, where the business is still carried on by his son. He died on March 28th, 1871, at the advanced age of 77, after a short illness, and was interred at All Saints' Cemetery, his funeral being attended by a large number of his friends and admirers.

The information in the above appeared in our 1872 edition, and was got partly from the poet and partly from his son. To it there is really little to add—steady and methodical, Emery's life was uneventful. Lambert's, in Grey Street, was the last place he worked at; and at Lambert's appears to have come to a head his wish to better his condition in life, as he left there to begin on his own account.

* Now dead ; died February 24th, 1874.

Amongst Lambert's old hands he is remembered as the laureate of the establishment, he furnishing them with a new song each year on the occasion of their annual trip. The following, on their trip to Warkworth, is probably the first:—

TRIP TO WARKWORTH.

Some love to sing of days gone by,
How warriors made their foes to fly,
A better theme I mean to try,—
    Our glorious trip to Warkworth.
Our lads were smart—the lasses gay—
The sun shone out to grace the day—
Each heart was eager for the fray,
And seem'd impatient at delay ;
At length we heard the signal clear,—
We thunder'd forth a hearty cheer—
The train rush'd on till we came near
    The bonny town of Warkworth.

Chorus—

For ne'er since days of "Auld Lang Syne"
Did youth and beauty e'er combine,
To journey from the Banks of Tyne
    With lighter hearts to Warkworth.

Ord's bugle sounded through the dell,
Which soon dissolv'd the magic spell
That bound the hermit to his cell,
    Who'd ages slept at Warkworth.
In merry mood, with staff in hand,
He from his little boat did land—
On Coquet's banks once more did stand,
And wish'd to join our joyous band—
The castle green he long'd to see,
Where loud resounded mirth and glee,
And Sons of Tyne, so kind and free,
    Regal'd their friends at Warkworth.

      For ne'er since days, etc.

The hermit mounts the castle wall,
And soon espied his old friend, Hall,
Dispensing cheer to great and small,
    Upon the green at Warkworth.
Bold Harry, too, with wond'rous skill
Performed his part with right good will,
And swore he'd take it very ill,
If we refus'd to eat our fill—

With that the bugle sounded clear,
When lots o' famous beef and beer
From groaning tables disappear,
    A glorious feast at Warkworth.
            For ne'er since days, etc.

A party reach'd the hermit's cave,
Where trees around so gently wave,
And chaunted many a pleasant stave,
    To charm their friends at Warkworth.
" The Boatie Row " with catch and glee,
Re-echoed over tower and tree ;
And Stephen's voice so bold and free,
Fill'd all around with melody :—
Back to the Castle we repair,
Enchanted with the scenes so fair :
The bugle's notes did rend the air
    Around us all at Warkworth.
            For ne'er since days, etc.

The hermit sprung upon the green,
And such a sight was never seen,
For mirth and fun each heart was keen
    To join the sport at Warkworth.
The band struck up and play'd so sweet,
Each lad and lass start to their feet,
And join'd the dance and waltz'd so neat,
Sure ne'er could joy be more complete ;
For tarsy-warsy some did cry,
While cricket balls around us fly,
One fairly knock'd Kay's head awry
    While drinking tea at Warkworth.
            For ne'er since days, etc.

Our merry day too soon flew past,
For mortal joys but seldom last :
The bugle sounds, we muster fast
    To join the train at Warkworth.
The hermit o'er us breath'd a prayer,
And slowly " vanish'd into air."
Then through the town we all repair,
In grand procession form'd with care—
The band so merrily did play,
We reached the train without delay,
But e'er for home we bent our way,
    We gave three cheers for Warkworth.

    For ne'er since days of " Auld Lang Syne "
    Did youth and beauty e'er combine,
    To journey from the banks of Tyne
        With lighter hearts to Warkworth.

EMERY.
                      " Bards of the Tyne," 1849.

The following verse, showing Emery's handwriting, is from a hitherto unpublished song of his :—

Answer to the Song called "Canny Shields."

By R. Emery, of Newcastle.

Tune — "The Ghister"

My Grandie, poor Body, has oft said to me
kind de to good folk as they should de to ye—
Altho' the awd wife had a will of her awn
Ye'll surely confess its a very fair plan.

Fol de rol.

The second verse runs—

> " Newcassel foaks like when ther neighbors de weel,
> And when owt gans wrang they hev hearts that can feel;
> But when gowks endevour wor gud nyem te rob,
> He's nowt but a calf that wad then haud his gob."

"Canny Sheels" (p. 156), to which he refers, certainly does not spare Newcastle. Unfortunately Emery, in replying, gives no information about the writer.

About 1829 he was with Edgar as a printer. This Edgar, some four years before, had brought out a small Collection of "Original Local Songs," mainly by Oddfellows, and in this collection we first trace Emery, his "Hydrophobie" and other songs appearing there.

In Marshall's 1827 edition of songs he is one of the trio of local bards—Mitford, Ross, and Emery—who break into song on the occasion of the fishwives being removed from their open stand on the Sandhill to the new covered market. This change they resented. A verse and the chorus runs—

> "O kind Sir Matt.—ye bonny star,
> Gan to the King an' show this ditty,
> Tell him what canny folks we are,
> And make him free us frae this Kitty.

> Oh ! hinnies, Corporation !
> A ! marcy ! Corporation !
> Ye hev duen a shemful deed,
> Te force us fra wor canny station."

In Fordyce (1842) "Jean **Jamieson's** Ghost" appears, and here and in slips printed by himself are to be found the rest of his songs.

The view given shows the old house in Silver Street, that in which some forty years of Emery's life was passed. In the heart of old Newcastle, it yet had a pleasant outlook, the trees and greenery of All Saints' being before it. Robert Emery's mild and genial disposition made him a general favourite. Metcalfe Ross, a master printer in the town, paid a tribute to him in the following ingenious play upon the letters of his name :—

TO ROBERT EMERY.

A health to Robert MRE,
Who handles oft his A B C ;
A friend presumes his name to UU,
And hopes the freedom he'll XQQ.
His well-known wit need I B telling,
In song or LEG XLing ?
He to XS ne'er went astray,
E'en with his shopmate ThomS K.
U cannot be the NME
Of honest Robert MRE.*

Photo.   Auty & Ruddock.

Joe Wilson, another printer-poet and friend, also compliments Emery in the following acrostic :—

E mery fill'd each breest wi' pride,
M irth-provoking songs he wrote,
E neuff te please a' far an' wide.
R ich an' racy tiv a note,
Y e'd hear his sangs a' roond Tyneside.

Joe's acrostic is interesting, not only as showing his kindly estimate of the old veteran, but also as being a connecting link between the old and new Tyneside.

---

* Robert Gilchrist, some fifteen years before, had done something similar in the shape of a sonnet addressed to Miss Bell.† The first four lines ran—

2 E D fy or even to M U's,
2 sing thy virtues, lovely M.A.B.,
Could I in terms proportionate F U's,
My song the fine L end of time would C.

† The daughter of his friend, John Bell, the noted antiquarian and book collector.

HYDROPHOBIE; OR, THE SKIPPER AND THE QUAKER.

TUNE—"Good-morrow to your Nightcap."

As Skipper Carr an' Markie Dunn
  Were gannin drunk through Sandgate,
A dog bit Mark and off did run,
  But sair the poor sowl fand it:
    The skipper in a voice se rough,
    Aw warn'd, says he, it's mad eneugh,
    Howway, an' get some docter's stuff,
      For fear of Hydrophobie!
        Fal de ral, etc.

The doctor dress'd the wound se wide,
  An' left poor Markie smartin',—
Then, for a joke, tells Carr, aside,
  Mark wad gan mad, for sartin.
    Now, skipper, mind, when in yor keel,
    Be sure that ye watch Markie weel,
    If he begins to bark and squeel,
      Depend it's Hydrophobie!
        Fal de ral, etc.

For Shields, next day, they sail'd wi' coal,
  And teuk on board a Quaker,
Who wish'd to go as far's Dent's Hole,
  To see a friend call'd Baker;
    The skipper whisper'd in his ear,
    Wor Markie will gan mad aw fear!
    He'll bite us a',—as sure's yor here,
      We'll get the Hydrophobie!
        Fal de ral, etc.

Said Quack, I hope this can't be true—
　Nay, friend, thou art mistaken;
We must not fear what man can do—
　Yea! I will stand unshaken!
　　　The skipper, to complete the farce,
　　　Said "Maister Quaker, what's far warse,
　　　A butcher's dog bit Markie's leg,
　　　　　And browt on Hydrophobie."
　　　　　　　　　Fal de ral, etc.

Now Markie overheard their talk,
　Thinks he, aw'll try the Quaker—
Makes P. D. to the huddock walk,
　Of fun to be partaker.
　　　To howl an' bark he wasn't slack,
　　　The Quaker owerboard in a crack,
　　　With the fat skipper on his back,
　　　　　For fear of Hydrophobie!
　　　　　　　　　Fal de ral, etc.

How P. D. laughed to see the two,
　Who, to be sav'd, were striving,
Mark haul'd them oot, wi' much ado,
　And call'd them culls for diving:
　　　The Quaker seun was put on shore,
　　　For he was frighten'd very sore,
　　　The skipper promis'd never more
　　　　　To mention Hydrophobie!
　　　　　　　　　Fal de ral, etc.

EMERY.　　　　　　　　*Edgar's Collection of Odd Songs, 1825.*

HACKNEY COACH CUSTOMERS;
OR, NEWCASTLE WONDERS.

January 25th, 1824, hackney coaches established in Newcastle. The stand appointed to be the square in front of St. Nicholas' Church.

TUNE—"Gee, ho, Dobbin."

SINCE the Hackneys began in Newcassel to run,
Some tricks hae been play'd off which myed lots o' fun:
For poor folks can ride now that ne'er rode before,
The expense is se canny, it's seun gettin o'er.
Gee, ho, Dobbin, etc.

'Mang the rest o' the jokes was a lad fra the Fell,
Where he lives wiv his feyther—his nyem's Geordy Bell;
For hewin there's nyen can touch Geordy for skill;
When he comes to Newcassel he gets a good gill.
Gee, ho, Dobbin, etc.

One day, being cramm'd wi' fat flesh and strang beer,
Left some friends at the Cock, an' away he did steer,
Wiv his hat on three hairs, through Wheat Market did
stride,
When a Coachman cam up, an' said—Sir, will ye ride?
Gee, ho, Dobbin, etc.

Wey, smash noo—whe's thou, man?—How? what dis
thou mean?—
I drive the best coach, sir, that ever was seen,—
To ride iv a coach! Smash, says Geordy, aw's willin'—
Aw'll ride i' yor coach though it cost me ten shillin'!
So Gee, ho, Dobbin, etc.

Then into the coach Geordy claver'd wi' speed,
And out at the window he popp'd his greet heed :—
Pray, where shall I drive, sir—please give me the nyem?
Drive us a' the toon ower, man, an' then drive us hyem!
Gee, ho, Dobbin, etc.

'Then up and doon street how they rattled alang,
'Till a chep wi' the news tiv and Geordy did bang,
'Bout his son in the coach, and for truth, did relate,
He was owther turn'd Mayor or the great Magistrate!

      Gee, ho, Dobbin, etc.

And Geordy did caper till myestly deun ower,
When Coachee, suen after, drove up tiv his door—
Young Geordy stept out, caus'd their hopes suen to
  stagger,
Said he'd paid for a ride just to cut a bit swagger.

      Gee, ho, Dobbin, etc.

To ride fra Newcassel mun cost ye some brass :—
Od smash, now, says Geordy, thou talks like an ass!
For half-a-crown piece thou may ride to the Fell—
An' for eighteen-pence mair, smash, they'll drive ye to H—ll.

      Gee, ho, Dobbin, etc.

And Geordy then thowt there was comfort in store,
For contrivance the coaches nyen could come before :
Poor men that are tied to bad wives needn't stick—
Just tip Coachee the brass an' they're off tiv Au'd Nick.

      Gee, ho, Dobbin, etc.

      Edgar's Collection of Odd Songs, 1825.

THE PITMAN'S RAMBLE.

    TUNE—" The Kebbuckstane Wedding."

Wor pit was laid in, an' but little ti de,
 Says aw, " Neibour Dickey, let's off te Newcassel,
   nd alterations aw's langin' te see,
   y thor se fine that they'll gar wor een dazzel."

We reach'd the *Black Hoose*, an' we call'd for sum beer,
　　When whe shud pop in but the landlord, se handy;
He wish'd us se kindly a happy new eer,
　　An' he rosin'd wor gobs wiv a glass o' French brandy.

We left wor gud frind, an' got doon te the shop,
　　That hes sum fine lasses frae Lunnin se cliver;
Astonished, aw stared till near like for te drop,
　　At thor greet panes o' glass that wad cover Tyne river
Says Dick, "It's been myed for greet folk like Lord 'Size,
　　It belangs te Broad Brim that myed brass at the
　　corner;
At poor folks like us, now, he'll cock up his eyes,
　　As he sits at the end there like Little Jack Horner."

We wheel'd reet aboot—spied a far finer seet,
　　As we went to the grocer's to get sum rag backey:
Lairge goold cups an' watches, se bonny an' breet,
　　An' fine *Fardin Pants* runnin' whisky an' jackey;
Aw wish'd aw cud get mi gob fair at the spoot,
　　Aw'd pay for a sook o' this liquor se funny;—
Says Dick, "The doors bowlted te keep the crood oot,
　　It's a place myed te glower at, but not te tyek munny."

We doon te the *Doctor's* that leeves i' the Side,
　　That cure's folks o' hairy-legg'd monsters like donkies,
Cull cheps for his worm kyekes frae far an' near ride,
　　Poor pitmen, an' farmers, an' keelmen, an' flonkies.
A chep at the window did offer te sweer,
　　For truth, that this doctor, se clivver an' cunnin',
Did tyek frae his sister, the varry last eer,
　　A worm that wad reach frae Newcassel te Lunnin!

At last, te the play-hoose aw swagger'd wi' Dick,—
    They've used the King's Airms an' the paintings most
        shockin';—
Yen said, since the hoose had been kept by *Awd Nick*,
    Wi' humbugs an' lees he'd Newcassel been mockin'.
Says aw, "Canny man, dis Awd Nick manage here—
    That cunnin' black fiend that gav Eve the bad apple?
Us Ranters will suen frae this place myek him sheer,
    An' we'll preach in't worsels, then we'll bang Bruns-
        wick Chapel!"

EMERY.   *Fordyce's "Newcastle Song Book," 1842.*

KING WILLY'S CORONATION.

Copied from an old manuscript of Robert Emery's, and sent to the *Weekly Chronicle* by Emery's son, 1879. The Coronation took place on September 8th, 1831. The song very fairly records the rejoicings on the occasion. It recalls the previous coronation—that of George the Fourth, in 1819—to which it affords a pleasing contrast. Marshall's and Fordyce's Local Collections have about a dozen songs on that coronation, in which George the Fourth and the authorities of the town are both severely lashed, as—

It adds but little to
    your praise,
To see your lavish,
    wasteful ways,
To see a keelman,
    from his huddock,
Within your wine
    trough wash his
    buttock,
Which ne'er before
    was drenched in
    wine,
But often plunged
    in Coaly Tyne.

What did your wil-
    ful waste avail?
Your fountains run-
    ning wine and ale?
The bronzed dome,
    the glitt'ring crown,
Torn by an enrag'd
    people down?
Who cheering hail'd
    Queen Caroline,
Borne by the bloom-
    ing fair on Tyne.

THE SANDHILL WINE PANT.

The song does not exaggerate; the rough scenes described actually occurred.

From another—

>   Hey! to the pants, where dribbling wine
>   And brewers' rot-gut beer distil;
>   With speed let every greedy swine
>   Swig what he can! aye, swig his fill.
>
>   Three royal fountains running beer,
>   And one to dribble wine, O,
>   Would make them flock from far and near,
>   To grunt like royal swine, O.
>
>   Two bullocks roasted whole, 'twas thought,
>   Would be a grand donation,
>   To toss among the "rabble rout"
>   At George's Coronation!

Disorder and riot characterised the whole of the 1819 festivities.

>   O MARROWS a', noo clear yor throats,
>   An' drop yor botheration;
>   Come, join me in a stave or two
>   Aboot the Coronation.
>   Whe wad refuse wi' me to sing
>   The praises o' wor canny king—
>   Of Brunswick House, the breetest star—
>   Newcassel's pride—a jolly tar?
>   Fra Mistor Mayor to wor P.D.
>   Extend yor jaws, an' sing wi' glee
>   King Willy's Coronation.
>
>   Fal de ral, etc.
>
>   Tho' Shield* may sing in magic strains
>   The mony happy days, man,
>   When wor Association lads
>   Engross'd the folks's praise, man:
>   In Blackett's Field we'd sic a feast,
>   Where sixteen hundred men, at least,
>   Did exercise wi' knife an' fork,
>   An' hew'd away at beef an' pork.

* See Shield's songs, page 62.

We'd loyal toasts, an' clivvor spokes,
Wi' music fine, an' funny jokes
    On Willy's Coronation.

Ma sarties, hed ye nobbit seen
    Green's bonny silk balloon, man!
Reet fra the Spital to the clouds
    It flaffer'd very suen, man.
Wi' starin' aw near lost ma seet,
Amang the crowd in Westgate Street;
Fra some aw gat an ugly thump,
They brak my nose agyen the pump,
    An' stole my hat, an' tore my sark;
    Becrike, but there was bonny wark
        On Willy's Coronation.

Off, helter-skelter wi' the thrang,
    Aw reach'd Newcassel Brig, man,
To view the boats that were to run
    Wor clivvor Sandgate gig, man.
Away they flew, 'mid noise and din!
Byeth Shields and Scotswood tried to win,
But Sandgate lads are just the breed,
Like hearts of oak they tuik the lead;
    To win the prize they warn't lang—
    Byeth sides o' Tyne their victory sang
        On Willy's Coronation.

Aw jump'd as aw went te the Garth
    Wi' cousin Dicky Reed, man,
An' at a stangie's shop aa bowt
    A cover for ma heed, man;

Then cruick'd wor houghs at the Blue Bell,
Talk'd ower the spree, an' smack'd the yell;
Then toddled hyem to wor dame Peg—
At scolding she is such a cleg—
    Aboot ma sark for years she'll chat,
    My broken nose, an' fine shag hat,
      On Willy's Coronation.

EMERY.   *Local Songs and Song-Writers*, "*Weekly Chronicle*," 1879.

SANDGATE PANT; OR, JEAN JAMIESON'S GHOST.

Jane Jamieson, a street vendor of fruit. Executed March 7, 1829, on the Town Moor, Newcastle, for killing her mother with a poker while in a fit of passion.

TUNE—"I'd be a Butterfly."

THE bell of St. Ann's toll'd two in the morning,
  As brave Skipper Johnson was gawn to the keel;
From the juice o' the barley his poor brain was burning,
  In search of relief he through Sandgate did reel.
The city was hush, save the keel bullies snoring,
  The moon faintly gleam'd through the sable-clad sky;
When lo! a poor female, her hard fate deploring,
  Appear'd near the Pant and thus loudly did cry,
    Fine Chenee oranges, four for a penny,
    Cherry ripe cornberries, taste them and try.

Oh, listen, ye hero of Sandgate and Stella,
  Jin Jemieson kens that your courage is trig;
Go tell Billy Elli* to meet me, brave fellow,
  Aw'll wait your return on Newcassel Tyne Brig.

* Billy Elli. In Cochrane's *Monthly Circular* for September 1891 "The Old Boy" tells the following :—"The 'fancy man' of the woman Jamieson was named Ellison. He was very ignorant. At the trial Ellison's name as a witness was called in vain. Forsyth, town marshall, got permission to call him in his own way; he cried out 'Elli.' At the sound of the familiar name the man stood up at once, and by his evidence proved the guilt of the half-witted creature, and so helped her to the place of execution."

Oh ! mercy, cried Johnson, yor looks gar me shiver,
  Maw canny lass, Jin, let me fetch him next tide,
The spectre then frowned, and she vanished for ever,
  While Sandgate did ring as she vengefully cried,
      Fine Chenee oranges, four for a penny,
      Cherry ripe cornberries, taste them and try.

She waits for her lover, each night at this station,.
  And calls her ripe fruit with a voice loud and clear;
The keel bullies listen in great consternation,
  Tho' snug in their huddocks they tremble with fear.
She sports round the Pant till the cock in the morning
  Announces the day, then away she does fly,
Till midnight's dread hour, thus each maiden's peace
      scorning,
  They start from their couch as they hear her loud cry,
      Fine Chenee oranges, four for a penny,
      Cherry ripe cornberries, taste them and try.

EMERY.   *Fordyce's " Newcastle Song Book," 1842.*

BAGGY NANNY; OR, THE PITMAN'S FROLIC.

A humorous account of the visit of the Great Fiddler "Paganini" to
Newcastle, September 9th-11th, 1833.

                              TUNE—"The Kebbuckstane Wedding."

COME, lay up your lugs, and aw'll sing ye a sang,
  It's nyen o' the best, but it's braw new and funny;
In these weary times, when we're not varry thrang,
  A stave cheers wor hearts, tho' it brings us ne money.
Aw left Shiney Raw,—for Newcassel did steer,
  Wi' three or four mair of our neighbours se canny,
Determin'd to gan to the play-house to hear
  The king o' the fiddlers, the great Baggy Nanny.
                              Right fal, etc.

We reach'd the Arcade, rather drouthy and sair—
 It's a house full o' pastry-cooks, bankers, an' drapers;
At the fine fancy fair, hoo my marrows did stare,
 On the muffs, hats, an' beavers, se fam'd i' the papers.
At Beasley's, where liquor's se cheap an' se prime,
 A bottle aw purchas'd for maw sweetheart Fanny,
We drank nowt but brandy—and when it was time
 We stagger'd away to see great Baggy Nanny.

       Right fal, etc.

We gat t' the door, 'mang the crowd we did crush,.
 Half-way up the stairs aw was carried se handy—
The lassie ahint us cried "Push, hinny! push"—
 Till they squeez'd me as sma' an' as smart as a dandy.
We reach'd the stair-heed, nearly smuther'd indeed;—
 The gas-letters glitter'd, the paintin's look'd canny;
Aw clapt mysel doon 'side a lass o' reet breed,
 Maw hinny! says aw, hae ye seen Baggy Nanny?

       Right fal, etc.

The lassie she twitter'd, and look'd rather queer,
 And said, in this house there is mony a dozen,
They're planted se thick that there's ne sittin' here,
 They smell se confounded o' cat-gut an' rosin.
The curtain flew up, and a lady did squall,
 To fine music play'd by a Cockney bit manny,
Then frae the front seats aw seun heard my frinds bawl,
 Hats off, smash yor brains! here comes greet Baggy
  Nanny.

       Right fal, etc.

An ootlandish chep seun appear'd on the stage,
  An' cut as odd capers as wor maister's flonkey,
He skipp'd and he fiddled as if in a rage—
  If he had but a tail he might pass for a monkey!
Deil smash a gud teun could this bowdykite play—
  His fiddle wad hardly e'en please my aud granny,—
So aw seun joined maw marrows, and toddled away,
  And wish'd a gud neet te the greet Baggy Nanny.

Right fal, etc.

On crossin Tyne Brig, hoo wor lads ran the rig,
  At being se silly deun oot o' thor money!
Odd bother maw wig! had he played us a jig,
  We might tell'd them at hyem we'd seen something
      quite funny;
But, law be it spoke, and depend it's ne joke,
  Yen and a' did agree he was something uncanny—
Tho, dark ower each tree, he before us did flee,
  And fiddled us hyem, did the greet Baggy Nanny.

Right fal, etc.

EMERY.   *Fordyce's "Newcastle Song Book,"* 1842.

THE SKIPPER'S VISIT TO THE POLYTECHNIC.

Written on the second Polytechnic Exhibition, commencing Easter
Monday, 1848. It was held in the same suite of rooms as the first (1840);
the entrance was from the Academy of Arts, Blackett Street; a gallery
crossing High Friar Street connecting the rooms with those in the Grainger
Street division. In the Exhibition, on a press worked by the author, Mr.
Emery, the song was first printed.

TUNE—"X, Y, Z."

    O, GEORDY, hinney, gan away,
      An' see what aw hev seen, man—
    The Polytechnic's such a treat,
      'Twad please wor very Queen, man!

Prince Albert tee, aw hev ne doot,
Wad swear that Lunnin oot an' oot
Was fairly be't with all her pride,
And give the palm te wor Tyneside.
E'en Billy Purvis an' his show
And Thorne's Theatre are no go
   To wor Tyne Polytechnic.

The paintings there wad make ye stare,
 Some awd an' some quite new, man,
And lots o' bonny China ware
 Of patterns not a few, man.
There's relics now not worth a groat,
Like Cuddy Willie's awd greet coat,
With arms and armour fra the Tower,
That sav'd wor lads in mony a stour;
There's coats and caps a' myed o' steel,
An' clubs wad make awd Horney squeel,
   In wor Tyne Polytechnic.

They've lantrens that can raise the deil
 An' myek him wag his tail, man,
With microscopes that turn at once
 A sprat into a whale, man.
There birdies sing an' look so nice,
Rare plants fra Eden's Paradise.
The incubcator scar'd me sore,
For bairns an' chickens by the score
It manufactures very free,
'Twad neither suit wor Peg nor me,
  At wor Tyne Polytechnic.

There's plows and harrows for the sod,
  An' mirrors—such a show, man,
At which a skipper and his men
  Might shave frae top to toe, man.
There's Armstrong, by some magic wand,
Makes great machines work at command;
The weavers they were thrang at wark,
Amaz'd—aw roar'd oot—smash my sark,
Wor Peg shall hev a posey gown
To mense her when she comes to toon
          To wor Tyne Polytechnic.

A water fountain in full play,
  Where ships o' war might float, man;
And on a stand not far away
  Was Harry Clasper's boat, man;
But here maw brains began te reel,
Enchanted at the organ's peal;
Its pipes like distant thunder roll'd,
Then squeek'd like mice i' wor keel's hold,
Aw'd sit an' listen half a year,
For music fine the heart does cheer
          In wor Tyne Polytechnic.

A chep was pulling at a thing,
  Its nyem aw cuddent guess, man;
He said te me se very free
  It is a printing press, man,
And if you do not take the hint,
I'll soon put all your thoughts in print,

An' sure enough, before 'twas lang,
He form'd maw thowts into this sang;
'Twas very like a magic trick,
But suen fra him aw cut maw stick
   At wor Tyne Polytechnic.

Aw've been at France, aw've been at Shields,
 An' likewise Shiney Raw, man,
Where aw've seen lots o' wondrous things
 Above grund and belaw, man;
But these greet wonders mun give in,
To say owt else wad be a sin,
The Polytechnic cuts the shine,
An' sheds a ray o'er Bonny Tyne;
E'en Cocknies ower their midnight bowls
Will toast with glee like jolly souls
   Wor Town and Polytechnic.

EMERY.   *Broadsheet printed at Polytechnic,* 1848.

MALLY AND THE PROPHET.

In consequence of the appearance of a bill announcing the arrival of a most extraordinary prophet in Newcastle,—whose dress was coeval with Adam, whose unshod feet and habits of teetotalism, together with his prophetic spirit, marked him as a sight worth seeing,—crowds of persons thronged the square of St. Nicholas in hopes of beholding this LUSUS NATURÆ,—when lo and behold!—the "chanticleer of the morning" strutted forth in all the majesty of the dunghill, and with his shrill clarion announces himself as the veritable prophet.—What a dress!—*Author's Note.*

TUNE—" Barbara Bell."

'TWAS rumour'd about that a wonderful Prophet,
 Who liv'd mony years afore Adam an' Eve,
Wad preach to the folks in Newcassel Wheat Market,
 Which myed them a' run his advice to receive;

20

The coat on his back fairly puzzles the tailors,
    An' deil smash a shoe or a stockin' he'll wear ;
He drinks nowt that's stranger than pure caller waiter,
    An' turns his nose up at wor Newcassel beer.
                                        Right fal, etc.

Wor Mally, determin'd to be like her neighbours,
    Suen dress'd her-sel' up in her fine chintzie goon ;
Thro' Sandgit she waddled as cliver as Lunnin ;
    To see this queer man she steer'd straight for the toon.
She hail'd Cuckoo Jack at the foot of the Kee, man :
    He caper'd an' roar'd like a cull silly block—
"O marrows ! see ! yonder gans crazy awd Mally,
    To glow'r like a feul at Hepple's gyem cock."
                                        Right fal, etc.

The keel-bullies nicker'd, but on Mally toddl'd,
    An' said tiv her-sel, "May the deil cock ye blind ;
Aw'll speak to the Prophet to send ye, the next tide,
    To the bottom o' Tyne iv a greet gale o' wind."
She reached the Sandhill, where Blind Willie was tellin'
    The truth 'bout the Prophet, yet thowt he did mock ;
"There's nowt there," says he, "but a few wanton huzzies,
    Thrang catchin' an' pullin' Bob Hepple's gyem cock."
                                        Right fal, etc.

Still Mally push'd forward, quite sure she wad see him,
    Not heedin' the jeers and the jokes that were pass'd ;
To laugh at a prophet she thowt it was cullish.
    Wi' sair tues she reach'd the Wheat Market at last ;
Cull Billy cam up, an' she ask'd for the Prophet
    (By this time St. Nicholas' had struck ten o'clock);
"There's no such thing, woman," said Billy, "I'm certain ;
    I fancy you want to see Hepple's game cock."
                                        Right fal, etc.

Aud Mally, enraged, was about to give battle,
    But Billy convinc'd her, which seun stopp'd her mouth,
That both cocks an' hens, he said, liv'd before Adam ;
    That each cock's a prophet is well known for truth.
The hoax thus explained, greet was Mally's vexation,
    To think she'd been made a complete laughing-stock ;
Then kilted her coats and trudg'd back to the Swirle,
    And often gets vext aboot Hepple's gyem cock.

Right fal, etc.

EMERY.   *"Bards of the Tyne,"* 1849.

THE CURDS-AND-CREAM HOUSE GHOST.

TUNE—"Walker, the Twopenny Postman."

O, THE neet was pick dark, and a strang wind did roar,
When abuen the Cat's Tail* wor aud keel ran ashore ;
And in tryin' te clear her we brak' wor sweep oar,
    So she stuck there as tight as a post, man.
Te get her afloat a' wor strength waddent de ;
Says Dick, "Let's a' hands back te toon on the spree,
And fast in the huddock we'll leave the Pee Dee,
    Te be freeten'd te deeth wi' the ghost, man."

They'd scarce jumped ashore when Pee Dee, the sly rat,
Gat oot, and ran doon to a stile, where he sat
Till the bullies cam up, then he squalled like a cat ;
    "O, marrows!" roared Dick, "that's the ghost, man !"
Such yells in the dark myed the brave bullies stop ;
And doon, deed as mutton, the skipper did drop ;
Cries Dick, "We're poor men nobbet gawn on the hop !
    Hev marcy on us, maister ghost, man !"

* The scene of the song—a small valley a little above the Shot Tower.

"Te the regions belaw," cried the ghost, "cum away!"
Then the skipper jumped up, shooting, "Pray, hinnies,
  pray!"
"Ye ken Gospel," ki Dick, "so kens best what te say,
  Speak ye te this monstrous ghost, man!"
Wi' thor hair reet on end, and thor blud like te freeze,
Myest deaved wi' greet yells, they dropped doon on thor
  knees,
And blubbered and cried, "We'll de owt that ye please,
  Nobbit leave us alyen, hinny ghost, man!"

When off the ghost flew wiv a terrible scream:
They ran into a hoose where they sell cruds and cream;
My sarties, astonished the wifie did seem,
  When they swore hoo they'd mawled a greet ghost,
  man;
But had they but knawn it was nobbit Pee Dee,
They wad hammered his ribs, just te letten him see
That te put them in fear he'd hev much mair te de
  Than te yelp in the dark like a ghost, man.

EMERY.   *Author's Copy,* 1862.

———

THE WIZARD OF THE NORTH; OR, THE MYSTIC POLICEMAN.

Mr. John Elliott, now Superintendent of the Gateshead Police Force, was
for several years the chief detective at Newcastle-upon-Tyne. He was
noted for his skill. The "Journeyman Tailor," a by-name by which he
was spoken of by the criminal classes—whose security he often disturbed—
is an allusion to his business before he joined the force.—*Note,* 1872 *Edition.*
Mr. Elliott resigned the office of Chief Constable, June 1891.

TUNE—"Hurrah for the Bonnets o' Bonnie Dundee."

Aw'VE cum fresh frae Mackie's tae sing ye a sang,
Aboot a queer chap—but aw'll not keep ye lang—
Of the prime cock-tail stingo aw just had my share,
When the Journeyman Tailor popp'd in, I declare.

Chorus.

He's a limb of the deevil, as sure as you're here,
For he's learn'd him the art to restore stolen gear;
But stop her there, Tommy—lang may wor boast be,
That the Journeyman Tailor's the top o' the tree.

He can flee through the air like a witch on a broom,
And bring a defaulter straight back to his doom;
In spite of all weather, blow foul, or blow fair,
The Journeyman Tailor is sure to be there.

> He's a limb of the deevil, etc.

He has cunning black eyes, and they shine in the dark,
For the thief thinks him near if he sees but a spark;
And he steps just as light as wor Granny's Tom Cat,
And springs on his victim as it wad on a rat.

> He's a limb of the deevil, etc.

His smell is so keen that he kens biv his nose
When a pick-pocket's near, and he's soon on his toes;
So ye light-fingered kiddies at races beware,
For the Journeyman Tailor is sure to be there.

> He's a limb of the deevil, etc.

The Cockneyfied runners of Bow Street may pine,
To think they're eclips'd by a son of the Tyne;
Let them bluster like Yankees, but little we care,
For wor Journeyman Tailor can make them all stare.

> He's a limb of the deevil, etc.

Three cheers for Newcastle! three cheers for the Tyne!
Where "had-away Harry," se often did shine!
And for peace and protection we'll never despair
As long as the Journeyman Tailor is there.

> He's a limb of the deevil, etc.

EMERY.   *Author's Manuscript*, 1862.

THE OWL.

In this song Emery contributes his share to the hubbub which some sixty years ago stirred Newcastle. T. Waller Watson brought an action at Newcastle Assizes, August 1828, against Thomas Carr, Captain of the Watch, for assault and false imprisonment. Carr was fined forty shillings and costs, evidently to the delight of the local poets, who, in some half-dozen songs, rejoice over his defeat. Mr. (afterwards Lord) Brougham was counsel for Carr, and Sykes, the compiler of *Local Records*, published a report of the trial.

Carr appears not to have paid the fine, hence the imprisonment of the Captain of the Watch, and the exuberance of the local poets. "Cappy," who was the Captain of the Watch in charge, and who is urged to "keep him tight," was keeper of the Old Castle, then used as the debtors' gaol of the town. See "Cappy," p. 141.

OLD CASTLE, 1810.

TUNE—"X, Y, Z."

Now, run away amang the snobs
　An' stangies i' the Garth, man,
An' hear about the great black owl
　That's let on Cappy's hearth, man.
Of sic a breed, the deil his sell
It's marraw canna' find in h—ll;
It hops about wiv its sloutch hat,
Can worry mice like wor Tom Cat;
　An' sic a yarkin blubber heed,
　It bangs X Y, that famous steed,
　Or ony thing ye like, man.
　　　　　Fal, de ral, etc.

Oft frev its nest, in Cabbage Square,
　It flaffer'd oot at neets, man,
'Mang sic a flock that neetly blare,
　An' carry crooks an' leets, man;
Then prowl'd wor streets in search of prey,
An' if a mouse but cross'd his way,
He quickly had it by the nose,
An' pawk'd it off to kuel its toes,
　　　Did Hoo! Hoo! wi' the blubber heed,.
　　　That bangs X Y, that famous steed,
　　　　So, Cappy, keep him tight, man.

To tell how Cappy gat his burd,
　Aw wad be rather fash'd, man.
Some say that, of its awn accord,
　It went to get *white-wash'd*, man;
So scrub him, Cap, with aw yor might,
Just nobbit make the lubbart white;
But if yor brushin' winna dee,
There's Waller Watson, Walton tee,
　They'll scrub him as they did before,
　An' make the bowdy-kite to roar,
　　　If Cappy keeps him tight, man.

St. Nich'las bells now sweetly ring,
　Yor music's se bewitchin';
Ye lads in Neil's, now louder sing,
　An' warble weel, Hell's Kitchen,
For yor awd friend is in the trap,
Alang wi' his awn brother, Cap.
Then shout hurra! agyen we're free
At neets te hev a canny spree.
　　　In gannin hyem, ne mair we'll dreed
　　　The lubbart wi' the chuckle heed;—
　　　　Mind, Cappy, keep him tight, man.

EMERY.　　　　　　　　　　　　　　*Marshall's Collection*, 1827.

THE SKIPPER'S DREAM.

This song we first find in *The Tyne Songster*, a choice selection of songs in the Newcastle dialect. The collection, one of 72 pages, was printed and sold by W. Orange, North Shields, 1827. The song appears without an author's name, but in Fordyce's, 1842, where it next appears, T. Moor is given as the writer. Moor was a shoemaker, who carried on business at Denton Chare. He was a good bass singer, and one of the choir of St. Andrew's. Mrs. Leybourne, yet remembered as a popular favourite, singing both at the Theatre Royal and public concerts, was his daughter. This seems Moor's only song, and about it there is related an odd fact. Robert Emery, the famous Tyneside writer, when he got a glass too much used regularly to break out with this song; it is just possible Emery had something to do with the writing of it. Silver Street, where he lived for so many years, is not the place to parade the spirit or the sentiments of "The Skipper's Dream." Moor (who used to sing the song), connected with the church, had associations more in keeping with it.

T'OTHER day, ye mun knaw, wey aw'd had a sup beer;
It ran i' maw heed, and myed me sae queer,
That aw lay doon to sleep i' wor huddock sae snug,
An' dreem'd sic a dreem as gar'd me scart me lug.

Aw dreem'd that the queerest man iver aw see'd,
Cam stumping alang wi' three hats on his heed;
A goon on like a priest (mind aw's telling ne lees),
An' at his side there was hingin a greet bunch o' kees.

He stares i' maw fyece, and says, "How d'ye de?"
"Aw's teufish," says aw, "canny man, how are ye?"
Then he says, wiv a voice gar'd me trimmle, aw's shure,
"Aw's varry weel, thank ye, but yor day is nigh ower."

Aw studdies awhile, then says aw, "Are ye Deeth,
Come here for to wise oot a poor fellow's breeth?"
He says, "No, aw'm the Pope, cum to try if aw can
Save a vile wretch like ye fra the nasty Bad Man.

He said, yen St. Peter gov him them greet kees
Te let into Hiven wheiver he'd please;
An' if aw'd turn Papish, and giv him a Note,
He'd send me to Hiven, without ony doot.

Then a yel heep o' stuff he talk'd about sin,
An' sed he'd forgi' me whativer aw'd deun ;
An' if that aw'd murther'd byeth fayther and muther,
For a five shillin piece, wey, aw might kill me bruther.

Says aw, "Mister Pope, gi's ne mair o' yur tauk,
But oot o' wor huddock aw's beg ye to wauk ;
An' if ye divent get oot before aw count *Nine,*
Byéth ye and yor keys, man, aw'll fling i' the Tyne."

So aw on tiv me feet wiv a bit iv a skip,
For aw ment for to give him an Orangeman's grip ;
But aw wakened just then in a terrible stew,
And fand it a dream as aw've teld ye just noo.

T. MOOR. *"Tyne Songster,"* 1827.

WILLIAM STEPHENSON, JUN.,

LIKE his father, has contributed to the songs of the district. Born in Gateshead, Sept. 2nd, 1797; he was to business a printer, beginning early on his own account, at the Bridge End, Gateshead; in 1824 he published a very interesting collection of "Original Local Songs," under the title of "The Tyneside Minstrel," Mitford, Oliver, his father, himself, and others contributing. His business seems partly to have been that of supplying hawkers with songs, slips, last dying confessions, etc., as these with his imprint turn up in the lots of collectors. In "The Tyneside Minstrel" appears his "Beggars' Wedding"; it is signed S. About a dozen sentimental pieces signed X. seem also to be by him, amongst them "The lass that shed a tear for me," and "Ellen," to the tune of "Robin Adair," the first verse of which may be given—

> "Who makes this life so sweet?
> 　　Ellen, my love.
> Who makes the hours so fleet?
> 　　Ellen, my love.
> But when her heart is sore,
> Time is to me no more,
> Unless in sighing for
> 　　Ellen, my love."

In 1832 he published his father's volume of poems and songs. About the same time he would be busy with his most important work, *The Gateshead Intelligencer.* This was a sixpenny monthly, a sort of half newspaper, half magazine. It began in 1830 and finished in 1833, but before it finished he had contrived through it to get into mischief with the Gas Company, and had to apologise for his remarks about them.

Giving up his printing, he commenced in his native town as an auctioneer, and succeeded in doing a good business. He died at a comparatively early age, the *Gateshead Observer* of May 26, 1838, thus briefly recording his death : "On Sunday (May 20), after a long illness, aged 40, much respected, Mr. W. Stephenson, printer."

THE BEGGARS' WEDDING.

TUNE—"Quayside Shaver."

WHEN Timber-legged Harry Crook'd Jenny did marry,
　　In fam'd Gateshead town—and, not thinking of blows,
Three ragmen did quarrel about their apparel,
　　Which ofttimes affrighted both small birds and crows.
This resolute prial, fought on battle royal,
　　Till Jenny spoke this, with hump back and sharp shins :
"Be loving as brothers, as well as the others,
　　Then we shall get orders for needles and pins !"

The bride-maid, full breasted, she vowed and protested,
 She never saw men at a wedding so rude;
Old Madge, with her matches, top full of her catches,
 Swore she would be tipsy e'er they did conclude;
The supper being ended, some part still contended
 For wholesome malt liquor to fill up each skin;
Jack Tar, in his jacket, sat close to Doll Flacket,
 And swore he'd drink nothing but grog and clear gin.

Black Jack, with his fiddle, they fixed in the middle,
 Who had not been washed since the second of June;
Old Sandy, the piper, told Nell he would stripe her,
 If she wouldn't dance while his pipe was in tune:
They played them such touches, with wood legs and
  crutches—
 Old rag-pokes and matches, old songs flew about;
Poor Jack being a stranger, his scratch thought in danger,
 He tenderly begg'd they would give up the rout.

Jack being thus ill-treated, he begg'd to be seated
 Upon an old cupboard the landlord had got,—
Like madmen enchanted, they tippled and ranted,
 Till down came the fiddler as if he'd been shot.
They drank gin by noggins, and strong beer by flagons,
 Till they had sufficiently softened each maw;
Then those that were able retir'd to the stable,
 And slept with their noses like pigs in the straw.

W. STEPHENSON, JUN.   "*Tyneside Minstrel,*" 1824.

———

THE SANDHILL MONKEY.

TUNE—"Drops of Brandy."

A STORY aw's gaun for t' tell,
   An' t' ye it may luik varry strange :
It was in a shop on the Sandhill,
   When the Craw's Nest* was on the Exchange,
A monkey was each day drest soon,
   Ahint the coonter he sat i' the shop,
Whe cam in an' their money laid doon,
   Jaco straight in the till wad it pop.

                              Rum ti iddity, etc.

A skipper he cam in yen day,
   He couldn't help luiking at Jackey,
On the coonter his money did lay,
   Saying, "Please, sir, an oonce o' rag baccy."
His money Jake popt in the till,
   The skipper kept luiking at him,
A' the time on his seat he sat still,
   An' he luik'd at the skipper quite grim.

                              Rum ti iddity, etc.

"Noo, pray, sir, will ye bear a hand ?
   For aw mun be at Sheels now this tide !
Now, pray, be as sharp as ye can,
   For wor keel she is at the Keeside ;

---

* In 1783 a pair of crows built their nest above the vane upon the spire
of the steeple of the Exchange, Sandhill. The iron rod upon which the
vane was fixed went through the centre of the nest, which turned with
every change of wind. They attempted to build it the year following, but
other crows pulled it to pieces before it was finished. In the years 1785-6-7-8,
the same crows, as it was thought, built on the same spot, or rather point,
and succeeded each year in rearing their young.

Aud man, are ye deef?" then he cried,
  An' intiv a passion he fell;
On the coonter lay some, ready weigh'd,
  Says he, "Smash! but aw'll help me-sel."
                              Rum ti iddity, etc.

Then he tuik up an ounce o' rag baccy,
  But afore he could get turned aboot,
Off his seat then up started aud Jacky,
  An' catch'd him hard fast by the snoot;
He roar'd and he shooted oot "Murder!"
  The maister he see'd a' the fun,
Not wishin the joke t' gan farther,
  Straight intiv the shop then he run.
                              Rum ti iddity, etc.

"What's the matter, my canny good man?"
  An' he scarcely could keep in the laugh;
"Take this aud man off me—bear a hand!
  For aw think now that's matter eneuf.
What's the matter, ye ax? Smash! that's funny;
  (An' he still kept his eye upon Jackey,)
Aw paid yor granfayther the money,
  But he'll not let me hae me baccy."
                              Rum ti iddity, etc.

"Now, mind ye, maw canny good man,
  If iver thou comes in wor keel, man,
For the trick thou hes play'd me the day,
  Wor pee-dee shall sobble ye weel—
Aye, for a' yor fine claes aw'll engage,
  An' for a' yor a sturdy aud man,
Tho' he's nobbut twelve years of age,
  He shall thresh ye till ye canna gan."
                              Rum ti iddity, etc.

W. STEPHENSON, JUN.   "*Tyne Songster*," 1827.

MERRY LADS OF GYETSHEAD.

‡ First appeared in the *Tyneside Minstrel*, 1824, published by W. Stephenson, Jun. There is no author given, only the initial B. It is the only song in the collection under that signature.

TUNE—"Sunny Banks of Scotland."

COME, lads, assemble in a ring,
And a' your flutes an' fiddles bring,
And join wi' me all ye that sing,
   To praise the lads of Gyetshead.
They are se frank, they are se free,
They please the lasses tiv a tee ;
They cry there's nyen that e'er aw see
   Can match the lads of Gyetshead.

Chorus—

Then fill the glasses up wi' glee,
And drink to them wi' three times three,
Lang may they live and happy be,
   The merry lads of Gyetshead.

The mothers warn their dowters fair
Of a' young men for to beware,
But myest of a', ma bairn, tyek care
   Of them blithe lads of Gyetshead.
They are se wily and se kind,
They seun wad win a lass's mind.
When aw was young 'twas rare to find
   A lad like them of Gyetshead.

Then fill the glasses, etc.

Whene'er they gan to tyek a gill
At Jenny Brown's, or where they will,
Ye find them blithe and cheerful still,
   The merry lads of Gyetshead ;

Or when at Kenmir's house they meet,
Se happily they spend the neet,
Say what ye will, there's nyen can beat
    The merry lads of Gyetshead.
                Then fill the glasses, etc.

At hoppin times, when fiddles play,
When lads and lasses dance a' day,
Abyun them a' they tyek the sway,
    The merry lads of Gyetshead.
The country lads to beat them try,
But na, na, na, they canna come nigh ;
The aud wives cock their thumbs and cry,
    Weel dyun, the lads of Gyetshead.
                Then fill the glasses, etc.

Aw henna power their worth to tell,
Abyun a' else they bear the bell,
And oh ! let me for ever dwell
    Amang the lads of Gyetshead.
Ye power abyun, to them be kind,
And keep them still in friendship joined ;
When life is o'er then let me find
    In Heaven the lads of Gyetshead.
                Then fill the glasses, etc.

B.
                " Tyneside Minstrel," 1824.

ROBERT NUNN.

ROBERT, familiarly known as Bobby Nunn, the author of
many popular Tyneside songs, was to business a slater. In
early life, while following his occupation, he fell from the
roof of a house, and unfortunately lost his eyesight from the
effects of the accident. Being unable to follow his business,
he afterwards supported himself and his family by his talents
as a musician, and attended with his fiddle the different merry-
makings, etc., in the town. A picture of his life at this
period is well drawn by his friend, Robert Emery, in the
song, " The Sandgate Lassie's Lament "—

Oh! hinny, Mall, aw's very bad, my heart is like to break ;
The dowley news, aw's greeved to say, hes nearly dyun the trick :
For Dick the Deevil on the Kee declar'd to me th' day,
While sobbin sair, that deeth had tyen poor Bobby Nunn away,
          Poor Bobby Nunn away !

Head-meetin' days were spent in glee when Bobby tyuk the chair,
Whene'er we saw his sonsie face wor steam got up for fair,
His merry sang an' fiddle good did banish care an' pain,
But cruel deeth hes stopp'd his breeth,—he'll never sing again !
          Oh ! he'll never sing again.

The happy days o' Christmas ne joy te us will bring ;
E'n Peter Nichol's bonny birds most dowley dirges sing ;
But while Tyne's stream runs to the sea, Nunn's fame can never set,
He always was Newcassel's pride, an' sae will he yet.
          An' sae will he yet, an' sae will he yet.

House in which Nunn died.

Besides the attractions of his fiddle, he was a good singer, and composed a great number of local songs, which he sung with great success. Many of his songs, written upon passing events, and sometimes rather coarse in consequence of the mixed companies he amused, are now forgotten, but several which appear in this volume have taken their places as standards amongst Tyneside songs, and are highly popular. He died at Queen Street, Castle Garth, Newcastle, on the 2nd of May 1853, aged forty-five years.

Robert Emery supplied the information about Nunn which appears above. W. H. Dawson, in his *Local Poets*, has further information. "Robert Nunn was eminently a Newcastle man, and had the 'burr' in all its delightful purity. He could not be considered a man of any intellectual culture, and it is therefore the more creditable that he has produced so many songs. Some of them will not bear a close inspection, on account of their approaching the questionable. There were circumstances to account for that; he had some talent as a performer on the fiddle, and being in the habit of attending women's boxes or benefit clubs on the occasion of their holding their head-meeting days, when the old ladies had plied themselves with a plentiful supply of stimulants they would disport themselves on the 'lightly-gay fantastic toe' to the pleasing scrapings of 'Bobby's' fiddle. To diversify their delight he would entertain them with a song, and a professor of moral ethics would have got a lesson had he seen how the more than innuendoes were received. No doubt this would urge him on the more in that direction. That was no reason, however, they should ever have appeared in print."

" 'Bobby Nunn,' as he was generally called, was a heavy looking man, a great favourite at resorts of which we have spoken, and no party of the kind was considered complete without 'Bobby' and his fiddle."

The bard, for Nunn is worthy of the name, did not confine his efforts in supporting his family to his musical abilities only; no honest work came amiss to him. His musical gifts were generally in demand at nights, and during the day Bobby, for Sopwith and other turners and cabinet-makers, turned the big wheels of their lathes. When not busy with that he indulged his love of birds, for which, blind as he was, he had a passion in making cages for them. That his home, despite his blindness, was a happy one, the following song, which he puts into the mouth of his wife, fairly shows :—

ROBY'S WIFE'S LAMENTATION.

(Second and third verses.)

When Roby's in my heart is leet,
  He tyeks the fiddle doon;
He drives away a winter's neet
  Wi' playin' a hearty tune.
He talks about th' happy neets
  He had when coortin' me,
Aside the burn among the corn
  Where oft we yuest to be.

Chorus.

Roby he's gyen oot th' neet
  Ti see his sister Jin;
It's now struck nine, he's past his time,
  Aw wish he wad cum in.

2 I

When sittin' bi the fireside,
  What pleasure div aw feel;
He smiles an' ca's me his dear bride,
  An' says he likes me weel.
An' when aw'm sittin' on his knee,
  He tugs at me for fun;
Lang may aw say, blist be th' day
  That aw was called a Nunn.

> Roby he's gyen oot th' neet, etc.

Some fifty years ago, at the annual treats to the aged poor of St. Nicholas' at Christmas-tide, Bobby was at home (St. Nicholas was his parish); and at the treats, after tea came the entertainment, thus described by one who saw and heard:—

"Bobby was great at the annual treats, his rendering of 'Jocker,' 'Newcastle is my Native Place,' 'The Ropery Banks,' and 'Drucken Bella Roy, O,' never failing to provoke the merriment of the old women. Occasionally he would compose impromptu verses on the company, and at such times the usually gravè clergy and the charming young ladies who ladled out soup in the kitchen in the Long Stairs in the winter time, and who always attended the Christmas party, could not by any means retain their gravity. There was, perhaps, a trifle of the blunt and uncouth in the language and sentiment of his songs that characterised the local poets of a former generation, but his inimitable drollery covered all blemishes and created a merriment that made his presence always welcome."—ELFIN, *Daily Chronicle*, *December 30th*, 1887.

Where poor Nunn lies, "after life's fitful fever," is uncertain. His sons have left the town, and his daughter is dead. Old neighbours of his say he lies in St. Nicholas' churchyard, but there is no entry of his burial there for 1853 (the year of his death), or for some years previous. The churchyard was closed in 1853, and the cemetery opened. The register of the cemetery has also been searched, but in vain. The uncertainty of his place of burial does not extend to the fate of his songs: they will live. Dawson writes of their being very melodious. It is a happy term, and some of his best, as the "Sandgate Lass on the Ropery Banks" and "Blind Willie's Death," richly deserve the name.

"Workmen's trips, now so common, were unknown until about 1847, when R. & W. Hawthorn begun them by giving the workmen at their famous engine works, Forth Banks, a two-days' trip to Edinburgh. It being the first of its kind (the factory band accompanying it), the trip made a great talk, and St. Nicholas' bells were rung in honour of the occasion.   Nunn, on the look-out for anything fresh, wrote a song about it, which he sung on pay-nights at public-houses near the works amongst the men.   It begins—

> " 'The twentieth of August the weather was fine,
>   When Hawthorn's mechanics went off from the Tyne,
>   To visit Auld Reekie.' . . .

The song was a lengthy one.   It described the journey, with the sights to be seen, and, as sung by Nunn, went well.   It would be about the last he wrote, as he died not long after."

Joe Wilson, in an acrostic on his death, thus gives his estimate of Bobby Nunn—

> N e mair will we hear him play a bonny teun ;
> U nequalled wes he when the dancin' wes deun.
> N yen cud chant like him, his sangs myed lots o' fun,
> N ebody pleased them like canny Bobby Nunn.

His songs we first find in Fordyce's 1842 volume ; in fact, Fordyce's may be said to be the only place, as the collection referred to by Dawson, and the broadsheets issued by himself, are about lost.

An imperfect copy of Nunn's songs, at the last moment, has been found.   The date (probably about 1840) is torn off. "The Poor Aud Horse" and "The Quarter of Currans," two songs much sung by Nunn, unfortunately are not in it. If they ever formed part, they must be amongst the missing leaves.   The songs here, as far as possible, are corrected from it.

THE PITMAN AND THE BLACKIN'.

The first song in Nunn's book is said to be the first song he wrote, and for which, the story runs, he got half-a-crown as his pay.   The McCrees, whose blacking he puffs, were some fifty years ago well-known tradesmen in Newcastle.   The Rev. T. McCree, about the first to devote himself to mission work amongst the outcast poor, was another brother.

TUNE—" Cole Hole."

O, BETTY, come and see my byuts,
  The upper leather's crackin' ;
It's a' wi' cleanin' them wi' syut,
  And niver usin' blackin'.

But, Betty, awl gan ti the toon
Ti-morn, and see my uncle Brown;
And if it costs me half-a-crown,
   Awl buy a pot o' blackin'.

For comin' hyem fra wark te neet,
   Aw met wi' Willy Dewar;
His shoes were glitterin' on his feet—
   He lyuckt like some heed viewer.
My eyes bein' dazzled at the seet,
Says aw, what myeks your shoes se breet,
He said to me, In Blackett Street
   Aw bought a pot o' blackin'.

It's myed, said he, by T. McCree,
   It's noted up and down, man;
It is the best, it heads the rest
   In a' Newcassel toon, man.
Byeth pyest and liquid ye may get
Te myek yor shoes as black as jet;
It will presarve them when they're wet,
   This celebrated blackin'.

There's Warren hes a vast o' slack,
   And cuts a deal o' capers,
But still McCree he hes the crack
   In a' Newcassel's papers.
Then if thou wants thy byuts ti shine,
Or shoes ti be as breet as mine,
Gan, Tommy, thou to toon in time,
   And buy a pot o' blackin'.

Then, Betty, jewel, if this be true,
   Awl gan ti-morrow mornin',
And awl bring hyem a pot or two,
   Awl not be lang returnin'.

Then Betty, it'll be a joke,
    When ye get on yor tartin cloak;
They'll tyek us for some better folk,
    Wor shoes being bright wi' blackin'.

NUNN.   *Author's Edition.*

THE NEWCASTLE LAD;

OR, NEWCASTLE IS MY NATIVE PLACE.

This song, in all probability, a little of Nunn's own early life.

TUNE—" An' sae will we yet."

NEWCASTLE is my native place, where my mother sigh'd
    for me,
I was born in Rewcastle Chare, the centre of the Kee;
There early life I sported, quite free from care and pain!
But alas! those days are past and gone, they'll never
    come again.
                    No, they'll never come again, etc.

They sent me to the Jub'lee school, a scholar to make
    me,
Where Tommy Penn, my monitor, learned me my A, B, C;
My master to correct me, often used his whip and cane,
But I can say with confidence, he'll never do't again.
                    No, he'll never, etc.

I left the school and to a trade I went to serve my time;
The world with all its flattering charms before me seem'd
    to shine;
Then there was plenty cash astir, and scarce one did
    complain,
But ah! alas! those days are past, and ne'er will come
    again.
                    No, they'll never, etc.

Like other youths I had a love to wander by my side,

And oft I whisper'd in her ear that she should be my
bride ;

And ev'ry time I kissed her lips, she cried "O fie, for
shame !"

But with "Good night," she always said, "Now mind you
come again !"

Now mind, etc.

At last to church I went away with Sally to be wed,

For thoughts of matrimony came, and troubled then my
head.

The priest that tied the fatal knot, I now can tell him
plain,

If I was once more single he should never do't again.

He should never, etc.

Now, like another married man, I've with the world to
fight,

But never mind, let friendship reign amongst us here
to-night,

Then with a bumper in each hand let every heart exclaim,

Here's happy may we separate and happy meet again !

And happy meet, etc.

NUNN.   *Author's Edition.*

LUCKEY'S DREAM.

TUNE—"Caller Fair."

THE other neet aw went t' bed,
   Bein' weary wi maw wark, man,
Aw dreamt that Billy Scott was deed,
   It's curious t' remark, man.
Aw thowt aw saw his buryin' fair,
   An' knew the comp'ny a', man,
For a' poor Billy's frinds were there,
   Ti see him levelled law, man.

Blind Willie slawly led the band,
  As beagle on the way, man,
A staff he carried in his hand,
  An' shook his heed se grey, man;
At his reet hand was Buggy Jack,
  Wi' his hat brim se broad, man;
And on his left was Bill the Black,
  Ti lead him on his road, man.

Big Bob, X Y, and other two,
  That leeves upon the deed, man,
They bore his corpse before the crew,
  Expectin' t' be fee'd, man.
His nyemsyek, Euphy Scott, was there,
  Her bonny Geordy, tee, man;
Distress'd, they cried, this happy pair,
  Ne mair we will him see, man.

Bold Jocker was amang them, tee,
  Brave Cuckoo Jack an' a', man;
And Hairy Tom, the keelman's son,
  And Bonny Dolly Raw, man;
And Bella Roy and Tatie Bet,
  They cried till oot o' breath, man;
For sair these twosome did regret
  For canny Billy's death, man.

But Hangy luickt above them a',
  He is see sma' and lang, man;
And Bobby Knox, the Dogbank ox,
  Was sobbin' i' the thrang, man.
And Coiner, wi' his swill and shull,
  Was squeakin' like a bairn, man;
And Knack-knee'd Mack, that drucken fyul,
  Like a monkey he did gairn, man.

Tally-i-oo, that dirty wretch,
    Was then the next aw saw, man ;
And Peggy Powell, Step-and-Fetch,
    Was haddin' up her jaw, man :
And frae the Close was Bobby Hush,
    Wi' his greet gob se wide, man ;
Alang wi' him was Push-Peg-Push,
    Lamentin' by his side, man.

And Roguish Ralph, and Busy Bruce,
    That lives upon their prey, man,
Did not neglect, but did protect
    Their frinds upon the way, man.
And Jimmy Liddle, drest in black,
    Behint them a' did droop, man ;
He had a coat on like the quack
    That feeds us a' wi' soup, man.

Now, when they got him tiv his grave,
    He then began to shoot, man,
For Billy being but in a trance,
    B' this time cam' aboot, man.
Then Jocker wi' a sandy styen
    The coffin splet wi' speed, man—
They a' rejoiced to see agyen
    Poor Bill they thowt was deed, man.

When a' his friends that roond him stood
    Had gettin' him put reet, man,
They a' went ti the Robin Hood,
    To spend a jovial neet, man.
Ne mair for Billy they did weep,
    But happy they did seem, man :
Just then aw waken'd frae my sleep,
    And fund it was a dream, man.

NUNN.   *Author's Edition.*

ST. NICHOLAS' CHURCH.

Mr. J. R. Boyle, F.S.A., in his recently published *Cathedral Church of St. Nicholas*, writes:—"Our only written authority as to the early history of this church is in the MSS. of Dr. Nathaniel Ellison, as these are quoted in Brand's *History of Newcastle*."

"A.D. 1091, in the fourth year of William Rufus, the Church of St. Nicholas was founded by Osmund, Bishop of Salisbury."—ELLISON.

Gray, in his *Chorographia*,1649, writes:—"Saint Nicholas, in the midst of the Towne; a long faire and high Church, having a stately high stone Steeple, with many pinakles; a stately stone Lantherne, standing upon foure stone Arches builded by Robert de Rhodes,* Lord Priour of Tinemouth in Henry VI. dayes. It lifteth up a head of Majesty, as high above the rest as the Cypresse Tree above the low Shrubs."

BEN JONSON.

My Altitude high, my Body foure
    square;
My Foot in the grave; my Head
    in the Ayre;
My Eyes in my sides; five
    Tongues in my wombe;
Thirteen Heads upon my Body;
    foure Images alone.
I can direct you where the Winde
    doth stay,
And I tune God's Precepts twice
    a Day.
I am seen where I am not; I am
    heard where I is not:
Tell me now what I am, and see
    that you misse not.

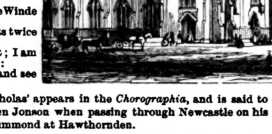

This riddle on St. Nicholas' appears in the *Chorographia*, and is said to have been written by Ben Jonson when passing through Newcastle on his way to visit the poet Drummond at Hawthornden.

TUNE—"Nae Luck about the House."

OH, bonny church, ye've studden lang
    Ti mense wor canny toon,
An' aw believe ye are se strang
    Ye niver will come doon.

* Mr. Boyle thinks not Prior Rhodes, but Robert Rhodes, Esq., who lived in Newcastle at the same time, built the steeple. He quotes Bourne as inclining to that belief, and adds that all more recent writers are of that opinion.

The Arkiteckts, wiv a' their wit,
   May say that ye will fa',
But let them talk, aw'll match ye yet
   Agyen the churches a'.

                                 Chorus.
                     Of a' the churches in our land,
                       Let them be e'er se braw,
                   St. Nicholas' of Newcassel toon
                     Completely bangs them a'.

Ye lang hae stud the bitter blast,
   But lang'r yet ye'll stand ;
And ye hae been for ages past
   A pattern for wor land.
Yor bonny steeple lyuks se grand,
   The hyel world speaks o' ye;
Ye've been the crack for centreys back,
   An' will be when we dee.

It's true they're patching ye aboot
   Wi' iron, styen, an' wood,
But let them patch, aw hev a doot
   They'll de ye little good.
But te be sure it's myekin wark,
   There's plenty lives on ye,
Not only tradesmen an' their clerks,
   But greedy black coats tee.

Yor bonny bells there's nyen excels
   In a' the country roun' ;
They ring se sweet, they are a treat
   When they play Jinny's tyun ;

And when all's still an' dark at neet,
  Ye, wi' yor fiery eye,
Can tell the travellers i' the street
  The time as they pass by.

O that King William wad cum doon
  To see his subjects rare,
And view the buildins i' wor toon,
  He wad crack on them sair;
But when he saw ye, canny church,
  Aw think how he'd admire
The ancient glorious Gothic arch
  That bears the lofty spire.

Now to conclude my little song,
  Maw simple local theme,
Aw trust that if aw've said owt wrang
  That aw will be forgi'en.
Then lang may fam'd St. Nicholas' stand,
  Oh niver may't come doon,
That when we dee wor bairns may see
  The glory o' wor toon.

NUNN.   *Author's Edition.*

THE KEELMAN'S REASONS FOR ATTENDING CHURCH.

TUNE—"Jemmy Joneson's Whurry."

Two keelmen, efter leeving church,
  Before me they were walkin';
When close behind them I did march,
  An' owerheer'd them talkin'!

The one cried, "Dick, me heart is sair,
   Since aw hev heard that sarmin—
It's enuef te myek me drink ne mair,
   For it surely was alarmin'!

"When he began ti tawk o' hell,
   As bein' a sinner's dwellin',
Faith, Dick! aw tyekt te meesel—
   It set maw heart a-swellin';
An' when he said each wicked man
   Wad leeve alang wi' deevils,
Aw surely thowt that aw wad gan
   For a' me former evils.

"Now, Dick, war ye not varry bad
   When ye heard him thus preachin'?
Now tell us, was your heart not sad
   When he se fine was teachin'?
Aw'm sure, Dick, aw cud roar'd amain,
   Had it not been wor Willy;
For he wad gyen an' tell'd wor men,
   An' they wad thought me silly."

Then up spoke Dick—"Aw divint knaw—
   Aw thowt it a' a folly.
Aw was thinkin' on the fad o' straw
   That Jack gae te wor Dolly;
An' then aboot the fight aw had
   Wi' Geordy i' the huddock,
When aw upset the clever lad,
   An' cut him on the buttock.

" Aw just gan there te see the preest,
  An' hear the bonny organ ;
Aw'd suener hev a haggish feast,
  Or drink wi' skipper Morgan.
Te tell the truth what myeks me gan,
  Wor maistor he's religious,
He'll think that aw's a godly man,
  An' mebbies raise me wages !

" For instance, just the tuther day,
  Aw heard it on the Kee, man,
A chep that lairns the folk te pray
  Drinks just as hard as me, man.
So, Tommy, if ye gan te hell,
  That preest 'ill gan there tee, man ;
Then come away, let's heh sum yell,
  An' let such things abee, man."

NUNN.   *Author's Edition.*

THE SANDGATE LASS ON THE ROPERY BANKS.

The Ropery Banks derived their name from the Ropery that was built on the first Ballast Hill that was formed outside the town. They were once a pleasant resort for the youth of the neighbourhood, but "now their glory is departed."—*Note,* 1872 *Edition.*

TUNE—" The Skipper's Wedding."

ON the Ropery Banks Jinny was sittin—
  She had on a bed-goon just new,
And blythely the lassie was knittin
  Wi' yarn of a bonny sky-blue :
The strings of her cap they were hingin,
  Se lang on her shoulders se fine,
And hearty aw heard this lass singin—
  Maw bonny keel lad shall be mine.

Chorus.

O wad the keel come doon the river,
    That aw my dear laddie could see ;
He whistles, he dances se cliver,
    Maw bonny keel laddie for me.

Last neet in amang these green dockins
    He fed me wi' gingerbreed spice—
Aw promised to knit him these stockins,
    He cuddled and kiss'd me se nice ;
He ca'd me his jew'l and his hinny;
    He ca'd me his pet and his bride,
And he swore that aw should be his Jinny,
    To lie at neets doon bi his side.

                    O wad the keel, etc.

That mornin forget aw will niver,
    When first aw saw him on the Kee,
The "Keel Row" he whissel'd se cliver,
    He wun my affections frae me ;
His drawers on his doup luik'd se canny,
    His keel hat was cock'd on his heed,
And if aw'd not gettin my Jimmy,
    Faith, by this time aw wad been deed.

                    O wad the keel, etc.

The first time aw spoke to maw Jimmy—
    Now mind ye it isn't a lee—
My mother had gi'en me a penny,
    To bring her a penn'orth o' tea ;
When a lad i' the street cried oot " Bessie ! "
    Says I, " Hinny, that's not my nyem ; "
" Becrike, niver mind," he said, " lassie,
    To-neet aw will see ye syef hyem."

                    O wad the keel, etc.

Since then aw hae been his true lover,
  Aw've lov'd him as dear as my life,
And in spite o' byeth fethor and mother,
  Aw'll suen be maw keel-laddie's wife !
How happy we'll be then together,
  When he brings hyem his wages ti me,
Wiv his bonny bit bairn cryin "Fethur,"
  And another one laid o' my knee.

O wad the keel, etc.

NUNN.   *Author's Edition.*

DRUCKEN BELLA ROY, O!

Bella Roy was a well-known street-vendor of fruit, fish, etc. Although in her latter days an object of pity through drink, when a young woman, some sixty years ago, she was noted amongst her class for her great personal attractions and neat appearance.—*Note*, 1872 *Edition.*

TUNE—"Duncan M'Callaghan."

WHEN Bella's cummin hyem at neet,
An' as she's walkin doon the street,
The bairns cry oot, "Whe pawned the sheet?
  Wey, Drucken Bella Roy, O !"

Chorus.

Then styens te them gans rattlin, rattlin,
They a' set off a gallopin, gallopin,
Legs an' airms gans wallopin, wallopin,
  For fear o' Bella Roy, O !

Noo, when she's gannin throo the chares,
The bairns begins an' shoots an' blairs,
An' cries, as she gans up the stairs,
  "Where's Drucken Bella Roy, O !"

Then styens, etc.

Noo, if she's had a sup o' beer,
She sets te wark te curse an' sweer,
An' myeks them run away for fear,
    Frae Drucken Bella Roy, O !

                Then styens, etc.

Then in the hoose she sits an' chats,
The bairns then hits her door such bats—
She calls them a' the dorty cats,
    Dis Drucken Bella Roy, O !

                Then styens, etc.

She'll myek the place like thunner ring,
An' down the stairs her things will fling,
An' cry, "Get oot, ye plagey thing,"
    Cries Drucken Bella Roy, O !

                Then styens, etc.

She shoots until she hurts her head,
An' then she's forc'd te gan te bed,
Which is a piece o' straw, doon spread
    For Drucken Bella Roy, O !

            Fal, lal, lal, etc.

NUNN.   *Author's Edition.*

JOCKER.

            TUNE—" O, gin aw had her."

HAE ye seen my Jocker?
Hae ye seen my Jocker?
Hae ye seen my Jocker
    Comin' up the Kee?
Wiv his short blue jacket,
Wiv his short blue jacket,
Wiv his short blue jacket,
    And his hat agee !

Spoken.—JIN. A! lyucka, noo, at clarty Nan, there!—what's she singin' at?

NAN. What is aw singin' at! What's that ti ye? What is aw singin' at! Ah, wey, noo—hev aw ti giv ower singin' for ye? Ah! wey, noo, there's a platter-fyeced bunter for ye!—there's a pink amang the pissy-beds! Ye'd mair need gan hyem and get the dust wesht off ye. Ah! wey, noo—what's that?

Chorus.

O, maw hinny, Jocker,
O, maw hinny, Jocker,
O, maw hinny, Jocker—
    Jocker's the lad for me!

Jocker was a keelman,
Jocker was a keelman,
Jocker was a keelman,
    When he followed me.

Spoken.—But he's exalted now—oh! bliss him! aye—for

He's a porter-pokeman,
He's a porter-pokeman,
He's a porter-pokeman,
    Workin' on the Kee.

Spoken.—NAN. A'say, Jin —hae ye seen owt o' wor Jocker doon the Kee there?

JIN. Ay; aw saw him an' Hairy Tom just gan inti the Low Crane there.

NAN. The Low Crane, ye clarty thing—whe are ye myekin yor gam on?

JIN. Noo call me a clarty thing, an' aw'll plaister yor gob wi' clarts.

THE KEE.

22

NAN. Ay! bliss us a', Jin, what are ye gettin' intiv a rage aboot?

JIN. Wey, didn't ye ax me if aw'd seen owt o' Jocker doon the Kee there, and aw teld ye the truth, an' ye wadn't believe us.

NAN. Wey, is he there?

JIN. Ti be sure he is.

NAN. Wey, aw'll sit doon here till he comes oot, then.

> O, maw hinny, Jocker, etc.

Jocker was a rover,
Jocker was a rover,
Jocker was a rover,
   When he courted me.
But noo his tricks are over,
But noo his tricks are over,
But noo his tricks are over,
   He tyeks me on his knee.

Spoken.—NAN. A! here he's comin'; here's maw jewel comin'. Cum inti my airms, maw tracle dumplin', an' giv us a kiss. Where hae ye been? Aw've been lukin' for ye all ower.

JOCKER. Where hev aw been! Aw've been walkin' up an' doon th' Kee here. Where hae ye been?—aw think ye've been i' th' Sun.

NAN. Wey, maw jewel, aw've just been i' th' Custom Hoose gettin' a glass, an' aw've com'd doon the Kee ti seek ye, ti gan hyem thegether.

> O, maw hinny, Jocker, etc.

NUNN. *Author's Edition.*

THE FIERY CLOCK FYECE.

The dial of the clock in St. Nicholas' Church first lighted with gas, December 5th, 1829. The dial blown out by a violent storm of wind, October 19th, 1862; re-lighted, November 15th, 1862.

TUNE—"Coal Hole."

O DICK, what's kept ye a' this time,
   Aw've fretted sair aboot ye,
Aw thought that ye'd fa'n in the Tyne,
   Then what wad aw duin without ye?

O, hinny, Dolly, sit thee down,
And hear the news aw've brought fra toon,
The Newcassel folks hes catch'd a moon,
    And myed it a bonny clock-fyece.

Thou knaws St. Nicholas' Church, maw pet,
    Where we were tied tigether—
That place, aw naw, thou'll not forget,
    Forget it aw will never.
'Twas there then, jewel, aw saw the seet,
As aw cam staggerin' through the street,
Aw thought it queer at pick-dark neet
    Ti see a fiery clock-fyece.

The folk they stood in flocks about—
    Aw cried, how! what's the matter?
Aw glower'd—at last aw gav a shoot
    For them to fetch some watter.
The church is a-fire, and very suin
That bonny place will be burnt doon;
Ye fyul, says a chep, it's a bonny moon
    They've catch'd and myed it a clock-fyece.

On Monday, when aw gan to wark,
    Aw'll surely tell wor banksman,
If we had sic a leet at dark,
    We'd never break our shanks, man.
Maw marrows an' aw'll gan ti the toon,
Ti see if we can catch a moon—
If we can only coax one doon,
    We'll myek't a bonny clock-fyece.

Then if we get it down the pit,
    We'll hed stuck on a pole, man,
'Twill tell us how wor time gans on,
    Likewise to hew wor coal, man.

So noo, maw pet, let's gan ti bed,
And not forget the neet we wed ;
Thi morn we'll tell wor uncle Ned
    Aboot the bonny clock-fyece.

NUNN.   *Fordyce's " Newcastle Song Book," 1842.*

SANDGATE WIFE'S NURSE SONG.

A, U, A, maw bonny bairn,
A, U, A, upon my airm,
A, U, A, thou seun may learn
    Te say dada se canny.
Aw wish thy daddy may be weel,
He's lang i' comin' frae the keel ;
Tho' his black fyece be like the deil,
    Aw like a kiss frae Johnny.
                  A, U, A, etc.

Thou really hes thy daddy's chin,
Thou art like him leg and wing,
And aw wi' plishure can thee sing,
    Since thou belangs my Johnny.
Johnny is a clivor lad—
Last neet he fuddled a' he had ;
This morn he wasn't varry bad,
    He luik'd as blithe as ony.

Tho' thou's the forst, thou's not the last ;
Aw mean te hae me bairns fast ;
And when this happy time is past,
    Aw still will luve my Johnny :
For his hair is broon, and se is thine ;
Yo'r eyes are grey, and se are mine ;
Thy nose is taper'd off se fine—
    Thou's like thy daddy, Johnny.

Thy canny dowp is fat and roond,
And, like thy dad, thou's plump and soond ;
Thou's worth te me a thoosen poond,
    Thou's a'tegither bonny.
When daddy's drunk he'll tyek a knife,
And threaten sair te tyek my life ;
Whe waddent be a keelman's wife,
    Te hev a man like Johnny?

But yonder's daddy cummin now,
He luiks the best amang the crew ;
They're a' gawn te the Barley Mow,
    My canny, gudlike Johnny.
Cum, let's now get the bacon fried,
And let us myek a clean fireside,
Then on his knee he will thee ride,
    When he cums hyem te mammy.

NUNN.   *Fordyce's " Newcastle Song Book,"* 1842.

JOHN BRODIE GILROY.

SOME forty years ago little was to be heard in the way
of street songs in Newcastle but Gilroy's " Noodle." This
clever parody was a palpable hit, the children shouting after
the old volunteers, when up for training, the lines (slightly
varied)—

    " Ye blue-tailed bumlor, cock-tailed tumlor,
      Ye durnet gan te war."

About the author, who appears only to have written this one
song, W. W. W., in the *Weekly Chronicle*, gives an interesting sketch :—"Foreman at Lambert's Printing Office, Grey
Street, he was a well read man, of ready wit and great
natural ability. He would say such extraordinary things
when vexed or annoyed—to the men or lads—that even the
recipients of these blessings could not refrain from laughing.
Warm-hearted and generous even beyond his means, he
was, in spite of his hot and fiery temper, much liked by those
around him. With all his peculiarities, few men led a more

pure and sinless life than Brodie Gilroy. He died at the beginning of the year 1853, at the early age of 35 years. Eccentric to the last, he was buried, at his own request, with his trousers and boots on. He lies in Westgate Hill Cemetery."

THE NOODLE.

TUNE—"Jeannette and Jeannot."

YOU'RE going to be a Noodle bold, a valiant Volunteer;
You think you'll have a lazy week, and get your swig of beer.
But you'll fight your battles o'er your pipe, and ne'er receive a scar,
You blue-tail bumbler, cock-tail tumbler, dare not go to war.

When you wear the dirty whites, and the sloggerin' jacket blue,
I fear that you will then forget what we may think of you.
With your musket backside first, and your bayonet, lord knows where,
You'll be marching like a hero, to make the lasses stare.

When the trumpet sounds for glory, you'll be madly rushing in
To Atkins' or to Thomas's, to spend your *hard*-earned tin:
And there you'll sit carousing till you're turned out at night,
Well knowing it is better far to fuddle than to fight.

I would I were our noble Queen, much better Matty Bell,
I'd send such would-be warriors to a place I dare not tell;
All the town should be at peace, and the fellows who compose
The swaggerin' volunteers should find themselves in meat and clothes.

GILROY.　　　　　　　　*Selkirk's Collection, 1852.*

JOHN PEACOCK.

MR. WILLIAM BROCKIE, in "Local Songs and Song Writers" in the *Weekly Chronicle*, gives the following sketch of John Peacock :—"A native of South Shields, he went to sea at the age of twelve, was taken prisoner during the French war and confined for several years in the north of France. He was a very remarkable man—a shoemaker, a chartist, a co-operative storekeeper, a second-hand bookseller, in South Shields Market Place ; sober, intelligent, sharp witted, verily, a public institution in the place. He was the author of several creditable pieces of poetry, most of which appeared in the *Shields Garland*, 1859. He died in 1867."

———

MARSDEN ROCK.

Marsden Rock is situated about two miles from South Shields. The shore is in the highest degree savage and terrible. Vast fragments of rock stand in every variety of grotesque form and combination. One enormous mass, riven from the parent beach, now stands detached about one hundred yards. The natural beauties of this romantic spot have long attracted pleasure parties. Mr. Peter Allen conceived the bold idea of scooping out for himself a habitation in the rock. In this he succeeded, and resided in this wild retreat for many years, continually adding to his accommodation, until he at length possessed fifteen apartments, all hewn out of the living rock, and fitted up as a public-house. He died in August 1850; his family still carry on the establishment.

TUNE—"Jockey to the Fair."

THE sultry sun aloft has roll'd,
And ting'd the hills and dales with gold ;
The sea her silv'ry robes unfold
    Her swelling bounds along.
Th' enraptured sky is calm and clear,
Come now to Marsden Rock repair :
Inhale the fresh and balmy air,
Which floats in cooling breezes there,
    The bright blue waves among.

The fruitful tree, and rustling corn,
Wave beauteous to the rosy morn ;
The birds, on rosy pinions borne,
    Proclaim it in a song.

In fleecy showers the pearly spray,.
From ocean's briny fountain play;
And, skimming o'er the watery way,
The Sea-mews strike their finny prey
    The bright blue waves among.

Let steamers gay with beau and belle
Chime up, for Seaton Delaval,
Or Warkworth's towers and hermit's cell,
    May fascinate the young;
But Marsden Rock has charms for me,
Reposing on a summer sea:
Their features wild I love to see,
And on the velvet beds to be
    The bright blue waves among.

The tumbling surge unrapts the strand,
Bespangled lays the beaming sand,
Your early footsteps to command,
    And pleasures to prolong.
Away! the fragrant fields in flow'r
Perfumes the path to *Allen's* bow'r;
With pealing mirth awake the shore
And ring old Marsden's rocky tow'r,
    The bright blue waves among.

Then crown the beach, enchanted roam—
And hail their *light-ships* to their home—
Our fostered seamen, now they come,
    And to its bosom throng.
With beauty graced in smiles divine,
We'll tribute pay to *Peter's* shrine,
And drink success to Wear and Tyne;
For long may their proud Commerce shine
    The bright blue waves among.

PEACOCK.   *" Bards of the Tyne,"* 1849.

JOSEPH PHILIP ROBSON.

OF Joseph Philip Robson, "Bard of the Tyne and Minstrel of the Wear," the author of some of our most popular local songs, we cannot pretend to give more than a brief sketch. To those wishing more information, his most interesting autobiography, recently published, will supply the want most agreeably. From this autobiography we learn he was born in Bailiffgate, Newcastle-on-Tyne, September 24, 1808. At an early age he lost his parents; his mother dying when he was six, and his father when he was only eight years of age. His father had studied at Stoneyhurst College for the Roman Catholic priesthood, but his health failing, he had been obliged to relinquish his

studies; and finally settled at Newcastle as teacher of the Catholic School. In due time our future bard was sent to learn a business, and apprenticed to a plane maker; but severely spraining himself by lifting a heavy log of wood, he took up the more congenial occupation of a schoolmaster.

He had, from an early age, been a lover and a writer of poetry, and now began to think of publishing the fruits of his muse, and in the year 1831 he issued his first volume, *Blossoms of Poesy*, his other works appearing as follows:— *Poetic Gatherings*, 1839; *The Monomaniac*, 1847; *Poetic Pencillings*, 1852; *Hermione the Beloved*, 1857; and *Evangeline; or, the Spirit of Progress*, 1869.

By the publication of his works he won a high reputation as a poet, and gained the friendship and praise of many distinguished writers, including Eliza Cook, Charles Swain, Lord Ravensworth, etc., etc. Of the latter he particularly speaks as a kind friend, and one ever ready to give his valuable critical assistance. Although it is perhaps as a local writer he will eventually be best remembered, it is singular that it was only at the solicitation of two musical friends that he took to writing in the dialect. The song he wrote being successful, he followed it by others: profit, as well as praise, being a consideration, he, like the majority of the "tuneful throng," having his share of the poverty generally accompanying the poet. On the publication of *Hermione the Beloved*, in 1857, through Lord Palmerston, the Queen sent him the handsome present of twenty pounds. This was but a transient gleam: he found it a hard fight to live by his pen, clever and ready as it undoubtedly was. In 1849 he wrote the life of Billy Purvis. In 1849-50 he edited the *Bards of the Tyne*, a collection of local songs, in which appeared some of the best of his own. On the visit of Prince Lucien Bonaparte to the North in 1859, he was engaged by the Prince to make a version of the Song of Solomon into the Lowland Scotch. This task he executed satisfactorily, the critics and the Prince alike being pleased. The latter years of his life were perhaps his most prosperous. He contributed to "Chater's Comic Almanack," and had a regular engagement on the *North of England Advertiser*, to which paper he sent his weekly Local Letter, signed "A Retiort Keelman." This letter he wrote in the local dialect, and it was eagerly looked for in the various towns and villages of the North: his great local knowledge and extensive reading enabling him to make it most interesting.

About the middle of 1869, while his last work, *Evangeline*, was passing through the press, he was seized with a paralytic stroke. After a time he slightly improved; but finally sunk under the attack on the 26th of August 1870, in his sixty-second year.

The following beautiful lines may be appropriately appended, as it was his wish that they should be regarded as his Parting Address to the people of Tyneside.

" When this hand that the harp of old Tyne oft awakened
  With lays rude and simple lies low in the earth;
When the Angel of Peace to his bosom has beckon'd,
  And called him from friendship, from music, and mirth ;
Let the sunlight of kindness in silence beam o'er him,
  And gild the dark spots on his mem'ry that lie ;
Let the radiance of love to a rainbow restore him,
  And hope spread her beautiful wings to the sky.

Let the strains that he warbled,—poor bird of the morning,
  Find echo in bosoms, the tender and true ;
And his spirit to earth in its gladness returning,
  In the Valley of Shadows his songs may renew.
O ye loved and true-hearted, forget all his errors,
  Clothe his mem'ry in robes of a penitent child ;
Let the grave where he slumbers be shorn of death's terrors,
  And love's daisies shall bloom in their gentleness wild. "

To this brief sketch, which appeared in 1872, we may add, " the grave where he slumbers " is in Jesmond Old Cemetery. Directly on entering the gates, turn to the left, then, about fifty yards along still on the left, you come to where he lies. The grave may be easily found, a neat tombstone marking the spot. On the stone which was erected by his many admirers are the following lines, taken from a piece to his memory by his friend, Mr. Joseph McGill :—

" ' Tho' dead,—in lamenting thee
  Still be it mine
To honour thy name, sweetest Bard of the Tyne. "

Joe Wilson, forgetting past differences, also contributed his offering to Robson's memory. In the following acrostic he praises him with no niggard hand :—

ACROSTIC.

R emember, ye Bards, the famous J. P.,
O v Tyneside,—a Poet ov highest degree ;
B ard o' the Tyne an' Minstrel o' the Wear,
S preedin the harmony we like te hear ;
O v a' the greet writers reet foremost he'll shine,
N oo an' for iver 'mang Bards o' the Tyne.

By the kindness of Matthew Mackay, Jun., we are enabled to give a *fac-simile* of Robson's handwriting and autograph. Other examples given here have had to be reduced by photography to fit the page. Robson's writing, small and beautifully fine, is reproduced exactly the size it was written.

Lincoln Grieves; or — Life Dreams.　By J. P. Robson

A rose-lipped, blue-eyed, baby lay,
Like a soft dream within 'he arms,
And on the bosom of sweet May —
'Twas but the miniature of charms
That had been infantine one day;
That thus had nestled from th'alarms
Of outward strife, like unto this
Rainbow of Love & hope & Bliss!

THE EXILE'S RETURN.

This, "The Return," is the last of the six "Lays of the Tyne Exile."
The first, "The Departure," opens—

" Soft fell the light of dying day on Tyne's fair flowing flood,
As on the shore, with burning breast. the hapless exile stood ;
To-morrow he must leave his home, his pleasures and his pride ;
Sad were his farewell strains of woe, as thus the mourner cried."

　　　·　　　　·　　　　·　　　　·　　　　·

Then comes " In Childhood we Wander," " Farewell, Fair Fields," " Maid of my Bosom," " Banks o' Tyne," and "The Return," last, but not the least, as it is by far the most popular of the whole, and written when he was in his seventeenth year. It appeared in *Fordyce*, 1842.

RECITATIVE—"The Old English Gentleman."

FROM wandering in a distant land, an exile had return'd,

And when he saw his own dear stream, his soul with pleasure burn'd ;

The days departed, and their joys, came bounding to his breast,

And thus the feelings of his heart in *native strains* expressed.

TUNE—"The Keel Row."—*Sung slowly.*

Flow on, majestic river,
Thy rolling course for ever ;
Forget thee will I never,
    Whatever fate be mine !
Oft on thy banks I've wander'd,
And on thy beauties ponder'd :
Oh ! many an hour I've squander'd
    By bonny coaly Tyne !

Flow on, etc.

Oh ! Tyne, in thy bright flowing
There's magic joy bestowing ;
I feel thy breezes blowing,
    Their perfume is divine !
I've sought thee in the morning,
When crimson clouds were burning,
And thy green hills adorning,
    Thy hills, oh, bonny Tyne !

When stormy seas were round me,
And distant nations bound me,
In memory still I found thee
    A ray of hope benign !
Thy valleys lie before me,
Thy woods are waving o'er me ;
My home, thou dost restore me !
    I hail thee, bonny Tyne !

Chorus.

Flow on, majestic river,
Thy rolling course for ever ;
Forget thee will I never,
    Whatever fate be mine !

J. P. ROBSON.   "*Bards of the Tyne,*" 1849.

THE WONDERFUL TALLYGRIP.

The following humorous account of that modern wonder, the electric telegraph, was originally sung at the **Wheat Sheaf Music Saloon, Cloth Market.** It became at once a great favourite.

TUNE—"Barbara Bell."

Iv a' the greet wonders that dazzles wor blinkers,
  The Tallygrip's sartin the king o' them a';
It bothers wor maisters, an' viewers, an' sinkers,
  An' hauds them as dumb as a cuddy's lockjaw.
Whei it's just a bit wire, like the string ov a fiddle,
  Gans alang biv some stobs for te ring a bit bell;
The leetnin', ye ken, runs alang by the middle,
  An' turns th' twe pointers se cliver te spell.

The Tallygrip travels by neet an' by day, man,
  An' sends a' the news te the man i' the meun;
If ye want te be wedded there's nowse for te pay, man—
  Wivoot ony parson the job can be deun.
Big Matty, wor keeker, was married at Howdon
  Wivoot ony ring but the ring iv a bell;
An' Mally, his bride, was then stoppin at Bowden,—
  Smash! the Tallygrip said a' the sarvis itsel.

Hoot, man, thor's ne prenter nor shorthandy writer
  Can scribble, like Tally, the speeches se fine;
She kens ivery blaw that can sobble a fighter,
  An' coonts ivery feul on the banks o' wor Tyne.
The "blue-bottle" cheps hes queer sprees on the rail, man;
  The Tallygrip catches folks 'fore they can leet;
That little clock fyece gars the "swells" hing their tail,
      man,—
  Ralphy Little ca's Tally the *Policeman's Beat.*   .

Rowley Hill, aw's aflaid, mun be knock'd on the heed, man,
    An' letters gan free by the Tallygrip's string;
Ne trouble o' writin', an' far quicker speed, man—
    Gox! we'll lairn a' the blackies "Pit Laddie" to sing.
But the negurs 'll ken that us whiteys is traders,
    When we cork a' wor jaws "Lucy Neal" for te shoot,
Wi' wor knackers an' drums, like aud Nick's sorrynaders,
    An' crawin' like Banties that's bad i' the moot.

Aw went, t'other neet, for te hear some fine singin',
    At Balmbra's grand consort, an' hear a' thor cracks;
An' there aw seun spied a' thor Cupid lads hingin',
    An' gas-leeters myed oot o' cannels o' wax.
A chep played Pianny, an' bonny she soonded:
    A leddy sung sweet, like a bird i' the skies;
A chep they ca' Spiers was the joker that croon'd it,
    But Charley, the fiddler, bang'd a' for his size.

Noo, what de ye think? it's as true as aw's stannin,
    Afore aw gat hyem te wor hoose on the Fell,
Aw met wi' Blue Bella, an' ca'd at the Cannon,
    An' just was beginnin o' Balmbra's te tell,
When a gentleman chep stopt me short i' me story,
    Says he, "Sir, ye heerd a grand consort last neet;
The news cam' te Lunnon—I knew it before ye,"
    Gox, smash! 'twas the gospel—the Tally was reet!

So aw'd hae ye, maw marrows, te mind what yor deein,
    An' not gan galantin wi' sweethearts an' that,
For the tellypie Tally 'ill seun send her fleein,
    An' mevies sum cheps might get inte the hat!

Whei dinnet ye knaw when wor Queen gat her bed, man,
    The couchers o' Lunnon scarce 'liver'd a son—
Aye, afore the young prince wi' spice boily was fed, man,
    The greet 'lumination o' the Tyne was a' deun.

WHEN WE WERE AT THE SKUEL.

TUNE—"Nae luck aboot the hoose."

I JUST maun chaunt a wee bit sang,
    An' play for yence the fyul;
An' tell the evils o' the days
    When we were at the skuel.
Ah! weel ye mind the wooden leg,
    An' think ye hear it stump;
Ye'll no forget the "Grey Meer Meg,"
    The name just gars me jump.

Chorus.

When we were at the skuel, my lads,
    We oft wished to be men;
We gat our wishes: now we lang
    To be at skuel agyen.

The Dom'nee lo'ed the "Quaker's Wife"—
    The sang, I mean—fu' weel;
He whistled as we sang for life,
    He drummed to make us squeel.
The dreadful "Clog" fast to the ring,
    An' "Ginglesby," the sprite,
That in the garret wav'd his wing,
    Filled a' our hearts wi' fright.

Ah, man ! to kneel two hours or sae
   Upon a ruler round
Was sic a pleasure in that day,
   The like's now seldom found.
An' then upon a desk to kick,
   Gripp'd fast by leg and arm,
Weel hammer'd wiv a clubby stick—
   It garred ye feel a' warm.

The maister was a canty chiel,
   At ba' in skuel he'd play ;
He did not heed the lads a deal,
   An' what could callants say ?
He'd fry us pancakes at a pinch,
   An' clout our heads when dull,
An' nip wor lugs, and gar us flinch—
   They were grand times at skuel.

Methinks I see the bonny spot
   Where pears an' apples grew ;
We didna like to see them rot,
   Sae kindly pluck'd a few.
Wor lads—the maisters kens it a'—
   Stuff bags down ilka back,
And if the cane should chance to fa',
   Ye'll never tent the crack.

Ye'll no forget the Washing Tubs,
   The burn's Green Water Pyul ?*
Ye'll maybe mind o' Tommy's rubs,
   When ye cam' late to skuel ?

* Both famous bathing places for boys at Jesmond Burn.

Your memory o' the battle speaks,
　　When foes were doom'd to fa';
Tho' Roman chiels, ye fought like Greeks,
　　But best—ahint the wa'!

The days are gyen—yet still we cling
　　To recollections dear;
We haud the bee without the sting—
　　The thought without the fear.
Oh! merry were the days o' yule,
　　When our good pastor came
Wi' grand prize buiks and cakes to skuel,
　　An' sent us dancing hame.

Where is that honoured pastor now?
　　His fate was like the lave:
Time laid his cauld hand on his pow:
　　We bore him to his grave.
An' when his image meets our ken,
　　The faithful tear is given;
But—let us never weep again,—
　　He'll no come back frae Heaven.

J. P. ROBSON.　　　　　　　"*Bards of the Tyne,*" 1849.

POLLY'S NICKSTICK.

Written on the second Polytechnic Exhibition, opened Easter Monday, 1848.

TUNE—"X, Y, Z."

SMASH, marrows! but aw's like to drop,
　　At summat aw mun tell, man!
Aw went te see wor Polly's shop:
　　Aw thowt te see hersel', man!

In Blackett Street the place aw fand,
For Poll's awn hoose 'twas ower grand ;
But in aw bowls :—when, in a box,
A chep says, "Sixpence, sir !" by gox !
"Hoot, man," says aw, "yor pickin' fun !
Aw's Polly's feyther's youngest son,
    Just com to see her Nickstick !"

Aw pays the lad the money doon
    (For brass aw niver cares, man !),
An' suen seed picturs stuck aroon',
    An' kissin' folks in pairs, man !*
A little lad, wi' greyhoond bitch,
Was gan a bonny bool te pitch ;†
A lass wes shiverin' wi' the caud,‡
An' bonny legs, poor thing, she had :
Says aw, "Maw bairn, gan hyem wi' me,
An' ye shall hae spice kyek and tea,
    An' leave wor Polly's Nickstick.

A chep was snorin' 'mang the trees,
    They said 'twas Charley King, man !§
Says aw, "Giv' ower wi' yor lees,
    Aw kens another thing, man !
For Charley's pluck for ony thieves,
And wadn't skulk amang the leaves.
So, freend, just drop yor Cockney craw,
Or mevvies aw may crack yor jaw."
So at his lug aw myed a spring,
Te tell him *aw* was Charley King,
    The freend o' Polly's Nickstick !

* Cupid and Psyche.   † Statue, by Gott.
‡ The Outcast, by J. H. Foley.
§ Charles the First in the Oak, by H. G. Townshend.

Queen Bess aw spied in Punch's box,
   Wi' ruffles roond her chin, man!*
An' Burley, slee as ony fox;
   An' Leester, luikin' thin, man!
A greet fat chep, wi' horns a pair,
Was dancin' wi' sum *hoo-hoos* there;
An' Fletcher, wiv his play-hoose crack,
Wi' aud rare Benny, drest i' black;
An' Shakspur, tee, that stole the bull,
Then ca'd the may'r a slaverin' cull,
   A' graced wor Polly's Nickstick.

Bill Martin wagg'd me tiv his side,
   Te prove his brother's skill, man!
Says he, "That king yence stopp'd the tide,†
   An' held the waves at will, man!
The chucks an' gravel luiks alive,
An' in yon wave a whale might dive!"
Says aw, "By gox! that's Cullercoats,
Except there is ne fisher boats;
An', smash! the sun is gan te fry
Yon cloods that luik like plucks on high,
   Te feed wor Polly's Nickstick!"

Noo, fra this show aw hows away,
   'Mang fishes, birds, and beasts, man!‡
An' certainly aw's boun' te say,
   Aw had a cliver feast, man!
Pall parrots, snipes, and kangaroos,
Redshanks, an' squarrels, an' cuckoos;

* Queen Elizabeth at the Globe Theatre, witnessing the play of "The
Merry Wives of Windsor."—D. Scott, R.S.A.
  † King Canute and his Courtiers.—John Martin, K.H.
  ‡ The Museum, Victoria Room.

White skulls o' bairns, or else baboons;
Stuff'd hedgehogs, otters, and racoons;
Tape worms, an' crabs, an' turtles rare,
Sea serpents, shorks, an' tyeds was there,
 Like live at Polly's Nickstick.

But when aw seed the engine grand,*
 That turns the 'lectric clock, man!
An' Lousyfilly's dune by hand,
 Upon a weaver's block, man!†
Says aw, "Why, Armstrang, thou's a king,
Thou'll suen gie Hudson's steam the fling:
For louse-traps here thou mykes o' wire;
Thy wetter wonders never tire;‡
Thou cracks steel nuts,§ an' figures glass, ||
Thaw engine does the world surpass:
 It graces Polly's Nickstick.

But, Lor! te tell ye all aw seed
 Wad fill a bible beuk, man!
Balloons was dancin' biv a threed,
 An' folks hung biv a heuk, man!
A CAN TELLS oot the chickens there;¶
Here's Cheeny folks wi' silver hair;
Fans, pipes, an' dwarfs, wi' heeds like bulls,
An' giants wi' greet iron skulls;
An' gowlden cups, an' bonny glass,
An' Clasper's skiff, an' forrin grass,
 Was at wor Polly's Nickstick.

* Mr. Armstrong's Water Pressure Engine.
† The Jacquard Loom.   § Shank's Screw Cutter.
‡ Card Machine. || Glass Engraving.
    ¶ Cantelo's Incubator.

An organ grand was bummin' lood,*
　　But nyen cud tell the tuen, man!
Aw paid maw penny wi' the crood,
　　Te see the glassy mune, man!
Wor Tommy's Ropes† they ca'd a thing,
Like rainbows runnin' iv a ring;
An' croods o' things wi' hairy tails,‡
An' ships wi' wings asteed o' sails;
Grace Darling, tee, cam iv her boat,§
An' saved the wreckers iv her float;
An' smash! wor Poll amang the mist
Peep'd oot, and said, " Gud neet,"—be blist!
　　Then vanish'd frae the Nickstick.

Aw left the place wi' sair regret,
　　Tho' aw had spoiled a gill, man!
But weel it's worth the brass they get,
　　Let folks say what they will, man!
Thinks aw, " By George! aw'll up an' see
Yence mair the engine an' the spree "—
When, gannin past, aw touched a wire, ‖
Why, smash! my neeves was a' afire—
The verra hair stud on my heed,
Away aw cuts wi' pith an' speed;
An' bools reet throo a rowley gate,
An' in a varry narvous state,
　　Aw left wor Polly's Nickstick.

J. P. ROBSON.　　　　　　　　　　" *Bards of the Tyne,*" 1849.

* Organ, by Nicholson.　　　‡ Oxy-hydrogen Microscope.
† Chromotropes.　　　　　§ Dissolving Views.
　　　　‖ Electrical Conductors.

THE HIGH LEVEL BRIDGE.

For long, all that was to be seen of the much-talked-of "High Level"
was the wherry from which boring operations were carried on.

TUNE—"Drops of Brandy."

Aw tyuk the cheap train t'other day,
   For wor Mally begun for to fidge, man ;
To Newcassel aw hastened away,
   To luik at the High Level Bridge, man.
The folks o' wor raw was aflaid—
   They tell'd us a brig was purjected
That wad spoil a' the colliery trade,
   For wi' Lunnon, they said, 'twas connected.

But when aw gets oot i' the train,
   Aw hows doon the stairs iv a hurry,
And the High Level seun aw seed plain,
   It was stuck o' the top iv a whurry.
But, man, when the Garth aw espied,
   Aw was nowther to haud or to bind, man,
For translators an' tailors aw cried,
   But the deevil a yen cud aw find, man.

Aw seed a chep dress'd up i' black,
   For the Garth, the folk said, he was mournin',
Aw ask'd him for Trimmel-leg Jack,
   'Cawse he had maw blue trousers in turnin';
He set up a terrible shout,
   Aw thowt the poor man was gawn daft, man,
Says he, " He is lost in the rout "—
   Aw luik'd at the feul an' aw laughed, man.

Aw dropp'd in at Jude's, o' the Cock,
   An' whe de ye think aw seed there, man?
Billy Purvis, as fresh as a rock,
   An' cursin' the brig, aw declare, man.

Says he, "They hae stopp'd the bug breed,
  The clocks is a' scrammil'd an' kill'd, man,
The snips is clean oot o' thor heeds,
  Since the Level they started te build, man.

"The claes-wives lost a' their fine goons,
  The silkies was torn in the laps, man;
The shifts sail'd aboot like balloons,
  An' they pull'd off the white trouser-flaps, man."
Says aw, "Then maw breeches is gyen!"
  Says Billy, "An' Trimmel-leg tee, man;
They've turn'd his sheep-shanks inte styen,
  Te striddle across the greet sea, man.

"The sweepers was forced for to brush,
  They gae the poor deevils the sack, man;
The chimleys cam doon iv a rush,
  An' Lumley was laid on his back, man.
The pie-men an' sassage-wives, tee,
  Gat notish ne langer te tarry:
The blackin' folks a' had te flee,
  An' the hatters was croon'd by awd Harry.

But spite o' their ravish an' root,
  Blue-styeny is still te the fore, man;
The apple-wives on her still shoot,
  Dandy-candy's still sell'd in galore, man.
Let the 'tractors an' beeldors purceed,
  An' cramp wi' greet bowlts ivery styen, man,
A secret aw hae in maw heed—
  We mun just start an' level agyen, man.

J. P. ROBSON.   *"Bards of the Tyne,"* 1849.

CALLERFORNEY.

A DIALOGUE.

TUNE—"Alley Croaker."

MALLY.
OH, hinny, Geordy, canny man,
  Thou kens aw likes thou dearly!
For thee aw turned off baggy Crooks,
  An' used Tim Targit queerly;
Billy Benson coax'd me sair to wed,
  But man, aw cuddent spurn thee!
Oh, hinny, canst thou think o' this,
  An' gan te Callerforney?
Oh, Callerforney! fuilish Callerforney!
Like honey blobs my heart 'll brust,
  If thou gans te Callerforney.

GEORDY.
Hoots, Mally, haud yor whinjin gob,
  Maw mind's myed up for sartin;
Maw peeks an' spyeds is i' my kist—
  The morn aw's sure be startin',
Aw'll seun be hykin on the sea,
  An' fleein' roond Cape Horney;
Aw kens the seam to hew for goold,
  When aw gets te Callerforney.
Oh, Callerforney, bonny Callerforney,
The vary clairts upon the street
  Is goold in Callerforney.

MALLY.
Thou's mevies rue, maw collier lad,
  When in the waves thou's sprawlin,
When crocidiles and unicorns
  Is at thaw hoggers haulin.

Thou's not hae luck like Joney, man,
    In some whale's guts to turn thee;
Thou'll lang to be wi' me at hyem,
    An' far frae Callerforney.
Oh, Callerforney, shem on Callerforney!
Bob Stackers sweers thor's nowt but fules
    Wad gan te Callerforney.

GEORDY.   Thou's rang aw tell thee, Mally lass,
    Just read the papers, hinny,
The place is verra like the mint,
    Another Coast o' Guinea!
Tho' mind thee, yence aw heer'd it tell'd
    The cannibals wad burn ye,
An' make goold ointment o' yor byens,
    When ye get te Callerforney.
Oh, Callerforney, whei noo, Callerforney,
Hoots, Mally aw can thresh them a',
    Aw'll conquer Callerforney!

MALLY.   Consither, Geordy, aw's thee wife,
    Aw divent gan contrary,
If thou mun gan, thou's tyek the lass
    Thou ca's thaw bonny Mary!
But weel aw kens afore thou gans,
    Thou's trim'lin at the journey;
Sea sarpints tee may cowp the boat,
    Then where's thaw Callerforney?
Oh, Callerforney, tice'n Callerforney!
Aw wish that folks was not se poor,
    To want thee, Callerforney!

GEORDY.   Cheer up, maw duck! thou'll gan wi' me,
              Aw niver heeds the danger!
          Poor collier lads works hard for nowt,
              An' still to deeth's ne stranger.
          Like Whittin'ton aw heers the bells
              That says, "Come on yor journey!"
          Goold's better far than howkin' coals—
              Oh dear, this Callerforney!
          Oh, Callerforney, we're comin', Callerforney,
          Fareweel to splint, choke damp, an' blast!
              Huzza! for Callerforney.

J. P. ROBSON.   "*Bards of the Tyne*," 1849.

THE PAWNSHOP BLEEZIN'

This celebrated song is written on Mrs. Trotter's Pawnshop, formerly situated in the Side, Newcastle, being entirely destroyed by fire, in the year 1849. Although a humorous composition, it faithfully describes the horrors and misery attending the use of such establishments, and is certainly one of the author's most popular productions.—*Note*, 1872.

TUNE—"X, Y, Z."

WOR Sall was kaimin' oot her hair,
    An' aw was turnin' dosy,
Whiles snot'rin' in wor easy chair,
    That myeks a chep sleep cosy,
When frae the street cam screams an' cries—
Wor Sall says "Wheest!" aw rubs my eyes;
An' marcy! shoots o' "Fire!" aw hears—
Aw myeks yen lowp doon a' wor stairs,
        An' smash, aw seed a queerish seet,
        Yel thousands crooded i' the Street—
        It was the Pawnshop bleezin'.

The wimmin folks 'twas sair to see
  Lamentin' their distresses ;
For mony a goon, an' white shemee,
  Was burnt wi' bairns' dresses ;
Peg Putty stamp'd an' cried, "Oh, dear,
Wor Geordey's breeks is gyen, aw fear ;
Maw bonny shawl an' Bella's frock—"
Says Betty Mills, "An' there's wor clock,
    An' a' maw bits o' laddies' claes—
    My pillowslips an' pair o' stays—
    Is in the Pawnshop bleezin'."

A dowpy wife wi' *borrow'd fat,*
  An' wiv a puggy beak, man,
Cam pushin' wiv her bonnet flat,
  And puffin oot her cheeks, man ;
Ye niver seed sic bullet eyes—
Her screams aw thowt wad splet the skies ;
"Oh Lord ! maw babbie's things is gyen !
Maw unborn babe hes claes noo nyen !
An' when wor Billy finds it oot,
There'll murder be, aw hae nee doot ;
    Oh dear ! what garr'd me put them in ?
    'Twas a' the races an' curs'd gin—
    That set my claes a-bleezin'."

"Oh, marcy, aw'll be hammer'd tee !"
  Cries Orange Jinny, blairin' ;
"Aw popp'd Ned's suit te hae a spree,
  But suen aw'll get me fairin',—
He thinks, poor sowl, his claes is reet,
He'll want yen suit o' Friday neet—

What mun aw dee? aw wadent care,
But, hinnies, watch an' seal is there;
    An' warse an' warse! he'll quickly knaw,
    That earrings, weddin' ring an' a'
      Is in the Pawnshop bleezin'!"

Lang Skipper Jack, wi' mony a sweer,
  Cam laingerin' up the Side, man,
Says he, "What's a' the matter, here?
  Noo, here's a bonny tide, man!
Why, marrows, sure it cannit be,
This isn't Trotter's place aw see?"
So oot his baccy fob he tuik,
Hawled oot some *tickets* frae a buik:
    "Why sink the sowls of a' the lot;
    Aye, d—n the yel scrape's gyen to pot,
      There's a' maw fortin bleezin'!"

The yells, an' blairs, an' curses lood,
  And cries o' stupefaction:
An' bits o' bairns amang the crood,
  Increased the mad distraction;
Aye, mony a wife will rue the day
She put her husband's things away;
An' men will groan wi' bitter grief—
(For Pawnshop law hes ne relief)—
    To find their labour, toil, an' pain,
    To 'pear like decent foaks is vain—
      There a' their goods is bleezin'!

The world was better far aw'm sure,
  When Pawnshops had ne neym, man;
When poor folks could their breed procure,
  Withoot a *deed o' shyem*, man!

Ther Boxes luik like cuddies' stalls;
There's hell-fire in ther hollow balls;
Their gains is large, wor chance is sma'—
They often's get wor pledges a'—
Just like the plagues ov Egypt sent,
They banish peace an' calm content—
Aw wish they a' were bleezin'.

J. P. ROBSON.   *" Bards of the Tyne,"* 1849.

———

THE USE AN' THE ABUSE;
OR, THE PITMEN AN' THE PREACHERS.

That there is another aspect to the drink question besides this, so
glowingly depicted below, Robson himself shows. "Maw marras, tyek
warnin' be me," of which the following is the first verse, shows it—

MAW MARRAS, TYEK WARNIN' BE ME.

Maw shift in this world nobbut lasts a few days,
    Then afore stairin' croods aw mun dee;
It's a' on iccoont o' my wild drinkin' ways,
    An' poor Nell's, for she lik'd a drop, tee,
Thit the rope o' cawd deith seun'll stop Matty's breeth,
    On a life crushin' hang-gallas tree.
Drink, drink was maw bane, aw repeat it again;—
    Then, maw marras, tyek warnin' be me!

.   .   .   .   .   .

(Last four lines.)

Oh! fra drink, marras awl, keep away, is maw cawl—
    Leest, like Matt, for fool murder ye dee;
It's the last word aw say—*fra strang drink bide away.*
    O, maw marras, tyek warnin' be me.

TUNE—*" Canny Newcassel."*

TEETO'LERS may jaw 'boot the drink as they will,
    An' preach till they're black i' the muzzle;
Maw feyther an' muther byeth lik'd a gud gill,
    An' ther son, tee, maun wheeten his whussel.
Gud yell has duen mair for te warm a man's breest,
    When Misfortin' hes cum wiv his hammer,
Then a thoosan' dry sarmins frae ranterfied preest,
    That gets paid for his lees an' his yammer.

Foaks gob aboot drink; wes the grapes sent for nowt
    But te stuff i' wor dumplins an' hinnies?

If the goold frae the yerth, man, had niver been browt,
  Smash! the mint cudn't coin monny ginnies.
Becaws a man's hung, mun we myek ne mair twine?
  Mun we starve 'cas some fules gormydises?
If a keel gets upset, maun we shut up the Tyne?
  Gox! such humbug maw reason surprizes!

Bill Wallis is turn'd a teetotaller, noo,
  An' lyeps up the fizzyfied wetter;
But aw find, on the slee, Bill his toddy can brew,
  For his beak is to brandy a debtor.
His wife, huiky Fan, gat the key ov his box,
  Iv a raw the black bottles were pleyc'd in;
Like as fizik frae doctors, a' labell'd, bi gox!
  But poor Fanny gat mortal wiv tyestin'!

Whei, it's deeth, mevies warse, if te Balmbra's ye gan
  For a glass, an' te hear the fine singin';
They sweer that the landlord's the deevil's best man,
  An' the band's nowt but imps ov his bringin'.
Man, ther spited te see that the "Wheat Sheaf" hes
    sprung
  Frae the seeds o' lang pashins an' murit;
Smash! ther awn duzzy consarts is shemfully sung,
  For ther sangs, like thersels, hes ne *spurit.*

Aw divent praise fules that, like pigs i' the muck,
  Gan gruntin' an' guzzlin' for iver;
There's ne cayshun te soom i' the drink like a duck,
  But just sup what'll myek a chep clivor.
Noo, ye ken verry weel what King Solyman says,
  An' he dissent mean gluttons te 'tice, man:
"Eat, drink, an' be merry, to lengthin yor days"—
  An', bi gox! but aw'll tyek his advice, man.

J. P. ROBSON.   *"Bards of the Tyne,"* 1849.

DAYS AND DEEDS OF SHAKSPERE.

TUNE—"The Old English Gentleman."

Aw'LL sing ye a braw new sang,
　　Aboot Bill Shakspur's plays :
A chep that kep wor toon i' tow
　　Wi' queerish neets an' days.
He wes born i' th' Swirl, i' Sandgate, man,
　　This poet ov a' natur ;
And hadded horses for ha'pennies,
　　Aside wor aud Theatur.

Chorus.

Oh ! a cliver chep wes Shakspur, lads,
　　An' the brag an' pride o' Tyne.

Ne lad like him cud heave a bool,
　　Or set the dogs away ;
For hingin' hares i' Fenim wood,
　　Bill wes the time o' day.
He had a kind o' conj'rin' gun
　　That browt the pheasans doon ;
He yence let flee at Crummel's hat,
　　An' wammel'd oot the croon.

O' gamkeepers Bill made his gam',
　　An' smok'd his cutty pipe ;
For poets, man, oft leeve on air
　　Or suction, like the snipe.
At hoppins Bill won the meat,
　　For he wes fond o' greese ;
He clamb the mast o' a ship ca'd *Fame,*
　　An' gat the goolden fleece.

Jack Ford, Rare Ben, an' Messenger,
   Fair deevils for a lark,
Went oot wi' Bill te Ravensworth,
   Yen neet when a' wes dark.
They rammel'd ower that bonny wood,
   Wivoot a sign o' luck,
Till Bill gat haud o' twe lang horns,
   An' haul'd away a buck.

The keeper-man poor Willy nail'd,
   An', gox! there was a spree!
He garr'd the pollis luik like fuils,
   Aye, may'r an' 'torneys, tee.
He tell'd them he had browt the horns
   The magistrate te fit:
Yen cock-eyed doctor laugh'd se lood,
   They say his jaws wes split.

Noo Shaksy went upon wor stage,
   An' acted tiv a won'er;
He grund the rosel for the leetnin',
   An' rowl'd big bools for thun'er;
He myed hell-fires o' reed an' blue;
   An', for a spreeish joke,
He popp'd up thro' a greet kale-pot,
   An' frighten'd a' the folk.

Yence Bill went on to act a pairt,
   But, man, he lost the words;
The trapper laddie lowsed the boult,
   An' Bill fell thro' the boards!
The owerman went stampin' mad,
   Te see the play disgraced:
So Shakspur cut the actor's life
   Biv thrawin' up the "Ghaist!"

24

Then Bill ran hyem an' scribbl'd plays,
  That pit lads like te read;
The Ranters said he was aud Nick,
  'Cas he cud raise the deed.
For, smash! he kenn'd a' things se weel,
  'Boot fairies, kings, an' fyuls;
Thor's mair grand sermons iv his buik
  Than cums frae Cambridge skyuls.

He tells us ov a blackeymoor,
  Wi' goggle eyes se queer,
That Dissymolly scumfished,
  For a handkercher, aw hear.
An' when the pollis tuik him up,
  He shooted for his wife;
Then stuck a gully iv his throat,
  An' stopped his gam for life.

Folks tawk o' conjuration sprees,
  An' dealings wiv aud Nick;
Noo Prossy Joe white spurrits gat,
  By waggin' ov a stick.
Fra Jarrow-Slek a lass he browt,
  Beside a monkey-man,
That liked a cask o' Jemmykay,
  They ca'd him Callerbran!

Fra thun'er cludes black witches cam,
  An' fairies frae the myun;
Green mermaids, tee, frae Hartley Pans,
  That kaim'd thor heeds like fun.
Will banged a' poets wiv his pen;
  But fules will gan astray;
They like wild beasts and lion kings,
  Far mair than Shaksy's play.

Yen neet aw heerd a spurit's voice,
　　It cried, "Save Shakspur's neck :
Translate him te the vulgar tongue,
　　An' crum'letators check.
There's Sherry Knowles can mind his hoose,
　　An' greet will be thaw blame,
If thou, Bob Stackers, divint start,
　　An' save Will Shakspur's name."

Se hinnies a', byeth leish an' sma',
　　An' lasses o' wor Tyne,
Poor Bobby comes afore ye noo,
　　Te favour his design.
An' if aw gets a greeter praise
　　Then mevvies is maw reet,
Aw cannit rob the bonny Swan,
　　Because his fame's cumplete.

J. P. ROBSON.　　　　　　　　　　*"Bards of the Tyne,"* 1849.

HAMLICK, PRINCE OF DENTON.

PART FIRST.

In these burlesque days, when H. J. Byron flourishes, and nothing seems
safe from the pen of the burlesque writer, it is no wonder that this clever
travesty, which gives to the melancholy Dane "a local habitation and a
name," should be highly popular. "Denton Burn," where the poet locates
the prince, is a small village, just outside Newcastle, on the West road.—
Note, 1872 *Edition.*

TUNE—"Merrily Dance the Quaker's Wife."

Ov a' the lads o' Denton Burn,
　　Young Hamlick had ne marrow,
He'd put or hew an' take his turn
　　Te drive the rolley-barrow.

His feythor kept a corver's shop,
   His muther teuk in sewin ;
But, man, they say she liked a drop,
   An' drunk gin like a new un.

Noo, Hamlick had a sweetheart tee,—
   Oh, Feeley, she was canny !
The weddin-day was seun to be,
   For Feeley lov'd her manny ;
The furnitary a' was bowt,
   The chairs wis polished bonny,
A German chep the clock had browt ;
   An' the bed wad challinge onny.

But iv a suddent a' was stopp'd,
   Misfortin cam se cruiket ;
The marridge meetin' seun was dropp'd,
   Aud Ham had kicked the bucket.
An' what was queer, afore a week
   The widdy wed agyen, man ;
The deed un's brother had the cheek
   Te coax her, it was plain, man.

Noo bonny gam' there was, aw sure,
   Yung Hamlick swore like Hector :
He vow'd he wad his mother cure,
   If biv hersel he neck'd her.
An' Clawdy, tee, might chucky oot,
   His jaws he'd surely plaister ;
Whei ! if he didn't gar him shoot,
   Then Ham wad own his maister.

'Twixt twelve an' yen, the meun was sma',
    As Hamlick hyem was gannin';
Just cummin past aud Denton Ha',
    He seed a white thing stannin.
Tho' freeten'd sair, says he, "Whe's there?"
    His kneebyens nack'd thegither;
It answered wiv a groaning blair,
    "Oh, Hamlick! aw's thaw feyther."

"What thou?" says he, "it cannit be!
    Aw seed thee fairly barried;
But, feyther, tell us what te de,
    For mother to uncle's married."
"Then listen, hinny, for the cock
    Aw's flaid 'ill seun be crawin'!
Ye ken it's lang past twelve o'clock,
    An' yen mun stop maw jawin.

"Ye'll mind that neet aw wun the pig,
    Aw went hyem like a lammie,
Tho Gurty sairly run her rig,
    An' shameful used her Hammy.
But warse, me lad—thaw Uncle Clawde
    Bowt ars'nic frae thaw cousin,
An' mixed it wi' some fat he had,
    An' aw lick'd up the puzzen.

"Ah man, aw cud sum queer things tell,
    But the deevil's verra jellis;
Tho aw've a fairish place i' hell—
    Aw's heed man at the bellis.

But, wheest! the banty's craw aw hear,
　Come, shake hands wi' yor daddie;
Thou'll mevies cuik thaw uncle's beer;
　Ta, ta—ta; ta—maw laddie!"

When Hamlick stuck his daddle oot,
　Te grip his feyther's paw, man,
He gav a kind o' croopy shoot,
　To find the caud styen wa', man.
The ghaist was gyen—but sic a smell
　Was fund like aud shoes burnin,
That Hamlick's niver been hissel
　Since yen o'clock that mornin.

PART SECOND.

Some strowlin' folks to Denton cam',
　A' ridin on thor donkeys,
An' conj'rin cheps wi' nowt but sham,
　Spy shows was there wi' munkeys.
The actors fund young Hamlick oot,
　An' spun him sic a yarn, sir;
Says Ham, "The gentlemen can spoot
　In Lissy Lambton's barn, sir!"

The play was made biv Hamlick's sel,
　His mother's sowl to press, man,
The scene was laid at Barley Fell,
　The lingo was Bosjesman.
" The Blighted Boar, or Puzzen'd Pluck,"
　The folks a' flock'd to see, man;
An' Feeley i' the front was stuck,
　Wiv Hamlick on her knee, man.

Up went the cloot—the crood sat mum—
  A pig-fyeced thing appearin;
Upon a' fowers 'twas seed to cum—
  By gox, it was a queer un!
It grunted thrice—thrice wagged its heed,
  An' hadded up his paw, then;
Then myed believe that it was deed,
  By droppin doon its jaw, then.

In popped a wife an' blubbered sair,
  Aboot her gissy's fate, then;
"*Wise pigs,*" says she, "*takes better care,
  Thou's lick'd a puzzen'd plate, then;
Aw'd seuner loss my man, the Turk!
  Aw wish that mine's was taken;
Thaw pluck to neet sall de the wark—
  There's ars'nic in thaw bacon.*"

Ham's mother dother'd like a duck,
  "Oh dear! oh dear! aw's drop noo!
Divent ye hear about the pluck?
  Howay! aw winnit stop, noo!"
An' frae the play like mad she flew,
  The crowd a' gyept an' won'er'd,
"Ho, ho!" shoots Ham, "the ghaist spak true,
  Play-actors for a hun'er'd!"

Next pay, Ham's feyther 'peared agyen,
  I' th' spot he elways haunted;
"Oh, Hamlick, Hamlick! tell us when
  Aw'll get maw wishes granted?

Thaw heart's like withered haws or hips:
  Revenge thaw feyther's deeth, then;
Ta, ta!"   Ham's een was i' th' 'clipse,
  He gyep'd clean oot o' breeth, then.

To Feeley's house, wivoot a stop,
  Throo puils, cross progly ditches,
Young Ham ran peltin neck an' crop,
  His sark ootside his britches.
He brak the door an' smashed the glass,
  Spanghewed poor Feeley's feyther,
An' tuik the coal-rake tiv his lass,
  An' jaw'd a heap o' blether.

The police cam wiv a' thor speed,
  But whe daur Hamlick tyek, then?
The crooner sat upon the deed,
  A verdick clear to myek, then.
Noo Feeley cam in rantin mad,
  Wiv a gyus's thropple screamin;
She ca'd her Ham, "Her bonny lad
  That set her daft wi' dreamin."

Her heed was dressed wi' docken leeves,
  Stuck roond wi' cabbage caskets,
An' milky thrustles in her neeves,
  An' rusher caps and baskets.
The crooner bad his men gie place
  Te let her view her feyther:
She smack'd the forsman on the face,
  Then chow'd sum bits o' leather.

She leeved on grass an' paddick's stuils,
　　Dry asks and tyeds she chorish'd;
An' Tommy-lodgers frae the puils,
　　Iv blackin-pots she norished.
Yen day she plodg'd to catch a duck,
　　A soomin seiz'd her heed, there,
An' in the slek poor Feeley stuck,
　　And "Cuckoo" fand her heed, there.

PART THIRD.

The winter efterneun was dark,
　　The winds, like bairns, was cryin,
The fun'ral folk had left the kirk,
　　Where Feeley cawd was lyin.
Yung Hamlick lowp'd oot frae a dyke,
　　Seiz'd fast o' Feeley's bruther,
An' Ham was Larty gan te strike,
　　When oot cam' Hammy's muther.

" For shem, ye feuls, on sic a neet,
　　Te set yor neeves for boxin,
'Twad sarve thee reet, Ham, varry reet,
　　To stick thaw shanks the stocks in:
Thou hes ne chance wi' Larty's fist,
　　Thou kens he was a ring-man;
He'll let the day-leet to thaw kist—
　　He is a second Spring, man!"

The match cam off at Throckley Fell,
　　Ham's uncle own'd the field, man;
His mother, tee, cam' there hersel,
　　Ham's fate she thowt concealed, man.

To wark they went, Ham drew first blood,
    Tho' Larty ken'd the science;
But Hamlick like a tarrier stood,
    An' grinn'd a blue defiance.

Hoot, Larty, hinny's fairly blawn,
    His breeth cums thick and shorter;
But what's that stuff Clawde's sleely thrawn,
    And mixed amang the porter?
But Larty's deun, the time is ca'd,
    Ham's mother seems a' queer, noo,
She grabs the glass and drinks like mad,
    She's drunk the pussin'd beer, noo.

"Oh, hinny, Clawde, what's this, maw lad?
    This porter's queerly fettled!"
Clawde blair'd oot, "Lass! put doon that glass."
    Poor sowl, her hash was settled.
Smash at his uncle's jaws struck Ham,
    Doon went the tyestral sprawlin,
Doon went his puzzen'd mistrest flam,
    The crood for help was bawlin!

Up stackered Larty for a blaw,
    Fair on Ham's jug'lar nibb'd him;
But Ham swung roond his iron paw,
    An' wiv a deeth-thraw fibb'd him.
The victims' bodies iv a dray
    Te their last hyem was sent on:
Oh! mourn for Hamlick neet and day,
    For he was Prince o' Denton.

J. P. ROBSON.   *Author's Vol., "Evangeline."*

THE PITMAN'S HAPPY TIMES.

Had this admirer of the "good old times" lived at the present time (1872), when pitmen's wages are advancing 10 and 15 per cent. at a bound, he even must have doubted whether the past was better than the present.—*Note,* 1872 *Edition.*

TUNE—"In the days when we went gipsying."

WHEN aw wes yung, maw collier lads,
    Ne man cud happier be ;
For wages was like sma' coals then,
    An' cheps cud raise a spree.
Wor pay-neet cam' wiv drink an' dance,
    Wor sweethearts luckt se fine ;
An' lumps o' beef, an' dads o' duff,
    Wes there for folks te dine.
An' then we spent sic merry neets,
    For grum'lin' we had nyen ;
But the times o' wor prosperity
    Will niver cum agyen.

Wor hooses then wes ower sma',
    For ivery nuik was chock ;
Wor drawers wes fair mahoginy,
    An' se wes chairs an' clock.
Wor feather beds, and powls se fine,
    Wes welcum te the seet ;
A man work'd harder i' the day,
    Wi' thinkin' o' th' neet.
Spice hinnies on the gurdle fizz'd ;
    Maw tea had rum in't then ;
But the times o' wor prosperity
    Can niver cum agyen.

Wor wives cud buy new shawls an' goons,
    An' niver heed the price ;
The spyed-yace ginnies went like smoke
    Te myek wor darlins nice.

The drapers used ne tickets then,
   The country gowks te coax :
They got thereckly what was ax'd,
   An' prais'd us collier folks.
The butcher meat was always best
   When Kenton paid thor men ;
But the days o' wor prosperity
   Can niver cum agyen.

When aw gat wed—gox, what a row !
   The bindin' brass aw spent :
Aw bowt new gloves an' ribbons, man,
   For aw the folks aw kent.
At ivery yell hoose i' this toon,
   We had a cocktail pot ;
Wi' treatin' a' the company roond,
   Maw kelter went like shot.
But smash ! we had a merry neet,
   Tho' fights we had but ten ;
Thor wes sic times for collier lads—
   They'll niver come agyen.

We didn't heed much lairnin' then,
   We had ne time for skyul ;
Pit laddies work'd for spendin's syek,
   An' nyen wes thowt a fyul.
Noo, ivery bairn can read and write—
   Extonishin' to me !
The varry dowpie on my lap
   Can tell his A B C.
Sum folks gets reet, and sum gets wrang,
   Biv lettin' buiks alyen ;
But this aw'll sweer, ne times like mine
   Can iver cum agyen.

J. P. ROBSON.   *"Bards of the Tyne,"* 1849.

THE HORRID WAR I' SANGEYT.

The following song most faithfully describes what the author terms "The Horrid War i' Sangeyt." The cause, the description, and the result of the horrid war are strictly in keeping with the newspaper reports; it only remains to add that this memorable war took place on Sunday evening, May 11th, 1851.

TUNE—"The King o' the Cannibal Islands."

THOR'S nowt se bad aw've heerd foax say,
Is let fyul preechors hae thor way,
An' that was proov'd the tuther day,
 Be the horrid war i' Sangeyt.
As Rantor Dick preeched frev a chair,
While singin' oot wi' cuddy blair,
An' gi'en the Pope a canny share
O' hell-fire comfort, aw declare ;
When Paddy Flinn set up a howl,
An' Squintin Dan wi' Ted McCowl,
Myed preest an' beuk an' styul te rowl
 I' the muck an' clarts o' Sangeyt.

Nan Dodds an' me an' Mettor Jack
Wes stannin be the preechor's back,
Says aw, "Ye thunderin Irish pack,
 Dor ye start yor gam i' Sangeyt ?"
Then, wi' me neeve, aw shuts a blaw,
An' levils Dan an' Cowley law ;
Wor Jack pick'd up the rantor craw,
An' tell'd him nut 'gyen Popes te jaw.
An' noo the bonny gam begun,
The Pats frev oot thor hooses run :
They poored be hundreds frae the "Sun,"
 Te start a war i' Sangeyt.

They cam frae loosy dens wi' howls,
Like harrin—man! they cam i' showls,
Wi' buzzum-shanks an' aud bed-powls,—
    Styens flew like shot throo Sangeyt.
The pollis cam wi' thor black sticks,
But sum gat fell'd wi' greet hawf-bricks,
Then rowlin-pins an' shafts o' picks,
Wes browt te de the naytivs' tricks :—
The Paddies screem'd till a' wes bloo,
" Let's slay the Saxon haythins, now ;
Down wid the Inglish thieves !   Hooroo !
    An' we'll be Kings i' Sangeyt ! "

They cam frae Quinn's an' Simpson's tee,
Frae Ford's, an' hoosis lang the Kee,
Frae Piporgyet an' Mill Intree,
    Te the horrid war i' Sangeyt !
The Irish force wes fairly quashed,
When on the Keeside porters dashed ;
Then tongs went up, bed-powls got smashed,
An' heeds wes crack'd, an' windors crashed ;
Then brave keel-laddies tyuk thor turn,
Wi' smiths an' potters frae the burn,
They cut the " White Boys " doon like corn,
    An' lyed them law i' Sangeyt.

The sweeps noo teemed wi' sic a rush,
The Paddies flew before the brush,
Ned Fish's heroes myed a push,
    An' blacked the boys i' Sangeyt.
Bill Johnson's crew an' Clarke's wes there,
An' Knight's an' Lumley's pack fowt sair ;

Jim Frame's bool'd frae the Cassel Square,
Wi' Blower's Blacks an' monny mair.
The landlords joined the jolly row,
Bob Carr got help frae "Barley Mow,"
Moor put his "Steam Boat" cheps i' tow,
 An' a' wes war i' Sangeyt.

Nell Prood chucked up her three-legged styul,
An' lyed it inte Dermitt's skull,
An' dog's-dort Peg whorled roond her shull,
 An' splet sum heeds i' Sangeyt.
Young Oyster Bet and Tatie Sal,
Gat three greet navvies gyen the wall,
Bet prickt them wiv a cobbler's awl;
Peg powsed thor jaws an' myed them squall.
An' when the Pats wis fairly deun,
Wor Sally for the pollis run,
An' te the stayshun they wor teun,
 For raisin war i' Sangeyt.

The pollis wad gyen doon aw fear,
If cheps like us had not been near,—
Man, Keeside blud's se full o' beer,—
 We'd fight the world for Sangeyt !
Wor Jack an' me te the Manors tyuk,
Just sixteen Pats be Scott's awn byuk;
We seized them like a grapplin hyuk,
An' caged them for sum mair te lyuk.
O' Mundor morn aw fand a' sair,
When aw wis cawled afore the Mare,
An' swore 'twas a' the Rantor's prayer
 That cawsed the war i' Sangeyt.

Te jale the dorty trash wis sent,
Wi' brockin skulls, an' fairly spent ;
They lyuk'd like owt but foax content
    Wi' raisin war i' Sangeyt.
Noo, when thor free, aw'll say agyen,
Just let us Inglish foak alyen,
Newcassel lads can rool a *main*,
In owther *seas* or *cocks*—that's plain.
Then let's away te sum yell-hoose,
An' hev a sang, an' gan on croose,
Let's proove us Keeside chaps is doose ;—
    The conk'rin blades o' Sangeyt !

J. P. ROBSON.   *Author's Copy, about* 1851.

BETTY BEESLEY AND HER WOODEN MAN.

TUNE—"The Bold Dragoon."

BET Beesley was a skipper's wife
    For twe lang years an' mair ;
They leeved a kind o' howstrow life—
    Smash, man, they fettled sair !
They gurn'd like cats—thor gob browt bats—
    Byeth often wished the yen was croakin' ;
So Deeth yen day stopp'd Tommy's chats,
    An' left the widow Bet heart-broken.
Oh, Betty Beesley !
    Dinnet break thaw heart, maw hinny !
No, Betty Beesley—get another man !

Bet Beesley had a bonny fyece,
    An' was a smartish queen ;
A fairy's foot an' leg o' grace,
    An' twe black roguish een.

Noo Nabob Tate, that had o' late
    Fra Indy cum wi' loads o' siller,
Teuk Bet to see his hoose an' plate,
    An' fairly popped the questin tiv her :
"Oh, Betty Beesley!
    Dinnet say thou winnet, hinney!
Oh, Betty Beesley, tyek me for thaw man!"

Smash! Betty wed this Nabob grand,
    Turned oot a leddy fine;
She gat silk gloves upon her hand,
    An' cut wi' rings a shine;
The happy day seun slipped away,
    An' neet cam on, ye ken—Oh, deary!
Tate's servant carried him, they say,
    To Betty's room, a little beery!
Oh, Betty Beesley!
    What a spree thou'll hae, maw hinney!
Oh, Betty Beesley, cuddle close thee man!

Poor Betty thowt a vast o' sheym,
    Else myed believe to de;
But Tate was jolly seun at hyem,
    An' clapp'd Bet on his knee.
Bet thowt his legs fand hardish pegs,
    Says she, "Oh, dear! what's thor things
        stickin'?"
"These are my stumps!"—and up he jumps—
    "Aw'll screw them off else they'll be breekin'."
Oh, Betty Beesley!
    Hes thee man ne shanks, maw hinny?
Oh, Betty Beesley—what a Wooden Man!
25

"Hoots! what's the use o' tryin', Tate,
　　To screw thaw legs, maw dear?
Ye men folks spoil the weddin' state
　　Wi' tyekin' se much beer!"
"Come thou, maw pet—this way, lass Bet,
　　An' when thou gets maw *pins* dissected,
Maw *airms* thou'll feel is *wood an' steel*,
　　So thou can lowse them as directed."
Oh, Betty Beesley!
　　Nouther legs nor airms, maw hinney,
Oh, Betty Beesley, thou's wed a *trunkey* man.

But Bet turned dwamy, like to fall,
　　"Oh dear, oh dear!" she cries;
Says Tate, "But, Bet, this isn't all,
　　Cum, tyek oot *teeth* an' *eyes!*
Then, to complete the screwin' feat
　　(Gox, what a thing to get a breed off!),
Just coup me backward in maw seat,
　　An' try, maw luve, to screw maw *heed* off!"
Oh, Betty Beesley!
　　What a job thou's deun, maw hinny!
Oh, Betty Beesley, thou hesn't *half* a man!

'Twas mair then mortal flesh cud stand,
　　Bet, shootin', cut her stick—
"Aw thowt to get sum *nabob* grand,
　　Aw's *bobb'd* wi' fair aud Nick."
"Cum back," says he, "it's nobbet spree,
　　The *heed* is fast upon yor mannie;
So now to bed thou's cairy me,
　　We'll sleep the-gether douce an' canny."

Oh, Betty Beesley !
    What a pairtner for thee hinny,
Oh, Betty Beesley, be canny wi' thee man.

The howdy nine muens efter this
    Iv hyest was summonsed late ;
Poor Bet gat through it not amiss,
    A bairn for Mister Tate.
Bet lyuk'd up, glad to see the lad ;
    Says she, "Peg, try the *airms an' legs on't,*
For if it's fashuns like its dad,
    Thou'll find steel airms an' wooden pegs on't."
Oh, Betty Beesley !
    Dinnet fret, maw bonny hinny,
For oh, Betty Beesley, the Nabob's proved a man.

J. P. ROBSON.   *"Bards of the Tyne,"* 1849.

EDWARD CORVAN.

" COMIC iv iv'rything, clivor at owt." So Joe Wilson aptly hits off the character of his versatile predecessor, Ned Corvan. Corvan, as a Tyneside writer, brings to mind De Foe's famous lines, which, slightly altered, might run—

" A mixture of all kinds began
    That heterogeneous thing, a Tyne-
      side man,"

English, Scotch, and now in Ned's case, Irish contributing to the roll of Tyneside writers. In the 1872 edition of this work it was stated that Corvan was born in the Stockbridge. On the authority of his widow, who outlived him twenty-five years, it should have been *not born*, but brought up in the Stockbridge, Liverpool really being his birthplace. Although

Tyneside thus cannot claim his birth, yet to Newcastle he belonged from an early age, his parents removing here when he was only four years old. Three years later his father died in Newcastle Infirmary, while undergoing an operation, and young Corvan (again quoting his widow) "was brought up by his widowed mother, who had many a hard struggle, the same as I have had myself." This may readily be believed, the family of three or four depending upon the widow's scanty earnings would have many a hard struggle, and there is little doubt Ned's early days are in the main truly told in his songs "Ne place now te play," and "The Death of Billy Purvis." There he has "Aw used te play the wag doon the Kee thonder. Aw've monny a time browt up three French apples at a time; but wor aud wife said if aw fell in an' got droon'd, she'd skin me alive when aw cum hyem, so aw played the wag doon the burn efter that. Some o' wor lads an' me petitioned the magistrates for a new playground, an' they tell'd us te gan te bordin skuels. What an idea! Wor aud wife hes sair tues te raise the penny for Monday mornin's; the maister seldom gets it tho'—aw buy claggem wid, then the maister hes te tyek't out in flaps. Aboot thirty years since them was maw happy days, when aw wad beg, borrow, or steel to get a luik at aud Billy's show. A've seen me gan aboot wi' me shart tail sticking oot behint; an' as for shoes, the ony pair aw had on me feet wer the pair the cobbler had away mendin'. But what did aw care aboot shoes, aw had big toes like styens. Oh, what music aw fund i' the bells of St. Nicholas' when the Easter halidays myed thor appearance. Hoo leet was maw youthful heart! ne stain wes there to mar maw happiness."

In this extravagance and nonsense with which Ned was so liberal in many of his songs, there can be little doubt are embedded many genuine bits of autobiography. But time went on, these happy harum-scarum days were to end. Young Ned was getting old enough to add his mite to the scanty family income, so to work he went, sail-making being the business he was sent to. But sail-making soon palled; he could not forget his early admiration for Billy's, or properly speaking, the Victoria, Theatre, which under Billy Purvis's management at that time made lengthened visits to Newcastle. So, smitten with a fancy for the life of an actor, he left his sail-making, and joined Billy Purvis's dramatic company. Here his duties were of a varied but scarcely of a dramatic character. He played the violin in the orchestra, sung comic and local songs between the pieces, took his turn at scene painting, bill - sticking, and made himself generally useful. With Billy he remained some years, but never made any figure as an actor, his efforts in that line being confined to small parts. His most successful hit at Billy's was in local songs; here was foreshadowed the line in which he was afterwards to make his name. "He wad be a Noodle" was a great hit. If not his first local song, it was his first markedly successful one, and Ned, now about twenty years of age, became a more important member of Billy's company.

About 1850 the Railway Company bought from the Newcastle Corporation its ancient public grounds, "The Forth," and let a part near the Infirmary to Madame Tournaire for the purpose of building a circus. After the circus season ended, the land still not being wanted,

CORVAN AS "CAT-GUT JIM."

the circus was altered into a concert hall, and named the
"Olympic," under the management of a Mr. Howard. This
was Corvan's chance : he left Billy, joined the Olympic Company as a local singer, and carried all before him. With Billy
it might be said he had been feeling his way ; here, sure
of his powers, he launched boldly out. "Oh, what a price
for sma' coals !" and "Ne place now te play," literally took
his audience by storm. And when, a little later on, he wrote
"Asstrilly; or, the Pitman's Fareweel," and "Asstrilly's Goold
Fields," they were so successful that for long he was almost
a permanent member of the company. Corvan was the
first who combined the writing and singing of Tyneside
songs as a profession, and who added to their attractions by
singing them in character. Finding concert business to be
his line, he devoted himself entirely to it, and left for good
his old dramatic associates.

A few words upon the after career of some of the fellow-
players along with him at Billy Purvis's may be interesting.
Spears and Stead, like himself, both left the drama for
the concert hall, Spears winning great popularity as a
singer of Irish songs, his "Black Turf" being a hit ;
and Stead becoming famous as the original singer of the
"Perfect Cure," the popularity of this song being almost
without a parallel, Stead by its success being placed
in the front rank of concert hall artistes. C. H. Stephenson kept to the drama, and from Billy's has risen to
fill almost every position in the highest theatres in the
United Kingdom. He is now living in retirement, and
only last year, under the title of "How I Interviewed
Myself," contributed to the *Newcastle Weekly Chronicle*
his most varied and interesting experiences as an actor.

Ned Corvan, as a popular concert hall artiste, now
travelled the North, making himself, by his Tyneside songs,
a favourite everywhere. After some years of this life he
settled in South Shields as a publican ; but this was
not a happy change. Ned was too fond of his glass,
and too many sought his company. After three or four
years as a publican and proprietor of Corvan's Music
Hall, Wapping Street, he gave it up, and returned to
his local singing, which he followed regularly until his
death. As a concert hall artiste, Ned had few equals, his
qualifications were so various. He was a fair singer and
an excellent performer on the violin. With that in his hand
he often occupied the stage agreeably for half-an-hour. In

many of his songs he introduced a deal of patter or speaking. This he did with such wit and humour, that it generally was the most "taking" part of the song. Again, with a bit of chalk he would draw on a black-board the portrait of his old master, Billy Purvis, accompanying the drawing with a running commentary, as "That's his heed, canny aud fellow! That's his mooth; mony a three-happorth's gyen doon there," etc. Ned, who was of Irish extraction, had the ready wit of his race, and once it stood him in good stead when singing his song on Billy Purvis. He was just about to begin the portrait of Billy, and all was still, when some one shouted out, "Myek us a cuddy, Ned." "All reet," replied Ned, without a moment's hesitation; "*stand up*," and he turned as he spoke, with the pencil in his hand, to where the voice came from, but the cuddy brayed no more. Ned had silenced him. "The Fire on the Kee" was a song his audience never tired of; its picturesque description of the great calamity, its variety of treatment, its wit and humour, all combined to make it a favourite. Once when singing it at Stanley's Tyne Concert Hall, Thomas Sayers, landlord of the "Blue Bell," a noted house which stood where the new Post Office now stands, was sitting in the pit. He was very stout, and Ned's humour and drollery as the distressed mother looking for her lost Jimmy, to use a common phrase, "convulsed him with laughter." The convulsing in this case was not a figure of speech, but a reality—he was really ill with laughing; but Ned's drollery was such that he was powerless to resist it. "Ned, for God's sake, drop; aw's killin' me-sel," at last he contrived to gasp out. Stopping his song and putting on a half-alarmed look, Ned came to the front. "Ye munnit de that," he said, "or they'll heh me up for *Tommycide.*" Another night, he was doing the last turn at the Tyne before closing for the night. He was at his best, and introducing new patter, which the character gave him every chance of doing, as in it he is dressed as a female street hawker seeking for her lost son Jimmy. With the fresh fun thus introduced he kept delighting his audience so long, that those who were behind the scenes waiting to be done for the night whispered from the side wings, "Ned, if ye'll finish, you shall have what you like at the Durham Ox over the way." "What's that aw hear?" says Ned, stopping his song suddenly, and making his way to the front of the stage, where, taking off his tattered bonnet and looking at his audience, he said, " Ye'll excuse the parental feelings of a poor muther, but aw've just got word the laddie's been fund ; he's ower at the Durham Ox. Gud neet." And so at once the perform-ance finished. Such are samples of the stories remembered of Ned. Towards the latter part of his life his voice failed considerably, and he had to rely more than before upon such extra attractions. Sitting in the audience part of the Oxford one night, not long before his death, Joe Wilson was on the stage singing "Aw wish yor Muther wad cum," then in all its freshness and making a great hit. A friend who was sitting beside him said, "A good song that, Ned." "Yes," said Ned in a voice which towards the end had become almost a hoarse whisper. "Yes," said he huskily, "a gud song, but aw'm writin' one that'll knock its end in." Poor fellow, he had then written his last song; the one that was to play such havoc with Joe's never appeared. It was not by any new song that he was to compete against his young rival. On his songs already written was his true reliance. These songs, whatever their worth, were the true outcome of his feelings and surroundings, and on them his fame rests. While comic undoubtedly was Ned's true line,

Corvan's handwriting slightly reduced. From photo by P. M. Laws.

yet in his " Hartley Calamity" and " The Caller," both sentimental songs, he made great hits.

THE CALLER.

Why sweet slumber now disturbing,
Why break ye the midnight peace,
Why the sons of toil perturbing,
Have their hours of rest to cease?

Ho ! marrows, 'tis the Caller cries,
And his voice in the gloom of the night mist dies.

The twinkling stars, through night shade peering,
Blink above with heavenly light
On the sleeping world, as a voice calls clear,
In the stilly air of the sable night,

Ho ! marrows, etc.

The collier sleeps, e'en now he's dreaming
Of a pure bright world and loved ones there,
He basks in the rays of fortune beaming
    In some far land, full and fair.

> Ho! marrows, etc.

Dream on, thou poor and ill-used collier,
For slaves should aye have visions bright,
There's one above who deems thee holier
    Than the wealthiest in his sight.

> Ho! marrows, etc.

Speed, thee, old man, let him slumber
When happy thoughts are in his breast;
Why should the world his peace encumber?
    Go, let the weary collier rest.

> Ho! marrows, etc.

Not long after Joe Wilson appeared, Ned's health, which had been failing, grew worse. After an illness of about three months he died at his residence, Newgate Street (a little below St. Andrew's Church, on the opposite side), on the 31st August 1865, in his 35th year, and was buried at St. Andrew's Cemetery. Twenty-five years have passed since Ned's death, and yet among Tyneside songs there are few so popular as his. An illustration of this is found in the fact that only last year, on the 23rd January 1890, at E. D. Archbold's Sunday Evening Lecture at the Tyne Theatre, the subject being Edison's Latest Phonograph, Ned's song, "The High Level and the Aud Bridge," was sung into the phonograph. And this, with Ned's song as a sample of Tyneside, will be taken by the lecturer to distant parts, and many a Tynesider at Australia, the Cape, and other English Colonies, will have old memories stirred as they listen to the familiar dialogue between the bridges.

As bearing out the following acrostic by Joe Wilson, it may be added, Ned was a good painter, and many, both sea pieces and landscapes, are from his brush.

ACROSTIC.

C omic iv iv'rything—clivor at owt
O v a' the professions—stickin at nowt,
R eal witty! as poet an' singer at hyem;
V ersatile Artiste, wes Corvan's reet nyem,
A s painter, fiddler, comedian, cloon,
N ed was the maister ov all i' the toon.

The above is Joe Wilson's tribute to Corvan's genius. When a boy some ten years of age Joe first heard Ned. Ned was then the rage at the Olympic, and Joe was taken by his uncle to see him. Years after they often came together, and of Ned Joe always had a high opinion.

Ed. Cowan 1862

HE WAD BE A NOODLE.

TUNE—"Gee wo, Dobbin."

WOR Geordy, won day—the greet slaverin' cull !—
He wad be a noodle, and act like a fuil ;
Wor aud wife advis'd him sic nonsense te drop,
But he wad be a noodle, nowt his notion cud stop.

> For he wad be a noodle, a sowjer-like noodle,
> For he wad be a noodle, the greet slaverin' cull !

To be a brave volunteer was Geordy's desire ;
Smash ! he langed for a gun at the pigeons te fire.
At neet he wad dream 'bout his gun an' fine claes,
An how a' the lasses his figure wad praise.

> When he was a brave noodle, etc.

When he first got his gun, man, aw'll niver forget
How he frightened te fits poor Black Puddin' Bet :
Wi' his kite full o' yell, an' his gun in his hand,
Gox, he ordered twe tripe wives te 'liver an' stand.

> For he wad be a noodle, etc.

Spoken.—The roguish animal ! te rob the poor tripe wife. But that's nowt. That varry efternuin him an' me had te gan tiv a tea party doon the Burn, at Mally Horne's. Aw wes followin' Jenny Hagishnose—(her fethur had ne nose ; but niver mind, aw had nose eneuf for ony family : for aw put a' thor noses oot that followed

maw Jenny); so aw wes sittin' amang them, thou knaws, when wor
Bob com rushin' in on tiv us, wiv his kite blawn oot wi' Mackey's
fowerpenny yell. The fuil wes noodle-struck, and so he riched
ower for a bit o' lump sugar, and cowped the cream jug, an' then
started te lickt up wiv his greet lang tung (and what a melt he
had !), afore a' the wives an' lasses; an' then tuik a moothful o'
scaddin' het tea—sent it fleein' oot agyen—an' burnt iv'rybody's
nose end roond the tyeble.

At the aud Ridin' Skyul he learned " reet aboot,"
But his knees they stuck in, and his toes they stuck oot.
His heart it was firm, and as teuf as his belt,
So, defyin' a' danger, te the Moor he did pelt.
For he wad be a noodle, etc.

When they gat te the Moor, for the prize they wad fire,
Then Geordy's ambition gat higher and higher;
So he tuik up his gun, gox, he cuddn't tell how—
He fired reet past the target an' killed an aud cow!
Unfortunate noodle, etc.

Geordy sent in his kit, for he'd noodle ne mair,
He thowt of misfortunes he'd hadden his share;
Six punds for the cow he laid doon;—lads, aw's sure
Geordy winnit forget when he march'd te the Moor.
For te be a brave noodle, etc.

CORVAN. *Author's Edition.*

THE TOON IMPROVEMENT BILL;
OR, NE PLEYCE NOO TE PLAY.

The Forth and Spital were favourite places of recreation for the young.
Belonging to the town, they were open to all; and the scene they
presented is faithfully described in the song. On them the Central Station
and its approaches now stand.

Noo, O dear me, what mun aw de?
Aw've ne place noo te play,
Wor canny Forth, an' Spital tee,
Eh, man ! they've tyuen away.

Ne place te bool wor peyste eggs noo,
  Te lowp the frog, or run :
They're elways beeldin' summick noo—
  They'll spoil Newcassel suen.

Spoken.—Thor's ne pleyce te play the wag noo; the grun's a' tuen
up wi' High Levels, Central Stations, an' dear knaws what else.
Aw used te play the wag doon the Kee thonder. Aw've seen me
fish for days tegither. The lads ca'd me the fisherwoman's boy.
Aw was a stunner. Aw've mony a time browt up three French
apples at a time ; but wor aud wife said if aw fell in an' gat drooned
she'd skin me alive when aw com hyem; so aw played the wag doon
the Burn efter that. But, noo to myek improvemints, they've filled
it up wi' cairt loads o' muck te beeld hooses on. Sum o' wor lads
an' me petitioned the magistrates for a new play grund, an' they tell'd
us te gan te bordin' skuels. What an idea ! Wor aud wife hes sair
tues to raise the penny for Monday mornin's : the maister seldom
gets it tho' : aw buy claggum wid : then the maister hes te tyek't
oot in flaps. But aw's broken hearted when aw think aboot wor
canny Forth, wiv its aud brick wall. What curious days aw've
spent there ! Man, aw've seen me play the wag for hyel days
tegither, wi' maw mooth a' covered wi' claggum an' clarts. What a
chep aw was for one-hole-teazer then ! mony a time aw've fowt an
oor for a farden bullocker. Aw used te skin thor knockles,
when aw won mee beeks. Aw used te fullock—man, what a
fullocker aw was ! But what's the use o' jawin' noo? the gams are a'
gyen. Thor's widdy-widdy-way-the-morrow's-the-market-day-slyater-
cummin-away and King-Henry's-boys-go-round—what a gam that
was !—aw used te be King Henry ! But aw'd better drop off, or
maw feelin's will set me on a bubblin'—for

Chorus.
  Oh dear ! what mun aw de?
  Aw've ne pleyce noo te play,
  Wor canny Forth, an' Spital tee,
  Eh, man ! they've tyuen away.

The Toon Improvemint's myed greet noise,
  But aw heard me fethur say,
Thor was summick mair than little boys
  Kept wor wise heed at play ;
Thor's bonny wark amang thorsels,
  But aw mun haud mee jaw ;
But still thor's folks 'boot here that smells
  The cash buik wiv its flaw.

Spoken.—Aw heard my fethur tell my muther yen neet all aboot the toon concerns. They thowt aw was asleep, but aw's a cute lad. Aw's elways waken when the tripe's fryin' for fethur's supper. Aw heard him say thor was a vast o' rates—sic as poor rates, leet rates, sewer rates, an' watch rates; but aw think, at ony rate, thor's ne first-rate rates amang them. Noo, thor's the watch-rate—that's the pollis. Noo, we cannit de wivoot pollis, but it's not fair te tyek a chep up for playin' at holes; but the magistrators isn't dein' fair wiv us at nowt. Aw's lossin' a' maw learnin' noo. What a heed-piece aw had yen time! Aw'd te use a shoe-horn te put my Sunday hat on, my heed gat swelled wiv knowledge se. Noo, a' thor days is gyen, so aw'll lairn te chow backy.

> For, O dear me, etc.

Bedstocks—that canny gam's noo duen,
  An' three hole teazer, tee;
They've duen away wor best o' fun,
  So, lads, what mun aw de?
Aw'll bubble tiv aw dee, begox!
  Or tyek sum arsynack,
Then corporation men may funk,
  When aw's laid on maw back.

> For, O dear me, etc.

Noo, a' ye canny folks that's here,
  Just think on what aw say,
And reckolect yor youthful days,
  When ye were fond o' play.
Ye say yor skuel days was the best,
  So help me in maw cawse,
An' cheer poor Bobby Snivvelnose
  By gi'en him yor applause.

> For, O dear me, etc.

CORVAN.   *Author's Edition.*

THE RISE IN COALS.

THE snaw fell doon fast, and poor folks seem'd shy,
Clos'd up in their hyems as the storm pelted by;
And they wish'd roond their nuiks such times suen wad
    pass,
For provisions was dear, and they'd sav'd little brass.
And as money and firing war meltin' away,
There seems nowt but caud dowps for uz sons o' clay.
The woman foaks flew te fill their coal holes,
To the depoe, but hang them, they've rais'd wor sma'
    coals.
        O what a price for sma' coals,
        Hinny how, they've raised wor sma' coals.

Goshcab, what caud weather, wor Dicky did shoot—
Muther, fetch some coals in, for wor fire's gawn oot;
Some coals, lad, thou's fond, and she gyep'd all amazed,
Thou maun eat less, and drink less, the sma' coals are
    raised.
But, hinnies, that's nowt, for aw's still sair beset,
Coals is thrippence a beetmint, and nyen for te get :
The only bit comfort maw aud body consoles
They've tuen off at last when they raised wor sma' coals.
        O what a price for sma' coals, etc.

Aw went te the depoe, aw think that's the nyem,
And aw stood tiv aw shivered, aw really thowt shem :
Amang sic a gang had ye seen me that day,
Thou'd mebbies come suener then aw did away.
They fit like fair deevils and far warse aw's sure,
For they ken'd what it was when the fire got poor;
But if poor folk had sense they'd fill a' thor holes
Wi' cinders, to spite them for raisin' the coals.
        O what a price for sma' coals, etc.

Yen jaws aboot seets, but aw gyep'd wi' surprise
Te see sic a queer squad wi' maw pair o' eyes;
There was scrushin an' pushin' sic a mixture o' folks,
Wiv sweels, pillow slips, cuddy cairts, and lang pokes;
But the aud wives bang'd a' as they scream'd wi' thor
    tins,
Canny man, gis a pennorth te warm wor aud shins;
Aw've tetties te boil,—says another, aw've stew,
Canny man, put your shuil in and gis a wee few.

                O what a price for sma' coals, etc.

Some keelmen 'bove the bridge, aw heard an aud wife
    say,
Had lang been frozen up an' scairsh could get away.
They thowt their fuddlin days were surely duen at last,
So they doon upon their knees te myek up for the past.
How, marrows, cries a bully, aw've an idea a some price,
We'll find Sir John Franklin if we howk throo the ice;
First, let us find the North Powl, it's some way aboot,
Then get on the top on't an' give him a shoot.

                Aw'll tell him they've raised wor sma' coals, etc.

They ken hoo te swindel poor folks wi' their loads,
Pretendin they're raised and the snaw stop'd the roads;
But a pitman tell'd me te stop up sic jaw,
For it niver rained hailstones nor snaw'd doon belaw.
And he said if thou'll tyek advice frae a fuel,
When there's a greet vast o' weather, get thaw holes
    chock full;
And while thou's warmin thy shins by the fire, as the
    snaw
Drops doon the lum, think o' pitmen belaw.

              For they toil hard an' sair for sma' coals, etc.
CORVAN.   *Author's Edition.*

ASSTRILLY; OR, THE PITMAN'S FAREWELL.

TUNE—" All round my hat."

Noo, marrows, aw's gawn te leeve ye, an' sair, sair 'twill
  grieve me
  Te leave wor canny Tyneside shores, where aw've had
    mony a spree;
Tho' it's sair agyen mee likin', tiv Asstrilly aw'll gan
  hykin',
  For wor maistors keeps us strikin', so what mun a
    pitman de?

Aw mind the time when collier lads cud work for goold
  at hyem, man;
  Dash! aw mind the time when collier lads cud spend
    a pund each pay;
But noo the times thor queer, man, we've nowther sangs
  nor cheer, man:
  When we cannit raise wor beer, man, it's time te gan
    away.

Greet men may de a vast, man, but wor fine times thor
  past, man;
  Gosh! aw waddent leave wor canny toon, but aw's
    forc'd te gan away:
So aw'll myek ne mair emoshun, but cross the salt sea
  oshun,
  Where aw've a kind o' noshun when aw howk aw'll
    get gud pay.

Aw'll bid fareweel te pit wark, an' howk for lumps o'
  goold, man;
  Goshcab! aw'll suen be rich aw've varry little fear;
So aw'll bid fareweel te mammy, an' maw sweetheart o'
  the Lammy;
  It's weel knawn aw's ne hammy—so tiv Asstrilly,
    lads, aw'll steer.

Spoken.—It's ne use stoppin' here; aw mun gan tiv Asstrilly. Still aw's kind o' flaid when aw cum te think o' bein' sea-sick, an' sailin' ower places where thor's ne bottom! Noo, if the sea was te run oot there, an' a' hands be lost, what—O Lord!—what a nibble aw'd be for a shark! An' thor's Geordie Hall, te; aw've con-swaded him te gan a' aw can. He'd myek a fortin oot there i' ne time! Sic a man for yarbs, tee! He can stuff bird cages an' canaries wiv onny man i' Northumberland. Thou shud see his tarrier bitch—she's a fair hare for rabbits! Sic a hunter! Geordie's a greet politishnist as weel: he says he'd suiner hev a reed herrin' at hyem than a beef-steak at Asstrilly. Aw say, what a slaverin' cull! Thor's nowt 'ill stop me frae gannin'. What odds if aw's drooned three or fower times, as lang as aw get there safe!

O, fare ye weel, ye happy scenes, where youthful days
    aw've spent, man!
  Fare ye weel! for better times 'boot here thor'll nivver
    be.
So aw munnet be a gowk, man, but for goold aw'll gan
    an howk, man,
  Tho' maw boiley aw may bowk, man, aw'll seun skim
    ower the sea.

CORVAN.   *Author's Edition.*

ASSTRILLY'S GOOLD FIELDS; OR, TOMMY CARR'S LETTER.

TUNE—"Marble Halls."

Aw dreamt that aw'd landed in Strilia's goold fields,
  Wi' Bessie, maw wife, by maw side;
An' aw also dreamt how aw toil'd i' the keels
  On the Tyne, still maw home an' maw pride.
Aw dreamt aw was howkin goold day an' neet,
  An' fand greet big lumps in galore,
Then aw thowt te mee-sel what a rich chep aw'd be
  When aw cum back te leeve doon the shore.

                    Aw dreamt that aw landed, etc.
26

Aw dreamt that aw saw some aud cronies there,
    All howkin for goold like mee-sel,
An' wishin', while sweetin' wi' byens stiff an' sair,
    For a swag o' good Newcassel yell.
Aw also dreamt aw'd sell'd a' maw goold,
    And gettin the brass, every scuddock ;
But aw waken'd an' fand mee-sel lyin', silly man,
    Fast asleep doon belaw in the huddock.

                    Aw dreamt that aw landed, etc.

Aw was rubbin' me eyes when the Pee-dee cries out,
    Aw say, skipper, the keel's gyen adrift ;
Where is aw ? says aw wi' a terrible shoot,
    Then aw gav his young backside a lift.
How, skipper, what's that for ? thou aud crazy fuil !
    The Pee-dee, the trash, bawls te me ;
Then aw spang-hew'd him weel, the gobby young cull,
    But he danced like an imp full o' glee.

Spoken.—Goshcab, the bit laddie went mad varry nigh.
What's the matter wi' thee? says aw. Wey, here's a letter frae
Asstrilly for thee. Blaw me rags, so it was; that was just maw
dream—what a queer thing dreams is, efter all. Aw say, what
gobby things laddies is nooadays: they think men's mice, or folks
is people—but aw stop a' thor jaws. Thor's a vast o' rats i' wor
huddock, sir,—but aw's forgettin' the letter—(*Opens the letter*) ;—
it's frae Tommy Carr; stop, aw'll read it ower.

            Melbourne, Octember, aw mean Septober the 35th,
                    18 hundred en eggs en bacon.
DEAR BOBBY,
        Afore thou opens this letter excuse maw bad spellin': pens
is varry bad here, en hoo can a body spell wiv a PHEMWHTN
(pen). [Marcy (*aside*), what a lot o' letters he hes for spellin' pen.
What a *schollar* he's turned; he must gan tiv a neet *skeul* through
the day: aw shuddent wonder.]
    Wor byeth i' gud health here, except me en Bob. Aw've teun
the Yaller fever wi' snuffin goold dust, en Bob's broke his three
legs, en can scairshly stand o' the tother; wishin' ye the same
benefits at hyem. Aw'll mebbies be deed the next time aw write
te thee.

There's bonny wark oot here wi' the Convicts, the Blackies, Robbers, en Bushrangers. Man, the time aw's writin' this letter aw've a loaded pistol i' one hand en a sword i' the tother, defendin' me heed. [(*Aside.*) The greet thick-heeded lubbert! What set him there? he wis deein' weel here, puddlin at Hawks's—three days a week overtime an' ne wages.] Give maw respects te Bill Scott, the Shingler, oot at Consett, en tell him te hev a luck at the tin bottle for maw sake. Ned Corvan says he's nobbit a reet un.

A' kinds o' provisions iz varry cheap here, except victuals en fustin jackets. We hae nee tripe, so we struggle wi' fustin—there's ne Butcher's meat here, except Wild Buffaloes en Yarmouth beef.

Little Jimmy's nowt like his feythor noo; some hungry convicts bit off the laddie's lugs; if ye saw him ye'd 'mawjin he'd been at Carson's drawing the Badger.

Nee more at present from yor Confectionate Brother,

TOMMY CARR.

P.S.—[(*Aside.*) Pint o' Soup!] Fat Hanna's mother's wife's cousin's brother's aunt's teun the measles.

Noo contented an' happy at hyem aw'll still be,
   Wi' Bessey, maw canny bit bride,
An' aw'll whiles hev a gill an' whiles hev a spree,
   Wi' comfort at mee awn fireside;
So excuse maw bit rhyme, for some other time
   Aw'll tell ye—though strange the tale seems—
'Bout the places aw've been, an' the wonders aw've seen
   I' the huddock, when lying 'mang dreams.

CORVAN.   *Author's Manuscript*, 1862.

TOMMY CARR'S ADVENTURES IN ASSTRILLY.

HERE aw is, byeth skin an' byen, in Asstrilly, O!
Man, aw wished aw'd stopt at hyem frae Asstrilly, O!
   Maw inside's a'most gyen,
   Tho' aw wonce weighed thirteen styen,
Noo aw scairshly can weigh yen in Asstrilly, O!

Aw sell'd maw keel for twenty pund throo Asstrilly, O!
Not a morsel o' gowld aw fund in Asstrilly, O!
    Sum natives com one day,
    An' brunt maw hut like hay,
An' Fat Hannah stole away in Asstrilly, O!

They tied me tiv a tree in Asstrilly, O!
But a Yankee set me free in Asstrilly, O!`
    Aw 'scap'd withoot a hurt,
    But they stript me te my shurt,
So aw rubbed mee-sel wi' durt in Asstrilly, O!

Aw paid for vittels wiv a froon in Asstrilly, O!
Three taties for a croon in Asstrilly, O!
    Sprats is sivenpence a dish;
    An' if a bit nice cod ye wish,
Fifteen shillins buys the fish in Asstrilly, O!

Few wives thor's te be seen in Asstrilly, O!
What thor is thor a' serene in Asstrilly, O!
    Thor beer hes a nesty tack;
    Coals is 'ighteen shillins a sack,
An' ye get them varry black in Asstrilly, O!

Sma' beer's ten shillins a quairt in Asstrilly, O!
Besides, it's soor an' tairt in Asstrilly, O!
    Six shillins a three pund brick;
    Butter's half-a-croon a lick;
'Sides they nivver gie ye tick in Asstrilly, O!

Spoken.—O Lord! O dear! aw wish aw was safe hyem wonce mair! When aw com to this cursed country, aw'd plenty ov ivverything: plenty o' munny, plenty o' claes; noo aw's nowt but rags. Aw'd myek a poor moothful for a wild beast, unless he's fond o' rags an' byens, for thor's ne flesh on mine. What a fuil aw was te leeve canny Newcassel te cum an' hunt for gowld! O Lord!

O dear ! 'steed o' me huntin' for gowld, they've hunted me frae one place tiv anuther, till aw heh ne place but this one, an' it's warse than ne place. What wi' bushmen, blackies, convicts, Indians, rattle-snakes, boa constructors, wolves, an' sic like human creatures, aw've had ne peace since aw left England. Just 'magine bein' tossed aboot on the ocean, an' then te be hunted like a kangaroo ! Aw had a hut. Fat Hannah, Jimmy, an' me happened te lie doon to rest wor byens, when aw smelled fire. Oot aw popped, and there was black divils shootin' ootside. They stole maw things ; cut off wi' Fat Hannah (ne bargain !) Then they walked off wi' me for supper, but aw've run for'd ; an' here aw've been wanderin' aboot five or six days amangst thorns, till aw hevin't a stitch o' claes left on me back, nor ne grub in me belly. Aw myed the last meal o' maw hat, an' aw felt it sair on me stomack. But it sarves me reet to cum oot here, for te loss me money and then te loss maw claes. O Lord ! aw'll loss me senses next ! Aw wish aw was safe back te canny Newcassel, if aw cud oney get oot o' this purgatory spot.

Aw'll return a rooind man frae Asstrilly, O !
Get on, whey ne man can in Asstrilly, O !
Noo here aw groan an' pine,
Aw's diddled up se fine—
O welcum, Coaly Tyne, frae Asstrilly, O !

CORVAN.   *Author's Edition.*

THE CULLERCOATS FISH-LASS.

TUNE—"Lilie's a Lady."

Aw's a Cullercoats fish-lass, se cozy an' free,
Browt up in a cottage close on by the sea ;
An' aw sell fine fresh fish ti poor an' ti rich—
Will ye buy, will ye buy, will ye buy maw fresh fish ?

Spoken.—Fine codlin's, hinny ; cheaper for hyem consumption thin butcher meat. There's fine mackerel. Come, Mistor, ye shall hae them at yor awn price, but the sea's up. Aw's sure, fish just noo's as bad to catch iz husbands ; and a greet deal warse ti sell.

(*Sings.*) Will ye buy, will ye buy, will ye buy my fresh fish ?
(*Imitate cries.*) D'ye want a—n—y fish ?

Byeth barefoot and barelegged aw trudge mony a week,
Wi' a creel on mee back an' a bloom on mee cheek;
Aw'll supply ye wi' flat fish, fine skyet, or fresh ling,
And sometimes pennywilks, crabs, an' lobsters aw bring.

> Will ye buy, will ye buy? etc.

Aw work hard for mee livin', frev a frind aw ne'er begs,
An' aw huff the young gents when they peep at my legs;
Aw's hilthy an' hansom, quite willin' and strong,
To toil for my livin', cryin' fish the day long.

Spoken.—That's what aw cawl fishin' for a livin'. But tawkin' aboot fish, thor's as queer fish on land as there's in the sea— Gladstone, Tom Sayers, and Blondin—aw cawl them star-fish, that baits the public ti sum tuin. Folks that neglects to buy the *Illustrated Tyneside Songs*, aw consider them flat-fish. Mackey's men, they're dry fish; ye can tell by their gills. Sailors, they're salt fish, that shud elways keep a wether eye on land-sharks. Volunteers, they're fresh fish, who, with wor sowlgers and sailors, myek up wor *sole* defenders. As for me, with yor kind favours, aw'd be like a fish oot o' wetter—aye, whei! Aw's a maiden fish oot iv her teens in sairch ov a husband to myek me comfortable. Aw want ti teyk moorins for life in the roads an' channels o' matrimony.

> Will ye buy, will ye buy? etc.

CORVAN.   *Author's Manuscript*, 1862.

BOBBY THE BOXER.

TUNE—"Pat's Curiosity Shop."

ABOOT "Fistiana" an' fightin' skull-bruizers may blether
   an' crack,
Aw's the lad the P.R. can enlighten—man, aw've walloped
   the yell o' the pack;
Tom Paddock, aw suin sent him muzy, Tipton Slasher
   aw knocked out o' time,
And Bendy aw doubled up mazy; smash! nyen can
   touch me in my prime.

Chorus.

On me thou mun place greet reliance, for boxin' thou'll say
    aw's a cure,
De ye think thit aw's not up ti science ? Howay oot ! aw's
    yor man for the Moor.

Wiv the bowld Johnny Wawker aw've won, tee, his
    backers they hoyed up the sponge ;
Bob Travers, the Blacky, aw've dune, tee, wiv a fine
    upper cut an' a lunge ;
The fighters ti me aw cums fleein, they aw ken me morit
    an' worth,
Aw trained Renwicks, Bill Cleghorn, and Heenan, an'
    a' the best men i' the North.

                        Chorus.

Jim Mace an' Tom Sayers may pass muster, byeth gud
    men we a' mun agree,
But for a' their greet battles an' bluster, they've byeth
    had to forfeit to me ;
Harry Powlson and Cobley, maw kitten, aw've hammered
    them black i' the face,
Dan Thomas and Jones's fine hittin' wi' this *Chicken* wis
    awl oot o' place.

                        Chorus.

Aw worry the pollis i' dozens, ti beat me they try a'
    they can,
But since aw mugged Inspector Cousins, they swear aw's
    the devil's awn man ;
Hoots ! fightin' to me's nobbit pastime, aw's elways first
    in for a pelt,
So Mace aw mun fight for the last time, then swagger
    aboot wiv a belt.

                        Chorus.

Wi' Jim Ward aw've had murry meetins, but then iv a
jovial way,

Their music an' toddy-care meetins aw drives the blue
divels away ;

Ti Langham's aw oft pay a visit, he's a decent aud covey
is Nat,

Gosh, his wife telled me when he hooked it to walk in an'
hing up me hat !

Chorus.

In Newbold's grand pictor awm stuck up wiv a' the
greet boxers aroond,

There aw stand wi mee eyes shut to luik up at the fight
for the four hundred pounds ;

Lads, there's not a gud fighter amang them, it's boonce
and mock courage they've got,

Nobbit giz a gud blaw oot at Mackey's, sowl ! aw'll
perish the yell o' the lot.

Chorus.

Like Tom Sayers, aw'll suin gan oot starrin' for a five-
pun note ivery set-to,

Gosh, cab ! aw's the genus for sparrin', Bobby the
Boxer's real Tyneside true blue ;

Aw defeated bowld Crawley an' Crockett, an' vanquished
wi' ease Jarry Noon,

An' aw've a challenge just now in maw pocket ti fight
wi' the man i' the moon.

Chorus.

But noo aw'll away ti me trainin', aw'll suin be i' fine
trim agyen,

Aboot three or fower styen aw want gainin', then aw'll
strip wi' the brightest o' men ;

So ta ta, ye bowld sportin' fellows, the time aw prepare
for the strife,

When aw knock oot the puff o' King's bellows, what a
worry there'll be for *Bell's Life.*

Chorus.

CORVAN. *Author's Manuscript,* 1862.

WARKWORTH FEAST.

TUNE—"Morpeth Jail."

Sum folks may jaw 'boot a fine breeze,
Praise Warkwith's shores an' hikey seas;
Praise steem-boat trips an' caller air,
Or spend a day devoid o' care.
They may tell o' wondrous things they see,
Sic as cassels, an' rooins, an' lots o' spree;
'Boot monks an' marmaids dein' queer feats,
An' rabbits dancin' polkas on the Coquet at neets.

But, lads, aw've got a different tyel,
For aw wonce had a trip doon there me-sel:
'Twas a ruffish morn—the wind nor-east—
When forst aw had a trip te Warkwith Feast.

Abord ov a steamer aw cruiked maw heugh,
An' things at the Kee went square eneuff;
So we got under way; but we haddent gyen far,
When an aud wife cries, "Wor on the Bar!"
"O, marcy me!" cries Jimmy Bell,
"Maw belly's sair—aw's quite unwell!"
Then bowkins o' boiley went fleein' aboot,
An' a lump o' chowed tripe catched me reet on the
snoot.

So if ye winnit believe maw tyels,
Just tyek a trip doon there yorsels, etc.

Half duzzy aw staggered alang the boat,
When a chep tossed a lump o' fat doon me throat.
Lord! says aw, thou's dyun maw job!
But says he, "Ye fyul, it'ell tyest yor gob!"

Then a' the things aw'd eatin last 'eer,
Fegs, grosers, reed herrins, an' yell, did appear ;
Eh, man, hoo aw trimmeled as aw stuck tiv a post,
Goshcab ! aw'd dyun fine te play Hamlick's ghost !

> So if ye winnit, etc.

Sic rushin', an' crushin', an' cryin' for drops ;
Sic rattlin' o' buckets, an' usin' o' mops ;
Sic pityful fyeces, an' cries o' distress,
Wi' screamin' an' shootin', an' spoilin' o' dress.
Aw wes creepin' alang as quiet as a moose,
Te try an' find the little hoose ;
Aw fell ower two aud wives, an' rowled on the deck,
An' nigh as a tutcher broke maw neck.

> So if ye winnit, etc.

At last we landed safe ashore,
Reet glad wes aw wi' monny a score ;
But syun maw wonders they increas'd,
When aw see'd three stalls at Warkwith Feast.
Nowt wes there yen's heart te cheer,
But a lot o' awful bitter beer :
'Twad puzzen rats—oh, maw poor tripes !
Aw's sartin 'twad gi'en a brass cuddy the gripes.

> So if ye winnit, etc.

Noo, a bit ov advice might be wholesome, I think,
When ye gan plishure trips, tyek yor meat an' yor
     drink ;
For thor's nivvor ne plishure where thor's nowt te
     eat,
If yor gyepin' at cassels frae morn till neet.

Lifetime's a trip, an' ivvery man
Mun battle throo the best way he can.
So excuse maw sang ; if ye doot the least,
Ye can gan next 'eer te Warkwith Feast.

So if ye winnit, etc.

CORVAN. *Author's Edition.*

THE KIPPER'D HERRIN'.

'Boot pitmen an' keelmen thou's heard some queer jokes,
What wi' blunders, mistyeks, an' thor queer funny spokes,
For when we get a drop o' beer we're a' full o' glee ;
Lads! we myek mony a blunder when we get on the
    spree.

Singing fal the dall, lall, etc.

Noo aw'll tell ye a trick we yence played on Jim Farrins,
Thit yen day bowt a cask o' the best kipper'd herrins,
Te eat tiv his coffee, his taties, and breed,
Determined a' winter te hev a cheap feed.

Reet fal, etc.

He tuik fower greet big uns yen neet doon the pit,
An' he waddent let yen doon belaw tyest a bit ;
So a pennorth o' Jalup we put iv his bottle,
An', lads! hoo we laffed iz it went doon his throttle.

Chorus.

He hewed half-an-hour tiv he felt summic ache,
Then he put doon his hands for te haud on the brake,
Cryin' oot—"Geordy Cairns, run away, thou's maw cuzen,
An' bring uz a docter, for aw've swallow'd some puzzin."

Chorus.

Noo, the bit trapper laddies they laff'd fit te borst,
An' menshun'd what myed the poor man bad at forst;
But he says—" Haud yor gobs, give ower yor leein',
Aw's speechless a'ready, aw's sartin aw's deein'.
Chorus.

" Aw's deein', aw's deein', aw's off, Geordy Cairns,
Protect when aw's gyen maw poor wife an' bairns;
Keep a' maw pit claes, cum draw thaw lugs near,
An' hear maw last words, for aw've supped maw last beer.
Chorus.

" Tell wor keeker aw deed wiv a pain i' maw booils,
Cawsed wi' eatin' some harrin' aw bowt frae Jack Snooils;
Tell wor preacher next Sunday te pray for maw *sole*,
Tell wor owners and viewers aw'll howk ne mair coal.
Chorus.

" Tyek maw picks tiv aud limpey, tell him aw's gyen,
An' come te maw funeral wi' cloaks ivery yen;
Tyek maw grandfethur's watch, keep that for theesell,
Aw's gannin'—ta, ta, Geordy—te Heaven or te H——ll!"
Chorus.

CORVAN.　　　　　　　　　　　　　　*Author's Manuscript,* 1862.

DEETH O' BILLY PURVIS.

William Purvis (better known throughout the North as "Billy Purvis")
was born in Auchindinny, near Edinburgh, but was brought to Newcastle
by his parents at an early age. After leaving school he was apprenticed to
John Chapman, joiner, Bigg Market. From an early age he showed a
decided inclination for the stage, and became a "call boy" at the Theatre
Royal, Newcastle, while it was under the management of Stephen Kemble.
After some coquetting with the muse as an amateur, and several peram-
bulations in the surrounding districts, as a conjurer, a clown, and a performer on the Northumberland bagpipes (on which he excelled), he finally
established himself as proprietor of a travelling theatre about 1818. With
his portable theatre he for many years travelled throughout the North of

BILLY PURVIS AS CLOWN AT HIS VICTORIA THEATRE.

England and Scotland, attending the various fairs, races, etc., until he became a familiar feature at each place. During the summer months, when the Theatre Royal was closed, being a freeman of Newcastle, he generally obtained leave to make a lengthened stay in the town; and often brought with him a superior company of performers, several of whom have since won a high rank in their profession. At Newcastle Races he was in his glory. Dressed in his now familiar clown's dress, and standing on the outside stage of his theatre, he would shout to the pitmen thronging round—"Are ye cummin' in te see wor show, Geordy? Ay, it's clivor, 'tis clivor! If ye dinnet like te cum ower the stage, ye can get in by Billy's backside! (pointing to the door at the back). Only a penny for trappers, an' tuppence for wappers! Ay, it's clivor, 'tis clivor!" With such like sallies he enlivened the proceedings on the outside stage between the dances, and generally succeeded in doing a large business. His life was a chequered one. Theatrical speculations are generally uncertain, and Billy had his share of its ups and downs. Despite his wandering life, Newcastle was always his home; and for nearly sixty-six years he resided in the same house in the Close, where he brought up his family in a most respectable manner. He died, while at Hartlepool with his theatre, on the 16th of December 1858, in his seventy-third year.

Shortly after his death, the Messrs. Sangers, on visiting Hartlepool with their circus, gave a benefit for the purpose of raising funds to erect a tombstone over his grave. A good sum was thus obtained, and a neat stone now tells his last resting-place.

TUNE—"Jenny Jones."

Aud Billy's gyen deed noo, frae worldly cares freed noo,
    Ne mair sports he'll heed noo on Wear or Tyneside:
Still his nyem leeves i' story, Tyne lads was his glory,
    For when he amused them his heart beat wi' pride.
But he's cut off at last noo, his days they are past noo,
    Ne mair, poor aud man, his *bundle he'll steal*:[*]
That *bundle*, for pastime, he's stole for the last time,
    For Deeth's corked him off te the land o' the leal.

Chorus.

    Aud Billy's gyen deed noo, frae worldly cares freed noo,
    For Deeth's corked him off te the land o' the leal.

[*] "Billy Stole the Bundle"—a piece he often played, in which he was constantly interrupted in his attempts to steal a bundle lying at the corner of the stage.

Ne mair tyels ye'll tell, oh, maw canny aud fellow !
    Hoo ye've swalleyed up crab-fish, an' locked up men's
        jaws ;
Ne mair thou'll dance neatly, or play your pipes sweetly,
    Nor perform *Hocus-Pocus*, that gained sic applause ;
For we'll see ye ne mair, man, at hoppin' or fair, man,
    Stand up i' yor glory 'mang actors ootside :
For that tyrant, King Deeth, man, hes stopt wor cloon's
        breath, man,
    And closed noo for iver poor Billy's *backside*.
                    Aud Billy's gyen, etc.

Ne mair at wor Races, friend Billy, thou'll grace us,
    Nor call Geordies in yor fine show to admire ;
For, oh ! 'twas his boast then, fine dramas an' ghosts
        then,
    Wi' pantomime plays full o' reed an' blue fire.
What troubles through life, man, what cares an' what
        strife, man,
    He had te amuse us—byeth aud folks an' young :
Oh ! aw think wiv emoshun, an' tears of devoshun,
    On the days when aw first lisped his nyem wi' maw
        tongue !

Spoken.—Yis, them was the days that we can nivor forget—wor skyul days. We had ne humbuggin' pollis then ; nobbit canny aud watchmen, that yen might heb knocked doon wiv a pipe-stopple. We had ne railways in Billy's youthful days ; an' times was far better than they are noo. Aw reckolect when Billy was an actor, aboot thirty eers since—them was maw happy days—aw wad beg, borrow, or steal to get a luik at aud Billy's backside. Poor canny aud fellow ! he used te be king o' the Spital. Them was maw youthful days, an' monny a yen's beside me. Aw've seen me gawn about wi' maw shirt-tail stickin' oot that far behint that aw've used it for a pocket-hankisher ; an' as for shoes, the oney pair aw had on my feet was the pair the cobbler had away mendin' ! But what did aw care aboot shoes ? aw had big toes like styens ! Oh ! what music aw fund i' the bells o' St. Nicholas', when the Easter hallidays myed

thor appearance! Hoo leet was maw yoothful heart!—ne stain was
there to mar maw happiness! Wi' what plishure aw booled maw
pyeste eggs on the green! That green's ne mair; but, like wor
favourite cloon an' Northumbria's jester, gyen for ivver. Where's
a' his funny sayin's, that set a' the Geordies in a roar? They are
gyen; but Billy 'ill nivver be forgettin'.

Aud Billy's gyen, etc.

But, oh! aw'll remember the sixteenth of December,
    In the eer '53, died wor aud king o' Tyne;
An' left us in mournin' withoot ony warnin',
    The frinds o' his yooth, an' the days o' langsyne.
But the frind we luv best noo, his byens cannit rest noo,
    So, Newcassel folks, think o' these words o' mine:
Let's hev him laid doon then, i' wor canny toon then,
    Else his ghost will be wanderin' at neets on the Tyne.

Aud Billy's gyen, etc.

CORVAN. *Author's Edition.*

THE GREET BULL-DOG O' SHIELDS.

**Written on the occasion of the gunboat *Bull-dog* lying at Shields, shortly
after the termination of the Russian War.**

TUNE—"Hokey Pokey."

WOR Dick an' me, last Curstmis day,
    Tuik i' wor heeds te gan away,
    Resolved te spend a yell week's pay
       Amang the fokes o' Sheels, man.
At Sandget end we had some yell
    Alang wi' Matt and Skipper Bell,
    Then doon te Sheels a' hands did speel,
    I' Skipper Johnson's bran new keel.
'Twas there aw hard young Geordy Carr,
    That kens se much aboot the Czar,
    Say, " What d'ye think's come frae the war,
       But a greet Bull-dog at Sheels, man?

Fall de dall, etc.

Says aw thou's leein fond aw's sure,
Yor idees mun be varry poor,
Thou wants to put on Tommy Moor,
    Wi' yor greet Bull-dog o' Sheels, man.
What, a bull-dog swalley Rooshin bears,
That's nobbit lees, cum speak for fairs.
He says then lissen ti' what comes—
He fired het snawballs at thor bums,
He peppered them all at Bummy Soond,
An' laid thor batteries wi' the groond;
That varry Bull-dog may now be foond
    Lyin' in Peggy's Hole i' Sheels, man.

Give ow'r says aw, wi' voice se gruff,
Or suen, by gox, aw may ye huff,
Wi' fiery snawballs me ti stuff
    An' yor greet Bull-dog o' Sheels, man.
Think weel, maw man, wi' whe ye play,
The fuil he laff'd and quick did say,
But mair than that, the dog lies reet
Chocked full o' guns and men complete;
He tuik Charley Napier, tars and all,
Ti Bummy Soond wi' Captain Hall,
And feyred them shells that made them squall,
    Did this greet Bull-dog o' Sheels, man.

He nipt thor tails and myed them shoot,
An' just like badgers drawed them oot,
He worried thor thropples wiv his snoot,
    Did this greet Bull-dog o' Sheels, man.
He fired them bullets het and thick,
Sayin' there's some pills, aud Mister Nick;
He myed them scamper duce'd quick,
An' levelled ivery steyn an' brick,

27

He myed their nasty tallow run,
Then wagg'd his tail an' barked like fun,
An' cam ti the Tyne when aw was duin,
        Did this greet Bull-dog o' Sheels, man.

Says aw, thou's stuffin me, maw man,
But when aw lands aw's sure ti gan
An' find this Bull-dog iv aw can,
        That's myekin sic wark at Sheels, man.
So when aw landed on the kee,
Away aw gans quite full o' glee,
Ti try and find this Bull-dog breed,
But hang a Bull-dog there aw se'd,
So aw axed a sailor stannin there,
If he saw a bull-dog ony where,
        He gyeped an' glower'd an' gave a blair.

Spoken.—An' let flee a chow o' baccy iz big iz a turmit—so aw
sets Nettle on tiv him (that's maw terrier), iv he was a Bull-dog
Nettle maniged him.   As for me, aw trotted, cas there was a dozen
bull-dogs i' nee time, an' nivor stopt tiv aw went bump agyen the
wooden dolly—aw thowt it was Jarrow. Wi' that aw heers the
sailors bawl oot—hie, shipmate, ahoy! shipmate, the deevil says
aw——
        (*Sings*) D'ye think we're fuils o' Sheels, man.

Sair vexed, begox! aw kept gawn back,
Determined Skipper Carr ti smack,
And let him see that aw cud snack
        Wiv ony bull-dog o' Sheels, man.
But, hinny marrows, guess maw surprise,
When aw twigs a steamboat sic a size,
Men an' guns aw did disarn,
Wiv B double LL bull-dog on her starn,
Aw seed her bonny colours flyin',
Wi' sowlgers an' sailors exercisin',
And sure enyuf the Bull-dog wis lyin'
        I' Peggy's Hole in Sheels, man.

Noo, may Sheels prosper, while the sea
Beats on her shores so wild and free,
May they niver lack prosperity
    Nor manly hearts i' Sheels, man ;
May blissins crown each happy home,
Wor sailors, tee, where'er they roam,
May we ever on old England's shore
Boast British Bull-dogs evermore.
Aw wish success tiv aw that's here,
May ye nivor want good health or cheer,—
Smash ! aw hope ye'll live for mony a year,
    Wi' greet Bull-dogs o' Sheels, man.

CORVAN.   *Author's Manuscript*, 1862.

THE FISHERMEN HUNG THE MONKEY, O!

"The Fishermen hung the Monkey, O!" These words are the greatest insult you can offer to the Hartlepool fishermen. It is supposed when Napoleon the Great threatened to invade England the fishermen were loyal and patriotic, and ever on the look-out for spies. A vessel having been wrecked about this time, all on board perished with the exception of a monkey, which was seized by the fishermen for a French spy, and hung because he could not or would not speak English.—*Author's Note.*

TUNE—"The Tinker's Wedding."

IN former times, 'mid war an' strife,
When French invashin threatened life,
An' all was arm'd te the knife,
    The Fishermen hung the Monkey, O!
The Fishermen, wi' courage high,
Seized the Monkey for a spy.
Hang him says yen, says another he'll die ;
    They did, an' they hung the Monkey, O!

Chorus.
(To sympathise with the unfortunate Monkey, altogether.)

Dooram, dooram, dooram, da, etc.

They tried ivery means te myek him speak,
They tortor'd the Monkey tiv he loud did squeak ;
Says yen that's French, says anuther it's Greek,
  For the Fishermen then gat drunkey, O !
He's all ower hair sum cheps did cry,
E'en up te summic cute an' sly ;
Wiv a cod's heed then they closed an eye,
  Afore they hung the Monkey, O !

Spoken.—Ladies an' cheps, a chorus this time to mark our disap-
probashin o' the Pugnaeshis Fishermen for closin' the ogle ov the
unfortunate Monkey.

            Dooram, etc.

Some the Monkey's fate they did bewail,
For all the speechless *pug* had his tail (tale),
He'd been better off i' Durham jail,
  For the Monkey wis tornin funkey, O !
They said he myed some curose mugs,
When they shaved his head an' cut off his lugs,
Sayin' that's the game for French humbugs,
  Afore they hung the Monkey, O !

Spoken.—Chorus in considerashin of the removal and total anni-
hilashin of the Monkey's auricular organ by all who have an ear for
gorilla sensashins.

            Dooram, etc.

Hammer his ribs, the thunerin thief,
Pummel his pyet weel wi' yor neef,
He's landed here for nobbit grief,
  He's aud Napoleon's Uncky, O !
Thus to the Monkey all hands behaved,
Cut off his whiskers one chep raved ;
Another bawled oot he's never been shaved,
  So they commenced to scrape the Monkey, O !

       Chorus.
   (After the style of " Lather and shave 'em.")
           Dooram, etc.

Now let us hope that ever at sea
We'll still maintain sovereignty,
May France and England long agree,
    An' nivor at each other get funkey, O!
As regards poor Pug aw've had my say,
His times they've past for mony a day,
But in Harlepool, noo, thou'll hear lads say—

Spoken.—Aw say, Mistor, mother says it, she telled me te ax ye, te tell me te tell her ; if ye tell me,—aw say, Mistor, can ye tell us—

(*Sings*)—Whe hung the Monkey, O?

                           Dooram, etc.

CORVAN.   *Author's Manuscript*, 1862.

THE COMET; OR, THE SKIPPER'S FRIGHT.

Written on the appearance of the Great Comet, 1858.

TUNE—"Polly Parker, O."

MARROWS, aw's pinin fast away, aw's freetin ivery day,
Aboot this awful danger noo impendin, O!
Aw's shakin a' te bits, wor aud wife she's tyekin fits,
Cawse the nibors say the world's upon an endin, O!

Says wor preacher t'other day, noo a' ye weak sowls pray;
An' te drop a' worldly care he did beseech us, O!
Says he, this mighty orth, wiv all int's but little worth,
If a fiery thing like a comet chanced to reach us, O!

Aboot Stronomists he bawled, then ower the reckinin hawled,
Te tell hoo lang a time we had te bide here, O!
Says he, sometime i' June, wiv a tail, it will drop doon;
Then a' the world i' mystery suin mun glide here, O!

Thinks aw, begum that's queer, wor preacher he's nee
  leer,
He's always on the reet side when he's speakin, O !
So aw'll sell off byeth maw keels, and tyek a ship at Sheels;
For a spot upon the new world aw'll gan seekin, O !

But first aw'll chawk a score ahint the Brown Jug door,
For it's little use o' passin when life's uncertain, O !
Like Robson, Bates, and Pawl, lads ! the kelter in aw'll
  hawl,
Then for flight like a' the swindlers aw'll be startin, O !

Noo, when aw cum te think, aw'd better spend maw chink,
Amang me Tyneside cronies, true and hearty, O !
For if we a' mun dee, thou knaws as weel as me,
The rich amang the poor mun join the party, O !

Then flow on wor Coaly Tide, spreadin wealth on ivery
  side,
Flow on, bright stream, wi' joy te croon maw giver, O !
That he may smile on thee for all eternity,
The light ov peace and harmony for iver, O !
CORVAN.   *Author's Manuscript*, 1862.

THE FIRE ON THE KEE.

The Explosion of October 6th, 1854, which took its rise from a fire in
Gateshead, was perhaps the greatest calamity that ever happened in the
North of England.

TUNE—" Wor Jocker."

OH ! hae ye seen wor Jimmy, oh ! hae ye seen wor
  Jimmy ?
Oh ! hae ye seen wor Jimmy ? for the lad's gyen on the
  spree,
He's pawn'd his coat an' troosers, he gans on as he
  chooses,
He can wallop a' the bruisers an' greet bullies on the
  Kee.

Chorus.

Oh ! hae ye seen wor Jimmy, oh ! hae ye seen wor Jimmy ?
Tell me, maw canny hinny, for the lad's gyen on the spree.

His nose is neat an' canny, he's a model of a mannie,
An' the pictor o' wor Fanny, oh, the nasty drukken
sow.
Aw'll yark his byens wi' skelpin, aw'll set the yelp a
yelpin,
Presarve us ! there's ne helpin byestin laddies now.

Oh, hae ye seen wor Jimmy, etc.

He hes a bull-dog wiv him, folks dorsent say owt tiv
him,
A good heart beats within him, for he knocks the pollis
doon ;
He hes twe nice black eyes, tee, an' a mouth for eatin
pies, tee ;
Folks say he's not ower wise, tee, an' call the lad a
cloon.

Spoken.—Aw wish aw could lay hands on him ; he went to seek wark
this morning—Wark ! he's been seekin wark this fourteen years an'
niver gettin a job yet—But that fire on the Kee ruined the lad's
mind ; a gyeble end iv a hoose fell on his head—He's been crack'd
iver since. Marcy, what a cutty fosty, but aw'll gie ye an account
on't efter the style ov the " Deeth ov Nelson."

TUNE—" 'Twas in Trafalgar's Bay."

It was a fearful crash, old buildings they went smash,
'Twas never so before ;
The haunts of " auld lang syne " burnt doon on Coaly
Tyne,
Laying waste the desolate shore :
For oh ! it was a fearful sight, and many a home was
lost that night,

For death's grim visitation brought ruin and devastation,
   And as from 'mid the flames they hie,
   Mercy! save us! hundreds cry—
      O! Firemen, do your duty!
      O! Firemen, do your duty!

TUNE—"Descriptive Chant."

Hurrying to and fro countless thousands might be seen,
Emerging after hairbreadth 'scapes from ruins where
   danger just had been;
The soldiers in solemn silence guard the dangerous way,
And firemen willing point the hose to where gaiety dwelt
   but yesterday.
The populace rushed forth half-dressed in day or night
   attire,
Like maniacs with maddened brain, from death's
   devouring fire.

Chorus.

For oh! the flames, Vesuvius-like, they spread o'er land and sea,
Laying desolate waste the spot where once had been Newcastle Kee.

Now many serio-comic scenes were enacted where poor
   people did dwell,
For goods and chattels from mysterious cribs came
   tumbling down pellmell.
Aw saw one poor deevil, mevies just gettin oot o' bed,
Hop varry quick to one side iz a wash-han' basin, a kyel
   pot, and a yetlin' fell a-top iv his head.
'Twas fearful to see the poor aud wives in narrow chares
   and lanes
Picking up their bits o' things, exposing life, aw's sure
   they spared ne pains.

Chorus.

Aw say, Pally! thraw the bed oot the window, niver
  mind the stocks,
Seize Ned's Sunday britches aw bowt last week, but niver
  mind the box.
Marcy! the floor's geen way,—noo whe wid iver think
That decent folks gan te bed 'boot ten o'clock shud be
  see close upon deeth's brink?
Search for Tommy's fustin claes, aw cannot see for smoke,
Luik sharp, ye platter-fyeced bunter, or else, begum,
  aw'll choke.

Chorus.

Search for the bairn's cradle, it's a claes-basket, niver
  mind, shove it to the door.
Let the auld clock stand agyen the wall, it's time it went
  'cas it waddent gan before;
A German for a shillin a week clagged it up agyen the
  wall,
He's got nowt yit, so faith his *tick* aw think'll suin be
  tickin small.
They say Ralphy L—tle's broke his legs, but that
  myeks little matter,
Cawse a glass o' brandy'll put him reet, wiv a bottle o'
  soda watter.

Chorus.

Pally, hinny, rush i' the crood an' shoot, for see the
  smoke an low gets dense,
And luik for Jimmy, maw canny hinny, for the laddie
  hez ne sense;
But there's a crood o' men there—Mister, can aw claim
  yor attention?
Aw've lost maw darlin son, an' what he's like aw'll
  mention—

He's nee scholar, bless the laddie ! but he smokes an'
  chows,
He's parshall ti military movements, espeshley Sangate
  rows ;
He's gat his *millishor* claes on, thou'll ken him iv a crack,
Besides sum stripes for good behavor, but they put them
  on his back.
His appearance commands respect—hae ye seen him
  gannin by ?
The skin's off his knockles wi' fightin', an he sports a
  lairge black eye !

Chorus.

CORVAN.

Author's Manuscript, 1862.

CHAMBERS AND WHITE.

The above most memorable race took place on the Tyne, April 19th, 1859,
between Thomas White, of London, and Robert Chambers, of Newcastle.
The latter fouled a keel after rowing about half a mile ; this accident
allowed White to obtain a lead of about one hundred yards, but Chambers
gamely followed, and caught him near Armstrong's factory, where he
passed the Cockney and defeated him very easily. This, the most wonderful performance on any river, stamped " Honest Bob " as the greatest
oarsman of the age.—*Note*, 1872 *Edition.*

TUNE—" Trab, trab."

THE Tyne wi' fame is ringin' on heroes old and young,
Fresh lawrels daily bringin', but noo awl men hez sung
In praise o' honest Chambers, ov Tyneside men the
  pride,
Who defeated White ov London for one hundred pund
  aside.

Chorus.

Singin' pull away, pull away, pull away, boys,
  Pull away, boys, se cliver ;
Pull away, pull away, pull away, boys,
  Chambers for iver !

They're off, they're off, the cry is, then cheers suin rend
    the air,
Like leetnin' they pass by us, the game an' plucky pair;
Greek meets Greek, then faster an' faster grows the pace.
Gan on, Chambers! gan on, White! may the best man
    win the race.

           Singin' pull away, etc.

Stroke for stroke contendin, they sweep on wi' the tide,
Fortune seems impendin the victor te decide;
At last the Cockney losin' strength, the fowlin gam' did
    steal,
He leaves his wetter ivery length, an' runs Chambers iv
    a keel.

Spoken.—What a hulla baloo! Hoo the Cockney speeled away;
ivery yen thowt the race was ower. Some said it was a deed
robbery, others a worry, an' wawked hyem before the finish o' the
race. There was a chep stannin' aside me wiv his hands iv his
pockets—aw'm sartin thor wis nowt else in—luikin' on the river
wiv a feyce like a fiddle-stick. He sung the following lament, efter
the style ov "There's nae Luck":—

      TUNE—"Nae Luck aboot the Hoose."
Ten lengths aheed! Fareweel, bedsteed! maw achin'
    byens nee mair
On thou mun rowl; no, this poor sowl mun rest on deep
    despair.
Wor Nannie, tee, she'll curse an' flee, an' belt me like a
    Tork,
For aw've lost me money, time, an' spree, an' mebbies
    lost maw work.

    Chorus.

For oh! dismay upon that day in ornist did begin,
On ivery feyce a chep might trace—(*Spoken*) Whe's forst—Bob?
(*Sings*) Oh! the Cockney's sure te win.

Says one poor sowl aw've sell'd my pigs, my clock, my
    drawers, an' bed,
An' doon te Walker aw mun wawk, when aw might a
    rode i'stead.
Gox! there's wor Jim an' a' the crews pawned ivery
    stitch o' claes,
An' they say thor's two cheps sell'd thor wives, the six
    te fower te raise.

For oh, dismay, etc.

Spoken.—Comin' doon efter awl wis ower, aw meets one i' wor
cheps, an Irishman; they cawld him Patrick, but aw cawld him
Mick for shortness. He wadent wait for the finish, altho' he
backed Bob; so aw hailed him, "Hie, Mick, whe's forst?" "Go
to blazes!" says he. "Nonsense, Mick; whe's forst?" "Och,
sure," says he, "the Londin man was forst half-way before the
race was quarther over." "Had on, Mick, that's a bull. Did ye
lay owt on tiv him—aw mean Bob?" "By my sowl, I did! an'
I'd like to lay this lump ov a stick on his dhirty cocoa-nut. The
next time I speculate on floatin' praporty may I be sthruck wid a
button on my upper lip as big as a clock face." "But Chambers
is forst!" says aw. "Arrah! de ye mane to say that?" says he.
"Didn't aw tell ye he'd win afore iver he started?" "Hurroo!
more power! fire away!"

Chorus.
Pull away, pull away, pull away, boys,
    Pull away, boys, se cliver;
Pull away, pull away, pull away, boys,
    Chambers for iver!

CORVAN.   *Author's Manuscript*, 1862.

THE DEETH O' CUCKOO JACK.

John Wilson (better known by the more familiar cognomen of "Cuckoo
Jack," which he derived from his father, who made "Cuckoo" clocks),
noted for his skill in recovering the bodies of the drowned, died December
2nd, 1860, aged 68.

FIRST AIR—"Chant."

IN wor celebrated metropolis o' the north, Newcastle-
    upon-Tyne,
A scullorsman leev'd, ca'd Cuckoo Jack, a genus o' the
    grapplin line.

The soorce o' Coaly Tyne an' all its curose channels
    well he knew,
So local fame suin crooned the nyem o' famous aud
    " Cuckoo."
His skill was greet in bringing up the deed, still what
    mair odd is,
'Tis said he little cared for sowls, so he but got the
    bodies ;
But noo aw'll end this little rhyme, to chant his dyin'
    strain,
Confident that aud Cuckoo's like we'll niver see again.

SECOND AIR—" Poor Mary Anne."
November winds blaw cawd, maw hinny !
    Deeth follows on mee track ;
The fall'n snaws will shrood me hinny,
    Thou's loosin' Cuckoo Jack.
Ta, ta, ti pay ; ta, ta, ti penshin ; maw ill deeds, nibors,
    niver mention,
But elways speak wi' gud intenshin 'boot poor aud
    Cuckoo Jack.

THIRD AIR—" Keel Row."
Fareweel tiv a' me cronies, Keeside and Sandgate Jonies,
For aikin ivery bone is, i' this aud skin o' mine.
Deed bodies frae the river aw've often tyun oot cliver,
Maw equal ther wes niver for grapplin Coaly Tyne.

FOURTH AIR—" Down among the Dead Men."
Luika here, luika here, doon belaw, doon belaw,
Pull away, lads, pull away, lads, aw've huiked him—
    (less jaw !)
This chep myeks a hundred and siventy-nine
Deed bodies aw've fund in the Coaly Tyne.

Aw's gannin noo, so frinds, good-bye—
Doon amang the scullormen, doon amang the scullor-
   men,
Doon, doon, doon, doon, doon amang the scullormen
   Let Cuckoo lie.
Aw mun rest wi' the rest that aw fund for my fee,
An' aw hope that aud Nick winnet grapple for me ;
Let maw eppytaff be, " Here lies on his back
The chep that fund the droon'd men, Cuckoo Jack."

                          Aw's gannin noo, etc.
CORVAN.   *Author's Manuscript*, 1862.

WOR TYNESIDE CHAMPIONS.

                          TUNE—" Billy Nuts."
THE Cockneys say uz keelmen cheps hez nowther sense
   nor larnin',
An' chaff aboot wor tawk, the fuils ; but, faix, they've got
   a warnin' ;
They thowt wor brains wis mixed wi' coals, but noo a
   change that odd is,
Alang wi' coals we send up men that licks the Cockney
   bodies.
Brave Harry Clasper aw'll nyem first amang wor stars
   that shine, man.
Lads ! here's the stroke that famis myed wor canny coaly
   Tyne, man.

(*Imitate Harry Clasper in position.*)

                Chorus.
                          TUNE—" Billy Patterson."
An' aw'll lay maw money doon, wi' reet gud heart and will,
Te back the sons o' coaly Tyne,—huzza for Tyneside still !
May Chambers lang his laurels keep, wor champion o' the world, man ;
His bonny rowin' adds fresh fame whene'er his flag's unfurl'd, man.

Of runners, tee, we've got the tips,—Tyne bangs the
    world for pacin',
Gox! White and Rowan, champion peds, bangs a' the
    lot for racin';
When little White means runnin', lads, he's shaped in
    fine condishin,
He dodg'd te get the start like this,—see graceful in
    position.
    (*Imitate the start.*)   Chorus as above.

                                 TUNE—" Chant."

When pay-week comes, wor collier lads for the toon they
    a' repair,
Then ower the moor, an' roond the coorse, ye'll fynd
    them boolin' there;
Hail, rain, or blaw, 'mang sleet or snaw, ye'll fynd wor
    boolin' men
Watchin' the trig, aw moves the twig, howe! let's hev
    her here agyen.

Saint, wor famis champion, with his bold eye keen and
    clear,
Like leetnin' sends oot mighty thraws, the best o' men
    scarce near;
Hollo! " Pies all hot!" upon the spot, ther're suin put
    oot o' seet;
"Some mair gravy," cries oot yen; "aw say, mistor, d'ye
    mean te say that's meat?

It's mair like deed pussey-cat "—war the bool there—less
    gob!
Six te fower on Broon—hie, men! six te fower on Broon
    agyen the Snob.
War the bool there, war the bool there, Harry Wardle's
    myed a throw;
An' when he hoyed his bool away he stood just so—
    (*Imitate position.*)   Chorus as above.

TUNE—" Bob and Joan."

Wor champion quoit players here thor match ye'll
    seldom meet with,
For ony length ye like, ye'll fynd men te compete with,
For quoits we've famis been since Julius Seasor landed ;
Man, for generations doon the gam's been duly handed.
McGregor plays weel, Lambert weel can fling her,
But Harle shapes like this when puttin on a ringer.
(*Position.*)

Chorus.

An' aw'll lay maw money doon, wi' reet gud heart and will,
    Te back the sons o' coaly Tyne,—huzza for Tyneside still !
CORVAN.   *Author's Manuscript,* 1862.

THE QUEEN HAS SENT A LETTER ;
OR, THE HARTLEY CALAMITY.

The falling of the large beam in Hartley Colliery, on the 16th January
1862, closed up the shaft, in consequence of which 204 men and boys lost
their lives.

TUNE—" No Irish need Apply."

OH ! bless the Queen of England, who sympathy doth
    show,
'Toward our stricken widows amid their grief and woe ;
Old England never had her like, nor never will again,
Then bless good Queen Victoria, ye loyal-hearted men.
She sent a letter stating—" I share your sorrows here,"
To soothe the aching hearts of all and dry the widow's
    tear.

Above two hundred miners are numbered with the dead,
Whose wives and children ne'er shall want their bit of
    daily bread ;
And while death's shadow overhangs the miner's cot
    with gloom,

Let us calm the widow's heaving breast for those laid in
    the tomb;
And ye that round your glowing fires life's comforts
    daily share,
Think of the helpless orphans and widows in despair.

We have heroes from the Redan and Inkerman as well,
Whose deeds of daring on the field a nation's thanks
    can tell;
But did they face the deadly stythe, where scarce a
    single breath
Held life to face eternity to rescue life or death!
Show me the page in history where deeds heroic shine
More bright than our Northumbrian men, the heroes of
    the mine.

The collier's welfare, as he toils, more interest might
    command
Among the wealthy owners and rulers of the land.
Are they like beasts of burthen, as Roebuck once did
    rave,
Will government in future strive the collier's life to save?
Why should the worn-out collier amid his abject gloom
Eke out the life his Maker spared to share the pauper's
    doom?

God speed the hardy collier, and Coulson's gallant band,
Who braved the perils of the shaft with willing heart
    and hand;
And ye that add to store the hive and feed the fatherless,
May He that watches o'er all things your earthly pros-
    pects bless.
The weeping and the wailing of widows let us end,
And with our Queen let all men see we are the widow's
    friend.

28

The sailor on the stormy sea life's perils often share,
Our soldiers 'mid the battle's strife what man can do
  they dare;
Yet both have got a chance for life, but ah! the miner's
  doom,
'Twas sad to sleep the sleep of death closed in the living
  tomb.
Then man to man, with heart and hand, let us still help
  each other,
With generous impulse to relieve a sister or a brother.

Oh! gather round, ye generous band, whose bounty
  caused a smile
To 'llume the face of dark despair throughout old England's isle.
Ye have ta'en the gloom from sorrow where rays of love
  will fall
On the widow and the fatherless, who pray " God bless
  you all! "
For the Queen has sent a letter, tho' she mourns a
  husband dear,
To soothe the aching hearts of all and dry the widow's
  tear.

CORVAN.   *Author's Manuscript, 1862.*

THE QUEEN'S VISIT TO CHERBOURG.

TUNE—"The Sly Old Fox."

Now Louis Napoleon, by-the-bye,—Tol lol, etc.
With great success a game did try,—Tol lol, etc.
Our gracious Queen, admired by all,
Forgot herself, and deigned to call
With an august assembly got up for a stall.
                    Ri tol de dol lol, etc.

No other crowned heads did he invite,—Tol lol, etc.

His game being to gammon John Bull at the sight,—
Tol lol, etc.

For ages past Kings, one by one,

And Emperors toiled, being bent upon

Showing up Britain as well as Vauben.—Tol lol, etc.

TUNE—"Spider and the Fly."

"Will you come into my Cherbourg?" sly Louis he did
say—

That is, he telegraphed, or else sent word some other
way;

"Mind, bring Field-Marshal Albert—we'll receive all
with *éclat*—

Your Majesty and Ministers, so Victoria, *bonswa*,

Will you, will you, will you, will you come in, British
Queen?"

TUNE—"Far, far upon the Sea."

All arrangements being made for this regal masquerade,
O'er the bright blue waters nobly on we go,

With our noble Channel Fleet, well manned, and fit to
meet
A friend upon the ocean, or a foe.

'Twas thus they left our shores, where a British lion roars
Far, far above the thunder of the seas,

Where Neptune's briny throng in triumph bears along
Old England's flag, that ever braves the battle and the
breeze.

Will you come into, etc.

TUNE—"Jonathan Brown."

Now a very true story I'm going to tell,

Well founded on fact, and you all know it well:

While the Queen and Prince Albert sailed along in their
yacht,

Albert says, "Vat's his game, *Vic*—vat can he be at?"

With his dumble dum deary, etc.

"Don't speak so loud, dear *Al*, if you please,
For Mollykoff's trying to cop every sneeze."
Now the guns commenced firing, they landed, and then
Napoleon seized *Viccy*, saying, "Velcome, mine frien."
> With his dumble dum deary, etc.

"Dere's my maritime wonder," in their ears he did bawl,
"And dis is my new naval arsenal;"
Then he showed them all round this monstrous plan,
And about our defences to talk he began.
> With his dumble dum deary, etc.

"You very mush back in England," said he.
"But we ne'er turn'd our backs yet," said Viccy, with glee.
"Dis is very large gun, Mrs. Albert, you see."
"Yes! but I've *larger* in Woolwich, so it's no treat to me."
> With your dumble dum deary, etc.

"With my fleet in my harbour I'm unequalled, no doubt,
And should war be proclaimed I could soon fit them out."
"Ho, ho! that's your game!" then the white of his eye
Turned round as the Queen said, "*You'd better not try.*"
> With your dumble dum deary, etc.

"My friends were not pleased with your queer British
        laws;
And I, too, thought Barnard* all but in my claws.
Chop de heads off such men." Says the Queen, "*Ah
        mon dieu,*
If we harbour assassins, we once harboured you."
> With your dumble dum deary, etc.

* Barnard, a French refugee, tried in London for being an accomplice of
Orsini in the attempt on the Emperor Napoleon's life; he was acquitted.

"Then let us be friends, Vic; for, when once unfurled,
Our flags, still united, can conquer the world;
I adore Albion's Isle—may ill ne'er beset it."
Says Vic, "*So did your uncle:* he tried hard for to get it."

                With his dumble dum deary, etc.

May our Queen take a hint from this Emperor's boast,
And strengthen old England, as needs round the coast;
For if we wish to have peace, I dare venture to say,
Be ready for war, lads—that's the true and best way.

                  TUNE—"Lucy Neal."

Ye loyal hearts in Briton's Isle, who ever true have been
To honour's cause and England's laws, now shout "God
     save the Queen!"
And may her Majesty and those connected with the State
Look a little more at home before it is too late.
Prepare our wooden walls—prepare our wooden walls;
We must complete our Channel Fleet—'tis threat'ning
     danger calls.
Britannia, rouse thy slumbering lion, and let all nations
     know
We are prepared for peace or war—to meet a friend or
     foe.
Let no vile hypocrite assume that Britons dread to meet
Napoleon or his Cherbourg forts, while floats our Channel
     Fleet.

Spoken.—And while we enjoy peace and good-will with our
neighbours on the opposite side of the Channel, let us at the same
time, with manly hearts and feelings of patriotic zeal, sing—

          "Rule Britannia."—*Finale.*

CORVAN.   *Author's Manuscript,* 1862.

STAGE-STRUCK KEELMAN.

TUNE—"Bob and Joan."

Aw's Jimmy Julius Hannibal Cæsar,
 A genius born for shootin';
Aw can recite Hamlick and King Dick,
 Man, aw's the lad for spootin'.

Spoken.—Besides, aw's an awther. Aw wrote a play entitled
" The Flash o' Thunder ; or, The Desolate Tree by the Roadside,
an' the Lonely Man o' the Lonely Mill o' the Blasted Heath, an' the
Fower-eyed Murderer." It's in fowerteen acts and a half. The
music's a' 'ranged by Frederick Jimmy Apollo Lumphead for nine
gugaws. Aw'll recite a dark passage oot on't, as a specimen.
 Scene 1st.—A Coal Pit—Blue Mountains in the distance (we'll
say the mountains is in America).
 'Twas a dark neet—a varry dark neet ; the sun peeped oot before
the skies ; the wind fell in fearful torrents ; the cloods fell te the
arth ; and the cuddies turned thor backs on the comin' storm, an'
wi' thor melodious noise gov a tarrific he ha ! he ha ! he ha !
'Twas then aw porsued maw way bi the Blasted Heath—medytatin',
codgetatin', and silly quisin', when sumthing seized me—a caud
swet com ower me sleeved waistket. Aw fell doon insensible ; an'
when aw recuvered, aw observed the Fower-eyed Murderer gazin'
upon me. Aw seized him an' cast him forth inte the boilin' het
caud watter. At that excitin' moment aw flew towards the Aud
Abbey. Hush ! what was that ? Hark ! I see a voice ! No, no,
'tis the wind whistlin' the air ! In this tent I'll pitch my field !
O let me behold the green fields o' Sandgate—the blue mountains
of Gyetshead and Jarrow—the Tripe Market, where youthful fancy
guided maw three-happence a week pocket-brass ! Egstacy ! A
shooer o' black puddins thickens maw imaginashun ! Light lights !
Richard's himself agyen !

      For I'm Jimmy, etc.

Play-acting's maw delight,
 Aw's called the Sandgate Spooter ;
Besides, the plays aw write
 Myeks me an oot-an'-ooter.
Love scenes, an' murders tee,
 Aw acts them up te natur ;
The cheps upon the Kee says
 Aw'll turn a real first-rater.

Spoken.—Yes, aw've anuther play entitled "The Two Thick-headed Bruthers; or, the Life and Adventures of Three Fardins' Worth o' Backey; or, the Keel Bully's Ghost." Thor's a' kinds o' characters in't : aw've ghosts, blue fire, reed fire, scufters, doddle hunters, organ weavers, cuiks, an' fower comic cheps. Here's a speech a bobby myeks te one o' the cuiks :—"Celestial, beautiful, divine creature ! star of my fancy ! staff of my existence ! lantern of my hope ! let me stand up and adore thee for ever on my knees ! Oh, ye crabs and fishes ! let me spout me blues ! Let me gaze upon thee ! O horrible agony ! Thy lovely features—that turnip nose —them saucer eyes—thy red luxuriant hair—that figure—thy quarter's wages—let me clutch thee !" Make way there ! 'tis the king who calls !

For I'm Jimmy, etc.

My talent will be seen,
    When actin' aw begin, sir ;
For aw'll play before the Queen
    Wi' Charles Kean at Windsor ;
Aw's sure te cut him oot,
    He'll heh ne chance wi' me, sir,
For when she heers me spoot,
    Thor's nyen like me will please her.

Spoken.—Aw just think she sees me in that scene in Hamlick, where the ghost cums—"Angels an' ministers of grease confend us ! Be thou sum sporits of earth or cobbler damned ; bring ye hares frae Ravensworth for me or thee to sell ; thou comest in such a drunken state, aw'll toss thee for a pint o' fowerpenny ! He's waggin' on me ; he wants te play at skittles at the Crystal Palace ! Gan on—aw'll follow thee."

For I'm Jimmy, etc.

CORVAN.   *Author's Edition.*

———

THE SOOP KITCHIN.

TUNE—"Lilla's a Lady."

THE soop kitchin's open—then cheer, Christians, cheer !
What glorious news for poor starvin' sowls here !
The soop kitchin's open for a' sorts in need ;
So rush in wi' yor tickets—ye'll get a gud feed.

Chorus.

O fine, het steem soop!   O bliss that steem soop!
Aw likes maw drop o' soop!

It's myed oot o' beef hoffs, fine barley, an' peas;
Smokin' het, it's dilishus te sup at yen's ease;
It's gud for the rich, an' not bad for the poor;
Gox! empty kite grumlers it's sartin te cure.

Spoken.—Drop that spoon, spooney!   D'ye want te myek maw
spoon the bone o' contenshun, eh?   Bring this chep a ladle,
mistress, an' a basin.   Next the bottom, he wants sum thick.
What a wite that soop's tyekin frae maw mind!   Begox! it's run
inte the channels o' maw corporation; an' now aw feel like an
alderman efter a gud feed!   It's a fine institushin; it suits maw
constitushin; an' tiv onny poor sowl in a state o' destitushin it's a
charitable contribushin.   Sum people's born wi' silver spoons i' thor
gobs, but it strikes me mine's been a basin o' soop.   They enjoy the
luxeries o' this world; A—whey, nivver mind—just gi'e me the
sweet soond o' spoons an' basins.   That's the music that bids me
discorse!   It fills me wi' delight!   Thor's nowt can lick't.

TUNE—"Merry Haymakers."

Then a song an' a cheer for the rich spreed o' steem
　O' the soop floatin' roond us on high;
For the givers an' the makers, the tickets an' the Quakers,
　An' subscribers that nivver tip shy.
We blaw oot wor bags on the cheep ivvery day,
　While happy as kings there we mess;
Gox! us poor starved sowls nivver heed the wind that
　　howls,
　For close roond the tyebles we press.

TUNE—"Cameron Men."

Roond tyebel and benches the bullies they stick,
　A' cled in thor feedin' array;
Sum coolin' het soop, uthers fishin' for thick,
　Uthers waitin' thor torns i' dismay.

Then we hear the spoons rattlin', rattlin', rattlin',
  We hear them agyen an' agyen ;
Thor knockin' thor basons an' brattlin',
  'Tis the voice o' the brave Sandgit men.

Bob Johnson cries, "How! becrike, men, what's that?"
  Wiv his spoon raised up high for te view;
"Begum! it's a rat, or a greet lump o' fat"—
  Says Ranter, "It's mebbies sum stew!"

Then we hear the spoons rattlin', rattlin', rattlin',
  Ye hear them agyen an' agyen ;
"Shuv the salt roond!" aw hear sum chaps prattlin',
  'Tis the voice o' the brave Keeside men.

The Paddies flock in wi' the rest iv a trice,
  Then doon to thor basins they stoop:
Says Mick, "It's cock turtle!" Says Barney, "It's nice!
  Made from raal Irish bulls—O what soop!"

Spoken.—"Long life t' the soop kitchin!" says Mick. "An'
hivven be his bed thit invinted it!" says Barney. "What's this?"
says Mick. "Och! it's only a bone. Be jabers! I thought it was
a lump of lane bafe. Some moor, misthress!"

Then ye hear the spoons rattlin', rattlin', rattlin',
  Once mair ye hear them agyen ;
Ye hear them prattlin', prattlin', prattlin',
  'Tis the voice o' the Callaghan men.

The Sandies, frae Scotland, they join i' the group,
  Sweerin' oatmeal's oot-dune wi' sic stuff,
As wi' gud Heelin' stamocks they swalley the soup
  In thor wames, till they scarcely can puff.

Spoken.—"It's capital stuff, Sandy; and vera economical." "A
capital remairk," says Watty.

Then ye hear the spoons rattlin', rattlin', rattlin',
   Ye hear them agyen and agyen ;
Ye hear them prattlin' an' prattlin',
   'Tis the voice o' the Cameron men.

CORVAN.   *Author's Edition.*

THE HIGH LEVEL BRIDGE, NEWCASTLE-UPON-TYNE. LENGTH, 1337 FEET.
HEIGHT, 112 FEET. OPENED AUGUST 15TH, 1849.

THE HIGH LEVEL AN' THE AUD BRIDGE.

A COMIC IMAGINARY DIALOGUE.

TUNE—"I'd be a Butterfly."

WON caud winter's neet, man, the leetnin' was flashin',
   And the wind through the High Level Bridge loud
      did squeel ;
The neet was pick-dark, an' the waves they were dashin',
   Man, we'd sair tues amang us to manage wor keel.
But amang a' the thunder what myed wor lads wonder,
Wis the High Level Bridge to the Aud Bridge bawl out—

TUNE—"Marble Halls."

" O ! ye crazy Aud Bridge, ye'll suin be pull'd down,
  An' yor styens in the river be hurled ;
Yor nee ornament, noo, but disgracin' wor toon,
  Luk at me—aw's the pride o' the world.
Hoo noble am I, reachin' up ti the sky,
  Lukin' down on a humbug belaw ;
There's yor blynd men an' cadgers stoppin' folks passin' by,
  An' yor Piperget wives wi' thor jaw."

Spoken.—An' a tidy lot o' gob they hev ; just gie them an aud
button for a happorth o' mince tripe, an' ye'll get some tongue into
the bargain. But, tawkin' o' the row 'tween the two Bridges.
Goggle-eyed Tommy heard them fightin' aside Lemington ; and
when aw gat aside the Meadows aw hears the High Level say ti the
Aud Bridge—"Yor neebody, poor aud fellow." Just at that time,
Jack Gilroy says ti the High Level—"Shut up, lang legs." That
nerved the Aud Bridge ; he showed fight, an' walked into the High
Level in the followin' style :—

TUNE—"Fine Old English Gentleman."

"Shut up, shut up yor skinny jaws," the Aud Bridge
    then did shoot ;
"For if thou's yung, Mistor High Level Bridge, just
    mind what thou's aboot,
An' dinnet wag yor jaws ower fast, like the men o'
    modern days ;
Just tyek advice fra a poor aud bridge, an' drop off a'
    self-praise.

Chorus.

" But mind yor locomotive things, an' let an aud bridge be.

" Wor Cassel Garth, where snips an' snobs wi' maid an'
    frinds did meet,
Ye've caused to be pulled doon, ye knaw, and banish'd
    oot o' seet.
Luk doon on me, lang sparrow shanks, ye half-bred,
    mean young pup,
If ye thraw yor engines doon on me, aw'll thraw some
    aud keels up.

But mind, etc.

"Before iver ye wor thout on, man, aw've stood here i'
   'maw pride,
An' lettin fokes wawk ower me 'tween the Bottle Bank
   and Side;
Besides ye charge a happenny, yor level's dearly bowt,
Man, aw stand maw grund es weel as thou, an' let fokes
   ower for nowt.

                              But mind, etc.

"When aw wis young we had ne jails or bastiles i' the
   toon,
Nor pollis wi' thor greet big staffs, ti knock a poor sowl
   doon;
But noo the mairch of intellect an' scientific ways,
Hez tyen away wor good aud times—we sigh for better
   days."

Spoken.—"Drop off tawkin' about sighin'," says Jack. "Shut
up," says Ralphy L—tle on the top o' the Mansion House, "or aw'll
wawk ye byeth off ti the kitty." There wad hae been manslawter if it
hadn't been for Ralphy; but the Aud Bridge kend him; they'd
gyen to the Jubilee Skeul together when they war lads. Says the
Aud Bridge, "What are ye gan ti' hev?" "Oh," says Ralphy,
"a bottle o' soda watter an' half a glass o' brandy in't." 'Twas an
awful dark neet, aw mind; that dark we cuddent see what we war
tawkin' about. Howsever, we byeth escaped, an' away we went
singin'—

     Weel may the keel row, etc.

CORVAN.   *Author's Manuscript,* 1862.

CAT-GUT JIM, THE FIDDLER.

TUNE—"And sae will we yet."

Aw'M Cat-gut Jim, the fiddler, a man o' greet renoon,
Aw play te myek me livin, lads, in country an' i' toon;
Tiv ivery fair an' ivery feast wi' maw fiddle aw repair:
Gox! where thor's ony fun or sport thou's sure te fynd
   me there.

Chorus.

For aw drive away dull care, aw drive away dull care,
So patronise poor Cat-gut Jim when ye've óny cash te spare.

Aw'll play ye ony tuen ye like, aw'll play ye "Cheer,
boys, cheer,"
Or te try an' keep yor spirits up, aw'll play the "Drop
o' Beer,"
The "Deevil amang the Tailors," "Peggy Pickin doon
the Shore,"
The "Lass that loves a Sailor," an' mony a dozen more.

> For aw drive away, etc.

Aw play "Mary Blane," an' "Lucy Neal," wi' "Poor
old Uncle Ned,"
"O! Nanny, wilt thou gang wi' me," "Scots wha hae
wi' Wallace bled";
Aw play "McCloud's" reel beautiful, "What are ye
gawn te stand?"
The "Keel Row," shaken a' te rags o'er this happy,
unhappy land.

Spoken.—Ony thing, frev an elephant's trunk tiv a lucifer match-box. Uz street fiddlers fynds times queer just noo—customers bad te fynd—but iv a' the customers aw meet gie me the sailors, them's the boys!—the bulwarks ov owld England. Aw'm a sailor; ye can see by the cut o' me jib. Aw sarved me time to be a ship-owner aboard o' the Dredger—what a gun-boat the Dredger 'id myek—when they run short o' cannon-balls they cud fire coal-skuttles at the enemy. An' then they're always weel supplied wi' Newcastle amonishen—clarts. Aw knaw a vast aboot the sea, but the next time aw gan it'll be iv a cab. Yes, aw'll hev a luik at it. Still, aw'm fond o' sailors; when aw sees yen aw generally play "Far upon the Sea." (*Play the tune named here.*) When aw see an Irishman—them's the boys, *Hatre genus men*—they'll gie ye tuppence if they hevent a fardin' i' thor pockets. Aw generally play them the "Exile of Erin" an' "Patrick's Day." One's full o' human nater, an' the other's full o' shillalahs an' life porsarvers—them's the things for layin a foundation for stickin plaister. (*Plays the airs mentioned.*) When aw see a Scotchman aw play "Auld Robin Gray" on the bagpipes, efter the style o' Sir Colin Campbell,

" Ye Deil's Buckie." (*Play here.*) But when aw join the fishwives
—them's the boys !—aw play sthem " Pop goes the Weasel," efter
the style o' Sir Walter Railly when he tossed a chow o' baccy at
Queen Elizabeth. (*Plays.*)

Chorus.

For aw drive away dull care, aw drive away dull care,
    So patronise poor Cat-gut Jim when ye've ony cash te spare.

CORVAN.   *Author's Manuscript*, 1862.

GEORGE RIDLEY

WAS a native of Gateshead, in which town he was born on
the 10th of February 1835. At the early age of eight years
our future rhymer was sent to Oakwellgate Colliery as a

trapper-boy. After but a brief
stay at Oakwellgate, he went
to the Goose Pit, or, according to its more familiar name,
" The Gyuess." There he remained ten years. He next
went to Messrs. Hawks, Craw-
shay, & Co., as a waggon-
rider, and remained there about
three years; an accident, which
nearly terminated fatally,
bringing his connection with
that firm to an abrupt termination.

While riding, as usual, his
train of waggons down the
incline (upon which his duties
principally lay), by some break-
age or mishap, the waggons became unmanageable, and,
being no longer under control, rushed at a great speed down
the incline. To save himself as much as possible from the
danger threatening, George jumped from his stand on the
runaway waggons, but, in doing so, he unfortunately got
himself severely crushed and injured.

For a long time he lay, incapable of work ; and when at
length he began to recover, it was only to find his strength

so shattered that anything like regular work he was totally unfitted for. Being thus forced to seek a new means of earning a livelihood, he fell back upon his powers as a singer, more especially of Irish comic and old Tyneside songs (in which he excelled); and thus was forced by accident into the path which afterwards led him to such a widespread popularity in the North. His first professional engagement was at the Grainger Music Hall, where he brought out his first local song, "Joey Jones." This, with the humour with which he invested it, and the local popularity of the subject (Joey Jones having just then won the Northumberland Plate), was a great success. At the Wheat-sheaf Music Hall (now the Oxford), his next engagement, he was equally successful; and, when engaged at the Tyne Concert Hall (at that time just opened by Mr. Stanley), he produced perhaps his greatest success, "Johnny Luik-Up the Bellman." The subject of this song being so well known, and George, imitating his peculiarities, and dressing in character, his success was unbounded. It is needless to detail his engagements at the various concert halls in the North. Everywhere he was a favourite. Cheap editions of

RIDLEY AS "THE BOBBY CURE."
(The cut which he had on his penny Song Books.)

his songs were printed, and had a large sale; "The Bobby Cure" (said to be a hit at a member of the police force) and "Johnny Luik-Up" being especial favourites, the children singing them as they ran about the streets.

In the midst of this success, after a short public career of about five years, his health began seriously to fail. He had never properly cast off the deadly effects of the accident at Messrs. Hawks', the severe crushing he had received on that occasion undoubtedly being the cause of his illness, which rapidly began to assume a dangerous appearance. After a brief struggle of little more than three months, he died at his residence in Grahamsley Street, Gateshead, on Friday, September 9th, 1864, aged 30 years. On the Sunday following, he was buried at St. Edmund's Cemetery, a large number of his friends and admirers following his remains to the grave.

As a song-writer it cannot be said that his productions have the literary merit of the older Tyneside writers; but, considering under what disadvantages he wrote, his premature death, and how little fitted his early life was to foster literary inclinations, his songs are exceedingly good. And it must not be forgotten that they were written for his own purposes as a concert hall singer, and there they did sing. At the present time— eight years after his death— at social meetings and private parties, where his songs are often sung, they never fail to please. As a public singer he was highly gifted; he possessed a fine voice, and, having great powers of mimicry, he swayed his audience at will; and there is little doubt, if he had not fallen at the opening, as it were, of his career, he would have left a still more indelible mark as a Tyneside song-writer.

RIDLEY AS "JOHNNY LUIK-UP."

Sketch from 1872 Edition.

Joe Wilson, whose acrostics on so many of his contemporaries have already appeared, did not forget Ridley. In the following he touches upon Ridley's successes, and regrets his early death.

ACROSTIC.

R eady wes he wi' the "Bobby Cure,"
I n Stanley's Hall, te myek secure
D elight tiv a' the patrons there,
L iked be them a',—but noo, ne mair
E nlivenin strains frae him ye'll hear,
Y e'll knaw ne mair poor Geordy's cheer.

George Ridley

Photographed by P. M. Laws.

———

JOEY JONES.

Joey Jones won the Northumberland Plate at the Newcastle Summer Meeting, 1861. His winning was a great surprise to the public generally, but a more popular victory could not have been achieved, his owners being well-known local sportsmen, who landed a great stake.

TUNE—"Pat of Mullingar."

Aw'M gan te sing te ye a sang,
   If ye'll but list te me,
Aw divent intend te keep ye lang,
   An' that ye'll plainly see ;
It's all aboot young Joey Jones,
   He wun the Northumberland Plate,
He was bred at Deckham Hall,
   Just up throo the gate.

Chorus.

For he jogs along, he canter'd along,
   He lick'd them all se fine ;
He was bred at Gateshead,
   He's the pride o' Coaly Tyne.

29

Joey ran at the Spring meetin',
  He was beaten by the Jim,
An' Hadlow, that belangs Gaylad,
  Said Joey wasn't game;
So they sent him off te Richmond,
  They knew he wasn't right,
Then Watson fetched him here,
  An' gov them a regular Yorkshire bite.

Noo when the horses started,
  An' was comin' past the stand,
Sum shooted oot for Peggy Taft,
  An' sum for Underhand;
An' when they reached the top o' the hill,
  Doyle heard Tom Aldcroft say,
" Aw dare lay a fiver that
  Aw win the plate the day!"

Comin' roond the Morpeth turn,
  Joey keepin' up his fame,
Says Doyle te Tommy Aldcroft—
  "Noo what's yor little game?"
Says Aldcroft—" Aw mean te win
  The plate this varry day!"
"Yes, but," says Doyle, " it's Joey Jones,
  A fiver aw will lay!"

Number eleven was puttin up,
  The people stood amazed,
Fobert he luiked varry white,
  An' Jackson almost crazed;
Little Osborne luik'd for his Wildman,
  An' Sharpe for Volatile,
Doefoot got a nasty kick,
  An' Joey wun in style.

RIDLEY.   *Author's Manuscript, 1862.*

BLAYDON RACES.

TUNE—" Brighton."

Aw went to Blaydon Races, 'twas on the ninth of Joon,
Eiteen hundred an' sixty-two, on a summer's efter-
noon ;
Aw tyuk the 'bus frae Balmbra's, an' she wis heavy
laden,
Away we went alang Collingwood Street, that's on the
road to Blaydon.

Chorus.

O lads, ye shud only seen us gannin',
We pass'd the foaks upon the road just as they wor stannin' ;
Thor wes lots o' lads an' lasses there, all wi' smiling faces,
Gawn alang the Scotswood Road, to see the Blaydon Races.

We flew past Airmstrang's factory, and up to the
" Robin Adair,"
Just gannin doon te the railway bridge, the 'bus wheel
flew off there.
The lasses lost their crinolines off, an' the veils that hide
their faces,
An' aw got two black eyes an' a broken nose in gan te
Blaydon Races.

O lads, ye shud only seen us gannin', etc.

When we gat the wheel put on away we went agyen,
But them that had their noses broke, they cam back
ower hyem ;
Sum went to the dispensary, an' uthers to Doctor Gibbs,
An' sum sought out the Infirmary to mend their broken
ribs.

O lads, ye shud only seen us gannin', etc.

Noo when we gat to Paradise thor wes bonny gam
    begun ;
Thor wes fower-and-twenty on the 'bus, man, hoo they
    danced an' sung ;
They called on me to sing a sang, aw sung them " Paddy
    Fagan,"
Aw danced a jig an' swung my twig that day aw went to
    Blaydon.
              O lads, ye shud only seen us gannin', etc.

We flew across the Chain Bridge reet into Blaydon toon,
The bellman he was callin' there—they call him Jackey
    Brown ;
Aw saw him talkin' to sum cheps, an' them he was
    pursuadin'
To gan an' see Geordy Ridley's concert in the
    Mechanics' Hall at Blaydon.
              O lads, ye shud only seen us gannin', etc.

The rain it poor'd aw the day, an' myed the groons
    quite muddy,
Coffy Johnny had a white hat on—they war shootin'
    " Whe stole the cuddy."
There wes spice stalls an' munkey shows, an' aud wives
    selling ciders,
An' a chep wiv a happeny roond aboot shootin' " Now,
    me boys, for riders."
             O lads, ye shud only seen us gannin', etc.

RIDLEY.   *Author's Manuscript,* 1862.

CHAMBERS.

Robert Chambers, Champion Sculler of the World, born at St. Anthony's, on the Tyne, June 14, 1831; died at St. Anthony's, June 4, 1868, aged thirty-seven years.

TUNE—"The whole hog or none."

Now, lads, ye've heerd ov Chambers,
    He's bet the Asstrilyen Green,
For pullin a skiff there is ne doot
    He's the best ther's ivor been.
He has regular locomotiv' speed,
    He's upright, honest, and true,
Wheniver he pulls wiv a pair ov sculls
    Aw puts on ivory screw.

Chorus.

Oh, ye Cockneys all,
    Ye mun think't very funny,
For Bob he gans an' licks ye all,
    An' collars a' yor money;
Wheniver he rows, he always goes
    The whole hog or none.

Bob struggled hard fra been a bairn,
    'Fore he got to what hee's now,
He puddl'd iv Walker Rowlin' Mill,
    But he's pull'd heessel safe throu';
An' aw hope each job he tyeks in hand
    Hee'l always hev fair play,
An' think a number one—that is—
    Never give a chance away.

Oh, ye Cockneys all, etc.

When Bob and Greeney pulled thor match,
    Green went away in style,
He tuik the lead of Bob at forst
    Till they got abyun a mile.

But Harry gov Bob the office then,
　　Saying aw'l lay ten to ite,
The Reporter of the "Chronicle" said
　　That Greeney then turned white.
　　　　　　　　　Oh, ye Cockneys all, etc.

Now Bob's licked Green and Kelly byeth,
　　An' White an' Everson laid law,
An' Cooper he put Mackey on,
　　And stopped the Cockney's craw.
This Green wad fain row Bob agyen,
　　But aud Harry he wants a bigger stake,
They munna think to catch him asleep
　　For he's always wide awake.
　　　　　　　　　Oh, ye Cockneys all, etc.

Tyek Bob all in all, as Shakespere says,
　　We'll ne'er see his like agyen,
He waddant de an unjust thing
　　To hurt poor working men ;
Win if he can, it is his plan,
　　So get yor money on,
For whenivor he shows he always goes
　　The whole hog or none.
　　　　　　　　　Oh, ye Cockneys all, etc.

RIDLEY.　　　　　　　　　*Author's Manuscript, 1862.*

THE SHEELS LASS FOR ME.

TUNE—" The whole hog or none."

THE uthor day we went to Tinmuth,
　　Some mair young cheps and me,
An' the first place that we called in
　　Was the " Cottage by the Sea."

There was a young lass sitting,
  They called her " Nancy Till,"
She was axin' " Aud Bob Ridley "
  To gan and hev a gill.

Chorus.

Oh, ye lasses all, the truth aw'll tell ye, hinny,
Tyneside's the place where the lasses are se bonny,
  An' if ever aw get married,
  There's a Sheels lass for me.

Now in cum " Billy Pattison "
  Alang wi' " Minnie Clyde,"
He said, just " Wait for the Waggon,"
  An' ye'll all get a ride.
Then in cum " Annie Laurie "
  Alang wi' " Robin Grey ";
The " Jolly Waggoner" brought in " Doran's
    Ass,"
  To tyek the waggon away.

Oh, ye lasses all, etc.

Then in comes " Peter Gray "
  Wi' " Rosalie, the Prairee Flower,"
An' the " Young Man from the Country "
  Alang wi' the " Perfect Cure."
Next in comes " Nelly Gray,"
  She was singin' " Dixey's Land,"
And " Widow Machree " was cryin'
  Oh! "'Tis hard to give the hand."

Oh, ye lasses all, etc.

Then in cum the " Artful Dodger,"
  He was on the " Low Back'd Car,"
He was gan ti " Limerick Races,"
  Wi' " Pat of Mullingar."

Then in comes "Gentle Annie,"
  She was singin' "Ole King Cole,"
"Pat Murphy" he was there too,
  Just come from the "Old Bog Hole."

                          Oh, ye lasses all, etc.

The "Young Man from the Country"
  Was sittin' on the floor,
He said if he'd a "Ragged Coat"
  He'd "Ask for nothing more."
"There is a Flower that bloometh,"
  'Tis the "Last Rose of Summer";
"Ben Bolt" cried from the "Old Arm Chair,"
  "What's a' the steer, kimmer?"

                          Oh, ye lasses all, etc.

The next aw saw "John Barleycorn,"
  He was there wi' "Nelly Bly,"
She sung "My own, my guiding star,"
  And "No Irish need apply."
Now it was "So early in the morning,"
  That we heard the "Postman's Knock,"
Then we all sung "God save the Queen,"
  An' the company up was broke.

                          Oh, ye lasses all, etc.

RIDLEY.   *Author's Manuscript, 1862.*

THE BOBBY CURE.

TUNE—"The Perfect Cure."

O, LADS, aw've turned a bobby noo,
  And disn't maw dress luk neat;
Aw've a greet moosetash abuve me gob,
  And aw'm on the Gyetshead beat. .

Noo all the jobs thor is aw've tried,
    But nyen aw can endure,
So noo aw've joined the Gyetshead force,
    And the kids call me the cure.

Aw mind the first neet that aw was on,
    It was doon in Pipergate,
An Irish row had started there,
    Thinks aw, aw'll knaw mee fate.
Aw rushes doon an' collars one,
    We fell in a common sewer;
As aw crawled oot the kids did shoot,
    "Just twig poor Bobby the cure."

The next neet aw was at the Bottle Bánk,
    Aw was on for a reglar spree;
There aw fell in win a nice young lass,
    She went inte the Goat wi' me.
Noo each of us hez a glass o' rum,
    At her expense, yor sure;
She was a married wife, and her man pop'd in,
    An' he mug'd poor Bobby the cure.

Aw huiked it off win a sheepish luik,
    And her man reported me;
The inspector com' an' says, "Noo, Bobby,
    This wark it winna dee!"
Aw was taken before the committee,
    And was heavy fined, aw's sure;
And still when aw's on the Oakwellgate beat,
    The kids call me the cure.

The next neet aw was on the Windmill Hills,
    Forget it aw niver shall;
They war smashin' the windows there like fun,
    And pushin' doon the wall.

Aw tuik ten te the stashon hoose,
   Withoot ony help, aw'm sure ;
Aw got these two stripes upon maw coat,
   And they still call me the cure.

A bobby's the canniest job in the world,
   He gets all his drink for nowt ;
Aw'm what they call drill-sarjant noo,
   Maw claes are ready bowt.
So noo aw've tell'd ye all maw tricks,
   Ye'll pity me, aw'm sure,
And niver call me when aw's on maw beat,
   And says there gans the cure.

RIDLEY.   *Author's Manuscript*, 1862.

JOHNNY LUIK-UP !

When this popular song was written, the subject of it, John Higgins, was,
and at the present time, 1873, still is, town crier or bellman. As a man he
is much respected, and carries on, in addition to his official duties as bellman, an extensive business as house agent. Like many others, he has his
peculiarities, which, to our local caricaturist (wanting a subject), were too
tempting to be resisted. The song was "a palpable hit."—(*Note* 1872.)

TUNE—"Sally, come up."

THOR was a bit laddie lost the tuther day,
And doon the Kee he'd stray'd away;
The muther was cryin' hard, they say,
   So she fund oot Johnny the bellman.
Says she, "Gan roond the toon,
Aw'll gie ye half-a-croon,
For if he's not fund it'll be maw ruin—
   Wor Jimmy he'll surely kill me !"

Chorus.
Johnny luik-up ! Johnny luik-doon !
Johnny gans wandrin roond the toon ;
He'll find yor kid for half-a-croon,
   Will Johnny luik-up, the bellman.

Johnny's a chep that'll not tyek a job,
Unless he's sure that he'll get a bob;
An' when he shoots he twists hee's gob,
     There's nyen can shoot like Johnny.
Noo the lads they de him scoff,
He hes such a nesty cough;
Aw doot sum fine day he'll pop off,
     An' then we'll loss poor Johnny.

Before he started te ring the bell
He used te gan wi' young lambs te sell;
He was a candy man, as aw hear tell,
     Noo a perfect cure is Johnny.
An' he used te sell claes pins,
An' sumtimes bairns' rings,
An' a lottery bag he used te hev—
     Mair blanks then owt had Johnny.

In these days he was a regular brick,
When he seld munkeys up the stick,
An' candy for the bairns te lick,
     A tin trumpet then had Johnny.
Ye shud only seen him blaw,
He fairly bangs them a',
It's like a cochin-china's craw;
     An' sic a beak hes Johnny.

Sum thowt Johnny was rang iv his mind,
When he used te gan wi' scissors te grind;
For hard wark he was niver inclin'd,
     For it niver agreed wi' Johnny.
Aw've seen him on a winter's day,
When he's been shullin' snaw away
Frae shopkeepers' doors, he'd lick a score—
     The soup-kitchen prop is Johnny.

Too aw propose when Johnny dies
  hat they tyek oot one of his eyes,
 n' put it inte cock-eyed Tom that sells the pies,
    Then we'll niver loss seet o' Johnny.
So, lads, gie yor lasses a treat
Te this place sum uther neet ;
Aw'll gie ye the Bobby on his beat,
    An' the life o' Johnny the bellman.

RIDLEY.   *Author's Manuscript*, 1862.

JOHN SPENCER.

A well-known character in Newcastle, extremely partial to changes. In his time he has played many parts, some of which are correctly referred to in the song. Perhaps the line in which he most delights is doorman at some travelling exhibition ; there, standing outside, with fluent tongue and an unfailing ready wit, which is none the less attractive through being occasionally wild and grotesque, he always gathers a large audience while he describes the wonders within.

TUNE—" Hamlet."

Maw nyem it is Jack Spencer,
  Aw hawk aboot the toon ;
Aw try to keep yor sporrits up,
  When ye are lettin' them gan doon.
Aw'm not like the priests that preach,
  An' tells ye hoo te get te heaven ;
Aw patter hard yor hearts te cheer,
  An' get me-sel an honest livin'.

Spoken.—Back combs, side combs, ear-rings, breast pins, steel pens.

Chorus.
Cock-a-doodle-dow, cock-a-doodle-doodle,
Cock-a-doodle-dow, cock-a-doodle-doodle.

Aw used te try the peep-show dodge,
  But that suin turned oot stale ;
And then a quack doctor aw turn'd,
  The flats aw used te nail.

But one day a bobby he nail'd me
 For stannin' i' the street,
And te the Manors he tuik me up,
 And kept me there all neet.
     Cock-a-doodle-dow, etc.

Aw gets oot the next mornin',
 An' gans up te Clayton Street;
Aw call'd inte Young's, the sign o' the *Clock*,
 An' maw box was there all reet!
The servant lass she says te me—
 "Aw say, John, d'ye want a wife?"
"No! no!" says aw, "d'ye think aw'm fond,
 Or tired of maw life?"
     Cock-a-doodle-dow, etc.

Aw used te follow a nice young lass,
 She leev'd up Westgate Hill,
Aw used te take her ower the moor
 To see the rifles drill.
Oft te Tynemouth, on her Sunday out,
 Aw've seen us byeth sail doon the Tyne,
We'd up agyen wi' the eight train,
 And get her in tiv her place at nine.
     Cock-a-doodle-dow, etc.

RIDLEY.   *Author's Manuscript*, 1862.

THE STEPHENSON MONUMENT.

TUNE—"John Barleycorn."

GEORGE STEPHENSON was as great a man
 As any in the North;
Ye'll find his Moniment stannin' now
 In a place it's near the Forth.

He was a poor body's bairn,
    And he used to drive a gin,
An' at neets he'd mend the nebors' shoes
    His daily bread to win.

Chorus.
Three cheers for Stephenson,
    George and Robert Stephenson,
Long may their names be heard
    On the banks of Coaly Tyne.

George once got a Fireman's job,
    He had fourteen shilling a-week;
An' next he got a Brakesman's job,
    He then for a wife did seek.
He married one Fanny Henderson,
    Love joined them hand in hand,
An' Robert he was ther only son,
    The cleverest in the land.
                    Three cheers, etc.

Ye shud oney see thor little thatch hoose,
    Aside Wylam waggon-way,
The walls were plastered up wi' clarts,
    An' the flors war nowt but clay.
There was three glass panes for windows,
    An' the rest war myed o' wood;
Now there stands a forst-rate beeldin'
    Where the aud thatch hoose once stood.
                    Three cheers, etc.

The first locomotive that he myed,
    The "Rocket" she was ca'd,
He said she'd run ten miles an hour,
    The folks thowt he'd gyen mad.

These days there was ne iron rails,
　　The waggon-ways were wood,
He said she'd run as hard agyen,
　　And they said she never could.

　　　　　　　　　　Three cheers, etc.

Now George he suen left Newburn,
　　For he knew he was reet clivor;
He shifted doon to Willington Quay,
　　That's ten miles doon the river.
He invented a steam ballast crane,
　　Which got him a gud nyem;
The aud ballast crane is stannin' yet,
　　At least aw'm told the syem.

　　　　　　　　　　Three cheers, etc.

Now ye see how clivor a man may be,
　　Tho' he's brought up very poor,
And Robert he was as clivor a man
　　As Tyneside bred, aw'm sure.
Now, think on what aw've telled ye, lads,
　　An' always try to shine
Like George and Robert Stephenson,
　　Wor two stars o' the Tyne.

　　　　　　　　　　Three cheers, etc.

RIDLEY.　　　　　　　　　　　*Author's Manuscript,* 1862.

JAMES REWCASTLE,

ONE of the old band of temperance workers who some sixty years ago welcomed the movement into Newcastle. A native, he was to trade a printer, and combined with that the business of bookselling. At his shop in Dean Street he published the *Temperance Advocate*, one of the earliest of temperance publications. When Paxton Hood began to enliven temperance meetings with his melodies, "As I 'woke one morning," "It was in dark December," and others, Rewcastle saw the wisdom of the step, and so to speak localised them by writing "Jackey and Jenny," etc., etc., Fenwick Pickup, another old temperance worker, singing them with great effect. Towards the latter part of his life he retired from bookselling, and accepted a responsible office in the Newcastle Corporation. He died October 4th, 1867, in his 66th year, and is buried at St. John's Cemetery (opened 1857, on the closing of St. John's Churchyard). His songs and recitations do not appear ever to have been issued in a collected form.

ST. JOHN'S AND VICARAGE.

JACKEY AND JENNY.

TUNE—"Come, fie, let us a' to the Bridal."

As Jackey an' Jenny sat gobbin
  About the fine things i' thor hoose—
Says Jenny, "By keepin' teetotal,
  It's myed us byeth cantie an' crouse.

When ye used te gan on the fuddle,
　　We then went byeth hungry an' bare,
But since ye hev joined the teetotal,
　　We noo hev eneuf an' te spare.
　　　　　　"When ye used te gan on the fuddle, etc.

" Wor hoose is weel stock'd an' weel furnish'd
　　Wi' dressors, an tyebles, an' chairs—
We've pots, pans, an' kettles, an' dishes,
　　And a' sorts o' crockery wares;
We've byeth bed an' beddin' i' plenty,
　　And we hev gud claes te wor back—
Wor cupboard is noo niver empty,
　　Thor's nowt really gud that we lack.
　　　　　　　　　　　　　　　Chorus.

" The bairns are byeth healthy an' hearty,
　　And blythsome as blythsome can be;
It myeks me heart joyful te see them,
　　For they are the pride o' maw e'e.
Aw try te keep a' things se canny,
　　Te myek ye a' happy at hyem—
An' what wi' wor curtains an' carpets,
　　Thor's nowt i' the hoose like the syem.
　　　　　　　　　　　　　　　Chorus.

" Noo, Jackey, aw'll tell ye a secret,
　　And myek me-sel sure ov a treat—
Aw wish te gan up tiv the concerts
　　That's held on the Seturday neet.
Aw'll dress i' maw best bib an' tucker,
　　An' ye mun put on yor best claes;
We'll show them hoo nicely teetotal
　　Has mended and better'd wor ways."
　　　　　　　　　　　　　　　Chorus.

REWCASTLE.　　　　　　　　　　　*Broadsheet, about 1860.*

30

EDWARD ELLIOTT.

IN 1862, when the first edition of this work was coming out in penny numbers, Edward Elliott, of Earsdon, left two songs for publication. They appeared at his request with his initials only, E. E. Both songs were new, and related to events of the day. The wit and humour of their author appeared in each, and they became popular. The writer, Edward Elliott, was a noted man in his day : in early life a victim to drink, he contrived to master the passion, and throwing himself with ardour into the temperance cause, soon became noted as one of its best advocates. At Newcastle he often spoke, and there his drollery and wit made him always welcome. His early drinking days had left him with plenty of material for the platform in the shape of stories, and these he told with great effect. In one, with pathos and humour, he depicted the drunkard's home, and by a happy turn showed its poverty by describing the mice sitting in the pantry with the tears in their eyes. Mr. Halliwell, in the *Weekly Chronicle*, has an interesting sketch of him. He tells of Mr. Taylor, the eminent engineer, once meeting Elliott and asking him " why he became a teetotaller," with Ned's answer—

"Aa've h'ard it said there's a certain quantity of drink brewed for evvory man, and a'am sure aa've drunk ma share lang since."

" If Yorick could 'set the table in a roar,' Edward Elliott could set the hall in a ferment when on a platform ; so much so, indeed, that the meeting was sometimes almost broken up with irrepressible laughter. He never attempted to refine his mother tongue, knowing full well that any attempt of the kind would only spoil the diamond."

He died April 29th, 1867, in his sixty-seventh year, and lies in Earsdon Churchyard.

THE SHEEP-KILLIN' DOG.

In October 1862 considerable alarm was felt by the farmers near North Shields, on discovering morning after morning that several of their sheep had been worried and left dead in the fields. Suspicion fell on several poor dogs, but, although closely watched, the offence could not be brought home to them. One dog was chased (on suspicion) all the way from Shields to his master's house in Percy Street. The offender is still at liberty.—*Note*, 1862.

Hae ye heard o' the dog that's been killin' the sheep,
How he baffled the watchers, and gae them the slip?
Sum says it's ne dog, but the ghost ov a glutton,
That when upon earth had a strang tyest for mutton.

> He's a bloodthirsty villin,
> We'll hunt him and kill him,
> And send his skin up te Newcastle museem.

Sum says it's a wolf just cum doon frae the hills,
To tyest a' the flesh meat they hev aboot Sheels;
Jack Proctor declares that he saw the beest runnin,
An' sweers 'twas the deevil or else 'twas a yungin.

Chorus.

Sum says it's a beest that nebody can tyem,
A laffin High Anna aw think is the nyem;
What iver it be, deevil, ghost, or wild beest,
It's clear it delights on gud mutton te feast.

Chorus.

He beats the bowld rifles, the pollis an' aw,
They sweer sic a beest in thor lives they neer saw;
He prowls oot at neets an' thor shanks he suin cracks,
An' leeves them caud deed on the broad o' thor backs.

Chorus.

Byeth aud wives an' yungins wi' greef the tyel lairns,
And feer the greet beest shud fall foul o' the bairns;
The perambulators they darn't set oot,
For feer they fall in wiv the sheep-killin' brute.

Chorus.

We've h'ard of hobgoblin, a witch, an' a warlock,
But surely he's givin the butchers pilgarlick.
Noo for the reward aw wad heh ye te strive,
And bring him te Sheels either deed or alive.

Chorus.

Elliott.   *Author's Manuscript,* 1862.

WHITLEY CAMP.

Written on the occasion of the Felling Artillery Corps camping on
Whitley Sands, September 1862.

HAE ye been doon at Whitley Sands
 Ti see the warriors campin'?
It's worth your while ti gan an see
 The Sangit lions rampin'.
They're just as feerce as untyem'd goats,
 An' all liked sowlgers dress'd;
They've a bunch ov hair upon their jaws
 Just like a yowley's nest.
     Whack, fal de ral, etc.

Their little huts, like sugar-loaves,
 All pointin' to the sky;
And woe betide the enemy
 If he gans ower nigh.
In the inside the warrior rests
 Upon his rusty spear;
He luiks as if he was distress'd
 Wi' backey and wi' beer.
     Whack, etc.

They talk they want ti hae them used
 Ti stand all kinds o' wether,
The whins and bents and strang sea air
 Will tan their hides like lether.
The enemy may fire away,
 An' try their utmost skill,
Nee shot 'll pierce their harden'd frames,
 They'll stand invincible.
     Whack, etc.

The neet was dark when Tommy Todd
 Was as th' sentry walkin',

An outlandish beast he thowt he saw
   Amang the tents was stalkin'.
In th' Queen's nyem, he cries "Whe's there?"
   He ne'er tyuk time to study—
Off went his rifle wiv a crack
   At Andrew Drummond's cuddy.
                 Whack, etc.

The poor beast ran, an' gav a yell,
   Tommy dropt on th' green;
'Twas said when he got up agyen
   He wasn't ower clean.
At last the grand review cum on,
   Ther surely was sum fun
Ti see the warriors fight the fish
   Wi' Willy Armstrang's gun.
                 Whack, etc.

The greet guns roar'd, the fire flew,
   It was a grand display;
The sea-gulls scream'd an' flapped their wings,
   An' flew far nor' away.
The greet round-shot went plish-for-plash
   Inti the tortured deep;
They myed the crabs and lobsters hop,
   An' the fish cud get nee sleep.
                 Whack, etc.

Jacky Scott, the pollisman,
   Wiv a fyece byeth black and cloody,
He sweers that nyen shall do them rang,
   Nee man shall hurt a noody.
Oh! they're the cream ov Britain's bowl,
   Them, ne uther troop surpasses—
In the canteen their valour's seen
   Amang the pots and glasses.
                 Whack, etc.

The French may brag ov body-guards,
    An' crack aboot ther warrin';
Giv our campin' lads but Willy's gun,
    They'll put them off their sparrin'.
Aw think we aw may safely say
    Ne mair we'll be neglected;
But wi sutch guns and valient men
    Wor shores are weel protected.

                  Whack, etc.

ELLIOTT.   *Author's Manuscript*, 1862.

MICHAEL BENSON.

Amongst the members of the "Stars of Friendship" (referred to in the notice of W. Armstrong) was the late Michael Benson, about the

Head of "The Side" (showing the Pant)
about 1830.

oldest master printer in the town. At the anniversary dinner, on Christmas Day, 1828, he delivered the following poetical address, which was generally admitted to be the best of the evening. At the same meeting, J. Selkirk, also a printer, and afterwards editor of the *Bristol Mercury*, delivered a poetical address on the same subject—"Friendship." —*Note*, 1872.

At the "Head of the Side" was a house much frequented by the local poets of the day. The *Northern John Bull* gives a mock report of one of their meetings (possibly a meeting of the "Corinthian Society"), and burlesques the proceedings, evidently pointing out Gilchrist and Oliver as two of the members.

THE BIRTH OF FRIENDSHIP'S STAR.

WHEN sleep its magic o'er me flung,
    Methought I scanned the sky,
And looked for some enchanting STAR,
    But none could I espy.

And still I gazed, but wherefore so?
    None blessed my aching sight!
All dark—all cheerless was the scene—
    All gloomy was the night.

I sighed to think that I should be
    Denied by Stars their aid;
But soon those bitter murmurings
    In transport were allayed.

For quick I saw a dazzling light
    That shed its rays on earth,
And seemed to fly the very power
    Which first had given it birth.

To me it seemed an exile, driven
    From heavenly counsels far;
At distance, too, from all its kin,
    To shine a lonely Star.

But soon another claimed regard—
    And still another yet;
And skies that late were darkly clad
    By orbs were quite beset.

And then, methought, such concord rose
    As ne'er had struck mine ear;
While, silent, I enraptured sat,
    Such heavenly strains to hear.

And angels sung, and bright stars shone—
  Nought woke their joys to mar;
And as the sound in distance fell,
  It spoke of "Friendship's Star!"

Yes! "*Friendship*" was the leading theme
  That burst from every lip;
And, as they sung, they oft the wine
  With god-like mirth would sip!

But morning broke the lovely charm—
  All—all had vanished far!
Except, indeed, an only one,
  The beauteous Morning Star.

I grieved to think "'twas but a dream,"
  And loud my bosom heaved;
But earth had caught the heavenly chords
  That lips of angels breathed!

And "STARS" adorn our native earth,
  Whose rays seem quite divine;
While round me now, in social mirth,
  The "STARS OF FRIENDSHIP" shine.

And may you e'er in Friendship live,
  Till Death's sad parting knell;
Possessing then an endless place
  Where "STARS OF GLORY" dwell!

BENSON.   *Author's Copy.* 1828.

JOE WILSON.

FROM an autobiographic sketch of Joe Wilson, which he published at the request, as he tells, of a few old friends, we extract the following, as furnishing, in the most interesting manner, the leading events in the life of this most popular Tyneside bard :—

"Me fether wes a joiner an' cabinet myeker, an' me muther a straw

bonnit mye-ker, an' byeth natives o' the canny aud toon o' Newcassil. Aw wes born on the 29th o' Novembor 1841, at the end o' Stowl Street; but *twenty minnits* efter aw had myed me forst ippeerince, te the stonishment o' neybors, *Wor Tom* showed his fyece, te dispute wi' me whe shud be the 'pet o' the family,'—an' he sweers he is te this day, *becas he's the yungist!*

"At fowerteen aw went te be a printer. Sangwritin' had lang been me hobby, an' at sivinteen me forst beuk was published. Since that time it's been me aim te hev a place i' the hearts o' the Tyneside people wi' writin' bits o' hyemly sangs aw think they'll sing. At twenty-one aw started business for me-sel as a printer; and at twenty-two aw myed me forst success i' publishing, wi' 'Wor

Geordy's Accoont o' the Greet Boat Race atwixt Chambers an'
Green;' an' next aw browt oot me forst number o' *Tyneside Sangs.*
Later on i' the syem eer aw wrote 'Aw wish yor muther wad

JOE WILSON IN "GEORDY, HAUD THE BAIRN."

cum,' throo seein' me bruther-in-law nursin' the bairn the time
me sister wes oot, nivor dreamin' at that time it wad turn oot the
'hit' it did.

    " ' The Row upon the Stairs,' 'The Gallowgate Lad,' an'

'Dinnet clash the Door,' wes me next successes; the last one (me muther bein' the subject) nearly lickin' 'Geordy, haud the Bairn.'

" Me forst perfessional ingagemint wes at Pelton, i' December 1864; me second at the Oxford Music Hall; an' me thord at the Tyne Concert Hall, Newcassil. Since then aw've been i' nearly ivry toon i' the North, an', aw's happy te say, wi' the syem success aw've had i' me native place."

Joe Wilson's Autobiography only comes down to 1867. Two years later he married; and although he still continued singing his songs as successfully as ever at the various concert halls in the North, yet the travelling from place to place, and the absence from home it necessarily caused, made it less agreeable now than before. This feeling strengthened with time, till, in the year 1871, he settled in his native town as landlord of the Adelaide Hotel.

Joe's career as a landlord was short. After little more than a year he gave it up, and started his concert life again. Never robust, his health began to fail, and after a lingering illness he died at his residence, Railway Street, in his thirty-third year.

Beyond all comparison Joe Wilson has been the most successful of Tyneside song-writers. His wish to have a place in the hearts of the Tyneside people by writing homely songs they would sing has been amply gratified. His name throughout the North is a household word; and far beyond the North, in distant lands, wherever North countrymen are settled, there his songs are prized; their truthfulness to Tyneside life vividly recalling the old home far away. The songs of the older local writers generally relate to particular occurrences, eccentric characters, and the like; Joe Wilson, while not neglecting these, has gone further, and has presented to us pictures of the everyday life of the great mass of the working classes of Tyneside. "The Row upon the Stairs," "Geordy, haud the Bairn," "Dinnet clash the Door," "We'll nivor invite them te tea ony mair," etc., are truly photographs in verse of Tyneside working-class life, and so faithful is the delineation, that they only, the subjects of his pictures, can fully appreciate their truth and accuracy. Although now the author of hundreds of songs, his later efforts show no falling off. "The Time me Fethur wes bad," "Be kind te me Dowtor," etc., only strengthen and increase a reputation that must ever remain one of the brightest in the annals of Tyneside song.

The above, to which a little has been added, appeared in

the 1872 edition of this collection. For a fuller life of Wilson the reader is referred to the new collected edition of his works (1890). Of that edition, it may be added, it has been noticed most favourably by the highest literary papers of the day—*The Athenæum, Literary World, The Spectator, The Saturday Review,* and others.

————

AW WISH YOR MUTHER WAD CUM;

OR, WOR GEORDY'S NOTIONS ABOOT MEN NURSIN' BAIRNS.

TUNE—"The Whusslin' Theef."

"Cum, Geordy, haud the bairn,
    Aw's sure aw'll not stop lang;
Aw'd tyek the jewel mesel,
    But really aw's not strang.
Thor's floor and coals te get,
    The hoose-turns thor not deun:
So haud the bairn for fairs,
    Ye've often deund for fun!"

Then Geordy held the bairn,
    But sair agyen his will;
The poor bit thing wes gud,
    But Geordy had ne skill:
He haddint its muther's ways,
    He sat both stiff an' num;
Before five minutes wes past
    He wish'd its muther wad cum.

His wife had scarcely gyen,
    The bairn began te squall,—
Wi' hikin't up an' doon,
    He'd let the poor thing fall.

It waddent haud its tung,
   Tho' sum aud teun he'd hum,—
" Jack an' Jill went up a hill—
   Aw wish yor muther wad cum ! "

"What weary toil," says he,
   " This nursin' bairns mun be ;
A bit on't's weel eneuf—
   Aye, quite eneuf for me.
Te keep a cryin' bairn,
   It may be grand te sum ;
A day's wark's not as bad—
   Aw wish yor muther wad cum !

" Men seldum give a thowt
   Te what thor wives indure :
Aw thowt she'd nowt te de
   But clean the hoose, aw's sure ;
Or myek me dinner an' tea—
   (It's startin' te chow its thumb :
The poor thing wants its tit—
   Aw wish yor muther wad cum !)

" What a selfish world is this !
   Thor's nowt mair se than man :
He laffs at wummin's toil,
   And winnet nurse his awn—
(It's startin' te cry agyen :
   Aw see tuts throo its gum ;
Maw little bit pet, dinnet fret—
   Aw wish yor muther wad cum !)

" But kindness dis a vast ;
   It's ne use getting vext :
It winnet please the bairn,
   Or ease a mind perplext.

At last, it's gyen te sleep,
  Me wife 'll not say aw's num ;
She'll think aw's a real gud nurse—
  Aw wish yor muther wad cum ! "

JOE WILSON.   *Author's Copy*, 1863.

———

DINNET CLASH THE DOOR.

TUNE—" Tramp, tramp."

OH, dinnet clash the door !
  Aw've tell'd ye that before,
Can ye not let yor muther hev a rest ?
  Ye knaw she's turnin' aud,
  An' for eers she's been se bad,
That she cannet bear such noises i' the least.

Chorus.

Then, oh lass, dinnet clash the door se,
Yor yung an' yor as thowtless as can be ;
  But yor muther's turnin' aud,
  An' ye knaw she's varry bad,
An' she dissent like te hear ye clash th' door.

Just see yor muther there,
  Sittin' feeble i' the chair,
It's *quiet* that she wants te myek her weel ;
  She's been yor nurse throo life,
  Been yor guide i' peace an' strife,
An' her comfort ye shud study an' shud feel.

She once wes yung an' strang,
  But bad hilth 'ill put folks rang,
An' she cannet bear the noise that once she cud.
  She's narvis as can be,
  An' whativor else ye de,
Ye shud study what ye think 'ill de her gud.

So dinnet clash the door,
Or myek ony idle stor,
For the stor 'ill only cause yor muther pain ;
As quiet as can be
De yor wark, an' let her see
That ye'll nivor give her causes te complain.

JOE WILSON.   *Author's Copy*, 1864.

BE KIND TE ME DOWTOR.

TUNE—"Die an Auld Maid."

ONE neet Jack Thompsin sat beside
His canny sweetheart's fethur ;
"We'll hev a crack," the aud man said,
"Since here we've met tegither ;
Ye've gyen wi' Mary two eers noo,
An' what aw'm gawn te menshun
Is—aw hope that yor gawn wiv her
Wi' myest hon'rible intenshun.

Chorus.

"For oh, Johnny, a canny lass is she,
An' aw hope ye'll be kind te me dowtor.

"She may be kind o' flighty : that's
A fault wi' a' yung lasses;
She may be kind a tawky on
Myest ivrything that passes ;
But if she wes ony uther way
She waddent be a wummin :
An' gox ! she's like her muther, an'
Her muther is a rum un !

For oh, Johnny, etc.

"Aw hope she'll be as happy as
    Her muther's been wi' me, lad ;
Tho' sumtimes we fall oot a bit,
    We varry seun agree, lad :
For te leeve as jolly as can be,
    Byeth her an' me's determined ;
An' when we hev a row or two,
    We nivvor see ne harm in't !

For oh, Johnny, etc.

"Ye'll treat wor Mary weel, me lad,
    An' always be kind tiv her ;
Ye'll nivvor rue yor bargain—no,
    Aw's certain that ye'll nivvor !
She can de the hoose torns clivvor,
    Just as clivvor as her muther ;
An' for sewin', knittin', darnin', whey
    Thor issen't such anuther !

For oh, Johnny, etc.

"We'll help ye ivery way we can
    Te set the hoose up decent :
The fethur bed an' ite-day clock
    'Ill not be a bed prisint ;
An' when ye've bairns we'll help ye tee,
    At borth, or deeth, or krissnin ;—
But noo, aw'd better haud me tung,
    For fear sumbody's lissnin ! "

For oh, Johnny, etc.

JOE WILSON.   *Author's Manuscript, 1869.*

THE TIME THAT ME FETHUR WES BAD.

TUNE—" Cum hyem te yor childer an' me."

THOR wes grief i' the hoose all aroond,
　　An' the neybors luckt in passin' by,
An' they'd whisper, "Hoo is he the day?"
　　Then hing doon thor heeds wiv a sigh;
An' they'd speak te me muther se kind,
　　Tho' whativer they said myed her sad;
An' she'd moan real heart broke tiv her-sel,
　　A' the time that me fethur wes bad.

As me fethur lay ill iv his bed,
　　As helpless as helpless can be,
Man, it myed me heart ache when he tried
　　Te smile at wor Johnny an' me.
For he always wes fond ov his bairns,
　　An' aw mind Johnny said, "Get up, dad!"
For the poor little fellow felt lost,
　　A' the time that me fethur wes bad.

Then me fethur wad say, "Me gud lass,"
　　Te me poor muther at his bedside,
"Lass, aw hevin't been half kind te ye"—
　　"Yis ye hev!" she wad sob as she cried.
Then he'd call me t' him, an' he'd say,
　　"Ye'll be kind te yor muther, me lad;"
For he knew that his day wes drawin' nigh,
　　Tho' we nivor thowt he wes se bad.

Then me muther wad sit up a' neet,
　　An' she'd nivor lie doon throo the day;
But wad spend ivry moment she cud
　　I' the room where me poor fethur lay:

31

Till the blow com at last, an' it fell
   On wor hearts, when he lay still an' ca'd;
An' tho' eers pass, aw'm sad when aw think
   O' the days when me fethur wes bad.

JOE WILSON.   *Author's Manuscript*, 1869.

RALPH BLACKETT

IN many respects resembles the unfortunate Selkirk. For
some years upon the Quay occupying a high position (this,
it may be added, he had won by industry and ability),
after a time reverses came upon him, and his position on
the Quay was lost. As a young man he had written many
beautiful hymns, and had published a small poetical work of
a sacred character. This poetical gift in the latter part of
his life he turned to account in another way, Chater's
Almanack and *Annual* finding in him a regular contributor.
John Taylor, another of Chater's band, writes of him—"His
first dialect song was 'Jimmy's Deeth,' a *Weekly Chronicle*
prize song, which was sung at the Tyne Theatre pantomime.
Reserved to strangers, he was kind and genial to those with
whom he was intimate. Prolific with his pen, he was
yet refined in all his ideas. He died at Middlesbrough,
December 29th, 1877, in his forty-seventh year."

JIMMY'S DEETH.

JIMMY WRIGHT deed se suddin, Mall thowt it but reet
To send to the krooner that varry syem neet;
So she sent up te Hoyle, an' accordin' te laws
He order'd post mortim te find oot the caws.

Syuen a doctor was browt, and wivoot much aboot,
He rowl'd up his sleeves an' had Jim open'd oot;
But all that he fund, an' as deed as a nail,
Was a small "eelea" wiv a queer brocken tail.

Now Hoyle was sair puzzled, an' scratch'd his awd heed,
Furst lyuked at the joory, then lyuk'd at the deed;
Swore the witnesses byeth—for thur only was two,
Poor Mally, Jim's wife, an' his marrow, Billoo.

Billoo was furst call'd for, an' said "Lyuk ye heer,
When Jim, like his marrows, drunk nowt else but beer,
He was reet as a trippet, an' riddy for owt,
But tyekin' te wettor, he syuen went te nowt.

"Aw mind weel one mornin', when aw cum te think,
The Whittle Dean stuff had a queer sort o' stink;
Jim, tyekin' a drink, said, 'Hoo strange aw dee feel,
Begox ! aw beleev that aw've swally'd an eel.'

"An' ivvor since then aw've notes'd he pined;
Oft tyun wi' the gripes, hoo he twitch'd an' he twined;
He gorned at the wettor, se seldim 'twas sweet,
An' tyuk on te porter, but nivvor gat reet."

Poor Mally blair'd loodly, an' swor "A' was troo
Wat had been browt forrid bi Billy Billoo;
But aw knaw 'twas a Sunday, ye awl may dippend,
That Jim gat the clincher that hyesten'd his end.

"We wor gawn up be Rye Hill, just like other folk,
And byeth fund the stink o' the nasty gas smoke;
Poor Jim held his breeth an' clapp'd his hand so,
Turn'd as bloo as gas-leet, an' nobbit sayed ' Oh !' "

The krooner then, in a few words, summ'd all up :
"The furst caws, nee doot, is the wettor we sup;
The eel mevvies lowp'd wi' the tyest o' the smoke,
And that was the way that his tailey gat broke."

The joory just whispor'd, an' haddin't lang sat,
'Twas varry syuen knawn when a vardick they gat,
For the foreman cough'd twice, an' said, when he spoke :
"The Whittle Dene wettor an' nasty gas smoke !"

MORAL.

Noo, all ye Newcassellors, mind what ye drink,
An' weer resporators te keep oot the stink ;
Or "eeleas" and sulfor ye'll find is nee joke,
Frev Whittle Dene wettor an' nasty gas smoke.

BLACKETT.   "*Weekly Chronicle,*" 1870.

WILLIAM HENDERSON DAWSON

WAS by trade a bookbinder, and carried on his business for some years at St. Nicholas' Churchyard, in the old workshop of Thomas Bewick, the wood engraver. Always a keen lover of Tyneside songs, in 1862, when Stephenson's monument was inaugurated, he wrote a song on the occasion, which was very successful. In the same year he was connected with, and had much to do in bringing out, the first edition of this song book, writing many of the notes on the old songs; this his wide local knowledge enabled him to do effectively. For some time he wrote a local letter for the *Newcastle Guardian.* The training he got there came in useful later on, when, on the death of J. P. Robson, he succeeded him in writing the local letter ("The Retoirt Keelman") for the *Advertiser.* Dawson was a free and easy writer, and while still carrying on his bookbinding, contributed "Walks round Old Newcastle," and being "native and to the manner born," he filled them with interesting references. He contributed also "The Local Poets of Newcastle," an interesting series of articles, biographical and critical, and a quantity of stories, songs, and poems. He died on January 25th, 1879, in his 52nd year, and was interred at St. John's Cemetery, Elswick.

THE PITMAN'S TICKOR AN' THE WAG-AT-THE-WA'.

TUNE—" Barbara Allen."

WOR Tommy was crissind, an' weel aw remembor
    We tuik worsels off for Newcassel toon ;
'Twis in the blithe munth iv bonny Septembor,
    Not varry lang 'fore wor bindin' cam roon.
The wifey cried oot for new shawl an' bonnit,
    The bairns an' the laddies they wanted new claes ;
An' wor awdist lass, Jinny, the slee witchin' donnit !
    Had coaxed her aud minnie te buy her new stays.

We gat te the toon, and gat wor brass ettled,
    An' then a' the bairnies war ower the muin
It the easy bit way that thor hashes was settled,
    An' glad te git drest in new duds varry suin.
They tuik thor ways hyem, an' aw wandered iboot,
    Tyekin stock iv the seets on a Settorday neet ;
For aw wis ditermined, 'fore the toon aw went oot,
    Hyem for me-sel te tyek sum fine treet.

Aw suin spied a chep thit wis sellin' a tickor,
    Thit he boastid wad beet a' the clocks i' the toon ;
Is he nobbit axed for'd what aw'd hev spent ippon likor,
    Aw suin struck a bargain, an' munny laid doon.
Aw tuik her off hyem, an' hung her up bi the wawl,
    'Side the wag-at-the-wa' thit had hung se lang there ;
But the crazy awd thing 'side it wad scairce gan it awl—
    Tickor bet Waggy kwite oot o' time, aw diclaire !

Says aw, " Thoo aud lump, what myeks thoo se feulish
    Te let a bit thing like that beat thee noo ?
Did aw ivor think aw had owt hawf se cullish,
    Is onny sic hoyt hawf is lazy is thoo ? "

Aw tuik up the hammer, an' levil'd her law, man,
  'Spite o' what wifey an' bairnies cud say;
Aw stuck te the tickor thit aw varry weel naw, man,
  Aw kin elwis dippend te gan thorteen oors i' the day.

DAWSON.   *Author's Manuscript*, 1862.

The Stephenson Monument, inaugurated October 2nd, 1862. In Newcastle and Gateshead there was a general suspension of business in honour
of the occasion.

THE PITMAN'S VISIT TO STEPHENSON'S MONUMENT.

TUNE—" Tallygrip."

OH! wor pit wes laid in, and we had nowt te de,
  Says aw te Tom Hoggers, " Let's off te Newcassel;

Thor's fine things te de—the toon's all astir;
    Newcassel, they say, 'ill be quite in a bussel.
For Stephenson's Monument's gawn te be shown
    By fine lords, and gents tee, and nobbies;
A greet lairge purcession's te mairch throo the toon;
    Gox! the noration 'ill myek sum fine wark for the
        bobbies.
                    Rite fal the dal lal.

We'd scarce gettin te toon when the music struck up,
    An' St. Nicholas's bells wor set ringin';
The folks in greet croods war a' flockin' aboot,
    The patters war threshin' away at the singin'.
Says Tommy te me, "Let's see what we'll de,
    We'll strike off te the place in a minnit;
For if we stay here till the purcession gets clear,
    Smash! we'll not heh the least chance te get in it."

We got te the Spital by drivin' amain,
    An' knockin' the folks on one side, man:
A dandified fellow he lifted his cane,
    An' thretten'd te pummel maw hide, man;
But aw up wi' me fut, an' aw gov him a fling,
    That suen myed the dandy a sloggers,
For amang a' the lads from Bill Quay te Tyne Main
    Thor's nyen can cum up te Jack Slack or Tom
        Hoggers.

Te hev a gud luik we suen moonted a styen,
    When we heerd the purcession wes cummin';
An' feyks! but the music suen myed the folks run,
    An' sairly sum heeds got a bummin':
For the folks they cam runnin' like waves o' the sea,
    Sum one way an' sum tiv anuther;
A dandy yung buck got a rap on the scaup,
    An' one went reet off in a swuther.

An' faiks! but the seet it suen dazed me, aw's sure,
    Te see the greet croods o' folks mairchin' se fine ;
Wor fitters an' viewers in greet numbers war there,
    An' enginemen an' workmen, the pride o' the Tyne.
But the volunteer riflers frightened us a',
    When they went past where Tom an' me stud ;
An' queerly dressed fellows war there cummin' thick,
    Besides, tee, the men o' bowld Robin Hood.

An' when the purcession got up te the styen,
    A chep began for te rowl up a cloot ;
A gentleman nob gat reet up aloft—
    The people aroond set up a greet shoot ;
An' aw wes the forst the figger te spy,
    An' aw said at wonce it wes Geordie the daddy ;
But aw thowt te mesel when they played "God save the
        Queen,"
    Aw wad weel heh liked for te hear the "Pit Laddie."

Ah, man! but the monument itsel it luiks grand,
    Te see the canny aud fellow up there ;
An' te hear a' the fine things the gentleman said,
    It varry near myed maw heart for te blair.
An' a wee trapper lad wes stuck in a corner,
    An' monny mair figgers se fine,
An' aw said lang might it stand here te Stephenson's glory,
    The wee trapper laddie, the pride o' the Tyne !

When the fray wes a' ower Tom an' me had a gill,
    An' loodly the haverils war tawkin' :
They said sic a seet they'd ne'er seen afore,
    Sic heeps o' fine folks thor wes walkin'.
Says aw, "Tommy, man, let's tyek wor ways hyem,
    An' tell te wor awn folks the story ;
For pit lads far an' near, frae the Tyne te the Wear,
    Lang may they rejoice in aud Stephenson's glory.

    DAWSON.   *Author's Manuscript*, 1862.

JACK'S WOODEN LEG.

Pilgrim Street Gate before its removal (1802).

John Stephenson, better known as Wood - Legged Jack, died October 15, 1862, whilst in the act of eating a morsel of food, which he had from two men in the White House, Pilgrim Street. Many carriers then frequented Pilgrim Street, and Jack picked up a living going messages for them. The following whimsical fancy was written at the time of his death, on hearing that it was intended to raffle his wooden leg.

TUNE—" Wonderful Tallygrip."

'TWAS in the White House some queer cheps did fore-
  gether,
  One Seturday neet when they war on the spree,
An' frae what aw cud hear 'mang the noise and the
  blether,
  There wis somethin' wonderful they had for ti see.
A duzen or mair war set at a tyeble,
  The head o' the company was stuck on a keg;
A cheppy tuik kelter as fast's he was yeble,
  There war gan for ti raffle aud Jack's wooden leg.

Aw joined in the set when aw herd what the gam was,
  An' blithely aw tyebled maw brass in a crack,
For i' maw young days when aw was a laddie
  Weel aw was liked bi' aud wooden-legged Jack.
An' sair, sair did aw greeve when aw herd ov his end,
  man,
  How for a bite the puir chep had ti beg;
He oft had sair wark for ti myek a bit fend, man,
  An' noo they wad raffle his aud wooden leg.

When the nyems war a' reckin'd, there wis a hundred duzen
  Ov fellows determined ti try at thor luck ;
The gam wis begun bi Bill Bowden's greet cuzen,
  Whe cawd us the cheps for showing British pluck.
He thrawed fifteen, which was considered a wunder,
  Another got five for ti hang on his peg ;
But Bill Thompson, the trimmer, gar'd Bill's cuzen
      knock under,
  For he thrawed eighteen for Jack's wooden leg.

Aw gat up the dice an' them aw did rattle,
  For aw felt sartin and sure for ti win ;
Aw thowt with the best aw wad gie them gud battle,
  For the leg ti gan past me wad be a greet sin.
Aw thowt o' the times when aw'd see him stot bi me
  Beside the Black House on his aud wooden peg ;
Aw'd gien him a hawpenny when he cam nigh me,
  Ti help for drink for his aud wooden leg.

Hurrah ! noo, me lads, aw've thrawn the two duzen,
  Come, try an' beat that thraw if ye can ;
Muckle-gobbed Mat he thrawed three-an'-twenty,
  But Bowdy-kites Billy's thraw showed him a man ;
For he took up the dice, an' he garr'd them a' jingle,
  He thrawed four-an'-twenty alang wi' Daft Peg.
The three on us paddled, but aw gaw them a tingle,
  For aw tuik off the prize o' Jack's wooden leg.

Aw ga'd ti the cheps that they caw *Anty Quaries,*
  That i' wor aud Cassel myek sic a gran seet ;
It's placed 'mang the steyns, and the greet nicky nackies,
  And for fowerpence ye may see'd ony haliday neet.
At thor varry last meeting me sair they did flatter,
  An' famed Dr. Bruce, tee, said he would beg
That they ask Robert White for ti tyek up the matter,
  An' gie them the History o' Jack's Wooden Leg.

DAWSON.   *Author's Manuscript,* 1862.

JOHN KELDAY SMITH.

THE *Monthly Chronicle* gives the following brief notice of this writer:—" Mr. J. K. Smith, bellhanger, died on the 12th of June 1889, at his residence, Temperance Row, Shieldfield, in his 54th year. He was a native of Orkney, but had lived in Newcastle almost since his infancy. As a writer of local songs, he showed his versatility in the composition of pieces for Chater's comic publication, Ward's Almanack, and the *Weekly Chronicle.* Besides this, he was the writer of a prize song on the Gateshead Working Men's Club, and the author of a prize essay on working men's clubs."

To this we may add the first and two last verses from one of his latest and best songs, " Whereivvor hae they gyen?" It happily hits off the changes made by a few years' absence from the old town.

WHEREIVVOR HAE THEY GYEN?

TUNE—" Perhaps she's on the Railway."

Aw'm a nativ ov Newkassil, but aw've been se lang away,
Aw divvint see the fyeces that aw met wiv ivvory day;
Aw miss the weel-knawn voices in the burly lokil tung;
Aw nivvor hear a single stave ov what me muther sung.
Thor's been such deeths an' weddins, an' changes gud an' bad,
Aw cannit finnd the foaks aw knew when just a Tyneside lad;
Aw had sum aunts an' cuzzins that war scattor'd awl aboot,
Aw've been ippon the hunt awl day an' cannit finnd them oot.

Chorus.

Whereivvor hae they gyen? Whereivvor can they be?
Aw've sowt them in the Tuthill Stairs—aw've sowt them on the Kee;
Aw've been throo lanes an' alleys, an' wandor'd up an' doon,
They're owther deed an' barried, or gyen an' left the toon.

. . . .

It's just the syem wi' public men whichivvor way aw torn,
Aw hevvint met a singil yen frae Elsick te the " Born ";
Aw clapp'd me hands for Larkin, the speaker ov the north,
Aw shootid oot te Johnny Fife, " the battle of the Forth."
Aw've shaken hands wi' Chambors—we awl liked " Honest Bob,"
An' said te Cockney boasters—he's the man te shut yor gob;
" Haud away, Harrie," for Claspor wonse yewsed te be the cry,
An' " Gan on, Renforth, hinny," when he myed the paddles fly.
Whereivvor hae they gyen? etc.

Bobby Allan, an' Rewcassil—the payntor, Tommy Carr,
Were elwis in the front te fight a stoot teetotal war;
Wor lokil bard in Robson, Joe Wilson wiv his rhymes,
Hes cheer'd the harts ov Tyneside men when far in distant climes.
An' monny mair aw yewsed te knaw tiv uther lands hev gyen,
The awd 'uns thit held langist oot hev dropt off yen biv yen;
Thor's nyen te say " Noo, hinney, Jack, hoo are ye gettin' on?"
They've melted like the wintor's snaw the sun hes shone ippon.
Whereivvor hae they gyen? etc.

SMITH.   *Author's Copy,* 1885.

THE FORST OV OWT YE HAD.

TUNE—"When the kye comes hame."

THERE's a happy time in awl wor lives, a plishur in the
    past,
When we wor stannin *forst* at skyul, instead of being *last;*
When ye went reet ayheed, an' beaten ivvory lad—
Can ye e'er forget the plishur ov the forst ov owt ye had ?

Chorus.

The *forst* ov owt ye had, the *forst* ov owt ye had ;
Can ye e'er forget the plishur ov the *forst ov owt ye had?*

When *forst* ye had te gan te wark, ye thowt yorsel a man,
And bowldly left yor cosy bed, and tyuk yor brickfist-
    can ;
When ye gat yor forst week's brass, and tyuk it te yor
    dad—
Can ye e'er forget the plishur ov *the forst pay that ye had?*

When ye dressed yor-sel in Sunday claes, te figgor roond
    the toon,
And cut a high toon swagger, bi wandering up an' doon ;
Te fit ye like a swell, an' myek the lasses mad—
Can ye e'er forget the plishur *ov the forst watch that ye
had ?*

And when ye met wi' bonnie Poll, when gawn up Jesmond
    Dene,
Ye thowt she was the finest lass that ivvor yit was seen ;
Ye gat a gud-neet kiss, that myed yor heart feel glad—
Can ye e'er forget the plishur *ov the forst lass that ye had?*

When sattled doon in married life, yor bliss wis *not*
    complete,
Ye wished a little Toddles for te play aroond yor feet ;
Ye tyuk it as it cam, if owther lass or lad—
Can ye e'er forget the plishur *ov the forst bairn that ye
had ?*

We get see yewsed te awl wor joys, thor's nowt ayboot
    them new,
They cum see nattoral in thor turn, we think it is wor
    due ;
But when they blissed us forst, we felt supremely glad—
Can you e'er forget the plishur of the forst of owt ye had?

    SMITH.   *Author's Copy*, 1885.

MATTHEW DRYDEN.

THE following letter, which appeared in the *Daily Chronicle*,
March 8th, 1890, gives a fair account of this writer :—

"While your columns day after day of late have been recording
the fall first of one 'Man of Mark' and then of another, and
recording also their struggles from comparative poverty to opulence,
perhaps a little space might be spared for one who, unnoticed,
except in your obituary columns, has just fallen, and, unlike those
whose careers you have recorded, has fallen as poor at the end of
his fight with fortune as at the beginning. Matthew Dryden,
author of 'Perseveer ; or, the Nine Hours Movement,' died a few
days ago, after a lingering illness, at his residence, Herbert Street,
in his forty-sixth year, leaving a widow and six children. He was
born at Belford, where his father occupied a fair position, having
an interest in some colliery about that part. While but a little way
into his teens, by his father's sudden death, Dryden, young as he
was, had to set to and fight the battle of life. Like many others
so engaged, he came to Newcastle, and, obtaining employment at
Sir W. Armstrong's, remained there until his death. In 1871 the
great nine hours strike occurred, and Dryden came out with the
rest. At once he set himself to work for the cause. He was a
good singer—local, Irish, and sentimental being alike to him. He
did all well, excelling in Joe Wilson's songs. He organised
concerts for the benefit of the strike funds, and for these concerts
wrote his popular song, 'Perseveer ; or, the Nine Hours Movement.'
Perhaps its literary merit is not great, but it suited his audience,
and the strike funds benefited. Another of his songs on 'Elliott,
the Pegswood sculler,' was also popular. At the end of the strike
he returned to Armstrong's, and at the time of his death had been
about thirty years in the service of the firm. His 'Perseveer' in all
probability will live as a memento of the great nine hours strike.
That movement, in its day considered almost revolutionary, is now,
so quickly times are changing, almost out of date by the rising of
the newer eight hours agitation."

PERSEVEER;

OR, THE NINE OORS MOVEMINT.

TUNE—"Nelly Ray."

Yen Munday neet aw went oot just te hev a walk,

When aw met a chep frae Sunderland, an' we got on
te tawk;

He says, "Wor workin clivvor noo, an' likely for te
thrive,

We've got the Nine Oors Movemint noo, an' we drop
wor work at five."

Chorus.

Perseveer! Perseveer! awl ye that's sittin' here!
Perseveer! Perseveer! they've gettin't on the Wear!
Ye men upon the banks o' Tyne, aw think thor's little fear,
But ye'll get the Nine Oors Movemint if ye only perseveer!

Says aw, "Me man, aw think yor reet biv aw that aw
can reed;

But mind ye myed a gallant fite before ye did succeed.

Se tell yor mates at Sunderland, when ye gan ower hyem,

That wor lads aboot Newcassel thor gawn te de the
syem!"

Perseveer, etc.

He says, "Yor tawkin like a man, for aw really think
it's time:

If the movemint pays upon the Wear it'll pay upon the
Tyne;

Yor workin men they've been lang famed, aw hope
they'll keep thor nyem:

They helpt us ower at Sunderland, so we'll help them
back agyen!"

Perseveer, etc.

Noo, strikes are what aw divvent like, but if they'll not
agree,

We'll heh te be like Sunderland, an' close wor factories,
tee;

The maistors then'll start te fret, and own 'it they were
    rang;
It's then they'll see they cannot de withoot the workin
    man.

Perseveer, etc.

Aw myek nee doot wor maistors think they'll just de
    what they like,
For they knaw it hurts a workin man when he hes te
    cum te strike;
But if we prove as true as steel wor maistors will be fast,
Thor contracts mun be finished, so they will give in at
    last.

Perseveer, etc.

DRYDEN. *Author's Copy*, 1871.

JAMES HORSLEY.

AMONGST the brightest of recent Tyneside song-writers
James Horsley must be classed. His songs and poems have
just been collected and published in a popular form. In that

edition his life, written by his
friend Mr. Hastings, appears; to
that interesting sketch the reader
is referred, as here all that can be
given is a brief summary. Belonging Alnwick, left an orphan in
Newcastle at an early age, when
little more than a child he had
to begin the battle of life. This
he fought as a stable boy, cabin
boy, anything that promised a
livelihood. About his stable
boy days he used to tell—mis-
timed and worn-out he has at
times fallen asleep on the horse's
back, and so been landed at the
stables in the Haymarket.
    Outgrowing his adverse cir-
cumstances, as a young man he was for a time with Robert
Ward, connected with his *Advertiser* and *Directory*, finally

engaging with Mr. Andrew Reid, where he continued until his death, *Reid's Railway Guide*, known all over the North, being his special line.

When, a little over twenty, he wrote his first song, a whimsical fancy, "Geordy's Dream; or, the Sun and the Muen," for twenty-five years that was his only song, as he was nearly fifty before he tried again. The second start knew no pause. With a free and fluent pen he continued writing until the last. Jesmond was his favourite theme: singing its praises he never tired. Perhaps in the following he is at his best :—

JESMOND.

I would the gift were mine in words to sing,
The beauty born of thee in early spring ;
Still more in summer would I long for power
To chant the birth of every opening flower ;
How blooming hawthorn with laburnum vies
In offering incense to the grateful skies ;
How rhododendrons with their " purpling " hue
Seem jealous of the heavens' translucent blue ;
How autumn's foliage in russet brown
Makes autumn's sun blush red as he goes down ;
How limpid ripples on thy purling stream
Smile shining dimples in the moon's pale beam ;
How rich profusion every sense rewards,
Made still more rapturous by songs of birds.
Much more thou hast that man hath kindly given,
Which makes thee seem a paradise from heaven.

Author's Volume, 1891.

Away from his favoured Jesmond, his lines " To the Angel of Death " possibly are his finest—

TO THE ANGEL OF DEATH.

O ! death, come softly to my side,
　And whisper low thy dread command ;
When I no longer here may bide,
　Then take me gently by the hand.
If thou must come, O ! then be kind,
And think of them I leave behind.

Come not in wrath nor in the storm,
　Nor in the pestilence nor war,
But rather in thy softer form,
　Of gentle swoon, or slumber's car.
If thou must come, O ! then be kind,
And think of them I leave behind.

Come not in treachery nor hate,
 Nor take me in some deed of sin,
But lead me to thy pathless gate
 In love, and bid me enter in.
If thou must come, O! then be kind,
And think of them I leave behind.

Come clothed in mercy, come in peace,
 While friends and loved ones round me mourn,
Whose voices may, as life doth cease,
 Accompany me to yonder bourne.
If thou must come, O! then be kind,
And think of them I leave behind.

Come when the flowers are blooming fair,
 In autumn or in budding spring,
When nature's perfume fills the air,
 And birds my requiem sweetly sing.
If thou must come, O! then be kind,
And think of them I leave behind.

I fear thee, yet I seek thee, Death,
 Thy wakeless sleep a rest doth bring;
May faith and prayer in my last breath
 Disarm thee of thy bitter sting.
If thou must come, O! then be kind,
And think of them I leave behind.

February, 1886.

O! come not when the driven snow
 Lies thick beneath the mourners' feet;
It seems so cold to be laid low
 Beneath a wintry winding sheet.
If thou must come, O! then be kind,
And think of them I leave behind.

Author's Volume, 1891.

The last verse was an addition, made not long before his death; its prayer was not to be granted. Snow fell heavily at the time of his death, and at the funeral lay so thick that a way had to be cut to the grave. Not for long at least was one to be left behind. Mrs. Horsley died six months later (September 1891), and was laid beside him in St. Andrew's Cemetery. Mr. Horsley's portrait is from a photo by P. M. Laws. _____

SHE'S SUMBODDY'S BAIRN.

ONE dark, dorty neet, as aw myed me way hyem,
 Aw passed a bit lassie se bonny;
She belanged tiv a class that aw'm frightened to nyem,
 An' aw grieve that wor toon hes se monny.

32

She'd dress'd hersel' up in extravagant style,
　　Wi' satins an' laces upon her ;
As she passed me her fyece had a strange sort o' smile,
　　That gliff'd me, it did, on me honour.
　　　　　　　　　Aw thowt, noo, that's sumboddy's bairn.

Aw wis struck bi her youth an' her bonny white skin,
　　An' the bloom on her cheek tho' 'twas painted,
As it flash'd on me mind, them's the trappins o' sin,
　　Oh, aw felt, ay, as if aw cud fainted.
Aw saw bi her walk, an' her heed toss'd se high,
　　An' her airtful-like manner se winnin',
Bi her ower-dressed style, an' the glance ov her eye,
　　That she'd myed, oh, that awful beginnin' ;
　　　　　　　　　An' aw thowt, noo, she's sumboddy's bairn.

Oh, lasses, remember yor feythers at hyem,
　　An' yor muthers, whe's hearts ye are breakin',
An' the bruthors an' sisters yor bringin' te shyem,
　　An' the awful-like future yor myekin' ;
Divvent hanker for plissure nor dresses se fine,
　　Nor be tempted bi fashin an' beauty ;
Think twice ere ye start on that dreadful decline
　　That leads ye fre' virtue and duty.
　　　　　　　　　Remember, yor sumboddy's bairn.

Ye lads that a muther hes fondled an' nurs'd,
　　That hes sisters that's gentle an' pure,
Nivver lead a young lass in the way that's accurs'd,
　　Nivver breathe in her ear what's impure.
Reyther try to protect her fre' danger an' harm,
　　And if wrang'd, see the injured one righted ;
For life hes been robb'd of its loveliest charm,
　　When a woman's fair fame hes been blighted.
　　　　　　　　　For mind, she wis sumboddy's bairn.

HORSLEY.　　　　　　　　　　　　　*Author's Copy, 1886.*

THE CHINESE SAILORS IN NEWCASTLE.

In 1881, at Armstrong's, a war vessel was built for the Chinese Government, and some hundreds of Chinese sailors came to Newcastle as her crew.
The song describes them as seen in the streets.

JOHN CHINAMAN hes cum te spy
 Wor canny Northern toon,
Wi' flatten'd fyece, an' funny eye,
 An' skin ov olive broon,
An' stumpy feet, an' lang pig-tails,
 An' claes o' clooty blue,
Alang wor street he slawly trails,
 Just like a live yule doo.

      Chorus.
  John Chinaman, John Chinaman,
   What hev ye cum te see?
   What de ye think o' wor toon lads?
   Hoo de ye like wor Quay?

Hev ye been to the Market yit,
 Wor cabbages te see,
Or " get a puddin' nice an' het,"
 Or hev a cup o' tea?
Or hev ye been te th' cutler's there
 Te get yor-sel a knife,
Or stroll'd th' length o' filly fair
 To choose yor-sel a wife?
      John Chinaman, etc.

Or hev ye had a swagger doon
 By Mosley Street at neet,
An' watched them myek th' bonny meun
 Wiv Swan's Electric Leet?
Or hev ye been te Laws's place,
 An' smiled yor biggest laff,
An' let yor pigtail hing wi' grace,
 Te get yor photygraff?
      John Chinaman, etc.

Or hev ye been te Barkas's
   The bicycles te try,
An' show'd th' Quayside marquises,
   Like them yor rethor " fly " ?
Or hev ye been te see th' shops
   Te spend yor English tin,
An' as th' money frae ye drops,
   Suspect yor tyek'n in ?
                      John Chinaman, etc.

Or hev ye had a ridy-pide
   Inside a Tramway Car,
Wi' grinnin' fyeuls at every side
   A' wunderin' what ye are ?
Or hev ye bowt a big ci-ga',
   An' tried to myek it leet,
An' gyen an' deun the La-di-da,
   Alang by Grainger Street ?
                      John Chinaman, etc.

Then trail alang, John Chinaman,
   Amang the crood ov bairns,
An' touchy tyesty all ye can,
   For that's th' way one lairns ;
But, mind, beware o' cheeky lass,
   An' whisky, John, and beer,
For if ye tyek an extra glass,
   Oh, John, 'twill cost ye dear !
                      John Chinaman, etc.

If ye shud tyek a drop ower much,
   An' it gets in yor eye,
An' ye get i' wor bobby's clutch,
   My sangs, he'll myek ye cry—

He'll tyek ye up before the " chief,"
    An' though yor skin be broon,
An' ye be neither rogue nor thief,
    He'll fine ye haaf-a-croon.
                    John Chinaman, etc.

But ye'll hev seen, John Chinaman,
    Barbarious English cheps
Disgrace the varry nyem ov men,
    Th' blackguard jackanyeps!
Should ony drucken cuddy, John,
    Dar smite ye in the gob,
We'll let ye break a saucer, John,
    An' fine him forty bob.
                    John Chinaman, etc.

John Chinaman, John Chinaman,
    Dressed in yor suit ov blue,
Ye've cum te see John Englishman,
    An' axee-how-he-doo.
Yor welcome here, John Chinaman,
    Te buy yor guns an' ships,
An' if ye bring yor munny, John,
    Ye'll find us jolly chips.
                    John Chinaman, etc.

HORSLEY.   *Author's Manuscript*, 1881.

GEORGE CHARLTON BARRON,

BORN at Gateshead, began his career on the Quay as a clerk
with his relative, Ralph Blackett (a Tyneside writer before
referred to). A mimic and elocutionist, like many so gifted,
when young he fancied the stage, but his career as an actor was

brief; he soon returned to Newcastle, where his dramatic abilities made him a great favourite. A commercial traveller with a wide circle of friends, for social gatherings he was much sought after. As an entertainer he was versatile; Scottish and Tyneside being his favourite lines, in these his stories were endless. In his prime, with apparently many years of life before him, he was suddenly struck down. For an abscess in the head he underwent an operation; it was successfully performed, but after a few days he took an unfavourable turn, and after a brief illness, died at North Shields on June 16th, 1891, in his 45th year, and was buried at Preston Cemetery.

Photo.   Auty & Ruddock, Tynemouth.

The Rev. H. Vian William, Congregational minister, in referring to his death said: "His life was marked by many fine traits, but most noticeable was his bubbling cheerfulness—an animated sunbeam, which brightened everybody and every place. His (Mr. William's) life during the last eighteen months had had its sorrows, and many a time Mr. Barron ministered to him some of this genial cheerfulness, and, as an act of gratitude, he would like to plant a flower on his grave." The general feeling at Mr. Barron's untimely death was shown by the way the subscription for his widow was taken up, about £400 being raised in a short time.

Apparently the only piece Mr. Barron wrote was "Bill Smith at Waterloo." Amongst the stories he told, many no doubt would be touched up by him, but in localising (assisted by his friend Mr. Spence) an American story into "Bill Smith at Waterloo," and making its hero a Tyneside man, he did his best.

BILL SMITH AT THE BATTLE OF WATERLOO.

THE following story is told to illustrate the prejudices of human nature in general, and Tynesiders in particular. You possibly never met a man yet, from even the most remote village, but who would in a few minutes' conversation assure you that it was the most wonderful place in the world for something or other.

A Scotsman might entertain a Tynesider for a month, take him up the Clyde and show him the latest wonders in machinery, etc.; yet it is ten to one that after examining it he would exclaim, "It's varry canny, but ye shud see the Tyne."

That we have prejudices I could give many proofs, but one will suffice. I remember well the late senior member for Newcastle (Mr. Joseph Cowen) delivering his first speech as a candidate for Parliament, giving as a reason, among many others, of his fitness to represent his native town, that he not only spoke the language, but "shared the prejudices of the people."

Two Newcastle workmen go to London, one of whom had been there before, so of course he was to be guide, friend, and philosopher of the other who had never been. When they arrived at King's Cross Station, after eleven hours' journey in one of those "cheap trips," the one who had never travelled before, stretching himself on the platform, said—

"By gox, Geordy, it's dry wark this travellin', and yon's a public-hoose open; let's hev a drink."

"Noo, Jack, thoo'll hae to be guided be me. If thoo gans in there, aw divvent knaw what thoo may get; thoo might get poisoned, where if thoo waits till we get into the next street, aboot six doors doon, thor's a hoose there kept by a reel Newcassel chep; they cawl him Bill Smith, and he hes a cupple of pot lads, and thor Newcassel cheps tee, an' we'll get a drop of reel Newcassel mild, and mair than that, he's a reel clivvor chep this Bill Smith; he's been oot at the Peninsula, kens Wellin'ton and awl them cheps, an' if he's i' the humour, he'll give us a grand crack."

"How-way, then, for aw's varry dry."

(*Smith's house supposed to be reached.*)

"Let's hae two pints o' mild. Is Bill Smith in, mistor?"

"Ay; he's in ahint there."

"Whie, tell him Geordy Taylor's heer frae Cramlington, and a friend of his. (*Smith supposed to enter.*) Hoo are ye, Smith?"

"Oh, varry canny; hoo's yor-sel'?"

"Wye, aw cannot complain. Here's a mate o' mine aw've browt up for the first time; an', man, Bill, he wes gannin' intiv that hoose at the corner to get a drink, when aw telled him te wait till we gat doon heer, and we'd get a drop o' gud stuff; and mair then that, aw wes tellin' him what a clivvor chep thoo was; that thoo'd been oot at the Peninsula, and kenned Wellin'ton and awl them cheps, and if thoo wes in the humour thoo'd give us a grand crack."

"That's just where thoo myed the mistake, Taylor. When a man's dyun the things aw've dyun it dissent dee for him te tawk aboot hees-sel."

"Whie, we knaw that weel eneugh; but he's nivvor been heer afore; giv him a stave."

"Weel, he's nivvor been heer afore, as yee say, or aw waddent be on. But thor's an awd corcumstance struck me this morning when aw wes shevvin mesel, if thoo dissent mind aw'll tell him that.

HOW WATERLOO WAS WON.

"Ye knaw when aw wes oot at the sowlgerin', aw wes up syun one mornin'—whie, aw wes up syun ivvery mornin' for the metter of that—when whe shud aw meet but Wellin'ton.

"Direc'ly he seed me he says, 'What cheer, there, Smith; hoo's things lukin?'

"'Oh, varry canny,' aw says, and with that he pulls oot a flask of French brandy he had on him.

"He always had a flask of nice brandy on him had Wellin'ton, just wi' the reet quantity of wetter in, neither ower much or ower little. We wor just hevvin a nip there, when awl of a suddint he torns roond te me and says, 'What's yon on the top of the hill there, Smith?'

"Says aw, 'Begox, thor Frenchmen.'

"'Whie, we mun hae them shifted.'

"'Shifted! we'll blow'd sharp shift them!'

"'Haud on noo, Smith, haud on. When ye gan tiv a job of that kind ye tyek ower few men. Ye'll be happinin something sum day. Noo, divvent ye gan wi less than twenty-five Newcassel cheps tiv a job o' that kind.'

"Aw went doon te wor cheps; they wor awl stannin iv a heep. Aw says, 'Did ye see them Frenchmen, lads, on the top o' the hill this mornin?'

"'Hoo many wad there be o' them?'

"'Oh, aw dar say thor'd be fower hundred.'

"' Ay.'

"Ay, and annuther chep thowt thor'd be fower hundred.

"' Whie,' aw says, 'hoo mony of hus Newcassel cheps wilt tyek te shift that lot? Wellin'ton thinks twenty-five. It's ower monny, isn't it?'

"' Ay! far ower monny; a duzzen's plenty.'

"' Wye, we'll tyek fifteen, just to humour him a bit.'

"So away we went tappy-lappy down the lonnin, awl iv a raw, just te myek wor-sels lyuk as big as possible, when, just turnin the bottom of the hill, whe shud aw see but Napoleon—hees awn sel, mind—on a lily-white horse, and a greet big telescope iv his hand. When he sees me cummin he torned pale as deeth, and efter he gat hes breeth he says—

"' Where ye gawn te, Smith?'

"Aw says, 'Aw's just gawn te shift yon Frenchmen yonder.'

"He says, 'Haud on noo, Smith, haud on. Are ye reely gawn te shift them, or ar ye only gawn te jossell them a bit?'

"' Thor's ne jossellin' aboot it noo, Napoleon; they'll hev te be shifted, 'cas Wellin'ton says se.'

"He torned his horse aroond and run up the bank, and says tiv his men, 'Back ye gan, ma lads, back ye gan; for heer's Bill Smith and fifteen Newcassel cheps cum te shift ye, and ye hevvent a happorth o' chance!'

"But aw divvent like te tawk about me-sel, Taylor; mine's half a rum."

BARRON. *Author's Manuscript,* 1891.

JOHN TAYLOR.

"DIED at Dunston on the 24th Sept., aged 51, John Taylor. Interment at Dunston churchyard." The above announcement appeared just as this volume was finishing at the press. It told that another of the old contributors of 1872 was gone, and that from the writers of the present another name had to be taken and placed upon the ever-increasing roll of the writers of the past. John Taylor began life as a clerk at the

Central Station. His father was an old North-Eastern man —the first man who printed the now familiar railway ticket,

being selected by the patentee to work his machine. His son, after being some years at the Central, finding promotion slow, thought of making a short cut to fortune. He left the railway company and became traveller for a large brewery. Like many other short cuts this, in time, he found had its drawbacks, and possibly the slower progress of the railway might in the end have been better. Besides the two songs in this collection, he wrote many for Chater's and Ward's Almanacks, being a prize-taker at each. Like Corvan, he was versatile, painting he was clever at, and the wood engravings of Blind Willy, Captain Starkey, Billy Purvis, J. P. Robson, and Geordy Black in this volume are by him. It was to him Joe Wilson said, "Jack, ye can write a sang aboot as weel as me, but yor sangs divn't sing, an' mine dis." This was said at the "Adelaide" in Joe's landlord days, when "Jack" was a regular caller. Dunston, where he lies, and where he was born, is just outside of Gateshead.

HARRY CLASPER AND HIS TESTIMONIAL.

Henry Clasper, famous in Tyneside annals as "Harry Clasper," was born at Dunston-on-the-Tyne, in the year 1812. While young his parents removed to Jarrow, and there young Harry was sent to work in the pits. After a time he returned to Dunston and worked as a cinder burner at the Garsfield coke ovens; and later on, when about twenty years of age, he became a wherryman for the same firm. From this period his aquatic career may be said to have commenced. At this time racing boats were heavy and unshapely, and the mechanical genius of young Harry was at once directed to their improvement, and such genius and perseverance did he bring to his favourite pursuit that it is a question whether his fame as an oarsman, or his renown as the inventor of the modern racing boat is the greatest. One of his earliest attempts at boat building was the *Five Brothers*, which he built at nights, after his day's work was done. In this boat, so appropriately named—the crew consisting of Harry, William, Robert, Edward, and a younger Clasper as coxswain—he for years was victorious at the annual gala on the Tyne, commonly known as Barge Thursday. On December 18, 1844, his victorious career was interrupted, he being defeated by R. Coombes in a skiff race on the Tyne for £180; but in the year following, with his brothers William and Robert, and his uncle, Edward Hawks, he won the champion prize of £100, and for the first time the Championship of the World was wrested from the Thames, one of the defeated crews being Robert Coombes, J. Phelps, T. Goodman, T. Coombes, and D. Coombes (cox.). On the 29th September he defeated Thomas Carroll on the Mersey, and on November 25 defeated W. Pocock on the Tyne, each match being for £200. Early in the following year, 1846, he was defeated on the Tyne by Robert Newell in a match for £200. In 1848, in the celebrated *St. Agnes*, he and his brothers with J. Wilkinson again won the champion prize on the Thames. On the Tyne, in a match for £100, on the first day of 1853, he with his brothers were defeated by the celebrated Elswick Crew— viz., Oliver, Bruce, Winship, and Spoor; these four, known as the Elswick Crew, were famous in the North, and in 1854 won the champion prize on the Thames. On July 22, 1858, Harry won the Championship of Scotland, defeating Robert Campbell on the Clyde in a match for £200, and again defeated him on October 6th, in another match for £200, on Loch Lomond; but on November 9th, 1858, he was beaten by Thomas White, on the Thames, in a match for £200. The races mentioned are but a few of his principal ones; he was engaged in several afterwards, but age began to tell upon him, and meeting younger men success did not crown his efforts, notwithstanding his great abilities as stroke in four-oared craft, in which he was generally victorious. In 1861 an influential committee of gentlemen combined to raise a testimonial to him (to which the song refers). Mr. T. Pringle, in a speech on the occasion, said—"the London watermen at first laughed at his boat, but after the race they quickly copied it, and now the lines of Harry's skiff have been adopted to sea-going clipper ships and screw steamers." The result of their efforts was that a handsome sum was raised, and a house in Scotswood Road was presented to him, where he carried on business as a licensed victualler; eventually he left it and removed to the Tunnel Inn, North Shore, where on Tuesday, July 12, 1870, he died of congestion of the brain, after a few days' illness, aged 58 years. On the Sunday following, July 17, he was buried in Whickham churchyard, an immense concourse of people gathering to witness the funeral, upwards of 100,000 being present at the various parts of the way. The funeral procession (which went part of the way by water), was three hours in reaching Whickham, where in the presence of a great assemblage the body was laid with those of various members of the Clasper family.—(*Note*, 1872.)

TIME's tried a', they say, and they're not se far rang,
Noo she's myed a tyuf trial, she's tested him lang—
Aw meen Harry Clasper, that weel chorised nyem,
For aw'm sure there's nee body can coupl'd wi' sh'em.

    Faithful aud Harry—plucky as ever,
    The still blooming posey iv wor coaly river.

Time's tried a' her dodges, and says he's a' square,
Byeth in mind and in body—he's sound iverywhere;
Nee better man iver tyuek haud iv an oar,
Nor can she fynd fault wiv him when he's ashore.

     Faultless aud Harry, etc.

Tyek him a' in a', as wise Shakespeare says
(Aw've clean forgot where—it's in one of his plays),
Ye'll not find his equal in Tyems or in Tyne,
For in life or in death Harry Clasper 'll shine.

     Matchless aud Harry, etc.

While larrels are still hingin' thick roond his brow,
He's tyen iv his head for to bid ye adieu;
He thinks of the young uns that's fond iv the skull,
And te ge them a chance he's nee mair gan te pull.

     Thoughtful aud Harry, etc.

For the honours he's brought to wor canny Tyne,
Folks talk aboot givin' him something that's fine—
A smart testimonial—an' aw think it's but fair,
For whe can ye think that deserves a one mair?

     Canny aud Harry, etc.

Noo, luk what he's dyun i' the boat-rowin' way,
What fine skiffs he's myed—ay, the best i' the day;
An' luk what a man he's trained intiv his place,—
De ye think there's a chep dur row Chambers a race?

     Wonderful aud Harry, etc.

Let's a' try wor best, noo, and see if we can
Raise somethin' to say that we think him a man,
That's chep iv respect: if to this ye agree,
To show ye are willin' join in chorus wi' me.

     Worthy aud Harry, etc.

If we divn't behave weel tiv him, ye see,
His ghost, when he's deed, 'ill be seen frae the kee

In a skiff, 'side the bridge, 'bout twelve iv'ry neet,
Till the mornin' cock craws, then he'll row oot iv seet.

Spirited Harry, the pride iv wor river,
Yor name it will flourish when ye're gyen for iver.

TAYLOR. *Author's Manuscript,* 1862.

———

THE FLAY CRAW; OR, PEE DEE'S MISHAP.

TUNE—" Warkworth Feast."

JUST as the darkness o' the neet
Began te hide a' things frae seet,
The Skinners' Burn a keel went past,
Wi' sails stritched wide, an' bendin' mast.
Strite as a craw she myed her way,
An' a' the keelmen thowt that they
Frae Leminton wad not be lang,
An' blist the wind that blew se strang.

Rite fal, etc.

But gud luck niver hes much last;
The Meedis Hoose they'd just gyen past,
When round aboot, te thor dismay,
The wind it crept—then slunk away.
As oney keelmen can, they swore,
An' cursed what they praised just afore;
One nipt the poor Pee Dee's bit neck,
Anuther kicked him 'cross the deck.

Rite fal, etc.

'Twas noo pitch dark; an' still thor lay
Two gud lang mile te gan: so they
A' lowered huik wi' little glee,
An' myed the Pee Dee tyek one, tee.
But suen, poor sowl! his huik gat fast
(Mind, game he was—ay, te the last);
He pulled an' twisted, till the keel
Left huik behint—an' lad as weel!

Rite fal, etc.

They niver missed him till close hyem,
Then shooted ov him biv his nyem.
Ne answer com; they sowt aboot,
But gyen he was, withoot a doot.
The skipper shuk his heed, an' said,
" The yung imp's drooned, aw's very flaid;
O' fault wor clear: aw'm shure he had
An angel's life wi' huz, poor lad."

Rite fal, etc.

'Twas summer time, an' suen the morn
Broke on the Pee Dee, a' forlorn;
But sowlger-like, tho' deed almost,
The poor lad stuck true tiv his post.
He watched the shore wi' watery eye
For folks that might be passin' by.
At last wi' joy a man he spied,
Wi' sumthin' hugg'd close tiv his side.

Rite fal, etc.

This chep (it turned out) tell'd had been
That sum big bords had there been seen;
So, wiv his gun, he sowt the spot,
For fond was Clarky iv a shot,
An' hopeful was he 'boot his luck,
Till he saw the Pee Dee on the huik;
Then, " Gox!" he cried, " for me te trick,
They've stuck that flay-craw on the stick!

Rite fal, etc.

" But dash, they'll get thor rags ne mair;
Te blaw them doon aw'll tyek gud care!"
He aimed and pulled—gud luck, a snap—
Just then the laddie waved his cap,

An' shooted, "Hey! hey! canny man!
Be sharp an' save us if ye can:
Aw'm nearly deed—aw'm stiff an' sair!"—
But lang the chep stud gyepin' there.

> Rite fal, etc.

When a' his ghostly doots were gyen,
An' he saw the lad was flesh an' byen,
Sharp as he cud, a boat he sowt,
An' suen ashore Pee Dee he browt.
As weel he might, the lad was pleased
Beyond a' boonds at bein' released.
He thenked the chep, se timely sent,
An', wiv his huik, off hyem he went.

> Rite fal, etc.

TAYLOR.   *Author's Manuscript*, 1872.

This finishes the selection from the dialect poets of the past; many more might have been included had space permitted; two, Dunbar and Cresswell, may be mentioned. William Dunbar, of Wardley Colliery, died young, being only twenty-one at the time of his death, February 23rd, 1874. The following extracts show that a writer of much promise fell in him :—

GEORDY'S PAY.

Mall Johnson last Friday i' wor hoose wis sittin',
    When somehow or other we got on te talk
Aboot the bad pays, an' we talk'd aboot quittin',
    Becaws they wor syun gan te force us te walk.
When Mall puts hor word in, an' says, "Divvent say nowt,
    If ye war i' maw place ye might talk that way:
Te sum that we deal wi' this time aw can pay nowt,
    For twenty-five bob is wor Geordy's pay.

> *Chorus*—Fal de la, etc.

Noo Mally when talkin' she keeps her tung gannin',
    Ye'd sweer that she's not gawn to stop ony mair;
When once she gets started she keeps ye all stannin',
    She'll not even let ye chime in here an' there.
The syem way last Friday she set away fleein',
    Aboot her affairs she kept rattlin' away;
She tell'd us awl things that she intended dein',
    An' hoo she wad mannish wi' Geordy's pay.

NOWT SE QUEER AS FOAKS.

Aw wundor sum's se fond te think that money myeks the man,
It dis for outside wrappin', but much farther cannot gan ;
Aw wundor hoo lang some wad live if money wad buy life,
Aw wundor if they'd like te see the "Last Day" end the strife ;
Aw wundor what myeks woman-folk se fond o' tawkin clash,
Aw wundor some fyuls hes the cheek te try an' cut a dash,
Aw wundor what gud baccy dis, an' hoo se mony smokes ;
But then aw needn't wundor when thor's nowt se queer as foaks.

Chorus.
Eigh sittin' by the fireside crakin' bits o' jokes,
Aw've heerd me awd gran'fethor say "Thor's nowt se queer as foaks."

In the year of his death, 1874, a collection of his songs,
recitations, etc., appeared.

Marshall Cresswell, of Dudley Colliery, one of Chater's
gold medallists, published in 1876 a collection of his songs,
and with them an interesting autobiographic sketch. He
died in 1889.

"Morpeth Lodgings," his prize song, is supposed to be
told by a "drunk and disorderly" who, unable to pay his
fine, had to do his fourteen days.

MORPETH LODGINGS.

Aw cam oot fra the yellhouse, an' lost byeth frinds an' feet,
An' knaw'd nowt till a boy i' bloo picked me up i' the street ;
But for the help he gov us a bit papor browt te say,
He wad meet me at the Moot-hall Coort upon a sartin day.
                        'Twas then aw thowt o' Morpeth.

Aw went just 'caws aw cuddint help't, was tell'd aw had te pay
A fine o' one pund two an' ten, but diddint knaw the way ;
What for bicaws ? aw haddint it, when te maw greet amaze,
They paid me fare te Morpeth, and me fare for fowerteen days.
                        Begims ! aw thowt o' Morpeth.

They sowt us oot a change o' claes, se kind like is thor way,
Tiv a' the guests they there invite is lent a suit o' gray,
Wiv a pair o' handsem stockins ov a' cullors, black te white,
One shoe a half a mile over lang, an' the tuthor full as tite.
                        Oh dear, aw think o' Morpeth,
                        Wi' ne idea o' Morpeth ;
                        Aw nivvor fancied Morpeth,
                        Nor a fortneet's wark for nowt.

LIVING WRITERS.

ROWLAND HARRISON.

ROWLAND HARRISON was born in King William Street, Gateshead, 23rd June, 1841. He first came into public notice as an author and comic singer when about 23 years of age, appearing at the Victoria Music Hall, Newcastle. The engagement proving a success, others followed in quick succession; amongst which might be mentioned, the Oxford Music Hall, Newcastle; the Alhambra, South Shields; and the Wear Music Hall, Sunderland; also at Stockton, Darlington, Glasgow, etc. The following extract from a local paper will show the estimation in which he is held as a popular singer :—

"Mr. Harrison's occasional visits to the 'Wear' are much appreciated, as was proved by the hearty manner in which he was received on making his appearance last evening. He sang, in his own peculiar and pleasing manner, 'The Coal Cartman ; or, I'm going down the Hill,' in which he displayed a great deal of pathetic power ; 'The Drum Major,' and 'The Lass I met at Shields,' in which his rich and peculiar humour found full vent ; and 'The Death of Renforth,' in the course of which the sympathies of the audience were frequently manifested. Mr. Harrison was listened to with great pleasure, and was apparently looked upon as an old friend."

His leading characteristic may be best defined in one word—" broad humour." The facial expression, attitudes, and alternations of voice impart such reality to the character he portrays, that his performances may, with truth, be said

HARRISON AS " GEORDY BLACK."

to be inimitable. The secret of his entertainments being so apparently well studied may arise from the fact, that whilst all the songs he sings are original, the music to them has been composed by himself.

The above appeared in our 1872 edition. Time, which has played havoc with so many since then, has spared Rowley (as he is familiarly called). Since 1872 he has written many songs and played many parts. Landlord of the "Geordy Black," Gateshead, The Commercial Hotel at Winlaton, manager of concert halls of his own at various places; and at Newcastle, at the Temperance Festival on the Moor he has had a large marquee devoted to singing and entertainments. The old concert halls, "The Victoria," "The Oxford," "The Tyne," are gone, but at "The People's Palace" and "The Empire" he still delights his Newcastle admirers. The old band, "Ridley," "Corvan," and "Wilson," all died young. Harrison, who was contemporary with them, survives, a link connecting the past with the present.

Rowland Harrison

GEORDY BLACK.

Maw nyem is Geordy Black, aw'm gettin' varry awd,
    Aw've hewed tons o' coals i' maw time;
An' when aw was yung, aw cud either put or hew—
    Oot o' uther lads aw always tyuk the shine.
Aw'm gannin' doon the hill—aw cannet use the pick,
    The maister hes pity on aud bones;
Aw'm noo on the bank; aw pass maw time away
    Amang the bits o' lads wi' pickin' oot the stones.

Chorus.

  Maw nyem is Geordy Black,—in maw time aw've been a crack,
    Aw've worked byeth i' the Gyuss an' i' the Betty;
  An' the coals upon the Tyne oot o' uthers tyek the shine,
    An' we lick them a' for iron doon at Hawks's.

When aw was a bairn, carried on my fethur's back,
   He wad tyek me away te the pit;
An' gettin' i' the cage, an' gannin' doon belaw,
   'Twas eneuf te myek a yungster tyek a fit.
Te sit an' keep a door, 'midst darkness an' gloom,
   Ay, monny an 'oor be me-sel;
An' hear the awful shots that rummel'd throo the pit,
   An' lumps o' roondy coal cum doon pell-mell.

Aw'll bid ye a' gud neet, it's nearly time te lowse;
   Aw shure aw've tried te please ye ivery one.
Yung lads that's here the neet, mind de the thing that's
     reet—
   In this world that's the way te get on.
But here's success to trade, byeth on the Wear an' Tyne!
   Aw dinnet like te see places slack;
For if wor pit lies idle, ne coal cums te day,
   It greeves the heart o' poor Geordy Black.

    HARRISON.   *Author's Copy,* 1872.

———

JACK SIMPSON'S BAIRN.

JACK SIMPSON'S bairn cried one neet,
   An' Jack cud git ne sleep;
The wife she wander'd oot o' bed,
   An' sighed reet hard an' deep.
She be'sh'd an' ba'd the bairn,
   To soothe its little grief;
An' then she said, "Wey, Jack, ye knaa,
   It's cuttin' its bit teeth!"

Chorus.
Jack says: "Oh dear! will mornin' cum,
   That aw may git te wark!
Aw'd syuner work than lie i' bed,
   Wide-waken i' the dark!"

Jack says: "Noo, Bess, just haud yor tung,
  The bairn's two eer awd;
Ye a'ways say it is its teeth;
  It's ye that myeks 'im bad.
Whativvor he shud cry for,
  Ye give 'im—what a farce!
I'steed o' mendin' wor forst born,
  Why, Bess, ye myek 'im warse!"

Bess torn'd aroond, an' then she said:
  "Jack, patience ye heh nyen;
The bairn he wad be far warse,
  If aw let him alyen.
Aw'd bettor walk aboot the floor,
  For then he finds relief;
He works sair on aboot his mooth,
  A'm shure it is his teeth!"

Jack laid his heed doon i' the bed,
  An' then he fell asleep;
He thowt he saw his bairn an' wife,
  An' sairly she did weep
Te think the fethur was se cross;
  That vishun myed Jack start;
For Jack had sworn before the priest
  Te tyek her tiv his heart.

That mornin', efter Jack got up,
  He torn'd another leaf;
He smiled at Bess, an' kiss'd the bairn
  That had te get its teeth.
Bess a'ways tried to please her man
  As they went on throo life,
An' that shud be the duty
  Of ivv'ry man's gud wife.

HARRISON.   *Author's Manuscript,* 1872.

HEH YE SEEN WOR CUDDY?

"George Guthrie, the author of many clever Tyneside songs, was born in Newcastle, 1842; but in his youth leaving the town, he has principally been employed at Wallsend and Sunderland as a blacksmith. His writings possess considerable merit, and are much admired."

This note was written by Joe Wilson for the 1872 edition. For that edition Joe set nearly all the type, and introduced Guthrie's song, thus showing the estimation in which he held it. Mr. Guthrie is still following his occupation as a blacksmith, down the river.

TUNE—"The King of the Cannibal Islands."

ONE neet, when gannin te the toon,
Aw met a wife called awd Bess Broon,
Wiv a raggy shawl an' durty goon,
　　Sayin' "Heh ye seen wor Cuddy?"
Her fyece was flush'd wi' pashun reed,
Her hair hung lowse aboot her heed;
Half flaid aw was when her aw seed,
Aw thowt it she was mad indeed.
She says, "Noo, Billy, ye mun gan
Wi' me, or else ye are ne man;
For find this beest aw niver can—
　　Aw've gyen an' lost wor Cuddy!"

Chorus.

Fal the dal, the dal, the da,
Fal the dal, the dal, the da,
Fal the dal, the dal, the da,
　　O, heh ye seen wor Cuddy?

"What culler is yor Cuddy, Bess?
Aboot that beest aw heh ne guess,
Maw heed swims roond in dizziness,
　　When aw think aboot yor Cuddy!
Is he broon? or is he grey?
When did ye loss him, d'ye say?
Or, how d'ye knaw he's cum'd this way?
Thor's uther roads the beest might stray.

What towl-gate did yor Cuddy pass?
Ye knaw doon here thor is ne grass;
It myeks ye luik a stupid lass,
    Te cum here te seek yor Cuddy!"

                   Fal the dal, etc.

"He's ginger heckled, Bill, ye knaw,
An' weers his hair reet roond his jaw,
An' a greet big tuft his chin belaw,
    Maw drunken ginger Cuddy!
He's been a trimmer mony a 'eer,
An' a reg'lar wet 'un for his beer,
Ye knaw as weel as me it's here,
Cud Broon, the trimmer, Bill, aw feer.
They get thor munny paid th' neet,
Ye knaw yorsel it's owt but reet,
Aw cannot get a bit te eet
    For that nasty, drunken Cuddy!"

                   Fal the dal, etc.

GUTHRIE.   *Allan's Collection,* 1872.

AW WISH PAY FRIDAY WAD CUM.

The author, a Northumbrian miner, is celebrated as the winner of several prizes for local compositions.—*Note,* 1872. "Pay Friday" won the prize in the *Weekly Chronicle* competition of 1870. To this competition Joe Wilson sent "Wor Geordy's Local Hist'ry." It missed the prize, but got honourable mention. Mr. Anderson still follows his occupation of a miner at Elswick.

                         TUNE—"Aw wish yor Muther wad cum."

'TWAS last pay Friday efterneun aw went an' drew my
    pay,
And, like a fyeul, unto the skeul aw surely bent maw
    way;
Aw suen lost all my money, and aw stood till aw was
    numb,
Then away aw went hyem, and wish'd te mysel that next
    pay Friday wad cum.

When aw went hyem an' teld my wife, she nearly broke
    her heart ;
She says, "Maw lad, such wark as this is sure te myek
    us part ;
Aw wadn't cared if thou'd cum'd drunk wi' strang beer,
    whisky, or rum ;
Aw wad tyen the rest, and dyen my best till another pay
    Friday wad cum.

Then she sobb'd an' sigh'd, and the bairns all cried, and
    aw was varry bad ;
A confused house, and a woman's abuse, is enough to
    drive a man mad ;
Aw knew varry weel what caus'd it all, so aw sat as if aw
    was dumb,
To speak aw was flaid, so nought aw said, but aw wish'd
    pay Friday wad cum.

The grocer, and butcher, and shoemaker tee, they all
    cam' smilin' in,
But what was maw poor wife to dee but tell them she
    had ne tin ?
Their smiles was all torn'd into frowns, it nearly struck
    them dumb ;
And when they went oot, aw couldn't say nought, but
    aw wish'd pay Friday wad cum.

On Saturday morn to be oot o' the way, aw took mysel
    off to the town,
But hevvin' ne brass to set me in, had to wander up and
    down ;
Aw met mony a ken'd feyce in the street, but they all
    appeared to be dumb,
And all the way hyem aw sang te mysel, aw wish pay
    Friday wad cum.

On Sunday morn, when aw got up,—the sun se bright
    did shine,
There was nought provided in the house to break wor
    fast, or dine;
The bairns was crying oot for broth and a greet marrow-
    byen made some;
They myed the house ring wi' tryin' to sing, aw wish pay
    Friday wad cum.

On Monday morn the miller cam' in, my wife began to
    cry,
He said if he couldn't get his tin, he wad surely stop the
    supply!
Aw's proud to remark that aw was at wark, and oot o'
    the way o' the hum,
And all the whole day aw was singing away, aw wish pay
    Friday wad cum.

We had nought to eat, neither taties nor meat, and the
    bairns was crying for breed,
My wife was freetin' away her life, and aw wish'd that aw
    was deed;
My bran new suit had to gan up the spoot, it's a regular
    practice wi' some,
But not a good plan for a hard-working man,—so aw
    wish pay Friday wad cum.

But next pay Friday, aw'll lay my life, aw'll not be such
    a fyeul,
Aw'll tyek my pay strite hyem to my wife, i'stead of
    gannin to skeul,
Aw'll treat mysel wiv a glass of good yell, and my wife
    wiv a good glass of rum,
And aw'll give her the rest, to manage her best, so aw
    wish pay Friday wad cum.

ANDERSON.   *Author's Copy, 1872.*

CUDDY WILLY'S DEETH.

Joshua I. Bagnall, one of the spirited proprietors of the Oxford Music Hall, some years ago published a small volume of Tyneside songs. Several in the collection became popular. Since he undertook the management of the "Oxford" (which he has raised to a high state of popularity), he seems to have confined his efforts solely to the Christmas pantomimes produced at that hall, which are understood to be from his pen.—*Note*, 1872.

The "Oxford" is closed, and has been for years (except as a free and easy), but Mr. Bagnall is still to the fore as landlord of "The Cannon," Low Fell. About local songs, he appears to have written none for many years.

Noo, Cuddy Willy's deed an' gyen,
   Aw's sure ye'll a' be sorry;
He was as hard as ony styen,
   An' a'ways was se merry.
His creels he used te cowp se fast,
   Till he was nearly silly;
But deeth hes tyun him off at last,
   Poor, harmless Cuddy Willy!

A fiddle Willy a'ways had,
   He used te play se bonny;
For fiddlin' Willy was the lad—
   An' what was varry funny,
A bit o' wood, tied up wi' twine,
   Wad please a Sandgate filly,
A tune he then wad play se fine,
   Wad cliver Cuddy Willy!

The blagaird lads upon the Kee,
   They used te treat him cruel:
They'd trip him oot just for a spree,
   An' hurt me canny jewel.
But, man alive! aw've seen him rowl
   Till he was soft as jilly,
An' get up a' reet, upon my sowl!
   Wad bonny Cuddy Willy!

A crust o' breed, an' drink o' beer,
  If he cud oney get, man;
An' if he gat ne better cheer,
  He nivver used te fret, man.
A bite o' tripe, or bacon raw—
  Stuff that wad nearly kill 'e—
He'd eat up crabs, an' shells, an' a',
  Wad bonny Cuddy Willy.

The fishwives a' poor Billy knew,
  They a' ca'd him thor pet, man;
O' wilks they wad gie him a few,
  Or a share or two o' skyet, man.
Poor Bill was nivver at a loss
  Te fill his hungry belly;
He'd drink aud milk at Sandgate cross,
  Wad canny Cuddy Willy

In jail Will offen used te be
  For sleepin' 'mang the cinders,
Or bein' drunk upon the Kee,
  An' smashin' folks's winders;
Or lyin' doon amang the durt
  Till he was ca'd an' chilly;
But still he did the folks ne hurt,—
  Poor, canny Cuddy Willy!

But iverythiag cums tiv an end,
  An' so did bonny Will, man:
Ne mair happy days he'll spend:
  He noo is lyin' still, man.

He nivver did ne body harm,
    For a' he was se silly ;
The toon seems noo te want a charm
    Since it lost poor Cuddy Willy !

BAGNALL.   "*Songs of the Tyne*," 1850.

William Maclachlan, better known as "Cuddy Willy," was a well-known eccentric of Newcastle. For years he wandered the streets without hat or shoes, and in clothes of the scantiest and most tattered description. He contrived to live by frequenting public-houses, and by playing his fiddle in the streets. His fiddle was a curiosity, made by himself : it was simply a flat piece of wood, on which he tied a few pieces of string. He was addicted to drink ; and his death was caused by some parties most shamefully, at a public-house, giving him brandy as long as he would drink it. The result was, he drank to such an excess that he died from the effects. His death took place September 27th, 1847.

THE TYNE EXILE'S LAMENT.

Mr. Crawhall, in his quaintly illustrated "Beuk o' Newcassel Sangs by deceased writers," includes "The Tyne Exile's Lament." Everything, it is said, comes to the man that waits, but in this instance Mr. Crawhall has not waited long enough : the writer is still alive.

TUNE—"Banks o' the Dee."

I SIT by the side of the broad rolling river,
    That sparkles along on its way to the sea ;
But my thoughts fly again o'er the wide heaving main
    To the home of my childhood so happy and free ;
The sun with rare splendour may brighten each scene,
    All nature in hues the most gorgeous may shine,
But all is in vain the fond wish to restrain,
    I wish I were again on the Banks of the Tyne.

How clearly before me again each bright scene
    Of my childhood appears to my sad longing eye,
The wild rugged banks where so often I've played,
    And listened the river roll murmuring by ;

Though brighter the river that rolls at my feet,
    And fairer the banks where I sadly recline,
All, all, I'd resign for the bleak hills of mine,
    Oh! I wish I were again on the Banks of the Tyne.

Oh fortune! befriend me, oh! list to the prayer ·
    Of the exile who mourns on a far foreign shore,
If here I must die 'neath the fierce blazing sky,
    And the home of my youth I must never see more ;
Take me far, far from here in my still narrow bier,
    And lay me where lie all the past race of mine,
With them would I lie where the river rolls by,
    On the banks dearly loved of my own native Tyne.

ANONYMOUS.   *Author's Manuscript*, 1862.

THE BOBBIES AN' THE DOGS.

In 1860 the police had orders to secure all stray dogs. To assist them in this rather difficult operation each policeman had a stick, with a wire noose at the end. The dogs, if not claimed within a given time, were destroyed. Much amusement was caused by the respective dodging of the dogs and the bobbies—the one to catch, and the other not to be caught.

TUNE—"Aud Cappy."

SINCE the days o' "Aud Cappy" thor's not been sic stor,
In Newcassel thor niver was sic like before ;
The poor dogs are howlin' an' madly rush by,
An' Bobbies, like leetnin', start off in full cry.

        There's a dog, Bobby! after him, Bobby !
        Dog hunting's the game—tallio! tallio!

Noo, the cause of a' this is wor Council's fine plan,
That a' dogs strowlin' lowse to the station mun gan ;
An' te catch them se cliver each Bob hes a stick,
Wiv a wire at the end for to gie them a click.

           There's a dog, Bobby, etc.

One day, beside Mackey's, a Bobby luk'd sly,
On a lost lukin' bull-dog he'd just clapt his eye :
Thinks he, Ye've ne maister, yor case is a' reet,
Yor byuk'd for a borth at the Manors this neet.

> There's a dog, Bobby, etc.

So he edged te the dog, myed a cast wiv his stick,
But his aim wasn't gud, or the dog wes ower quick ;
For the dog sav'd his neck, catch'd the wire iv his jaw,
An' then tugged it amain, an' the Bobby an' a'.

> There's a dog, Bobby, etc.

Noo, the end of the sport was, the wire, wiv a crack,
Snapt in two, an' the Bobby went flat on his back ;
But he up in a rage, on the dog myed a spring,
An' he color'd him fast as the bairns did sing,

> There's a dog, Bobby, etc.

Wi' the dog in his airms, he thowt a' was won,
When a Pitman came runnin'—"What hes maw dog
    duen ?
He's an aud un—near blind—an' he quietly follis "—
Shouts X21, " He's resisted the pollis ! "

> There's a dog, Bobby, etc.

" An' wise was the beest, so ye'd best let him be ;
Maw nyem's on his collor—aw pay for him, tee,
Ye've had eneuf sport, noo, se let the dog gan ; "—
An' the Bobby, bein' wise, thowt it was the best plan.

> There's a dog, Bobby, etc.

A' ye that hes dogs, noo, ye'd better luk oot ;
Beware hoo ye let them gan strowlin' aboot.
Dog hunting's the gam' noo all ower the toon,
An' X21 laffs when he grabbs yor half-crown.

There's a dog, Bobby, etc.

ANONYMOUS.   *Author's Manuscript,* 1862.

ROBERT CHAMBERS.

ROBERT CHAMBERS, the renowned aquatic champion of the
Tyne and Thames, whose sterling integrity won for him
the happy distinction of " Honest Bob," was born at St.
Anthony's, on the 14th of June 1831.   His earlier years were
spent at Hawks's, in
whose extensive iron-
works on the Tyne he
worked his way up until
he reached the position
of a puddler. Having a
fancy for the water, and
delighting in rowing, he
attracted the attention of
Harry Clasper, who saw,
in his well-built, strong,
and muscular form, the
elements of a first-class
oarsman ; he standing
about five feet ten inches,
and in rowing generally
weighed   about   11½
stones.   His after career,
under the guidance of
Clasper,   was   unparal-

leled.   He rowed in 101 races, winning 89 times ; he
started 45 times in skiffs, and won 34 times ; he took part
in 45 four-oared races, and won 40 ; he rowed in 19 pair
contests, and won 15.   For six years he held the championship of the Thames, and was the first Tyneside oarsman that

ever won the proud title of the "Champion of the World."
Early in 1868 his health began to fail; consumption, induced
probably by the incessant training he underwent for his
various matches, attacked him, and, after a brief illness, he
died at St. Anthony's on the 4th of June 1868, in his thirty-
seventh year.

BOB CHAMBERS.

Written on the occasion of the great scullers' race for the championship
of the world, between Robert Chambers, of Newcastle, and Richard
A. W. Green, of Australia, June 16th, 1863. Chambers won easily by a
quarter of a mile.

TUNE—"Kiss me quick and go."

Aw left Bill Blakey's late last neet,
    An' weary wandered hyem,
Fair tired at last te hear the noise,
    The cry was still the syem—
It's two te one aw'll lay on Bob,
    Wor Tyneside lad for iver,
He's champion o' the saucy Tyems
    And Tyneside's Coaly River.

Chorus—It's two te one, etc.

When hyem aw reached aw off te bed,
    An' funny though 'twad seem,
Nee suener doon aw'd laid me heed
    Then aw'd this queerish dream :
Aw thowt aw stood in London toon,
    Wi' thoosands croodin' near,
And Bob and Green were in their skiffs,
    When oot a chep bawls clear—

It's two te one, etc.

The start was myed, away they went,
  Byeth strove wi' might and main,
But Greeny, lad, had little chance,
  For Bob began te gain ;
And as he pulled his famous stroke,
  The Cockneys a' luk'd queer,
But uz Tynesiders cheered him on,
  An' shooted far near—
                    It's two te one, etc.

The race went on, Green struggled game ;
  But, hoots, it waddent dee,
The Princess Alexandra
  Through the watter fair did flee ;
And Bob cam' in the winner,
  As he's always dyun before,
And as wor lads haul'd in the brass,
  We one and all did roar—

                    It's two te one, etc.

Now half the world they've travell'd ower
  Te lay wor Tyneside law,
The 'tother half they now may try,
  And still we'll keep the craw.
Aw says aw'll lay me brass on Bob,
  And work the winnin' seam.
·Just then aw wakened wiv a start,
  And fund 'twas all a dream.

          But still aw'll lay me brass on Bob, etc.

ANONYMOUS.   *Author's Manuscript, 1863.*

———

34

RICHARD OLIVER HESLOP,

WHO is widely known in connection with "Northumberland Words," appears here as a writer of Tyneside Songs and Readings. These—probably thrown off as a relaxation from

From a Photo by James Bacon.

the labours of his greater work —have become popular, and for some time have been out of print. "Northumberland Words," Mr. Heslop's work, which week by week for years has been appearing in the *Chronicle*, has been happily described as a "monumental work." It must have been to its author a work entailing toil and application of no ordinary kind, only possible, perhaps, as "a labour of love." This literary work Mr. Heslop has contrived to find time for, while carrying on a large business as an iron merchant; business and literary work combined must have made him a busy man. A native of Newcastle, an old Grammar School boy, Mr. Heslop was born on March 14th, 1842. In the prime of life, with his great work half accomplished, there seems every probability of his carrying it successfully through, and so completing his dictionary of Northumberland words, past and present.

HOWDON FOR JARROW.

TUNE—"Chapter of Donkeys."

O, ye taak aboot travels an' voyages far,
But thor's few beats the trip fre' the toon te the bar,
As ye gan doon te Tinmuth ye'll hear the chep shoot,—
" Here's Howdon for Jarrow, maa hinnies loup oot !

Chorus.
Howdon for Jarrow, Howdon for Jarrow,
Howdon for Jarrow, maa hinnies loup oot ! "

When yen hes been doon bi' the side o' the Tyne,
An' seen all the smoke an' the chimlies se fine,
There's mony a voice that is welcome nee doot,
But the bonniest soond that Aa knaa is " Loup oot !

Howdon for Jarrow, Howdon for Jarrow,
Howdon for Jarrow, maa hinnies loup oot ! "

Sin' Aa knew the banks o' wor aan bonny river,
There's been changes gawn on, an' there's noo mair nor iver;
But the finest ov aa', barrin' change o' the wind,
Is when the soft voice caalls, an' then ye aal find,

" Ye mun change here for Jarrow, Howdon for Jarrow,
Howdow for Jarrow, maa hinnies loup oot ! "

There's chemicals, copper, coals, clarts, coke, an' stone,
Iron ships, wooden tugs, salt, an' sawdust, an' bone,
Manure, an' steam ingins, bar iron, an' vitr'ol,
Grunstans an' puddlers (Aa like to be litt'ral),

At Howdon for Jarrow. Howdon for Jarrow,
Howdon for Jarrow, maa hinnies loup oot !

Besides, on wor river we hev the big dredgers
That howks oot the muck, man, Aa's sure we're nee
        fledgers,
An' then the greet hopper works like a wheelbarrow—
Ye'll see'd if ye come doon te Howdon for Jarrow.

Howdon for Jarrow, Howdon for Jarrow,
Howdon for Jarrow, maa hinnies loup oot !

Aa yence wis at London, and h'ard a chep shoot,
"Yor tickets!" Aa "Howdon for Jarrow!" caaled oot;
He leuked se teun back that, ses Aa te me marrow,
"Here's a chep, mun, that dissent knaa Howdon for
    Jarrow!"

> Howdon for Jarrow, Howdon for Jarrow,
> Howdon for Jarrow, maa hinnies loup oot!

Thor's Jack Scott, the puddler (just hear what a caaker),
Uphads that there surely is nee place like Waaker;
But Aa've elways thowt, for't's the place Aa hev grow'd in,
Yen may range thro' the world, but thor's nee place
    like Howdon!

> Howdon for Jarrow, Howdon for Jarrow,
> Howdon for Jarrow, maa hinnies loup oot!

HESLOP.   *Author's Edition*, 1879.

NEWCASTLE TOON NEE MAIR.

Dr. Ernest Wilberforce, the first Bishop of Newcastle, consecrated St.
James' Day, 1882.

TUNE—"Nee good luck aboot the hoose."

Wiv aal the "toon improvement" hash,
    New fangles yit they'll fish up;
So noo they've fund, wi' aal thor clash,
    The Toon mun he' a Bishop.
They say he'll he' te weer white goons,
    An' laan sleeves, leuk ye there!
But when he comes they say the Toon's
    Newcastle Toon nee mair!

Chorus.

> We like the soon' o' "Canny Toon."
>   We like wor aad Toon sair;
> But ivverything is upside doon,
>   Newcastle Toon nee mair!

Aad Nichol's chorch, an' steeple tee,
  The clock feyce, an' the Beadrel,
They've set the heyl consarn agee,
  An caal it noo "cathedraL"
Thor'll be a Dean an' Chapter seun,
  Te put the job aal square,
We'll not dar say, when aal is deun,
  Newcastle Toon nee mair!
Chorus.

Hoo can the Bishop he' the flum
  Te caal the pleyce a City?
The Toon's been Toon afore he cum;
  Te change it mair's the pity!
He mevvies thinks wor nowt but cloons,
  An' he' nee wit te spare,
But what's the odds? for O, wor Toon's
  Newcastle Toon nee mair!
Chorus.

"Maa fellow Toonsmen," noo fareweel,
  Maa heed is teum, nee wit is in,
Thor's nowther sense, nor mense, nor feel
  In "Hum—maa fellow citizen!"
For aa this fancy change o' soon'
  Aa waddent hev a care,
But, O me lads, it's wae! the Toon,
  The canny Toon's nee mair!
Chorus.

HESLOP.   ————   *Broadsheet, 1882.*

A TOW FOR NOWT.

OH, wor cargo we'd got oot, away doon at Whitehill Spoot;
But the wind an' tide wis both on them contrairy, O!
An' it seemed we'd hae te lie till the tide wis comin' high,
So the keel we moored, an' leuked aboot se wary, O.
Chorus.
So the keel we moored, etc.

Just then, te wor delight, a tugboat hove i' sight,
An' backed astarn close by where we wor stannin', O.
Ses aa, noo aa'l accost hor! so aa hailed, " Hey, Mistor
    Forster,
Wad ye gie's a tow as far up as wo'r gannin', O ? "

Then the tugboat-maistor torned, an' he leuked, an' kinda
    gorned,
Ses he, " Hoo dis thoo knaa they caal me Forster, O ? "
" Man," ses aa, " yor dad afore wis a chep aa did adore,
An' yo'r just like him, maa canny Mistor Forster, O."

Iv a frindly kind o' way, aa got a tow that day ;
An' off we set, wi' nowt at aal te cost hor, O.
Aa bargaint wivoot doot, as aa past wor towlin' oot,
" At the Mushroom hoy hor off, please Mistor Forster, O."

So we cam' up spankin' fine, an' past aal on the Tyne—
Sic a tow for nowt aa waddent then he lost hor, O.
An' we just hed past The Geuse, an' aa thowt o' gettin'
    lowse ;
So, ses aa, " Just hoy hor off, please Mistor Forster, O."

Wi' the tiller 'tween his legs, just like twee wooden pegs,
He nivvor torned, but oney went the faster, O.
Aa shoots oot, " Here we are, yor gannin' ower far ;
Aa telt ye 'twas the Mushroom, Mistor Forster, O ! "

What wis deein noo wis clear, so aa couldn't help but
    sweer.
" Yo'r a bad 'un, yo'r as bad as ony coster, O !
An' so wis yor aad dad—gosh, he wis just as bad !
Where the smash, man, are ye towin's te, ye Forster, O ? "

But it aal wis o' nee use, owther sweerin' or abuse;
For a joke there Forster steud as deef as dummy, O;
An' he waddent hoy us free till past Newcastle Quay,
So, thinks aa, *a tow for nowt* is sometimes rummy, O!

HESLOP.   "*Newcastle Weekly Chronicle,*" 1882.

THE SINGIN'-HINNEY.

TUNE—"The One-Horse Shay."

SIT doon, noo, man alive!
Te tell ye aa'll contrive
O' the finest thing the worl' hes ivver gin ye, O.
It's not fine claes nor drink,
Nor owt 'at ye can think,
Can had a cannle up ti singin'-hinney, O.
    Sing hi, the Puddin' Chare an' Elwick's lonnin', O!

Newcassel's fame 'ill bide
Lang as its coaly tide;
But it winnet rest on what makes sic a shinney, O.
The pride o' a' the North
Is 'cas it forst ga' borth
To the greetest charm o' life—a singin'-hinney, O.
    Sing hi, the Spital Tongues an' Javel Groupe, hi O!

Fre the day we forst draa breeth
To the day 'at brings wor deeth,
Fre the forst day ony on us ken'd wor minnie, O,
We gan on step bi step,
An' each gaady day is kep,
Wiv a cheer 'at's elways crooned wi' singin'-hinney O!
    Sing hi, for Denton Chare an' the Big Markit, O!

Wor weddin' feast wis spreed
Wi' menseful meat an' breed,
An' ivverything wis theer for kith an' kin, ye O !
As aa sat doon wi' me bride,
Aa wad say aa felt a pride
Te hear them praise her aan-made singin'-hinney, O.
    Sing hi, the Bottle Bank, an' the Team-Gut, hi O!

The day the bairn wis born
Wis a snaay New Eer's morn ;
Se caad yee'd scarsly feel yorsel' or fin', ye O !
But we put the gordle on
The rousin' fire upon,
An' we whistled as we baked wor singin'-hinney, O.
    Sing hi, the Dog-Lowp Stairs an' the Darn Cruck, hi O !

At christnen, tee, se fine,
Another wife an' mine
Gans oot an' takes the bairn, see spick an' spinney, O.
Wi' spice cake an' wi' salt,
The forst they met te halt,
An' gar him stan' an' tyest wor singin'-hinney, O.
    Sing hi, the Friars' Geuse an' the Aad-Faad, hi O !

An' se on, day bi day,
As we trudge alang life's way,
We've troubles roond—like stoor—eneuf te blin' ye, O !
But whiles thor comes a stop,
An' wor tools we then can drop,
Te gan hyem, lads, an' hev a singin'-hinny, O.
    Sing hi, the Close, Waal-Knowl, an' the Cut Bank,
        hi O!

An' when we can enjoy,
Amang wor hivvey 'ploy,
A day 'at brings huz not a single whinney, O;
Let's elwis drop wor cares,
An' set worsels, for fairs,
Te celebrate it wiv a singin'-hinney, O!
Sing hi, the Mushroom, Forth, an' Heed o' Side, hi O!

HESLOP. *"Newcastle Weekly Chronicle,"* 1885.

———

THE TYNESIDE CHORUS.

HADAWAY, Harry! Hadaway, Harry!
Them wis the days on wor canny aad Tyne!
Clasper afore him could ivverything carry,
Back'd bi the cheer 'at we hard lang sin syne.
Hadaway, Harry, lad! Hadaway, Harry!
Pull, like a good 'un, through storm or through
shine.
Gan on, wor canny lad—Hadaway, Harry!
Come te the front for the sake iv aad Tyne.

Where's like Tyneside cheps for warkin or owt?
Buffin away, heart an' sowl like te teer;
Hewin' or puddlin', thor beaten bi nowt,
Their owerword's still "How there, lads, what cheer?"
Hadaway, Harry, lad—Hadaway, Harry!
Afloat or ashore, or doon the coal mine;
Gan on, maa canny lads, Hadaway, Harry!
Teuf 'uns for wark is the lads iv aad Tyne!

Doon the black pit shaft thor's brave lads at wark;
Doon dunny Tyneside the fornaces lowe;
Workers is busy, through dayleet an' dark,
Singin', me hearties, though tired they may grow.

Hadaway, Harry, lads, Hadaway, Harry!
  Cheery, me marrows, an' nivvor a whine;
Gan on, maa canny lads, Hadaway, Harry!
  Gan like th' aad 'un for pride o' the Tyne.

'Way ower the seas wor Tyneside lads afloat,
  Brave as thor fethors, still fight wi' the storm.
Nee paril flays them; thor prood o' thor boat,
  An' marrily cheer as they show the aad form.
    Hadaway, Harry, lads, Hadaway, Harry!
      Still te the fore; let yor hearts nivvor crine.
    Gan on, maa canny lads, Hadaway, Harry!
      Where is thor braver nor crews fre the Tyne?

So, noo, canny cheps, let's nivvor forget,
  I' life's course reet on, come good or bad luck,
Whativvor we dee, wor motto be yet,
  Like aad Harry Clasper, the pictur o' pluck—
    Hadaway, Harry, lad, Hadaway, Harry!
      Pull like a good 'un, through storm or through
        shine,
    Gan on, wor canny lad, Hadaway, Harry!
      Come to the front for the sake iv aad Tyne.

HESLOP.   "*Newcastle Weekly Chronicle,*" 1886.

HIS OTHER EYE.

I MET him on board a steamboat. There was a
comical look about his face which struck me, and I was
glad to find an empty seat alongside him, where I quietly
sat down. He was filling a broken and blackened cutty
pipe with some tobacco, which seemed to need a deal of
work before it could be got ready. It was carefully cut
up with a jack-knife; then it was rubbed in the palms of
his hands; and finally it was thrust home with the fore-
finger. He looked all the time as if he were talking

inwardly without knowing it, and yet were fully busied with the work on hand. The face betokened a mind wandering in dreamy thoughtland, whilst the eye—his own eye—stared with a sternly fixed purpose upon the pipe. Here was the face of a philosopher, but with it an absurd intenseness which gave the comical look I first noticed in him.

His other eye was covered with a leather patch—the same patch which gives the evil look to the comrade of the idle apprentice in Hogarth. A small half-round patch of black, covering a sightless socket, and held on by two straps passing aslant round the head.

His face otherwise was like that of a canny man, and, as I had expected, he soon saluted me by saying, "It's been a fine day, Mister!" This led on to further talk between us, and the man's confidence grew when he found he had a ready listener. So it became easy to lead him on to speak of his own history.

I found that my friend had been a pitman; that whilst at work in the Billybottom Pit he had had an eye destroyed. The accident caused him great suffering and laid him up for months. Thus his means were clean gone, and his handicraft became an impossible thing for him hereafter. Besides this, the horror of the wolf at the door was aggravated by the unsightly look of the face with the lost eye. His pressing need, however, soon stirred him in a new effort to "pick up a canny bit living," and in this his mates helped him in their best ways. Amongst other devices they clubbed together funds to buy him an artificial eye, and this done, he was told to go to a certain shop in Newcastle to get his new eye fitted in.

"Wey," said he, continuing, "Aa gets the eye putten in, an' the chep i' the shop haads up a leukin' glass. Aa wondered at forst whe's portrait it wes he wis haddin' up. True as Aa's a leevin' man, Aa duddent ken mesel, but Aa kinda cam forrad a bit, an' begox, ses Aa, *it's me.* Man, but that's clivvor noo, ses Aa—twee as good eyes as ivver man had iv his heed! Forst Aa keeked this way, then Aa keeked that way, then Aa torn'd half roond an' tries to keek ower me showlder. Aa saa mesel i' the glass aa wayses, fore ways, side ways, hint ways. They wor that beyth alike, them twee eyes, 'at ye waddent he' kenned yen fre the tother. Then Aa leuks strait forenenst us, an' Aa covers up me good aad eye wi' the flat o' me hand, an' Aa glowers hard at the man wi' the new eye 'at he'd putten in; but, man alive! Aa fund 'at when Aa shut up me good aad blinker Aa could see nowt w' the new yen. That's a queer 'un, ses Aa. So Aa oppened me gud eye ageyn an' Aa could see mesel i' the glass leukin clivvor, an' reet as owt. Beyth eyes leuked the yen better nor the tother. Ses Aa, mum! ses Aa, had on a bit. She mebbe oney wants to be wrout a bit, so Aa sayed nee mair but cam oot an' gans up Grey Street.

"Aa med strait ower to the bonny shop set oot wi' picturs an' potographs an' cum close up to the window, lays the flat hand ower me good eye ageyn an' tried to keek wi' the new yen. Nee use, hoosivver, Aa wis blinnd as a bat. Thinks Aaa, it's owther he hesn't getten her reet put in or she's nobbut a dummy eye he's putten on to me. Ye see Aa'd nivver bowt a thing o' the kind afore, an' nee wonder then if Aa wis teun in.

"We'll gi'd a fair try, though, thinks Aa, an' away ower the street Aa gans—cuttin' an' lowpin' i' front o' the horses like a geuse nicked i' the heed—till Aa comes to the shop that hes the big clock abeun the door, an' aa the watches an' clocks an' greet plates an' dishes nowt but solid gowld. (Hinnies, what a things is i' that shop!) Noo, ses Aa, for me new peeper!—an' Aa made a paas. Gosh cab! ses Aa, when Aa'd shutten up me aad goggle an' put all my full seet on to the new eye—Aa's just i' the dark as ivver. She *mun* be a bad'n this new blinker —Aa canna see nowt wid. An' just when the leet flashed as Aa oppened me good eye ageyn, it cam ower me 'at the man hed played off on me a second-hand eye oot o' a blamed waax work. Aa'll gan reet back an' hev her swapped for a good yen.

"So Aa comes back to the man, an' waaks strait up to where he steud ahint his coonter.

"'Thor's summat wrang aboot this eye ye've putten in,' ses Aa; 'an' Aa mun tell ye 'at Aa notished it afore Aa went oot forst, but Aa thout it mun be 'at Aa wasn't reet hanted wid, and hadn't getten the way on't. When Aa fund 'at wiv aal me gornin' and glowerin' Aa wis still blinnd o' yen eye, ses Aa to mesel', it mun be wrang putten in; but efter seein' me feyce deflected iv a shop window, ses Aa, smash, man, ses Aa, it's the eye oot o' an aad waaxwork. Ye see, Aa's plain-spoken wi' ye, sor, 'cas ye leuk like a canny chep (ses Aa ti the shopman). But ye see, Aa mun he'd swapped for a good yen, 'cas Aa can see nee mair wid nor nowt.'

"That chep stared at me as if he'd been struck aal iv a heap. Then he sets his sel back—still glowerin' at me —as if he wis teun bad iv a suddent—an' then he laft an' laft till Aa gat reed i' th' feyce. But as he wis a plisent chep, he torned aal at yence quite kind like, and ses—

"'As it's artificial, you cannot expect to see with it.'

"'Yartifeecial,' ses Aa; 'Aa thowt it wis glass—ony-way ye'll he' to fix in yen 'at Aa can see wi'—'cas this is nee use. Aa might as tight deun wivoot an eye as hev what ye caal a yartifeecial.'

"'Stay till I show you,' ses the shopman. 'Now, sir, I remove your eye—look at yourself in the glass. I replace your eye—look now at your personal appear-ance.' There he haads up the glass ageyn.

"'At me *parsonal appearance*,' ses Aa; 'dee ye mean at me yartifeecial?'

"They've fine names for aa things nooadays, as the pig sayed when he corled his *narrative*. An' so this pattent side leet 'at Aa getten' put inte me heed's like the rest. Me glass eye, Begox! Aa wis made up aboot gettin't when Aa forst com' in to get fitted on. But noo, hinnies, ay, Aa did feel a prood man yenoo to taak aboot me yartifeecial or me parsonal appearance. Aa might see through'd or Aa might not see through'd; me blinnd blinker might be blinnd as blazes; nivvor mind, Aa'd getten a *yartifeecial*—a parsonal appearance. Glass eye, Becrikes! Divvent taak to me!

"At that time Aa knew nee mair nor Aa's tellin' ye. An' hoo mony men is thor 'at dissent yen time or other get thor heed torned wi' dandy words? Aa mind when they'd getten the brass clubbed 'n bowt the cork leg for Jackey Humble—Jackey elways caad it ' the yartifeecial limb.' He waddent hear tell o' 'cork leg.' Aa fund oot then 'at the chep i' the shop'd been putten't on to *him tee*.

"But Aa's forgettin'. When Aa cum heym sic a stoor wis on. Aa lifted the sneck an' waaked reet in, sits doon, thraws me heed weel back, leuks strait inte the wife's feyce, an' ses Aa—'Noo, hinney, what dis thoo think o' me new parsonal appearance?'

"'Wey, lad,' ses she, 'thoo leuks as brisk as a lop an' mair nor ten 'eers young'r wi' tha new glass eye.'

"'Me yartifeecial,' ses Aa, drawin' mesel up, 'or me parsonal appearance, if thoo likes, but ye munna caa'd a glass eye.'

"'Aa canna get ma mooth roond thor fine words,' ses she; 'but, nivvor mind, lad, thoo's browt a new leet inte the hoose, an' here's the bairns aa'sittin' up waitin' for thor dad.'

"Sec a dance them bairns led thor fethor that neet; thor wis nee getten' them te bed. They wad he'd in, an' they wad he'd oot, an' they wad see'd foreside, an' they wad see'd backside, an' little Bobby wanted to touch't, but, ses Aa, 'Hands off,' ses Aa', an' a shoved it in tiv its pleyce ageyn, quick.

"'Oh, fethor, thoo's squintin'!' ses Bobby.

"'Aa'll yark tha hide, thoo young brat, thoo.' An' Aa myeks a dab at the bit imp, and clears aa off te bed iv a jiffey.'

"Sure eneuff Aa hed shoved it in aal' askew, an' when Aa torned roond te the wife she sniggered an' laft, an' as Aa wis iv a kind o' a tift, Aa ses, 'Aa cum past folk bi' the hundreds i' Newcastle the day, but thoo's the forst 'at's laft at me parsonal appearance!'

"'Divvent be vext, hinney,' ses she, 'sit thee ways doon and he' thee pipe.'

" ' It's aal me eye ! ' ses Aa, an' Aa fund Aa wis getten grumpy, but Aa cruicked me houghs on the cracket, an' the bit blast o' baccy gat me inte better fettle agyen.

" By-m-by, Aa'd getten canny inte the hant o' weerin' me new blinker, an' Aa hadded up me heed, when the mates com by wiv a ' How there ! ' and Aa gis them a ' What cheer, there ? ' wiv a air 'at could oney be putten' on biv a chep wiv a parsonal appearance. But nivver mind that ! Them bairns o' mine's hemps ; tho'r fair deevils wiv thor skylarking, an' yen neet we'd tusseled an' larked till Aa wis sair wi' laffin' an' tewed to deed wi' them climmin aboot. Aa wis glad when the wife puts the supper breed on the teyble, an' Aa teuk the chance to sit doon on me hunkers to leet me pipe. Just as Aa puts me heed doon, Odsmash ! oot drops me pattent goggle. Flap doon it went on the hearth steyn, an' cracked aal to bits. Aa've getten mony a gliff i' maa lifetime, but nivver owt like this. A caad sweet wis ower me heyl body, an' aa felt like a lifelike corp. That put me pipe oot, Aa can tell ye. But nivver mind that ! Doon Aa gans on me marrow byens, an' picks up ivvery bit, an' lays them oot on a newspaper. The fine new eye wis nowt noo but a heap o' bits o' boodies. The wife skriked oot an' myest teuk a fit at sic a mishap. Noo or nivver ; Aa mun play the man, hoosivver, when Aa fund she wis warse putten aboot nor me, an', ses Aa —' Hoots, hinney ! Had thee gob. Aa can sewer*ly* dee wi' me game eye as she is. Efter aal, Aa nivver could *see* nee better wi' this pattent eye.'

" ' It's thee parsonal appearance 'at's brokken', ses the wife, an' she fair blaired and cried agyen.

" ' See'st tha, hinney,' ses Aa, ' Aa he'd aal gethered up i' the paper here, an' Aal seun get her fettled.'

" Neist mornin' Aa gans to the cobbler an' gets a bit o' his waax, waps't up, an' puts't i' me pocket, an' that varra neet Aa sweeted ower them bits o' boodies till Aa gets them aal clagged t'gither agyen wi' the cobbler's waax. It teuk oors te dee efter the bairns wis abed, but Aa dud it, an' when Aa puts't in agyen neebody wad knaan nowt.

"This wis aal weel eneuf; but a few neets efter this, when Aa com in Aa could see 'at the wife wis wrowt sair —what wi' mindin' the bit shop 'at we hed, and hevin' te bake mair breed for the shop than common that day, forby hevin' a lairge brewing o' pop to watch, not to speak o' them hemps o' bairns gaan oot an' in, and besides the babby nivver oot o' her airm wi' the bits o' tuttles fashn't. But nivver mind that! Aa'd puttin the bit horse an' cairt in, coonted ower the brass 'at Aa'd tyen tha' day, getten me bit bait—an' Aa tyecks had o' the bairn oot o' the wife's airms an' claps mesel doon bi' the fireside. Aa mun he' sitten rether close up te the fire— cuddlin' and crooin' ower the bairn, but Aa nivver knaas till oot drops me yartifeecial, bit bi' bit. The waax hed melted.

"'Smash, man!' ses Aa, 'she's deun noo.' Aa puts the bairn doon quietly i' the credle an' scraffles amang the cinders till Aa'd getten howcked oot yen an' another o' the bits. What a seet! The bits wis aal clagged wi' the soft waax, an' stuck wi' cinders an' dort. Aa wis just gaan te hoy them inte the fire when the biggest bit torned ower i' me hand. It wis the star o' me aan eye! It leuked me strait i' the feyce as much as to say—'Aa isn't like the stang o' an aad teuth 'at ye wad burn—Aa's pairt o' yorsel.' Aa thowt it leuked reet through me an' kend mair aboot me nor Aa kend mesel. Aa knaa what conscience is, an', man alive! that glazy bit o' boody wis me conscience. It wis mesel leukin at mesel.

"Neyn o' yor cobbler's waax nee mair. Aal buy a stick o' reed sealin' waax, an' fettle her fair this time. An' so Aa did!

"Ye see Aa've getten a leather patch o' me eye yenoo, but Aa hev me other eye i' me pocket wapped up i' shammy leather. It's here! Aa he' to be varry canny wid. O' war days Aa put on me leather patch an' keeps me yartifeecial i' me pocket. O' Sundays an' o' boat-race days Aa puts me pattent keeker iv her pleyce, an' then, man, ye should see me parsonal appearance. Ye waddent knaa me wi' *me other eye.*"

HESLOP.   *Author's Edition,* 1880.

JOHN ATLANTIC STEPHENSON.

BORN in "Mid-Atlantic" on Waterloo Day, 1829, Mr. Stephenson owes his second Christian name to that circumstance. His father—well known some seventy years ago in the chemical trade on the Tyne —was on his way to India as superintendent in the service of the East India Company when his ocean child was born. Mrs. Stephenson belonged an old Newcastle family, being a daughter of Dr. Brummell, famous in local song. Many are the allusions to him. Blind Willy, so often referred to in this volume, in one of his songs used to sing—

THE SANDHILL.

"Dr. Brummell upon the Sandhill,
He gov Sir Maffa a pill."

And it is about Dr. Brummell, Oliver, in his famous song, "Newcastle Props," thus writes (Blind Willy supposed to be singing)—

"O weel aw like te hear him sing
'Bout young Sir Matt and Dr. Brummell."

After some twelve years in India Mr. Stephenson returned to Tyneside. His son in due course went to business. Beginning at Sowerby's Glass Works, Gateshead, he now occupies the responsible post of representative of John Rogerson and Co. Possessing artistic and literary tastes,

35

Mr. Stephenson has been a member of the Bewick Club from its beginning, and at present holds the office

of hon. treasurer. The annual exhibition finds him as an amateur regularly contributing. His pictures, mostly water-colours, are scenes of rural beauty, farmhouses, half-ruined cottages, etc., and bits of old Newcastle; some secured just before their destruction. At the conversaziones of the club Mr. Stephenson's humour, mimicry, and elocutionary powers make him a great favourite. He delights in the local, Tyneside, Wearside, and other North-country dialects being alike to him.

Photo by Bulman, Gateshead.

For charitable and other purposes he is much in request, and there giving in Tyneside some of his racy pieces which follow, he never fails to please.

Yours sincerely
J. H. Stephenson

HAWKS'S MEN AT THE BATTLE OF WATERLOO.

MAN, aa fell in wi' Ned White the other day. Ye knaa Ned and other twenty-fower o' Haaks's cheps went out te the Peninsular War, where Wellin'ton was, ye knaa. Se, as we wor hevin' a gill tegithor, aa says te him, "Ned, d'ye mind when ye wor in the Peninsular War?" "Aa should think aa de," says he. "Did ye ever faall in wi' Wellin'ton?" says aa. "Wellin'ton!" says he; "wey, man, aa knaa'd him. Wey, just the day afore the Battle o' Watterloo he sent for me. 'Ned,' he says; 'tyek yor twenty-fower cheps,' he says, 'an gan up and shift them Frenchmen off the top o' yon hill.' 'Aal reet,' says aa, 'but it winnit tyek all the twenty-fower,' aa says. 'Ah, but it's Napolean's crack regiment,' he says; 'ye'd bettor tyek plenty.' 'Aal reet,' aa says, 'we'll suen shift them.' So doon aa cums te the lads, an' aa says—'Noo, ma lads, Wellin'ton wants us te shift yon Frenchmen off the top of yon hill.' 'Heor, Bob Scott, come here; hoo mony Frenchmen are ther up yondor?' 'Aboot fower hundred,' he says. 'Hoo mony on us will it tyek te shift them, Bob?' 'Oh, ten,' says Bob. 'Wey, we'll tyek fourteen,' aa says, 'just te humour the aad chap.' 'Aal reet,' they says. So off we set at the double alang the lonnen; but just as we turned the corner at the foot of the hill, whee should we meet but Bonnipart hees-sel on a lily-white horse, wiv a cocked hat on. 'Where are ye off te, Ned?' says he, 'Wey, te shift yon Frenchmen off yon hill!' 'Whaat!' he says; 'wey, that's maa crack regiment,' he says. 'Nivor mind that,' aa says; 'Wellin'ton says we hev te shift them, and shifted they'll be noo!' 'Get away, man, ye're coddin,' says he. 'Ne coddin' aboot it,' aa says; 'cum by!' 'Haud on, then,' he says; and he gallops reet up the hill on his lily-white horse, and shoots oot, 'Gan back, ma lads, gan back! Heor's Ned White frae Haaks's and fourteen of his cheps comin' up te shift ye. Ye hevvent a happorth of chance!' Did aa ivvor see Wellin'ton? Wey, man, ye should think shyem!"

J. A. STEPHENSON.   *Author's Copy,* 1890.

A TOW FOR NOWT.

A TYNESIDE STORY.

A WELL-KNOWN steamboat man named Forster, belonging to the Tyne, was about to proceed up the river to Newcastle from Jarrow in his tug-boat, when he was accosted by an impecunious keelman, who wanted a tow up to the Mushroom "for nowt." "Mr. Forster, hinney!" he shouted, "give us a tow, hinney; give us a tow up to the Mushroom, hinney!" "How do you know my name's Forster!" "Oh, aw knaw yor nyem's Forster, hinney. I've knawn ye awll yor life. I knew your fether afore ye. He was a canny chep, yor fether. He was particlar fond o' me, yor fether was. Give us a tow, hinney!" "Well, fling us yor rope." "There ye are, hinney. Yor the model o' yor fether, hinney; the model o' yor fether. Fling us off at the Mushroom, hinney!—at the Mushroom! Aye! yor the model o' yor fether." So Forster made the tow rope fast, and began to steam up the river. Now Forster was rather fond of a practical joke, and he thought it would be a good one not to fling the rope off at the Mushroom, but to tow him up to the bridge, about a mile higher up. So, on approaching the Mushroom, the keelman sang out, "Now, Mr. Forster, hinney, fling hor off, hinney, fling hor off." Forster took no notice. "Fling the rope off, hinney; fling the rope off. Here's the Mushroom." Forster steered steadily on. "Fling the rope, Forster. Why, man, fling the rope off. Why! ye mun be a bad 'un. Ye are a bad 'un. Ye always war a bad 'un; and yor fether was a bad 'un afore ye."

J. A. STEPHENSON.   *Author's Manuscript, 1891.*

A RECOLLECTION OF NED CORVAN.

Patter given by Ned in " Heh ye seen wor Jimmy?"
An early version of "The Fire on the Kee."

OH, hinnies, what iver is aw gannin to de with that lad o' mine? His gawn to ha' maw life—aw's sure he is; it's wor Jimmy aw mean, ha' ye seen owt on him? He's an awful lad. Wark! he'll work nyen. He's been gannin oot every day for the last six months te seek a job, and niver getten one yet—not likely—while I keep him, he knaws better, hinney. Now, his fether wes a man, his fether was. If ye had only seen his fether cummin alang the quayside iv a Sunday mornin

wiv his white hat and his wooden leg, and a blue han-
kitcher round his neck; he was the varry spittin immige
o' the Duke o' Wellinton — umph-m, about the small
o' the back, hinney. Oh dear me, when aw think o' his
fether it reminds me of wor early days, when he used te
cum sweetheartin me, in the spring-time o' the year,
when the cock robbin and the kitty wren and the moudy
warp all joined together in a grand chorus o' delight—
umph-m, it was lovely. He used to take me to Jesmond,
down by the green water pool, him walkin on in front
and me behint, an' aw didn't like that, ye knaw, and aw
wad say, "Give ower lettin me a-be," and then he put
his airm round me waist, and, oh, such things he wad
say tiv us! He once said 'at aw was varry like Mary
Queen o' Scots—umph-m, about the back o' the neck,
hinney! But he's deed and gyen now, hinney, and these
lovely times is ower; but aw've still getten his wooden leg
hinging aback o' the door as a mementer of the dear
departed. Things is changed now, hinney. Aw heh te
gan oot washing five days a week, eighteenpence a day an'
me meat—little enough, aw think. If it wasent for a
little drop o' gin aw get wi' a little drop of watter—not
ower much watter, ye knaw, for it niver did agree with
me—aw divent knaw what aw wad de.

Weell, hinney, whe de ye think aw seed the uther day?
Aw was cummin doon the Groat Market, and aw just
popped into H——l's kitchen—aw beg yor pardin, hinney,
but ye knaw where aw mean—where they keep the poker
chain'd up for fear they knock one another on the heed
wi'd, ye knaw; and aw'd just gettin a half o' gin when
whe should cum in but Hillar Thompson—Geordy
Thompson, ye knaw, but they call him Hillar; he was
brother te Billy Thompson—ye knawed Billy—they byeth
used te be wi' Billy Purvis, ye knaw. Hillar's just aboot
the height of six pennorth of copper, ye knaw, and
always drunk—aw believe he was born drunk, aw niver
saw him sober i' maw life. He just gans aboot spootin'
for beer—spungin', ye knaw; so when he came in a
chep says, "Let's hev a recitation, Hillar." Why,

that's just what he cum in for, de ye see? so he gets on te the table and starts,

" A chieftain to the highlands bound,"

and then he stopped. " Aw knaw what he wants," says the chep; "fetch him a quart o' beer, misses." And she did, and Hillar slockened it off, hinney, ay, to the last gasp, and then he started off afresh.

"A chieftain to the highlands bound
Cried, boatman do not tarry,
An' I'll give thee a silver pound "—

him give onybody a silver pund, he niver gov onybody a copper fardin iv his life—niver !—

" To row me o'er the ferry.
Oh, who is this wad cross Lochgyle—
This dark, this stormy water?
Oh, I'm the chief of Ulva's Isle,"—

him the chief of Ulva's Isle! Why, his father and mother selled apples and pears in Denton Chare—

" And this Lord Ullin's daughter.
And fast before her father's men,
We two have fled together ;
Oh, should they meet us in the glen,
My blood would stain the heather."

His blood stain the heather! Why, his blood was nowt but beer; and just then, ye knaw, he stepped back on the table, te give a bit elocution tiv his words—de ye see? when he went reet ower intiv a basket of eggs and biscuits belangin' tiv an au'd wife, and myed a bonny smash. "Whe's gawn te pay for these?" says the wife. "Haud yor gob," says Hillar; "aw'll eat them all when we're deun."

From J. A. STEPHENSON'S *Manuscript,* 1891.

THE POSTPONED GOOSE.
A WEARSIDE STORY.

AN idle, loafing, lazy sailor, belonging to the port of Sunderland, one of those fellows who never would work while he had a penny in his pocket, or as he termed it, " A shot in his locker," was lounging about the Pottery Bank, at the foot of the High Street. He had been out

of a ship for three months, and was very hard up.
Meeting one of his mates, a rather crusty old salt, he
sang out, "Luik hiar, man, Gowdy, what's aw gawn te
de; aw'se bine out iv a ship for three munths, and aw
heven't a shot i' the locker, eh?" "Why, get a ship,
man! get a ship!" "Why, ye knaw varry wiel there's
ne ships in." "Why, the Mary Jane's in, and they want
a cuik." "A cuik! Why, ye knaw varry wiel aw canna
cuik nean." "Get away, man, onybody can cuik; had
away and tell the maister ye can cuik, and ye'll get the
job." So the fellow went and applied to the captain for
the job. "What can you cook?" asked the captain.
"Cuik, mister, cuik owt—cuik owt, mister." So he was
engaged as cook. The first thing he had to do was to
boil some rice for the men. "My eye, aw'se glad aw'se
getten sec a easy job as that; onny body can boil a bit
o' rice." So he got a bucketful of rice and put it into
the copper, filled it up with water, and set the fire away.
Soon the water began to boil and the rice to swell, a
thing he had not calculated upon, and presently to rise
up to the rim of the copper. "Dear me, aw wunder
what's the metter wi' that rice." It boiled over, so he
got a bucket and threw a bucketful overboard; but it
came up again, away went another bucketful, and then
another, still it came up; then he got a piece string and
tied on the lid, but it burst it away. Then he gave it up
and shouted out, "Some o' you fellows hes been
puttin some marcary i' that rice; aw put one bucketful in and aw'se thrawn three bucketfuls out, and its
bigger than iver." Well, he expected dismissal for this,
but it seems never to have come to the captain's ears.
The next day the captain expected some gentlemen to
dinner in the cabin, and had provided a beautiful goose
for their entertainment, but they sent word to say they
could not come that day, so the dinner had to be put off.

The captain then went to the cook and said, "Cook,
postpone that goose, and do me a steak." "Pospone
the geuse!" said the cook. "Yes, postpone the goose,"
said the captain. "Aal reet, mister, hit el be riddy—

what time, mister?" "Three o'clock," answered the captain. "Aal reet, mister;" and the captain went on shore, leaving the poor perplexed cook standing scratching his head. "Aw wunder how they de pospone a geuse," he muttered to himself. "Hire, carpenter, come hire, mun. De ye knaw how te pospone a geuse?" "Pospone a geuse, man! Why, ye'll spoil the thing. Roast it, man; roast it." "No, no," said the cook, "onybody can roast a geuse, but the maister wants it posponed, and posponed it il heh te be." "Why, aw niver heard tell o' such a thing; but yonder's Billy Whimple gean intiv yon public-house on the quay. Had away; give him a glass o' rum, and ax him; he'll tell ye, he's been a ceuk aal his life."

So away went the cook, and followed Billy into the public-house. "Hev a glass o' rum, Bill?" asked the cook. "Ay, aw diven't care if aw de," answered the thirsty Billy. "Tow glesses o' rum, misses." "Billy, des thou knaw how te pospone a geuse?" "Why, man," said Billy, "onybody can pospone a geuse." "Ay, how de ye de'd?" asked the cook. "Why," answered Billy, "ye knaw ye get a geuse, and ye plote it, an' ye clean it, and then put it intiv a canvas bag, and lay'd doon on the deck and hammer'd wiv a handspike for half a our; then ye put it intiv the copper wi' some wetter and onions and pepper and salt, and sarve it iv a tureen—that's the way te pospone a geuse!" "My eye, Billy, aw'se glad aw'se sein ye. Hev anuther glass o' rum, Bill."

So cook went on board again and did as the man had told him, and when the captain returned at three o'clock he put the tureen and a steak before him.

"What's in the tureen, cook?" asked the captain. "That's the posponed geuse, mister," answered the cook. He was presently ejected from the cabin, his exit being accelerated by the captain's boot.

Well, he was sure of the bag this time, but the next morning the gentlemen sent word they were coming that day, so the captain went to the cook and said, "Now, here's a fine job you have made. The gentlemen are coming to dinner to-day, and there's nothing for them."

"There's the haar, mister, there's the haar." "Oh, I forgot the hare," said the captain. "Now, let me have that hare properly roasted this time." "Aal reet, mister; hit'll be aal reet this time. What time, mister?" "Three o'clock," said the captain. "Aal reet, mister; hit'll be aal reet."

Well, three o'clock came, the table was laid, the guests arrived—everything was in readiness—*but the hare.* The captain at length told the cabin boy to go to the galley and see why the cook did not bring the hare. He returned and said, "He'll nut speak tiv us, sir. He hes the galley door locked, an' he winnet speak tiv us." "Confound the fellow," roared the captain. "Go and tell him if he does not bring it here at once I'll kick him overboard."

Then the unfortunate cook came slowly down the cabin stairs, his hands covered with fur and blood.

"Is that hare not ready?" shouted the captain. "No, sir; hit'll nut be riddy te-morn at this time. Aw'se been ploatin' that blowed thing since nine o'clock this mornin', and hit's nut haaf dune yet." This time he "got the bag for fairs."

J. A. STEPHENSON.   *Author's Manuscript,* 1891.

————

ADAM AND EVE.

A WEARSIDE STORY.

MANY years ago two very fine pictures, representing Adam and Eve in the Garden of Eden—"The Temptation" and "The Expulsion from Eden"—painted by Dubouffe, were exhibited in the Victoria Rooms, in Grey Street, Newcastle, and also at and about the same time at the Athenæum in Fawcett Street, Sunderland. While at the latter place two Sunderland pilots meeting at the corner of High Street, one said to the other, "Where ye gawn tee, Gwordy?" "Why, te the Thinium te see the picters." "Ay, are they wuth owt?" "Why," answered the other, "they say they're cliver, and it's nobbit sixpence te gan in." "Why, blow! it's nobbit the price iv a quart—aw'll gan wi' ye!" So they went and saw them, and on coming out, one said to the other, "What de ye think iv yon, Gwordy?" "My eye! yon's a fine woman," says Gwordy, "but what's it awl aboot?" "Why, Adam and Eve," said the other. "Ye'v hierd tell iv Adam and Eve?" "Why, yes," said Gwordy, scratching his head thoughtfully. "I hev hierd tell iv Adam and Eve, but I've forgetten whe tha ware." "Why," said the other, "Adam was the fust man—but ha'way doon te the Grace Darlin' and we'll hev a quart, an aw'll tell ye all aboot it." So away they went and had the quart in. "Now then aboot these picters," said Gwordy. "Why," answered the other, "Adam was the fust man, and Eve was the fust woman, and they war put intiv a greet big gaaden—ay, a big 'un—aboot as big as fra hier te Ryhope. An' this gaaden was full iv all manner iv fruit trees and vegatables—apple trees and peir trees and peiches and grosers, and tormuts and carrots and taties, and rubab and leiks, and iverything. An' ye knaw they had parfec liberty te eat ony iv these fruit or vegatables, except the apples off a cartain tree. They hadn't te eat ony iv them, ye knaw, or they wad get kicked oot. Se one day Adam gits up frev his brikwest, and he says, 'Eve,' he says, 'aw'm gawn doon te the summer-hoose te hev a smoke,' he says, 'an' ye'd better get on yor apron an' yor straw hat an' gan doon te the tormit bed an' gether sum tormits an' leiks for the broth; but mind,' he says, 'divent ye gan nigh yon tree,' he says. So away he went te hev his smoke; an' Eve put on her apron—aw'se warn'd it wis te carry the tormits an' leiks in—an' her straw hat, an' doon she went te the tormit bed; but ye knaw she had te gan reet bye yon tree. An' ye knaw Eve. Why, Eve was a woman, an' iverybody knaws 'at a woman's chock full o' curosity. She'd offen wondered what them apples was like; an' she cuddent help gettin' a clot an' knockin' yan doon; an' she had a bite oot on't. Man! it wis the finest apple ever she tasted. So doon she gans te the summer-hoose tiv Adam. 'Teast that,' she says, an' he had a bite, an' then they finished it, an' went up tiv the tree, an' aw'se warn'd they had sum mare. 'Asiver, they got kicked oot." "Kicked oot," cried Gwordy; "kicked oot for eatin' a apple! Why, man! aw'd eat a ship-load iv apples for a woman like yon!"

J. A. STEPHENSON.   *Author's Manuscript*, 1891.

THOMAS KERR,

WHO was born in the Black Gate, under the shadow of the Old Castle, may justly claim to be a native of the old town.

THE BLACK GATE ABOUT 1830.

In Newcastle, some twenty-five years ago, Mr. Kerr was in business. Had you called upon him then, the chances were you might have had a chat with Joe Wilson, who was one of his early friends, and a regular caller. Leaving Newcastle, Mr. Kerr settled in Blyth, where, his literary inclinations leading him to press work, he acted occasionally as reporter for the *Blyth Weekly News*. To the *News* for some seven years he contributed the local letters of "An Awd Trimmer," and during that time, in the letter, hundreds of songs appeared, most of them of a fugitive character, but some, taking the popular taste, became favourites, and are still sung. While at Blyth he appears to have gone into Chater's competitions, winning several prizes, amongst them a gold medal for the best local song for his Annual. Taking entirely to press work, Mr. Kerr has now for about twelve years held a prominent position on one of the Newcastle daily papers. This seems fully to occupy his time, as for some years now, no local songs by him have appeared.

WHEN THE GUD TIMES CUM AGYEN.

TUNE—"The Captain with the Whiskers."

In sweet anticipashun o' the gud times cummin' back,
Let's join in ruminashun on the days se bad an' black,
That the myest o' foak are troubled, aye, byeth wimmin',
    bairns, an' men,
That wor joys may awl be dubbeld when the gud times
    cum agyen ;
Fur wheriver we may be, on the land or on the sea,
The retrospect 'ill point oot awl things we shudent de,
An' warn us te forsyek sum ways wor footsteps used te
    ken,
Pointin' us te purer pleshors when the gud times cum
    agyen.

If specalayshun wis yor forte, an awl yor brass wis lost,
Throo some famed bubble company that sair yor temper
    crost ;
Or if on bricks an' mortor, lads, yor 'onest hopes war set,
Till ye fund yor cash wis ganning an' yor hooses wadent
    let ;
Oh, it's dinnet pine an' fret, an' get intiv a swet
Ower the twenty-five percentage ye wor hopin' for te net,

But quietly keep plodding on, till mair cotterds ye get, then

Look before ye lowp, lads, when the gud times cum agyen.

If drinking wis yor hobby, when the wages they wor flush,

An' ye spent yor hard 'arned money ower idleness an' lush,

Till ye hardlys had a suit o' claes, a tyebbil or a press,

An' ye stud imang the foremist that wis suf'rin fra distress;

Though the triawl wis seveer, it 'ill still yor future cheer,

If it learns ye te be steady, te be canny wi' the beer,

Ti save up for a rainy day, an' leeve the drink alyen,

Thit troo comforts oft may cheer ye when the gud times cum agyen.

If gamilin engrost yor mind, an' thowts o' dorty greed

Had o' yor heart possesshun tuen, 'twis pitiabil indeed,

Fur dreed remorse mun sair 'a tried yor conshience neet and day,

When plunged in poverty ye mourned the brass ye'd hoyed away;

Then be sure ye dinnet fail, ti forsyek the heed an' tail

That may land ye i' the wark-house, the mad-house, or the jail,

An' seek healthier recreashun mair suitabil te men,

Te improve yor mind an' body, when the gud times cum agyen.

Aye, thor's lessons fra the bad times that every yen may larn,

Wiv a littil bit o' thinking, an' a mind that can discern,

Fur vile extravagense wid ceese if foak had only sense

Fur te note the crime an' fuilishness iv useless expense;

Then the gud we mite exert, wiv a pure an' noble
    heart,
In the workshop, in the cottage, in the mansion, in the
    mart,
Wid guide wor future footsteps i' the paths o' wisdom,
    then
Wi mite myek this world an Eden when the gud times
    cum agyen.

    KERR.   *Author's Copy.* 1879.

AW'S GLAD THE STRIKE'S DUIN.

TUNE—"It's time to get up."

" OH, aw's glad the strike's duin," shooted lang Geordy
    Reed,
Ti the groop thit wis stanning iroond,
" Fur the care an' anxiety's ni' turned me heed,
An' am gettin is thin is a hoond ;
Fur ye knaw me an' Jenny had promist te wed
When the money te start hoose wis won,
But the unlucky stop cawsed wor sports te drop,
So aw's glad, very glad, the strike's duin."

"Oh, aw's glad the strike's duin," said a hawf-grown
    lad,
"Fur wor brass it wis gettin' se short,
An' the boolin' an' runnin' wis gan te the bad,
An' we'd ni' seen a finish te sport.
Noo te Newcassel Races, se merry an' blate,
We'll yet start like shot iv a gun,
An' it's nyen ower late te back one fur the ' Plate,'
So aw's glad, very glad the strike's duin."

" Oh, aw's glad the strike's duin, for the sake o' my wife,"
Said a brave little man in the crood,
" Fur the pinchin' an' plannin' an' sorrow an' strife
Neerly had her, poor lass, in her shrood.
Noo wor canny bit bairns ill luik tidy an' trim,
When te chapel on Sundays thor tuin ;
An' hoo thenkful," said he, " iverybody shud be
That the unlucky strike is noo duin."

"Oh, aw's glad the strike's duin," cried oot shopkeeper Jack,
An' he's words they exprest awl he said,
Fur he's fyece wore a smile, an' he's lips gov a smack,
Is he tawk't o' "the prospects o' trade."
Hoo the business wid thrive, is it yence did before,
An' the wheels iv prosority run ;
" Ay, an' awl get me whack," said shopkeeper Jack,
" So aw's glad, very glad, the strike's duin."

Then the crood awl agreed, wi' a nod o' the heed,
They war pleased the bad job wis put strite,
An' a wummin or two, is the crood they passed through,
Gae full vent te thor happy delite ;
While the bairns in the street, wi' thor voices se sweet,
In the hite o' thor glory an' fun,
Shooted " Hip, hip, horray ! it's settiled the day,
An' wor glad, very glad, the strike's duin."

KERR.   *Author's Copy*, 1880.

———

ALEXANDER HAY,

BORN in Newcastle on December 11th, 1826, has had a roving and many-sided career. Apprenticed to a cabinet-maker, his restless nature rebelled at the restrictions then

From a Photo by A. D. Lewis.

common, and he took to the sea as a ship carpenter. Clark Russell, the popular novelist, in the preface to his work, *Sailor's Language,* writes—"A ship carpenter once told me that he had been clapped into irons, and lay manacled for six weeks, in a voyage to China, for writing the words of a song which the sailors sung on every occasion when the captain was on deck. He gave me a copy of the words, which I found to be a rude enumeration of Jack's troubles, every stanza winding up with a shout of 'Board of Trade, ahoy!'" The ship carpenter who wrote and gave Mr. Russell the song was Alexander Hay. Russell prints the song in his book, but falls into an error about the carpenter being put in irons; he was brutally used, but the irons were only threatened. A verse or two perhaps will best show the nature of the song.

> " I snubb'd skipper for bad grub, rotten flour to eat,
> Hard tack full of wevills ; how demon chandlers cheat !
> Salt junk like mahogany, scurvying man and boy.
> Says he, ' Where's your remedy ?' *Board of Trade, ahoy !*
>
> Can ye wonder mutiny, lubber-like, will lurk
> In our mercantile marine, cramm'd with measly pork ?
> Is it wonderful that men lose their native joy,
> With provisions maggoty ? *Board of Trade, ahoy !*"

Some time after this incident Mr. Hay had the honour of reciting his " Board of Trade, ahoy ! " at a great public meeting at Limehouse, the sailors' friend, Samuel Plimsoll, in the chair. About this time a kindred piece by him, "The Shoddy Ship," appeared in the *Nautical Magazine.*

As long ago as 1856 Mr. Hay contributed to the *Northern Poetic Keepsake.* Thomas Doubleday, Robert White, L. Goodchild, R. Storey, and R. Fisher (the publisher of the volume) being amongst his fellow-contributors. The following striking lines are taken from his sonnet on "Time."

TIME.

Time hath no age—as vigorous to-day
As when Creation started. . . .
.   .   . His menial is the sun ;
The blazing stars that plough the azure skies
And glass their semblance in the dallying sea ;
The silver moon that levers up the tides
And gilds the surface of the glimmering leaves,
Are all subservient to the pulse of time.

On land Mr. Hay's experiences have been varied—at Liverpool a tutor in a school, and connected with the press, at London engaged in the building of the Great Exhibition, 1862, and also a journalist, these are a few of the parts he has played. For some years now he has been back to his native town. In connection with this volume he has been ever ready to help. He has joined in the search at Ballast Hills, for the graves of Selkirk and Gilchrist; at St. John's he assisted in seeking out the poet Thompson's half-forgotten grave. His latest help has been in reference to Nunn, and finding the mutilated copy of his songs. A ready writer, his contributions in prose and verse to the Newcastle press have been numerous. The following are examples of his dialect work.

———

THE DANDYLION CLOCK.

TUNE—"Days we went a-gipsying."

WHEN wor aud toon was the aud toon,
  Wi' mony a grassy nyuk,
And posies ivvoreewhere adorn'd
  It like sum pikter-byuk;
We lay above the sighin' burn,
  On hills ov fern and rock,
To blaw thaw balloon life away,
  Maw "dandylion clock."

Two bonnie lasses and me-sel,
  But bairns—dash ! hoo we play'd
Wiv buttercups and daisies pure,
  And babby-hooses made.

36

Before the manly cares cam oot
  To gie won's heart a shock,
We lay and blaw'd to tell the time—
  The " dandylion clock."

Luk! the dear sunshine's teeming doon
  Neagarrays of joy,
On Lizzie's bonnie curly heed,
  Like dolls her lovin' toy.
It sparkles like the goold itsel—
  Aw might hev had a lock
Is easy as aw blew for her
  The "dandylion clock."

And there wis little Katie, tee,
  Whe's figur aw wad paint;
But God saves me the trubbil noo,
  He's tyun hur to the saint.
And Lizzie tee's an angel gud,
  Iv her brite lalock frock;
Aw think aw see her blawin' yit
  The " dandylion clock."

HAY.   *Author's Copy*, 1879.

————————

THE ILLEKTRIC LEET.

Written on Mr. J. Swan, the inventor of the incandescent lamp, lighting
with electricity his (Mawson and Swan's) chemist shop, Mosley Street.
The first shop in Newcastle lighted by electricity (1880).

TUNE—"Billy O'Rooke's the Boy."

AAVE seen sum queer things in maw time,
  When gas did oil eclipse, sor,
For, aa remembor Neshim's men,*
  Whe myed wor mowls an' dips, sor,

* About fifty years ago Mr. Nesham had a famous tallow-chandler's
works on the site of Handyside's shops in New Bridge Street.

The tindor box an' rag isteem'd
   Begat the loosifors, sor;
Yit still wor greet inventive brain
   Is floororie as the Gorze, sor.

Chorus.

   The illektric leet ! the illektric leet !
     The pet ov aal the seasin ;
   We'll he'd hung up th' morrow neet
     Or else we'll knaa the reasin.

We've had sum clivor cheps it hyem,
   Ye'll knaa what they wor worth, sor ;
The lion gob ov steem snores oot
   The glory ov the North, sor.
Its ingins push the ships aboot
   Faster nor the breeze, sor ;
It helps to win wor wives and bairns
   Thor bits ov breed and cheese, sor.

     The illektric leet ! the illektric leet ! etc.

Noo Stevinson an' Watt, ye knaa,
   Sent Geordies ower the seas, sor,
To teach mankind to de the trick,
   Myek steam de as they please, sor.
Ye'll find wors in Astrillia,
   In aal the isles aboot, sor ;
Fur aa'll be bund ne class ov men
   Mair blabbed the secrit oot, sor !

     The illektric leet ! the illektric leet ! etc.

So here's te Swan, wor canny man ;
   His 'llektric leet is fine, sor,
That burns away an' rivals day
   In honour ov wor Tyne, sor.

The aud wax candels håd thor time,
   The gas wor sarvant, tee, sor;
But seun Swan's leet 'll blink like stars
   Frov Sanget te The Kee, sor.

                    The illektric leet! the illektric leet! etc.

HAY.   *"Weekly Chronicle,"* 1880.

JOHN CRAGGS

WAS born at North Sunderland in 1849, and was for years engaged as a clerk on the Tyne. He was one of the Bohemian coterie of local authors which included Joe Wilson, Rowland Harrison, John Taylor, and Ralph Blackett. While in Newcastle Craggs contributed largely to the local press under the *nom-de-plume* of "Mrkg. Fudjjv" (a cryptogram of his name). In 1874 he was awarded Chater's gold medal for his sentimental song, "The Old Cot on the Tyne." He is also the author of "The M.P. for Jarra," "The Letter from Hannah," etc. In 1877 he migrated to the metropolis, where he has long been a prominent member of the detective police.

Photo by Taylor, Newcastle.

TH' LASS THAT SELL'D GROZERS UPON THE AAD BRIDGE.

SINCE aa wis a lad aa hev had an ambishin
   Te distingwish me-sel' wi' th' rod an' the line;
An' that's how it cums aa's se offins fund fishin'
   Aboot oot-th'-way places on wor canny Tyne.

Thor wis yen Friday neet aa had tripe te ma supper,
　　Then aa turned inte bed an' went reet off te sleep,
When aa dreemed that aa won a cuddy's new crupper,
　　For ma skill i' landin' th' fry fra th' deep.

But what 'stonished me myest wis th' place where th'
　　　　match wis,
　　It was on the aad bridge that aa stud wi' ma line.
Thor wis croods lookin' on, an' cheps singin' snatches
　　Ov the "Amyture Fishor," th' pride o' the Tyne.
Thor's anuther queer thing aa mite as weel menshin,
　　Aa thowt that aa baited ma hyuk wiv a midge,
An' there wis aa 'tractin' aal fokes's attenshin,
　　Fishin' for trooties upon th' aad bridge.

Next mornin' you're sure aa wis properly bent on
　　Testin' th' trooth ov ma wunderful dreem ;
Se aa gat up ma tackil an' cam' in fra Kenton,
　　An' wis varry s'yun soondin' th' aad-fashint streem ;
But aa didn't catch owt, an' it wassint sorprisin',
　　For aa saw summick else put me aal in a fidge—
'Twis the bonniest lass that aa ivvor clapt eyes on,
　　Sellin' apples an' grozers upon th' aad bridge.

Wi' ma rod i' ma hand an' ma line iv the river,
　　Te where she wis stannin' aa elbid alang,
An' when aa had gettin up close enyuf tiv her,
　　Te tyek hor attenshin aa *whussted* a sang.
Ses aa, " Canny hinney, how is grozers sellin' ? "
　　Ses she, " Thor a little bit cheapor nor troot."
Ses aa, " Aa's not weel, an' aa dinnit mind tellin'
　　The seet ov ye torned ma heart reet roond aboot."

" If ye hev owt te say," ses she, " give ower fishin';
   Speak yor mind like a man an' say what ye mean ;
But please yor aansel' noo ye knaa the condishin,
   For aal aa sell grozers, aa's prood as th' queen."
Aa tell'd hor reet oot ma h'yemly posishin,
   Th' brass that aa myed an' th' tin that aa had.
" Eigh," ses she, "th' faa't that ye hev is yor fishin',
   But for aal that ye lyuk like a decint young lad."

She sed that ma luv she cuddint weel doot it,
   Oney she diddint fancy te change her aan nyem,
But she promist at last te consider aboot it,
   An' tell es next week, if that wad de aal th' syem.
Noo yung cheps cannit fancy how happy ma life is,
   Free fra a landledy's fashin' an' fidge,
An' ye'll not be surprised when aa tell ye ma wife is
   Th' lass that sell'd grozers upon the aad bridge.

     CRAGGS.   " *Newcastle Weekly Chronicle*," 1881.

MATTHEW TATE

AT an early age showed his fancy for poetry. In 1854, when only seventeen, he begun his writing. About twenty years later, in 1874, he published his volume, *Stray Blossoms*, and since has contributed largely to the local press. He comes off an old mining family, and was born at Benton Square on September 5th, 1837. Northumberland all his life has been his county. At present, and for long, his residence has been Waterloo, Blyth.

THE FORE SHIFT.

OH, the fore shift dark and dreary,
   Oh, this lonely two o'clock ;
Limbs may ache, and hearts be weary,
   Still there comes the caller's knock ;

And each blow upon the panels
Bids us up and don our flannels,
By the light of lamp or can'les
   Batter at the grimy rock.

Just to get a bare subsistence,
   Little earn'd and nothing saved,
With the Workhouse in the distance
   After we for years have slaved.
Some look on with holy horror,
At each pitman's little error,
But 'twould much abate their terror
   Could they see the dangers braved.

To the coal's grim face we travel,
   And again our flannels doff;
Can they wonder if we cavil
   At the ones much better off?
Like a snake our bodies coiling,
Weary hours incessant toiling,
Through each pore the sweat comes boiling:
   Think on this, ye ones that scoff!

Up while stars are dimly peeping
   Through the midnight's sable gloom;
Up while pampered ones are sleeping
   In their snug and cosy room.
Fore shift visions need not haunt them,
Nor the pit's grim danger daunt them;
Oh, 'twas kind of fate to plant them
   Where they could so safely bloom!

TATE.   *" Newcastle Weekly Chronicle,"* 1886.

RALPH DOWEY,

ANOTHER miner-poet, was born at West Holywell Colliery, October 11th, 1844. Local song-writing has long been his hobby, and what he is at his hobby may be judged from the number of prizes that have fallen to his pen, some eight having at various times been awarded to him. His pieces principally have appeared in Frazer's and Tweedy's Almanacks, and *The Blyth Weekly News*, where the piece selected here appeared.

THE PICNIC DAY.

CUM hinny, Jane, maw bonnie lass,
    Get thoo the bairns ready,
An' hand me here what pocket brass
    Thoo ettles for thee Teddy.
Because the time is creepin on,
Thoo knaas the speaking starts at one,
Thor's not much time te play upon
    An' dress them aal for Morpeth.

An' dress thee awnsel up te dick,
    Put on thy last new bonnet ;
We'll myek them stare at wor picnic,
    Thoo may depend upon it.
Awl link wi' thoo, me bonnie lass,
An' through the croods we'll dash an' pass,
An' mevvies dance upon the grass
    When we get there te Morpeth.

Cum let us catch the special train,
    Neer freet iboot the weather ;
For if the cloods splash doon thor rain
    We'll hooze inside together.

We'll meet wi' cronies mony a one,
An' crack o' times an' days that's gone,
Iboot percentage off an' on,
    An' feast wor-sels at Morpeth.

Just lissen there, dis thoo hear that ?
    Wey that's wor drum what's beatin ;
It's just iboot the time they sat
    An' pointed for their meetin.
Ay, thon's the bandmen torning oot,
An' croods are flocking aal iboot
Just waiting for the marshall's shoot,
    An' then they're off te Morpeth.

Aw knaa thoo's not been weel for lang,
    An' Doctor James is cummin ;
But he'll not clash nor myek a sang
    Iboot thoo an me, maw woman.
So let's away te see the sport
An' hear wor Fenwick an' wor Bort ;
Aw'm sure thoo cannot tyek much hort
    Imang the trees at Morpeth.

    .   .   .   .   .

What's that thoo says, maw canny Jane ?
    Awm pleased te hear thoo's gannin ;
Awm sure thoo'll not feel ache or pain
    Thi time that thoo is stannin
Imang ken'd foaks fra far an near
That's laid aside pit duds an' gear,
Te meet each other once a year
    On picnic day at Morpeth.

DOWEY.   "*Blyth Weekly News*," 1891.

It was intended to have had at the end of this volume a fairly representative selection from the living dialect writers of the day. As the volume progressed, however, that was found impossible; the writers of the past took up more of the volume than was expected, and so those of the present were crushed out. The late Mr. Chater, with his almanacks and annuals, his gold medals and prizes, brought out many good dialect songs; and the *Weekly Chronicle*, with its local song competitions, brought out more. At the Stephenson Centenary, 1881, a good song appeared in the *Weekly Chronicle*, signed A. F., Leadgate. It opens—

WYLAM GEORDY.

Come, Billy, lad, let's tiv the toon,
This glorious sunny Ninth o' June;
Te-day aa'll lay ma tools aal doon
    In memory o' Geordy.

For just a hunnor summers syne
This varry day began te shine
In yon wee cottage by the Tyne
    The Railway Star in Geordy.

"Indeed," said Bill, "aa's on the way;
Man, whe wad bide at hyem te-day?
The varry trains are full o' play,
    Sae prood ower Wylam Geordy."

They reach Newcastle, all decorated in honour of the occasion,

An' see the ancient fortress toon
Hes dressed horsel' in sic a goon
Of gowld an' glittor up an' doon,
    An' aal for Wylam Geordy.

Here's miles o' rolleys on the move,
An' miles of men, whese presence prove
A brotherly discarning love
    For men o' brains like Geordy.

About a year after "The New Keviling* Monday" appeared. This came also from Leadgate, and was signed A. Frazer, little doubt the A. F. of "Wylam Geordy."

"The Kevils's draan at Parrington Pit,
An' Mat an' his marra hev myed a bad hit;
Doon the Sooth Crosscut we're shiftin' wor kit—
    Oh, bother the Kevilin' Monday!"

---

* "Kevils," or "cavells," are the lots cast by miners in the distribution of "places" to the workers in a given pit. The coal in some parts of the mine is worked more easily than in others; in order, therefore, that the "marras" may have a fair chance of getting a good place, "kevils" are cast at stated times.

On the Stephenson Centenary another local writer, MATTHEW C. JAMES, of Walker (who has written largely), also has a good song—

THE STIVVISON CENTENNERY.

Noo, how thor, marra! had thy jaa,
Aa's just cum frev th' toon ye knaa,
Aa'll tell ye aboot th' seets aa saa
    Et Stivvison's Centennery!

Newcastle toon luiked fine th' day,
Wi' bonny flags th' streets se gay
Quite 'mazed th' folk, as weel they may,
    Et Stivvison's Centennery!

Wor pit lads marched amang the rest,
Th' Buffloes i' thor sleeve-hats dressed,
Salvation Army! aa'll be blest!
    Et Stivvison's Centennery!

Th' banners waved, th' bands did play,
But whaat'n tuen aa couldn't say;
Aa nivvor shall forget the day
    O' Stivvison's Centennery!

Another miner, ROBERT ELLIOTT, of Choppington, has written "A Pitman gawn te Parliament," and of this pitman—Thomas Burt—he thus writes :—

" Becaas he's not furward, in fact he is blate,
Considerin' the knowledge he hes iv his pate.
He's a man we respec for his sense an' his worth;
He's the king o' the howkies, an' pride o' the North;
An' the papers confess thit thor cuddent weel be,
For a lot o' bold howkies, a better M.P."

In another piece, "A Pitman in Parliament," he begins—

" Wor Tommy, wor member, wor canny M.P.,
Hes been myekin' a speech, an' a clevvor yen tee;
He struck oot see hard, thit he myed Mr. Hoker
Believe he had clutched the rang end iv a poker."

The piece is a reply to the stories of champagne and costly pianos so current some years ago.

" The champane, Mr. Hoker, will be rather weak,
Iv the man that just myeks twenty bob i' the week.

The peanny ye speak of for dowters an' wife,
Tyek't oot an' put in a tin whussle or fife."

Mr. Elliott published an interesting volume of his poems and recitations in 1877.

Mr. R. USHER, of the Felling, reflecting the subjects of the day, sings of the Salvation Army, or, as he calls them, "The Hallayuyes." His "Hallayuye Convert" tells how, listening at their open-air meeting, he follows them to their "Mishin Hall," is impressed with the service, and finally follows one of the Hallayuye Lasses, who comes to him saying—

> "Cum this way, maw canny man,
>   And join the Hallayuyes.
>
> Aw begun te think the lass wis reet,
>   Fra maw evil ways aw shud turn, man;
> Aw myed up maw mind that varry neet,
>   Te gan up te the penitent form, man.
> At forst aw thowt aw'd lost me tung,
> For aw reely felt as if aw wis dumb—
> But when aw went doon upon maw knees,
> It wis just as if fra chains released,
> Aw got up and wad maw experience speak,
> And then aw thowt aw cud talk't a week,
>   For aw fund faith in Hallayuye!
>   *Chorus.*"

Mr. Usher has written a good many songs, which have been printed in slip form.

———

R. J. WILKINSON, a bookseller in the Market, a place famous for its gatherings of second-hand books of all kinds, has published a small collection of dialect and other songs (1886). In "Tommy on the Bridge" he sings of a well-known character.

> "Wor Charlie, just the tuther day
>   Wis wawkin on the kee,
> When he thowt he'd gan alang th' bridge
>   An' poor blind Tommy see;
> He haddint seen him for a time,
>   An' thowt he'd like te heer
> What he'd gat to say aboot
>   The toppicks ov the eer.

Charlie fund Tommy it his reglor post, and is usual workin hissel is if he wis gannin bi machinery. 'Noo, Tommy,' ses he, 'hoo are ye gettin on noo?' 'Whei,' ses Tommy, 'very badly; heer hev aw stud awl this blessid day, and ony myed tuppince-hapney oot ov awl the hundrids ov folks thit's gyen ower the bridge. Aw'm gannin te pitishun the corporashun te get the bridge altor'd; it dissint suit me, for whenivor there's a ship cummin eethor up or doon, aw hev te move off the swing; aw waddint mind if they paid is for'd, but aw get *ne* compensayshun, an' aw think it's a blow'd shyem ov onnyboddy tryin' te prevent a man myekin' a livin'.'

>   *Chorus.*
> So, if ye want te hev a treet
> Awltho' he's not a judge,
> Ye'll heer words ov wisdim
> Frae Tommy on th' bridge."

From the Shieldfield, "Havadab" sent to the *Weekly Chronicle* "Ma Singin' Freend."

MA SINGIN' FREEND.

Gannin on for six, when aa maun start
  Ma day's wark, aa dee often meet
  A chep cum singin' doon the street,
Cum singin' wi' a leetsum heart ;
In sleet or snaw, in leet or dark,
  Nee mettor if it's wet or dry,
He gans on singin' tiv his wark,
  Wi' cheery voice he passes by.

.   .   .   .

Aa often weary went te wark,
  Kind o' heart sick ; but, nivvor mind,
  It nivvor left a trace behind
When he passed singin' like a lark.
Aa wunder if he ivvor thinks
  Thet, while he's cheer'd thor's others te ;
Aa knaa one heart thet sometimes sinks,
  Thet's lifted by his melody.

Sing on ! sing on ! ma hearty freend,
  Aa hope ye'll nivvor knaa the day
  When misery will drive away
Yor sang, or put it tiv an end.
O, still gan singin' te yor wark,
  Wi' leetsum heart an' cheery voice,
An' knaa that when it's sometimes dark
  Ye myek anuther heart rejoice.

That the dialect is not this writer's only gift, the following, also from the *Weekly Chronicle*, shows—

GONE!

Her harp is mute : were it to wake,
The sadness of its strains would break
  My heart, because it mourneth for
  The hand that never more shall stir
Its silent strings for love's dear sake.

The song that charmed away my cares,
Her laugh, her footfall on the stairs,
  And every sound that banished gloom
  Is hushed, and in the silent room
My heart is full of voiceless prayers.

Yet oft at night she comes again
In dreams, and sings an old refrain
  To soothe my soul in deeper rest ;
  I turn to clasp her in my breast—
And wake, and look for her in vain.

.   .   .   .   .

572

Mr. R. USHER, of the Felling day, sings of the Salvation Ar... Hallayuyes." His "Hallayuy... at their open-air meeting, he... Hall," is impressed with th... of the Hallayuye Lasses, w...

"Cum this w...
And join...

Aw begun...
Fra ma...
Aw myel...
Te ga...
At for...
For aw...
But...
It w...
Aw...
An...

Mr. Usher h...
been printed i...

R. J. W...
famous for i...
has publish...
(1886). I...
known ch...

Fro·
Chrc

Courant, about a year ago, there appeared

ID PITMAN'S PO'TRY TIV EES MARRAH.

Ah's eighty, Tom! an' frae me poo
The hair 'at yance o' th' top on't groo
Hez te the fower win's ahl gyane,
An' noo there's nowse bud skin an' byane.

. . . . .

Me limbs wis strang, me back wis lythe—
Cud run an' lowp, an' be as blythe
As ony youngster o' my age,
An' play at owt 'at was the rage.

. . . . .

Ah cannit run, bud toddles yet,
An' hez te mind the styens,
Me apple cairt itz syun upset,
I' spite ov ahl me byens.

. . . . .

ьh anonymous, Dr. Embleton, so long a prominent
, is credited with the authorship.

———

pley, a South Shields painter, seeing the popularity of
ew sensation—the parachute descent from a balloon—
ıssfully accomplished it at South Shields, on April 5th ·
7th, 1890. A song by "Geordie" in the *Shields Gazette*
ѳrated their townsman's success.

SHIPLEY'S DROP FRAE THE CLOODS.

Noo had on, mee hinnies, and whisht till aw tell ye
Hoo Shipley hes proved his-sel fairly a man;
He up wiv his brushes and hivenward rushes,
And leaves us awl gyepen as hard as we can.
Sum called him a hero, an sum a greet ass,
Sum said wi' poor Shipley its awl up a tree.
Says he, "Noo awl show them it isn't awl gas,
Awl syeun let them see what a painter can dee."

> Hurrah te wor rockets, hurrah te wor lifeboats,
> Hurrah te wor gud-tempered star-gazin' croods;
> Hurrah te wor Shipley, wor awn painter Shipley,
> Hurrah te wor Shipley that dropt frae the cloods.

Miss Bomont wis clivor, but dropt in the rivor,
And doon a high chimler she vary nigh fell;
So wor Shipley wis on, and syeun bet ten te one
If he had a balloon cud dee bettor his-sel.
He wid stonish the toon wiv a rush te the moon,
An' wid fetch doon the man that had been there see lang;
He wid paint up the stars, and wid rub up awd Mars,
An' the Clerk o' the Weather kick doon wiv a bang.

. . . . .

Mr. HENRY JACKSON commemorates the Free Education Act in a song beginning—

> " O Sal, aa've heord sum wondrous news,
>   Wor Parlymint's left thor ' Irish stews,'
>   Thor baldordash 'boot tax an' dues,
>   An' aal sic bothorashun.
>   Ay, lass, they've wakened up at last,
>   An' aal sic things aside are cast,
>   An' noo a bran' new Act they've passed
>   Te gie Free Eddikashun ! "

Mr. J. HARBOTTLE's "A Newcastle Sang" appeared in the *Weekly Chronicle* a few months ago. It is what the *Chronicle* truly calls a racy production.

A NEWCASTLE SANG.

Oh ! cum' ma canny lads, let's sing anuthor Tyneside sang,
The langwidge ov each Tyneside heart, wor aad Newcassel Twang.
Ne doot it's strange te stuck-up folk, and soonds byeth rough and
       queer,
But nivvor mind, it's music sweet untiv a Tyneside ear.

Wey, bliss yor heart, thor's ivvorything a Tyneside chep can boast ;
Wor Tyneside tongue is spoke and sung on ivvory foreign coast.
On sea or lan', where'er ye gan, when Armstrong's cannon roar,
It is the voice o' Tyne that's hard resoondin' frev her shore !

.   .   .   .

The ancient langwidge o' the Tyne hes sayins awfu' queer !
They say aad Nick torns pale as deeth when real Tynesiders sweer !
An' Adam spoke in Tyneside tee, when he cried te Mistress Eve,
" A bonny mess ye've myed on't noo ; begox, we'll hev te leave ! "

An' when a muthor scolds hor bairn, she'll sheyk her fist and froon,
" Noo, haad yor jaw," " aa'll skelp yor lug," or sum plyece lower doon ;
But if she's in the humour fine, it's " Cum, noo, hinny, cum ! "
An' if ye want te hear the burr, wey, mine's a haaf o' rum !

An' when a chep's sweethartin' like, it's " Cum, lass, gie's a cuddle ! "
Or when a man is drinkin' sair, it's " Tommy's on the fuddle ! "
The bairn that cries is "raimin on," things paaned they say's "in pop,"
An' then a feythor says wi' pride, " The bairn's peart as a lop ! "

An ear's "a lug," a mooth's "a gob," and then a hand's "a paa" ;
Te hev a smoke it's "here's a low, sit doon and hev a blaa."
It's "howay here" or "had on thor," "what cheer, my lad ! " they'll say,
" It's kittle wark," " what fettle noo ! " "it's dowly like the day ! "

Noo aa might crood a thoosand things inte this Tyneside sang ;
But sum will say, " Hi ! had yor han', yor myekin't ower lang."
Aa've said enough ; aa'll leet ma pipe, ma rhymin' pen lay doon,
An' pray wor speech may ne'er depart fra wor aad CANNY TOON !

Besides this racy song, Mr. Harbottle is the writer of the "Pitman's Song," which in the "Royal" pantomime, 1890, was such a hit. Before this he had been successful in a different line; in 1889 the *Weekly Leader* offered a prize for the best poem on the "Tyne," and Mr. Harbottle carried it off. The poem describes the Tyne from its source to the sea, and is full of fine passages; one, the opening, may be given here as an example of the writer's graver vein:—

> "Dear is the heart . . ,
>
> And sad my own, if e'er the image fade
> Of those fair scenes wherein my childhood played,
> Where all the joys of life have found their birth,
> And spread their wings around a Tyneside hearth,
> Home of all Northern hearts, my Muse's shrine;
> Once loved, still loved, the dear old banks of Tyne."

APPENDIX.

Page 58. JOHN SHIELD.—Amongst the stock of the late W. Dodd, bookseller, sold September 1891, was a manuscript signed John Shield. It begins "Dear Kit," this Kit probably Christopher Myers, chemist, is told that his lozenges have saved the writer's life, but they are done, and unless renewed, his cough may return, and

Think, should this cough, bring on a hiccup,
And finally, my heels I kick up,
    What sadness will prevail,
How will the laughter-loving throng,
When, ceas'd for ever, is my song,
    The dread event bewail

J. Shield.

Then he goes on humorously depicting his friends lamenting him, and Black Bob, the undertaker, "listening keen my knell to hear"; but all to be changed when Kit sends more lozenges. From this manuscript the autograph and handwriting here given are reproduced. The piece has all the wit and brightness of Shield, and there is little doubt is his,

Page 99. JAMES STAWPERT.—In a volume of odd broadsheets in the Reference Library, Newcastle, we find one in memory of James Stawpert, of Newcastle-upon-Tyne, brewer, who died March 12th, 1814, aged 39 years. On the broadsheet are three verses lamenting him. One runs—

> " Now that his generous soul to heaven has fled,
>   Here weeping friends, recalling former years,
> Will oft, revisiting his turfy bed,
>   Let fall a flood of sympathetic tears."

Unfortunately, the broadsheet does not give the place of his burial.

Page 126.—"NEWCASTLE ON SATURDAY NIGHT." By W. Stephenson, Sen.

Page 153.—"THE HALF-DROWNED SKIPPER" first appeared (signed D.) in the *Tyneside Minstrel,* 1824.

PAGE 221. — "BILLY OLIVER'S RAMBLE." A small early edition of Marshall, 1823 (bought at Dodd's sale) gives Thomas Moore as the author. In the larger edition, 1827, Moore's name is dropped, and the song appears anonymously.

F FOR FANCY
  I FOR NANCY
    N FOR NICHOL BOE
      I FOR JOHN THE WATERMAN, AND
        S FOR SAVILLE ROW.

A rhyme common amongst children fifty years ago.

FINIS.

THE WALTER SCOTT PRESS, NEWCASTLE-ON-TYNE.

20/3/12- 2/6

Lightning Source UK Ltd.
Milton Keynes UK
21 July 2010

157278UK00001B/73/P